Innovators in
Battery Technology

D0947982

ALSO BY KEVIN DESMOND

Gustave Trouvé: French Electrical Genius (1839–1902)
(McFarland, 2015)

Innovators in
Battery Technology

Profiles of 95 Influential Electrochemists

KEVIN DESMOND

Foreword by MICHAEL HALLS

McFarland & Company, Inc., Publishers
Jefferson, North Carolina

LIBRARY OF CONGRESS CATALOGUING-IN-PUBLICATION DATA

Names: Desmond, Kevin, 1950–
Title: Innovators in battery technology : profiles of 95 influential electrochemists / Kevin Desmond ; foreword by Michael Halls.
Description: Jefferson, North Carolina : McFarland & Company, Inc., 2016. | Includes bibliographical references and index.
Identifiers: LCCN 2016015957 | ISBN 9780786499335 (softcover : acid free paper) ∞
Subjects: LCSH: Chemists—Biography. | Electrochemistry—History. | Electric batteries—History. | Energy storage—Research.
Classification: LCC QD21 .D47 2016 | DDC 621.31/24240922—dc23
LC record available at https://lccn.loc.gov/2016015957

BRITISH LIBRARY CATALOGUING DATA ARE AVAILABLE

ISBN (print) 978-0-7864-9933-5
ISBN (ebook) 978-1-4766-2278-1

Front cover (top right) Alessandro Volta, (middle row, left to right)
Zempachi Ogumi, Humphry Davy, Ernest B. Yeager, Pieter van Musschenbroek,
(bottom row) Gaston Planté, Benjamin Franklin, Thomas Edison, Stanford R. Ovshinsky

Printed in the United States of America

*McFarland & Company, Inc., Publishers
Box 611, Jefferson, North Carolina 28640
www.mcfarlandpub.com*

Acknowledgments

The author wishes to thank the many battery innovators who helped him with their respective entries for this book. In particular, Professor Detchko Pavlov and Dina Ivanov; Jürgen Garche; Alex Karpinski. "Un grand merci" to Damien Kuntz, Director of Archives at the Musée EDF Electropolis, Mulhouse, France, for his patient and ever fruitful assistance.

Very special thanks to Mike Halls of *Batteries International*, without whose regular publication of my articles this book would never have been conceived; and to my long-suffering wife Alex and our two children for their unswerving support.

Table of Contents

Foreword
by Michael Halls

Little did I know when Kevin Desmond approached me eight years ago with the idea of publishing a historical article on battery inventors in *Batteries International* that a long and fruitful relationship was about to develop. His first piece, on Gustave Trouvé, proved more than just worthy or readable—our subscribers loved it. Engineers who had been involved in lead-acid batteries for most of their lives told us they knew so little about Trouvé, the father of the first recognizably rechargeable battery, that they'd like more.

Kevin's next idea was for a feature on Gaston Planté, who developed Trouvé's ideas and put them into practice with an inventiveness that would be hard to match. That, too, was warmly greeted by our readers. This puzzled me. What I thought was arcane had proven to be mainstream! So, given that our readers had liked it so much, we dedicated a section in the magazine to the unsung heroes of the battery world. As time went by, we realized that this rich vein of history did not need to be confined to stories about long-dead inventors or energy storage pioneers. We quickly found that we had almost two generations of battery inventors who were still alive and working.

Two contemporaries, for example, stand out: John Devitt, the inventor in the 1970s of the VRLA battery, the workhorse of today's automotive industry and back-up power; and John Goodenough, the pioneer of the lithium cell, which inspired a revolution in the way we live, powering the mobile phone, the laptop and much more.

Once the decision was made to research living scientists or technicians, an interesting thought emerged: this field had hardly been studied and it was clearly worthy of attention. Since then, Kevin has researched and interviewed a huge number of the great and the good, and that has proved to be the genesis of this book.

So I welcome this compendium of some of the articles that he's written and abbreviated from our magazine. I also warmly commend his extra research outside of *Batteries International* in creating these extra entries, not just because of my long friendship with the author, but because this is an important book cataloguing mankind's inventiveness in dealing with energy storage. And that is an issue that is more than likely to be one of the defining features of the 21st century.

A journalist for three decades, Michael Halls has worked for newspapers and magazines. For the past 10 years he has been publisher and editor of Batteries International, *a magazine examining the energy storage market—automotive, stationary, uninterruptible power source—worldwide. He helped relaunch* Energy Storage Journal, *a magazine focusing on the role energy storage will play as solar and wind power are integrated into electricity grids.*

Preface

It may not seem entirely logical to create a book about battery innovators organized alphabetically, where one of the earliest pioneers, Alessandro Volta, is placed near the end! For this reason, the reader will find a timeline as an appendix, and page cross-references between different innovators. This book is not an exclusively technical history of electrochemical progress and formulae. That has already been done in countless learned papers and books, some of which the reader will find in the bibliography. In all my previous books I have tried to present the human aspect of my protagonists—not merely who and what initially inspired them, but their personal lives and their pastimes. This is a group photo of more than 90 men and 5 women from 19 countries. There are, of course, bound to be omissions. During the past two centuries, hundreds of people have made outstanding contributions to battery technology, often summed up here by the phrase "et al." or "and co-workers."

As the world population demands ever more electrical energy, it will be the innovative skills of brilliant electrochemists that enable us to responsibly use the mineral reserves available on this planet—and maybe beyond—as economically and efficiently as possible. The good news is that, even as this book is printed, it will be slightly out of date, because battery innovation has never before been as intense and promising as it is today. My thanks to all those who have assisted me in the assembling of this book.

THE INNOVATORS (A–Z)

André, Henri-Georges
(1896–1967)
Rechargeable silver-zinc battery

Henri-Georges André, born in Fontainebleau, Paris, in 1896, came from an academic family: his father Paul André was a Paris-based violinist and arranger of military music, who forbade his son from making any technical studies until he was 21 years old. So he taught himself electricity.

In 1915 he was recruited into the army and was posted to an aerodrome on the Western Front. During his spare time, by 1917, André had assembled a DC voltage regulator using carbon resistances and electromagnetic adjustments. It was used successfully during World War I by the French Air Force. Following Armistice, he went to work at the Laboratoire Central d'Electricité in Paris. There he met the electrical engineer Joseph Bethenod, who encouraged him to research electrochemistry. From the Paris-Rhône Company, he joined the French Radio-Electric Company. Here he developed surface junction conductors—today known as transistors. Thanks to radio pioneer General Gustave-Auguste Ferrié, André was able to communicate his findings to the French Academy of Science.

In 1922 André invented a dry condenser using silver and silicon alloys. He devoted his time to perfecting this, publishing his findings in the *Bulletin de la Société Française des Electriciens* (August 1939). By this time, his unit was being manufactured to his specifications at the Industrial Condenser Company in Colombes, in the northwestern suburbs of Paris.

From his rectifier experiments, André's thoughts turned to batteries. His choice of materials was influenced by his condenser work. In his first experiments in 1927 he used a silver oxide positive electrode with a porous separator and zinc negative. Experiments with these had already been carried out by Volta (see Volta entry) and Jungner (see Jungner entry).

André chose zinc because he considered it to be the last element in the electrochemical series capable of giving reversibility. He experienced difficulties with solubility. His previous experience with colloids (around 1925) made him believe that part of the trouble could be resolved by a regenerated cellulosic membrane. At first he made his own, by treating nitrocellulose and acetocellulose, in order to obtain a semi-permeable membrane. His first membrane patent was issued in 1932.

After an almost endless series of experiments, written up in almost 3,000 pages of notes, the first industrial operation of his silver oxide-zinc couple was made on September 14, 1936, when a cell delivered 5 amps for 75 minutes. This cell weighed 377g.

3

Up to that time, André constructed all his cells with soluble negatives. After 1940, however, he reduced the amount of electrolyte to make a more insoluble zinc electrode. In André's first U.S. patent, granted in 1943, cellophane was used as a separator to retard the migration of silver specks from the positive to the negative electrodes, which had caused the early failure of previous versions.

It was another Frenchman of Russian origin, Michel N. Yardney, who commercialized André's battery and obtained worldwide patents for it. When, aged 35, he escaped from occupied Paris in 1940, Yardney had approximately $500; degrees in electrochemical engineering and electronic engineering from the University of Caen and Ecole Supérieure d'Electricité; patents of a remote control device he had invented; and a personal motto, "Cherchez et tu trouveras," "Seek and you shall find."

Shortly after his arrival, Yardney built a working model of the remote control unit, demonstrated the device to the U.S. Navy, and received a $20,000 prototype development contract. That first small contract was the beginning of the Yardney Electric Corporation in New York City.

Back in France, Yardney had spent a lot of time working with his colleague, Henri André, and in 1948 persuaded his compatriot to join his company. Yardney began to manufacture the rechargeable silver-zinc battery. Later, Yardney International increased its range to silver cadmium, silver metal hydride, silver hydrogen, magnesium silver chloride, aluminum silver oxide, aluminum air, zinc-air, magnesium-air, lithium-air, cadmium-air, lithium-ion, lithium thionyl chloride, lithium manganese dioxide, and nickel cadmium and nickel hydrogen cells and batteries. Such batteries would be used in air-to-air missiles, satellites and submarines.

Postwar, Henri André returned to France. In 1954, the first automobile that worked using silver-zinc was a Dyna-Panhard, equipped with a Yardney-André 56-cell, 256-ampere battery and a special André electric motor. André was frequently seen driving this silent car around Paris for the next decade.

By this time, the Soviet Union had become interested in silver-zinc, and the intensive work was done at the Moscow Academy of Sciences in the battery group of Prof. Vladimir Bagotsky (see Bagotsky entry). In 1957, the world's first artificial satellite, Sputnik, was launched, powered by a silver-zinc battery.

André was a man who lived for his work. He was made a Chevalier of the Legion d'Honneur in 1949, awarded the Ampère medal by the Société Française d'Electriciens in 1953, and the Gaston Planté medal in 1960. He once confided to his friends that his supreme satisfaction would be to see the fulfillment of his work and their application. He died of a heart attack on October 6, 1967, in his home in Montmorency, France. He was 71 years old.

••

Bacon, Francis Thomas
(1904–1992)
First practical hydrogen-oxygen fuel cells

Francis Thomas "Tom" Bacon was born December 21, 1904, at Ramsden Hall, near Billericay, Essex, UK. He was a direct descendant of Francis Bacon, 1st Viscount St. Alban,

QC, the 17th century English philosopher, statesman, scientist, jurist, orator, essayist, and author. He was educated at Eton College 1918–1922, specializing in science and winning the Moseley Physics Prize in 1922, and at Trinity College, Cambridge, obtaining a third class in the Mechanical Sciences Tripos in 1925.

During the next decades, Bacon served an apprenticeship at the electrical company C.A. Parsons & Co. Ltd., Heaton Works, Newcastle upon Tyne. A few years into his job, Bacon became intrigued by a couple of articles he read in the magazine *Engineering*, which described ideas for electrolyzing water with off-peak electricity and using the resulting hydrogen and oxygen to power a vehicle. He was immediately struck by the potentialities of whether it might be possible to make power electrochemically from the hydrogen and oxygen, rather than feed them to an engine.

He tried to convince his employers to back fuel cell research but was rebuffed because it was not relevant to the business. So while earning his keep at the Parsons Searchlight Reflector and Research and Development Departments, Bacon proceeded to experiment at home.

The principle of the fuel cell had been demonstrated by Sir William Grove in 1839 (see Grove entry), and other investigators had experimented with various forms. However, unlike previous workers in the field, as an engineer, Bacon was comfortable working with machinery operating at high temperatures and pressures.

He began experimenting in the late 1930s with Grove's use of activated platinum gauze with a sulfuric acid electrolyte, but quickly moved on to use activated nickel electrodes with an aqueous potassium hydroxide electrolyte (KOH). KOH performed as well as acid electrolytes and was not as corrosive to the electrodes. Bacon's cell also used porous "gas-diffusion electrodes," rather than the solid electrodes Grove had used. Gas-diffusion electrodes increased the surface area in which the reaction between the electrode, the electrolyte and the fuel occurs. Also, Bacon used pressurized gases to keep the electrolyte from "flooding" the tiny pores in the electrodes.

However, while the experiments went well enough, the corrosive chemicals, high pressure and temperatures involved made them ill-suited to being carried out at home on the coffee table. He secretly moved his experiments to work, but was eventually found out. Faced with the ultimatum of stopping work on his fuel cells or leaving the company, Bacon resigned.

During 1940, he was able to start full-time work on the hydrogen oxygen fuel cell at King's College, London, with the financial support of the consulting engineers Merz and McLellan. He developed a double cell, with one unit for generating the hydrogen and oxygen gases and the other for the fuel cell proper. This could be reversed so that it acted as both an electrolyzer and a fuel cell. Problems were encountered due to the high operating temperatures and pressures and the corrosive nature of the chemicals.

From 1941 to 1946 Bacon was temporary experimental officer at H.M. Anti-Submarine Experimental Establishment, Fairlie, Ayrshire, working on ASDIC, the underwater submarine detection system. In 1946, under new funding arrangements, his work moved to the Department of Colloid Science at Cambridge University. There, Bacon's team were shown a sample of porous nickel sheet whose origins were so obscure they were protected by the Official Secrets Act. They used this sheet to develop electrodes with large pores on the gas side and finer ones on the electrolyte side, which created a much more stable interface than had existed previously. As funding levels increased, the apparatus was moved again to what was then the Department of Chemical Engineering.

Fellow researcher John Davidson recalled, "When you first met him he would ask what you were interested in. If it had any relevance to his fuel cell he was deeply interested, otherwise he would switch off. Not that he was aloof, he was very approachable. I never got involved with his project but we used to meet and talk. He was in the lab every day of the year. I don't think I've met anyone more single-minded."

Developing the fuel cell was an arduous task. With temperatures raised to 200°C and pressures of up to 600 psi, gaskets were prone to deteriorate and the asbestos diaphragm frequently failed. Bacon's target of 0.8 V per cell at 100 mA/cm2 was proving to be elusive. The team eventually overcame problems of corrosion of the oxygen electrode by soaking the new nickel electrodes in lithium hydroxide (LiOH) solution followed by drying and heating. Tom Bacon was able to proudly present a working six-cell fuel cell battery at an exhibition in London, producing 0.8 V per cell at 230 mA/cm2. In 1949, with support from Marshall of Cambridge Ltd. (later Marshall Aerospace), a 5 kW forty-cell battery, with an operating efficiency of 60 percent, was demonstrated publicly.

The patents for the fuel cell were ultimately licensed by Pratt and Whitney as part of a successful bid to provide electrical power for NASA's Project Apollo. The fuel cells were ideal in this regard because they have rising efficiency with decreasing load (unlike heat engines), hydrogen and oxygen gases were already on board the spaceship for propulsion and life support, and the by-product water could be used for drinking and humidifying the atmosphere of the capsule.

In January 1954, Bacon, residing in Little Shelford, England, assignor to E.R.A. Patents Limited, Leatherhead, Surrey, England, was awarded U.S. patent application Serial No. 403,393. For "Alkaline primary cells.... An electrical primary cell comprising a container, an electrode of nickel mounted in said container and having a coating of nickel oxide, in which lithium is incorporated and an alkaline electrolyte in contact with said electrode."

Over the course of the following twenty years, Tom Bacon made enough progress with the alkali cell to present large-scale demonstrations. One of the first of these demonstrations consisted of a 1959 Allis-Chalmers farm tractor powered by a stack of 1,008 cells. With 15,000 watts of power, the tractor generated enough power to pull a weight of about 3,000 pounds. The tractor was later donated to the Smithsonian. Allis-Chalmers maintained a research program for some years, building a fuel cell–powered golf cart, a submersible, and a fork lift. The U.S. Air Force also participated in this program.

Bacon continued to seek new applications for fuel cells as a principal consultant to the National Research Development Corp. (1956–62), Energy Conservation Ltd. (1962–71), and U.K. Atomic Energy Authority (1971–73). He regularly predicted that fuel cells would be the energy solution of the 21st century. Towards the later part of his life, Bacon was a consultant for both the engineering firm Energy Conversion Limited and Johnson Matthey.

As his achievement came to be recognized, Tom Bacon was made an Officer of the Order of the British Empire (1967) and elected a fellow of the Royal Society (1973). In 1978 he received the Society's Vittorio de Nora–Diamond Shamrock Award at the Electrochemical Society's meeting in Seattle. He was awarded the first Grove Medal (1991). He was a founder fellow of the Fellowship of Engineering and the first honorary member of the European Fuel Cell Group.

Tom Bacon died where he had been born, at Ramsden Hall, Little Shelford, Cambridgeshire, on May 24, 1992.

Bagotsky, Vladimir Sergeevich
(1920–2012)
Batteries for Soviet spacecraft

Vladimir Sergeevich Bagotsky was born on January 22, 1920, in Bern, Switzerland, the son of Sergey Yustinovich Bagotsky and Regina Eduardovna Birenbaum. In 1914, his father, an activist of the Russian social–democratic labor party, had moved to Switzerland. After diplomatic relations between Russia and Switzerland were severed in 1918, he became the Soviet Red Cross representative in Geneva, and it was through those offices that political contact was maintained between the two states until 1936.

In 1938, after the teenage Bagotsky had completed his secondary education in Switzerland, the family returned to Russia, where he continued his studies at Moscow State University (MSU), during the hostilities of World War II. From 1944 to 1949, he held a research position at the Department of Electrochemistry, headed by A.N. Frumkin, at MSU, and was involved in fundamental studies of electrode kinetics.

In 1947, Irina Evgenyevna Yablokova began to work with Bagotsky as a diploma student. They married and were to continue to work together throughout their long professional life.

Bagotsky's publications during this period are related to hydrogen evolution (with Zinovy A. Iofa), the concentration polarization, and the oxygen reduction at a mercury electrode. The most important result of this period was publication, in 1952, of the monograph *Kinetics of Electrode Processes*, together with A.N. Frumkin, Z.A. Iofa and B.N. Kabanov (see Kabanov entry). This was the first textbook on electrochemical kinetics.

Between 1949 and 1965, Vladimir Bagotsky worked at the All-Union Research Institute of Power Sources. He contributed substantially to the development of a series of innovative batteries for submarines, aircraft, and spacecraft, most notably silver-zinc batteries, mercury-zinc batteries, water-activated batteries, and thermal reserve batteries. The first space satellite, Sputnik, which was launched on October 4, 1957, was equipped with three silver-zinc batteries made under Bagotsky's supervision. The Sputnik-1 transmitted signals for 22 days before its batteries failed. Later, other Soviet spacecraft, including the Vostok with Yuri Gagarin in 1961, were equipped with these batteries. For these achievements, in 1959 Bagotsky was awarded the degree of Doctor of Technical Sciences (honoris causa) without even being required to present a thesis. By this time, he had been twice awarded the Order of the Red Banner (1956 and 1957), and in 1961, he was finally awarded the Order of Lenin, the highest decoration bestowed by the Soviet Union.

When Frumkin founded the Institute of Electrochemistry in 1958, he invited Bagotsky to work as a head of the power sources division. It is during this period that systematic studies of various basic aspects of electrochemical power sources—electrocatalysis, electrode kinetics on porous electrodes, electrochemical intercalation—were initiated. From 1960, Bagotsky became a leader of fuel cell development in the Soviet Union, and from 1980 he supervised the Russian R&D related to lithium batteries. He was also the only electrochemist who had a perfect command of the artificial language of Esperanto!

After retirement, Bagotsky moved to the USA and continued his work on monographs. He kept numerous professional contacts in the USA and in Europe.

He continued his uniquely long professional activity into his eighties. After publication of the second extended edition of *Fundamentals of Electrochemistry* (Wiley, 2006), he published the treatise *Fuel Cells: Problems and Solutions* (Wiley, 2009).

In October 2010, as part of the 218th meeting of the Electrochemical Society in Las Vegas, a special session was presented in his honor, titled "Professor V.S. Bagotsky—65 Years in Theoretical Electrochemistry, Electrocatalysis, and Applied Electrochemistry."

V.S. Bagotsky authored more than 400 scientific papers and six monographs. He was a kind and considerate teacher, and a scientist with an incredibly broad outlook in various fields of fundamental and applied electrochemistry. He died in Colorado on November 12, 2012, at the age of 92. His wife Irina died two years later, aged 89.

Sources: Alexander M. Skundin and Galina A. Tsirlina, V.S. Bagotsky's contribution to modern electrochemistry, *Journal of Solid State Electrochemistry* (2014) 18:1147–1169; Dr. Natalya V. Bagotskaya, who provided the photos and other original materials.

••

Bagshaw, Norman Ernest
(1933–)
Development of lead-acid battery alloys

Norman Ernest Bagshaw was born on May 25, 1933, in Kettleshulme, Cheshire, England. His father worked at Ferodo Brake Linings, Chapel-en-le-Frith. He attended

Norman Bagshaw, key researcher at Chloride, Manchester, UK in 1968 (Bagshaw Collection).

primary school at Whaley Bridge, where he won a scholarship to Kings' School, Macclesfield, becoming interested in physics and chemistry. He studied the Natural Sciences Tripos at Downing College, Cambridge. In part 1 of the Tripos his main subjects were chemistry, physics and math, with some lectures also on history and philosophy of science. In part 2 of the Tripos his subject was metallurgy, including corrosion and protection.

During this time, Bagshaw played cricket and hockey for his school, then his college. He also played cricket for Whaley Bridge in the Derbyshire and Cheshire league.

Bagshaw's first appointment was with M.E.L. (Magnesium Elektron Limited) at Clifton Junction, the major magnesium company in the UK. He took part in the development of new cast magnesium alloys, used in the aircraft industry, which had the advantage of being lighter than aluminum alloys. A notable example was magnesium-zirconium alloys.

In 1957 Norman Bagshaw married Norma Bradley: they would have four children, one of whom, Melinda, would follow in her father's footsteps as a metallurgist.

In 1958, he moved to the Chloride Group in Manchester, where he spent the next 29 years. Working alongside Montefiore Barak (see Barak entry), Bagshaw was head of materials research and also later assistant director of research of the labs. He was also a part-time lecturer in corrosion and surface treatment at Manchester Technical College.

In the early years (1958–1963), his work included a detailed examination of lead-antimony-arsenic alloys, the grain refining effect of selenium on these alloys, and the first use of selenium as a grain refiner. Between 1963 and 1968 he investigated the properties of lead-calcium and lead-tin-calcium alloys and discovered a method of preventing oxidation of calcium from molten lead alloys by addition of aluminum. He also researched lead-barium and lead-strontium alloys and compared these with the properties of existing lead-calcium alloys, as well as developing lead-antimony-cadmium and lead-antimony-cadmium-silver alloys. In addition to the alloy work, Bagshaw and his team carried out X-ray and microscopic analysis of active materials in battery plates. The structures of lead oxides were clarified by X-ray and neutron diffraction analysis, and the ways in which alpha and beta lead dioxide could be formed were elucidated.

In 1968, he was awarded the Hoffmann Memorial Prize at the 3rd International Conference on Lead in Italy, for his findings on lead-antimony-cadmium alloys. Of this honor, he remarked, "I was never particularly concerned with patents (although I recognised their importance) and left that to the patent office in Chloride. I don't even know how many patents have my name on them."

In 1968, Norman Bagshaw transferred to C.I.B.L. (Chloride Industrial Batteries Limited), the company manufacturing lead acid batteries for standby applications, and also for submarines and aircraft. In addition the company made special silver oxide-zinc batteries for torpedoes. Following a reorganization, he was made technical director and given the technical responsibility for all standby, submarine, aircraft and torpedo batteries, with all the technical managers and also the quality manager reporting to him. A further reorganization allowed him to concentrate on defense and aircraft batteries by giving him overall control (including sales and marketing) of these products.

Chloride had always been the supplier of batteries to the British Navy since diesel-electric submarines were first introduced. Chloride also made batteries for submarine-launched torpedoes. Bagshaw extended this to include batteries for air-drop torpedoes. These batteries had magnesium and silver chloride as electrodes and used sea water as the electrolyte. The batteries were prepared with dry plates and when the torpedo was dropped into the sea, the electrolyte (sea water) entered the battery. Thus the weight of the electrolyte did not have to be carried by the aircraft. One of the disadvantages of the flow-through system is a fall in voltage as the battery discharges. This was overcome by recirculating some of the sea water to increase the temperature and therefore the voltage during discharge.

In 1982 Bagshaw authored the 203-page book *Batteries on Ships*, published by John Wiley & Sons, 1982. It was translated into Russian in 1986. He edited a series of books titled *Power Sources Technology* for Research Studies Press. He also published 60 scientific papers for professional and technical journals.

In 1988, Bagshaw, who had left Chloride to become an independent consultant, was awarded the Frank Booth Medal by the International Power Sources Symposium Committee for contributions to battery research and development. During the next decade, he carried out many projects for companies and government departments in various countries throughout the world. This included expert witness in many battery and patent disputes; in one notable case, his name as expert witness was enough to make the opposing company withdraw. Bagshaw conducted an examination of a "failed" submarine battery for the Canadian navy; presented battery tutorials and workshops held in the UK, USA, Canada, Holland and South Korea; worked closely with HBL (Hyderabad Batteries Limited) in India on some of their new battery projects; gave advice to Magneti Morelli, an Italian battery company, on their phase oxides of titanium and new method of formation (in large coils). In addition, Bagshaw carried out a critical survey of all ILZRO lead-acid work; conducted a mission to Syria on behalf of the United Nations to advise on batteries for PV (photovoltaic) systems; and provided advice to the House of Lords Committee on zero emission vehicles, to mention but a few of his activities.

Norman Bagshaw served as chairman of the British and IEC Standards Committees on Aircraft Batteries over many years; was an Industrial Fellow at Nottingham University for 6 years; and since 1987, has been a member of the Council of the University of Manchester Institute of Science and Technology. In 1999 the Bulgarian Academy of Sciences awarded him the Gaston Planté medal for fundamental contributions to the development of lead-acid battery technology. In 2003 he received the medal for sustained and outstanding work for the University of Manchester Institute of Science and Technology.

Source: information provided by Norman Bagshaw, January 7, 2015.

Bain, Alexander
(1810–1877)
Electric clock, earth battery

Alexander Bain was born on October 12, 1810, the son of John and Isabella Bain of Leanmore farm at Watten in Caithness in the far north of Scotland. He had a twin sister, Margaret, and grew up alongside six sisters and six brothers. Bain did not excel in school, and between 1829 and 1830 was apprenticed to John Sellar, a clockmaker in Wick, Caithness. Having learned the art of clockmaking, he went to Edinburgh, then in 1837 to London, where he obtained work as a journeyman in Clerkenwell. Bain frequented the lectures at the Polytechnic Institution and the Adelaide Gallery and later set up his own workshop in Hanover Street.

In 1840, desperate for money to develop his inventions, Bain mentioned his financial problems to the editor of the *Mechanics Magazine*, who introduced him to Sir Charles Wheatstone. Bain demonstrated a model of his electric clock to Wheatstone, who, when asked for his opinion, said, "Oh, I shouldn't bother to develop these things any further! There's no future in them."

Three months later Wheatstone demonstrated an electric clock to the Royal Society, claiming it was his own invention. However, Bain had already applied for a patent for it. Wheatstone tried to block Bain's patents, but failed. When Wheatstone organized an Act of Parliament to set up the Electric Telegraph Company, the House of Lords summoned Bain to give evidence, and eventually compelled the company to pay Bain £10,000 and give him a job as manager, causing Wheatstone to resign.

Bain's first patent was dated January 11, 1841, and was in the names of John Barwise, chronometer maker of 25 St. Martin's Lane, Charing Cross, and Alexander Bain, mechanist. It describes his electric clock, which uses a pendulum kept moving by electromagnetic impulses. It was not the first galvanic clock; this had been devised by Carl August von Steinheil in Munich in 1839.

Soon after this, Bain improved on this invention in later patents, including a proposal to derive the required electricity from an "earth battery." His Patent No. 9745, granted on May 27, 1843, deals with the production and regulation of electric currents, electric timepieces, electric printing and signal telegraphs. This patent showed a method of insulation by embedding wires underground in asphalt; a pendulum worked by zinc and copper plates buried about 1 yard apart in moist earth.

Between 1843 and 1846, he is also credited with having worked on a chemical mechanical facsimile machine, able to reproduce graphic signs in laboratory experiments. Around 1848, Bain went to America and came back to London about 1852. Initially Bain made a considerable sum from his inventions but lost his wealth in poor investments. In 1873, Sir William Thomson, Sir William Siemens, Latimer Clark and others obtained a Civil List pension for Bain from Prime Minister William Ewart Gladstone of £80 per year. He died January 2, 1877, in Kirkintilloch Scotland.

Source: Alexander Bain, *A Short History of the Electric Clocks*, London: Chapman & Hall, 1852, p. 3.

••

Barak, Montefiore
(1904–1989)
Chloride battery innovator

Montefiore ("Monte") Barak was born on August 18, 1904, in Blenheim, on the east coast of New Zealand's South Island. Soon after, the family moved to Taranaki, a region in the west of North Island. His mother, Mary, was a teacher and later became headmistress at a primary school in a tiny settlement called Warea, in Taranaki.[1]

In 1918, aged 14, Monte qualified in the Junior National Scholarship to study at the Junior Free School, and from there graduated to the New Plymouth Boys' High School, where today, in view of his subsequent career as a battery innovator, a residential house is named after him. It was here that he first played rugby football as a hooker. He continued his love of sport while he read chemistry at the University of Canterbury, Christchurch, New Zealand, obtaining a B.S. in 1925 and graduating with a M.S. (with honors) in 1926, when he published an 82-page paper "Hydrates and Complexes in Solutions of Zinc Chloride."

He was then awarded a Rhodes Scholarship to Hertford and then Balliol College, Oxford University, England, where he obtained a PhD in chemistry in 1929. His doctoral topic was the electrical conductivity of non-aqueous solutions. Alongside rowing, he played rugby for the Oxfordshire Nomads and towards the end of the 1929 season as center-threequarter for Northampton.

From there, Monte won yet another scholarship—a Commonwealth Fund Fellowship (today, a Harkness Fellowship) that took him to Princeton University, New Jersey, for the next two years. Here he worked on the photochemical reaction between hydrogen and oxygen.

Already a first-class player at all of the colleges he had attended, in October 1930, Monte and another British graduate student, H. Cooper, re-established the Princeton Rugby Club. Over 5,000 people attended the inaugural Harvard–Princeton game in 1931. Not only did Princetown win, but they went on to beat Harvard again and Yale twice during the rest of the season. The club has been playing ever since.

In 1931, Barak returned to the UK and took up a position as assistant lecturer at the University of London, Kings College. From there, in 1934, he moved on to begin a professional scientific career in British industry, initially as works chemist at Chloride Electrical Storage, based at Clifton Junction, Manchester. In 1941 he became chief chemist of that company.

He continued to play rugby, firstly for Northampton, and then in 1932 he joined the Saracens, elected captain for the seasons 1933 and 1934, playing for Middlesex v. Berkshire in 1933. On his posting to Manchester, he joined the Sale Rugby Club. In 1942 Monte married Josephine Pollitt; they would have two sons, Adrian and Nigel.

Chloride Electrical Storage Co. was by far the dominant battery maker in the UK. It had acquired other companies: Pritchett and Gold at Dagenham; DP Batteries at Bakewell; Tudor UK in Cheshire; Alkaline Batteries in Redditch; Lorival, who made rubber and plastic containers and separators; and some emergency lighting and UPS makers. Chloride also had major plants in all the British Imperial countries, some of them quite large.

Montefiore Barak, battery researcher and rugby man (Barak Collection).

The Chloride Works at Clifton saw many decades of battery innovation (Peters Collection).

At the largest plant, in Manchester, over 3,000 workers were employed making automotive, industrial and defense batteries. It produced submarine batteries for many navies and was sole supplier to the Admiralty for torpedo batteries. It was owned by the Electric Storage Battery Co. (ESB) of Philadelphia, some of whose senior managers Monte had come to know at Princeton. ESB was as dominant in the U.S. as Chloride was in Britain.

In 1945–46 Monte was part of an Allied investigation team who visited German battery plants to assess and "acquire" know-how and plant. AFA was similarly dominant in Germany. In 1947 he was made a fellow of the Royal Institute of Chemistry.

In 1953, Chloride Group established a moderately large R&D operation, later moving to grand new premises and called Chloride Technical Ltd. This was the ivory tower policy of the 1950s and '60s, and both ESB and AFA had similar new laboratories and workshops. Barak was in charge of Chloride Technical for about 10 years before moving to Chloride Group head office in London, where he was appointed research director for the whole group.

Barak's principle function around that time was to transfer ESB's technology—new alloys, new designs, especially for telecom activities, many new recruited expert specialists—from the operating companies to Chloride Technical. He was instrumental in guiding the work in the right direction. Whilst continuing improvement and development of the main product lines, lead acid, and nickel iron, and nickel, Barak was always prepared to look at and initiate research into innovative power sources.

One of the patents for which he was co-assignor, with Ken Peters (see Peters entry), concerned the "Method of and means for applying additive material to the place of electric accumulators" (Filed Apr. 23, 1962, Ser. No. 189,464).

In 1953 Chloride became a wholly-owned UK company, breaking away from ESB. The following year, the three major companies (ESB, Chloride and AFA) signed a technical exchange agreement. Ken Peters notes, "We had regular meetings exchanging data and results until 1968 when the U.S. State Department judged it illegal."[2]

In 1954, Barak was elected a member of the Royal Society of Chemistry. Two years later, he was instrumental in establishing the International Power Sources Symposium, the first major conference for discussing battery technology. It would function from about 1956 until 2008, when it was surpassed by many other battery meetings and discontinued.

Ken Peters recalls, "In the early '60s we had a team developing fuel cells and then in 1974, with Barak's initiative, a joint venture company, Chloride Silent Power Ltd, was formed to develop molten salt, Sodium/Sulphur NaS batteries. The fuel cell work was wound up about 1970 but Chloride Silent Power continued for 20 years when parts of the technology were sold off. These technologies are still being developed by many organisations."[3]

In 1962, Barak, still the keen rugby man, published *A Century of Rugby at Sale*, an official history of the Sale Shark professional Rugby Union Club, located at the Heywood Road ground in the Manchester suburb of Sale; for several years he had played center forward for this club. He was also an external examiner at the nearby Salford Royal College of Advanced Technology.

From 1965 to 1969, Barak was scientific adviser to the Chloride Group Ltd., as well as being a director of EPS, Alkaline Batteries Ltd. and Chloride Overseas. He was chairman of the Society for Electrochemistry, and a member of the IEE committee on novel methods of power storage. He also became a fellow of the Royal Society of Arts. In 1970 he was awarded the Frank Booth Medal at the Power Sources Symposium.

Barak wrote a history of Chloride in 1974. During the next six years, he contributed to various books, including the editing of a seminal 500-page book *Electrochemical Power Sources: Primary and Secondary Batteries (IEE Energy Series)*. It was published in 1980 by the Institution of Engineering and Technology.

Retiring to Burgess Hill, Sussex, Barak became a member of the Board of Governors at the local Oakmeeds Comprehensive School, and Chairman of the Park and Community Centre. He died in 1989, aged 85.

Notes

1. Communications to the author by Adrian and Nigel Barak, November 2014
2. Communication from Ken Peters to the author. See page xx of this book.
3. Ibid.

••

Bode, Hans Heinrich Christian
(1905–1989)
Lead-oxide in positive active mass

Hans Heinrich Christian Bode was born on January 18, 1905, in Kiel, Germany, the son of a foreman. In 1923, having graduated from high school, he began to study chemistry under Professor Gerhard Preuner. His PhD dissertation, which he received in 1928 from the Christian-Albrechts-Universität of his native city, was the subject of his first patent, one of seventy. Two years later, he took out his second patent, about the refraction of alkali hydrides—with at least two patents following each year. In 1937, after four years as an assistant at the Chemical Institute of Kiel University, Bode qualified as a recognized university teacher when he acquired the *venia legendi* in chemistry. His main interest at this time concentrated on problems of the physical chemistry of phosphonitrile compounds, in particular on reaction kinetics. In 1938 Hans Bode married Ruth Beckmann, an engineer's daughter. In 1940, he occupied the post of senior assistant at the Chemical Institute.

In January 1942, Bode was drafted into the Wehrmacht as a chemist in Hellmut Walter's rocket fuel research unit. At the end of the war, he was an officer in charge of town planning. In April 1945, Bode was made prisoner. But by 1947 he had returned to Kiel University, where he became professor of inorganic chemistry, and whence he resumed his succession of patents. In 1949, Bode was appointed Professor at Hamburg University.

At the well-known State Institute of Chemistry he continued his work on fluorine chemistry, which he had started already in Kiel in cooperation with Professor Wilhelm Klemm. Numerous papers on the synthesis and structure of alkali fluorometallates, mainly published in *Zeitschrift für anorganische und allgemeine Chemie*, are evidence of his ingenious research work. For example, in 1952 he applied for and was awarded a patent for alkali metal and alkaline earth perfluorides. By this time he had been joined by Ernst Voss (see Voss entry), who would work with him in the years to come.[4]

In 1955 Hans Bode became director of the Central Laboratory of the Accumulatoren-Fabrik Aktiengesellschaft (AFA, now VARTA Batterie AG), established at Frankfurt-am-Main. Although aged 50, he did not hesitate in accepting this challenge. He left the university and within a short period of time he succeeded in creating an industrial research institution which rapidly won an international reputation while he simultaneously obtained a widely-acknowledged professional authority within the company.

Under Bode's directorship and with his active participation, a number of significant contributions to the knowledge of various electrochemical energy storage systems were made.

A representative selection of these might be: first proof of a-PbO_2 in the positive electrode of a lead-acid cell (1956), evaluation of partly sulfated lead oxide pastes for electrode production (1959), impedance of Leclanché cells (1959), reactions in sealed NiCd cells (1958–1960), current distribution in porous MnO_2 electrodes (1963), phase analysis of MnO_2 (1962), cathodic reduction of MnO_2 in alkaline solutions (1965), knowledge of the NiOOH/ Ni(OH) electrode (1966–1969), current distribution in porous PbO_2 electrodes (1969), and effect of electrolyte flow-through on the material utilization of porous PbO_2 electrodes (1970). Simultaneously he developed relations with many universities and renowned electrochemists (K.J. Vetter, H. Gerischer) and most importantly entered into an exchange of battery science with laboratories of major battery companies in the U.S. and UK.

One of Bode's key patents was for an alkaline storage battery and the process for making the same, taken out at home and abroad in the early 1960s.

Hans Bode retired from VARTA Batterie AG in 1969. He immediately took advantage of his freedom from managing a large laboratory to undertake a variety of activities. He was invited to give lectures in foreign countries and his technical knowledge was required by a number of institutions in Europe. He also continued his research in the early 1970s into the electrochemical behavior of nickel-cadmium hydroxide.

Finally, he started to write a book on the lead-acid system. After 7 years of laborious work, his important 408-page tome *Lead-Acid Batteries* (Electrochemical Society Series) was published by John Wiley and Sons in 1977. Translated by R.J. Brodd and Karl Kordesch, it came to be respected as a comprehensive summary on the science and an introduction to the technology.

After this exceedingly great effort, it appeared that Bode felt he had accomplished his life's work. Although still in contact with VARTA and in particular with the Research and Development Centre in Kelkheim, he now "really" retired. The remaining years of his life were devoted to his family, to visiting friends, to excursions and walks in the beautiful forests around the city of Königstein im Taunus, and to travels and studies of fine arts with his wife Ruth.

Through his personality and spiritual approach, Hans Bode inspired students, coworkers, friends and visitors with candor and confidence. Hans Bode died on September 27, 1989, at the age of 84.

NOTE

4. Landsarchiv Schleswig-Holstein Abt. 47. Nr 6455.

....

Böhnstedt, Werner
(1945–)
Battery separators

Werner Böhnstedt was born on March 3, 1945, in Stendal, a town in Saxony-Anhalt, Germany. "My interest in natural science topics—already in school—was primarily focused on Physics, more than on Chemistry, but later on their partial interaction in the field of Electrochemistry fascinated me."[5]

Böhnstedt studied mathematics, physics and chemistry at the University of Göttingen between 1967 and 1971, concluding with a diploma in physics. Professor Oskar Glemser then offered to him to work on a doctorate thesis about the impact of a magnetic field on the deposition of zinc from alkaline solution. This study was aimed at avoiding growth of dendrites in order to improve the cycle life of nickel-zinc batteries for electric vehicles. Böhnstedt obtained his Dr. rer. nat. (Doctor in Natural Sciences) in 1973.

By this time, he was working for Friemann and Wolf GmbH / Silberkraft GmbH in Duisburg as head of electrochemical research, researching alkaline battery properties mainly for silver oxide-zinc and nickel batteries. He was later promoted to head of R&D for this group of companies. Main development areas were special batteries for military submarines and aircraft as well as for space applications. Böhnstedt's scientific interest additionally concentrated on aluminum alloy electrode reactions in alkaline electrolyte[6] and early lithium metal battery development work.

In 1980, Böhnstedt joined W.R. Grace & Co. Battery Separators Europe in Norderstedt as director of R&D. Whereas in 1980 almost all automotive starter batteries still used stiff leaf separators and containers with mud spaces, Grace Battery Separators introduced microporous polyethylene separator envelopes, thus avoiding the mud space and improving high performance SLI batteries.

In 1994 Grace Battery Separators was acquired by the Intertec Group based in Charleston, South Carolina, and renamed Daramic, Inc., which was the already established brand name of their main product polyethylene separators. Böhnstedt was promoted to vice-president of technology with worldwide responsibility.

His work at Grace and Daramic concentrated on improving polyethylene separators in various aspects, such as low electrical resistance, high oxidation stability, and low water consumption, resulting in the so-called Daramic High Performance Separator family.[7]

A topic of special interest for Böhnstedt has always been the question of antimony poisoning in lead-acid batteries, especially in industrial traction batteries, which results in high water consumption, sulfation, and less cycle life. Fundamental insights were achieved[8] leading to a patented product for deep cycle batteries (U.S. Pat. 5,221,587).

Together with his co-workers, he achieved another breakthrough with the so-called AJS (Acid Jellying Separator; U.S. Pat. 6,124,059). The extraordinary properties of this product were extreme porosity and almost no compressibility, allowing improved battery cycle life.[9]

Daramic, Inc. was acquired in 2004 by another financial investor and is nowadays an affiliate of Polypore International, Inc. Daramic is the major supplier of the world's demand for high performance polyethylene battery separators to the lead-acid battery industry, for automotive as well as for industrial batteries. This is largely due to the work put in by Werner Böhnstedt over the years.

With over 10 internationally granted battery separator patent families and about 30 scientific papers presented at international battery conferences, Böhnstedt also contributed to encyclopedias and textbooks on batteries.[10] He finally retired in 2010 and founded Battery Separator Consulting at Henstedt-Ulzburg in Schleswig-Holstein, Germany. He enjoys playing tennis, and is married to Carola.

Notes

5. Communication to the author November 8, 2014.
6. *Journal of Power Sources* 5 (1980) 245.
7. Progress has been reported frequently at international conferences and published, e.g., J. Power Sources 67 (1997) 299, J. Power Sources 95 (2001) 234, or J. Power Sources 133 (2004) 59.
8. *Journal of Power Sources* 19 (1987) 301 and 117th BCI Convention 2005 Presentation, The Battery Man Magazine 47 (2005) 28.
9. *Journal of Power Sources* 78 (1999) 35.
10. *Handbook of Battery Materials; Separators,* (1999); 2. Edition, (2011) 285–340.

Brush, Charles Francis
(1849–1929)
Wind-powered battery generator

Charles Francis Bush was born on a farm on March 17, 1849, in the township of Euclid, near Cleveland, Ohio. A child prodigy, by the age of 15, he had built electrical gadgets and microscopes and telescopes for school chums. Brush attended Central High School in Cleveland where, inspired by Humphry Davy (see Davy entry), he built his first arc light, and graduated with honors in 1867. His high school commencement oration was on the "Conservation of Force." An uncle of Charles from his mother's side of the family provided a loan which enabled him to continue his education at the University of Michigan, where he graduated in June 1869 at the age of twenty with a degree in mining engineering. At Michigan, Charles was a member of the Delta Kappa Epsilon fraternity (Omicron chapter).

Returning to Cleveland, Brush struggled as an analytical and consulting chemist for the first few years of his career. In 1873 he decided that there was not enough demand in Cleveland for his services as a chemist, so he tried his hand at marketing Lake Superior pig iron and iron ore. The iron ore business turned out to be more profitable for Brush. Now that he was earning a comfortable living, his thoughts turned toward marriage. He courted Mary Ellen Morris, and they were married on October 6, 1875.

Having obtained U.S. Patent No. 189,997, "Improvement in Magneto-Electric Machines," in 1877, during the next decade, Charles Brush developed a range of dynamo and arc lights, which first illuminated a Cincinnati physician's home in 1878, then Cleveland Public Square in 1879. His generators were reliable and automatically increased voltage with greater load while keeping current constant. By 1881, New York, Boston, Philadelphia, Baltimore, Montreal, Buffalo, San Francisco, Cleveland and other cities around the world had Brush arc light systems, producing public light well into the 20th century. These and more than 50 patented innovations made Brush a wealthy man.

In 1884, Brush built a graystone mansion at East 37th Street and Euclid Avenue in Euclid that showcased many of his inventions. There he raised his family and lived the remainder of his life. The basement housed Brush's private laboratory.

In the winter of 1887, Brush designed and built an automatically operated wind turbine generator in the back yard to charge the 408 dry cell batteries, as developed by Gassner (see Gassner entry), stored in the cellar of his mansion. Its 60-foot, 40-ton wrought iron tower rested on a gudgeon that extended 8 feet into the masonry. The windmill's wheel measured 56 feet in diameter, had 144 blades and a sail surface 1,800 square feet. The tail was 60 feet long and 20 feet wide. A 20-foot shaft inside the tower turned pulleys and belts, which at top performance spun a dynamo 500 revolutions per minute. This dynamo was connected to the batteries, which in turn illuminated 350 incandescent lamps, ranging from 10 to 50 candlepower, and operated three electric motors and two arc lights. The whole contraption produced 12 kilowatts at its peak. This made Brush's home the first in Cleveland to have electricity.

While Brush was a busy man, he did find time for relaxation, especially after his children were grown. He enjoyed golf, playing 3 or 4 days a week at one point in his life. Duck hunting was another sport he enjoyed at the Winous Point Shooting Club. After his son went to college, Brush spent most of his weekday afternoons at Cleveland's exclusive Union Club. Here he would play his favorite card game, bridge, and catch up on personal correspondence.

For the next twenty years, until 1909, his turbine never failed to keep the home continuously powered. Brush's batteries lasted until his death on June 15, 1929.

In his Will he stipulated that the mansion must be demolished when it was no longer occupied by a family member. The windmill was left standing. In the early '30s, Henry Ford attempted to purchase the mill for his museum in Dearborn, Michigan, but a Cleveland city councilman opposed the sale, hoping that Cleveland would save the windmill as an historic landmark. Unfortunately there was no resolution as to who should get the mill, and it was removed to make way for a new road.

Source: Eisenman, Harry J. III. 1967. *Charles F. Brush: Pioneer Innovator in Electrical Technology.* PhD dissertation. Case Institute of Technology, Cleveland, Ohio.

• •

Bullock, Kathryn R.
(1945–)
Battery modeling

Kathryn and Judith Rice, identical twins, were born in Bartlesville, Oklahoma, in September 1945. Bartlesville was the headquarters of Phillips Petroleum and Cities Service oil companies. The twins' paternal grandfather was an engineer who led the development of the first Phillips refineries and developed the natural gas business. Their father, a geophysicist, had studied music and mathematics in college and did his graduate work at Ohio State University. He and his father were also avid gardeners who provided wonderful places to play, and the twins' maternal grandfather was by hobby a naturalist who liked to take them on discovery walks in the woods. By profession their maternal grandfather was a mechanical engineer and inventor who owned a small company that made liquid level gauges for railroad tank cars. Kathryn and Judith were always welcome to explore his machine shop whenever they visited his company.

"Our grandmothers had both taught school before marriage and continued to teach as volunteers in community educational programs," Kathryn recalls. "Our mother was a creative artist when she could find the time for it, but keeping her twin daughters out of trouble took much of her time. (Two heads are better than one!)"

As the Rice twins grew up, their elders shared their many interests with them and taught them to use both the right and left sides of their brains. Kathryn was interested in studying the stars and collecting rocks. When she was ten years old, her father took a job at a new Marathon Oil Company research laboratory near Denver, Colorado. She learned shorthand and typing so that she could work there in the summers during college, filling in for secretaries on vacation. This gave her an opportunity to learn about research in different areas, including geology, chemistry and other physical sciences.

Kathryn recalls:

My father and his colleagues encouraged me to pursue a scientific career, and I decided to focus on chemistry. Girls were not given chemistry sets in those days, but I had ample opportunity to experiment with food chemistry in the kitchen. At Colorado University, I was the only female in a laboratory of fifty male students. My lab partner told me that I was in the wrong field for a girl, and the lab instructor was not encouraging either, even though I got good grades. I finished a Bachelor of Arts degree at Colorado University with honours in English literature and writing and minors in French and Chemistry.

In 1967, Kathryn married Ken Bullock. She also started looking for a job:

Fortunately I applied to Gates Rubber Company and was interviewed by John Devitt [see Devitt entry], who was organizing a battery development group. He decided to hire me to do a combination of secretarial and technical work, since his new department was too small to need a full-time secretary.

I enjoyed working on nickel oxide-zinc batteries so much that I decided to go to Northwestern

University near Chicago to get a master's degree in Chemistry while my husband studied at an Anglican seminary there. Although I had been accepted to the Graduate School in the English Department, they told me that they had a policy of not giving fellowships to married women. I had no money to fund graduate work, but the Chemistry Department offered me a laboratory job and outlined the courses that I would need to take to enter the graduate chemistry program.

Kathryn worked on their staff full time for nine months, doing computer programming for Professor Donald Smith, and took enough math and chemistry courses to enter the graduate program the following autumn. Smith provided her with a stipend for teaching and doing electro-analytical research, and in 1972, Kathryn Bullock earned a PhD in physical chemistry and electrochemistry. In her graduate research, she used alternating current polarography to study the kinetics of organometallic reactions and experimentally verify the electrochemical models of homogeneous chemical processes coupled with electrochemical reactions.

Her twin sister Judith was to follow another path, majoring and then lecturing in English literature, specializing in the Renaissance writers at the University of Saskatchewan in Canada.

After 5 years in the Chicago area, the Rev. Ken and Dr. Kathryn Bullock returned to Colorado and she rejoined Gates. By that time, John Devitt and his team had developed the VRLA battery, and Dr. Don McClelland was leading the work to test and refine the design and develop the manufacturing processes. The first sales of the first VRLA item, the Gates D-cell, was to makers of portable medical equipment. Notably, the very first was to a human blood pump company in New York State. The pump was part of a portable haemdialysis system for use in ambulances and the like. Kidney-failure patients were the beneficiaries of this device. The ride they undertook might be long and the pump was a high-current electrical load on the battery power supply. So they correctly concluded that Gates cells were the answer.

Lead-acid batteries with silica gel added to the acid could be used in some portable applications, but the gel limited the power. Although lead is heavier than nickel and cadmium, they could use three lead-acid cells to replace the voltage of a battery of four nickel-cadmium cells. When lead-acid batteries are discharged, the state of charge decreases as the acid concentration decreases.

Many large stationary applications, such as at telephone central facilities and electric power plants, typically used to use large, vented, "flooded" cells. These had top openings for gas escape and adding water. But the vented gases contained acid mist in quantities large enough to cause harm to people and equipment. This hazard has been a large driving force causing switchovers to VRLA batteries.

Battery condition can still be measured without the use of a hydrometer, which carries its own problems with it. One simply measures the cell voltage, regardless of what discharging or charging operations are occurring. Good management of this system implies that a suitable level of expertise is present. If a cell is in a state of equilibrium (no charging, discharging or gas potentials), the voltage is a measure of state of charge, being around 2.1 volts or more at full charge and around 1.7 volts or less at complete discharge. Beginning at least as early as 1904 (Dolezalek), this relation was observed and measured. Tables of voltage vs. state of charge are found in all good texts since. The original ones were based on limited experience and improvements have been offered up to the present time.

With her background in computer modeling and physical chemistry, Kathryn was able to develop a model and numerical tables that would allow customers to convert the open circuit voltage of a VRLA battery to the acid concentration and battery state of charge. She was also able to use thermodynamic data from the literature to correct the state of charge for the internal battery temperature.

Kathryn recalls: "To maintain my skills and increase my knowledge of lead-acid batteries, I began reading articles in the *Journal of Electrochemical Society* on corrosion reactions at the lead-acid positive grid by Paul Ruetschi [see Ruetschi entry], Jeanne Burbank [see Burbank entry], Detchko Pavlov [see Pavlov entry], and others. With electrochemists from local universities, I also founded a local chapter of the Electrochemical Society."

In an evening graduate course on corrosion at the Colorado School of Mines, Kathryn learned about potential-pH (Pourbaix) diagrams. Since positive grid corrosion reactions are dependent on both sulfate (S) and hydrogen (H) ion concentrations at the corrosion interface, she now developed a three-dimensional potential/pH/pS diagram that could be used to better understand and reduce the corrosion of the positive lead grids.

In 1977, after about five years in Denver, Bullock's husband wanted to accept a position as a minister in Wisconsin. So she applied for and accepted a job at Globe-Union, a large battery company in Milwaukee that became part of Johnson Controls, Inc. She worked there for nearly 15 years, first as a research scientist and then, beginning in 1980, as manager of the battery research group. Her team worked on many different kinds of lead-acid batteries, including flooded, gelled and acid-starved designs for all types of automotive, stationary, and portable applications [see Pierson entry].

At Gates, Bullock had worked on a project to determine how much phosphoric acid should be added to the VRLA battery electrolyte and had presented a paper on her results at an Electrochemical Society meeting. Phosphoric acid was added to lead-acid gel batteries to increase their cycle life. She used cyclic voltammograms (CVs) to study the effects of phosphoric acid on lead battery reactions. Based on her CV data, the amount of phosphoric acid added to the Gates cells was reduced to a very low level. At Johnson Controls, she continued to study phosphoric acid effects on the positive electrode in lead-acid batteries and published additional work on the subject. In 1980 the Electrochemical Society Battery Division presented Kathryn Bullock with their Research Award for this work.

Bullock's research group was partially funded by the U.S. Government Department of Energy to work on electric vehicle and load-leveling batteries. The battery research group also supported development work on nickel-metal hydride and zinc-bromine batteries. She began to file some patents at Johnson Controls on her ideas of ways to improve lead-acid battery performance and on ways to decrease battery production times.

One of her first projects was to find an alternative way to make a dry-charged battery. Johnson Controls had a method of charging an acid-filled battery and then dumping out the excess acid and centrifuging the battery to eliminate as much moisture as possible. Unfortunately, the shelf life of this battery was not as long as for dry-charged batteries due to the residual acid left in the battery.

To solve this, she innovated putting a sealed plastic bag of highly concentrated acid on top of the battery electrodes after the centrifuging process. Since concentrated sulfuric acid is a good desiccant, water from the battery self-discharge process would slowly move from the residual acid in the battery through the wall of the plastic bag. The highly concentrated acid in the bag was gradually diluted and the battery's open circuit voltage remained high. She thought that this approach would extend the shelf life of the positive plate and that she could easily add the diluted acid to the battery by puncturing the bag. When she tested the battery after about a year on the shelf, it still had a high voltage and the positive plate had good capacity, but now the negative plate limited the battery's performance. She observes, "But from this experiment I did learn a useful lesson: If one electrode doesn't fail, the other one will! Paying attention to chemical reactions in both positive and negative electrodes and the interactions between them is still very important if we want to understand and predict failure modes in VRLA designs for hybrid electric vehicles."

The Johnson Controls Battery Division had a very good engineering department, along with a technical library, a materials research group and an analytical group that provided very good support for battery research and development. Many of their projects were cosponsored by the U.S. Department of Energy. They built a new R&D laboratory and worked on lead-acid, zinc-bromine, and nickel-metal hydride battery development projects for applications such as load leveling and electric vehicles. Kathryn notes, "Our electrochemical engineers and scientists had studied at well-known graduate schools such as the Universities of California, Texas, and Wisconsin. The University of Wisconsin had electrochemical programs on both the Milwaukee and Madison campuses, and so we had a good local source of new employees."

One of those whom Kathryn brought into her R&D Group at Johnson Controls was University of Texas PhD, George Brilmyer:

> When Kathryn hired me it was back in the early '80s, not too long after Johnson Controls had purchased Globe Union. I was new to the industry, one of the new additions to an established R&D group that she was expanding. What I admired about Kathryn was that she was not only as a very good scientist but was also an outstanding manager. Yes, she did some ground-breaking work to understand the functioning of non-antimonial alloys, but she (and Bill Tiedemann) assembled a top-notch R&D team and soon built a new world-class R&D laboratory (that has now morphed into JCI's "Battery Technology Center").
>
> Back then we were working on many of the right subjects such as grid corrosion, battery thermal management, EV batteries, grid design, plate curing and even load-leveling. I'll never forget our work designing the new lab and purchasing some of the first computer-controlled battery cyclers from Bitrode (and it was all done without email)!

As continuing education was also important to their success, Kathryn taught several short courses to her staff. The Electrochemical Society had a Chicago local section, but it was a long, cold evening drive in the winter. "So we organized a local Wisconsin section with alternating meetings in Madison and Milwaukee. One meeting each year was a symposium of papers given by local graduate students. I also accepted invitations to speak annually at a graduate course in batteries at the University of Wisconsin in Madison and to teach a course in electroanalytical chemistry at Milwaukee. These activities helped us to maintain an excellent research group."

In 1991, AT&T Bell Labs asked Kathryn to lead the move of their battery group from New Jersey to Texas. The AT&T power systems group had already moved to Texas, but most of the battery group in New Jersey did not want to move. Fortunately, she was able to retain a few of the battery engineers in New Jersey and hired others in Texas. Her husband had earned a master's degree in social work at the University of Wisconsin and found a position near Dallas. AT&T also agreed to let her accept a nomination to run for vice-president and then president of the Electrochemical Society.

The Bullocks worked in Dallas for five years, until Bell Labs became part of Lucent Technologies. At that time Medtronic, Inc., invited Kathryn to lead a group developing an aluminum electrolytic capacitor design and factory and designing new lithium primary batteries for implantable medical equipment. At the end of 1999, she accepted a position as executive vice-president of technology at C&D Technologies in Philadelphia.

John Devitt holds a high opinion of Kathryn Bullock: "My working contacts with Kathryn were quite early on, but we have remained close friends. She is fine, throughout. Her many papers, some penetrating the theoretical labyrinth of lead-acid science, are, I believe, highly valued by all who count in this business. She is particularly interested in imparting education to worthy folks." In 1996, she was awarded the Gaston Planté medal.

In 2003, Kathryn Bullock founded a consulting business called Coolohm, Inc. There, supported by the Advanced Lead-Acid Battery Consortium, she has been working on many interesting projects since, including the UltraBattery (see Lan Trieu Lam and Rand entries). She also teaches a graduate course in electrochemical power sources at Villanova University. Husband Ken continues to work as a priest in the Diocese of Philadelphia.

Bullock is the author and co-author of more than 60 scientific papers, chapters and books and has eleven U.S. patents in battery, fuel cell and capacitor technology. Since 2002, she has also been a heritage councilor for the Chemical Heritage Foundation, a nonprofit organization whose aim is to strengthen the public understanding of chemical sciences and technologies; to increase the flow of the best students into the chemical sciences and chemical process industries; and to instill in chemical scientists and engineers a greater pride in their heritage and their contributions to society.

Batteries aside, since a 21st birthday trip to the England Lake District, Kathryn Bullock has been an inveterate globetrotter, not only exploring the entire North American continent with husband Ken, but also taking advantage of scientific meetings in Europe and Asia to take cultural "days off." Alongside this, in her spare time, she has followed a family tradition of singing in church choirs and playing music, and of researching her family's genealogy, tracing her ancestors back to the 16th century: "I am writing down our family stories to share with my son and daughter and their two young sons. Genealogy is also a very good way to meet new people and make new friends."

Sources: From an article by the author, published in *Batteries International*, based on information provided by Kathryn Bullock.

....

Bunsen, Robert Wilhelm Eberhard
(1811–1899)
The Bunsen battery

Robert Wilhelm Eberhard Bunsen was born at Göttingen March 30, 1811. He was the youngest of four sons of the University of Göttingen's chief librarian and professor of modern philology, Christian Bunsen. Robert once recalled that he had been a wayward child at times, but that his mother kept him in line. After attending high school in Holzminden, Bunsen matriculated at Göttingen in 1828 and studied chemistry and mathematics with Friedrich Stromeyer as well as mineralogy with Johann Friedrich Ludwig

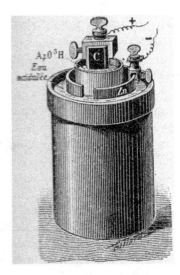

Left: **Robert Bunsen of Marburg University.** *Right:* **Bunsen's battery (Musée EDF Electropolis, Mulhouse).**

Hausmann and mathematics with Carl Friedrich Gauss. In 1831, aged 19, Bunsen obtained his PhD with a dissertation on hygrometers.[11]

Aided by a grant from the Hanoverian government, Bunsen toured Europe from 1830 to 1833, visiting factories, laboratories, and places of geologic interest in Germany, France, and Austria. In 1836, he succeeded Friedrich Wöhler at the Polytechnic School of Kassel, where he taught for three years. In October 1838 he was appointed professor *extraordinarius* of chemistry at the University of Marburg, where he continued his studies on cacodyl derivatives. He was promoted to full professorship in 1841.

Through the 1840s and 1850s, Bunsen made a number of improvements in the galvanic battery. In 1841 he assembled a battery with carbon, instead of the prohibitively expensive platinum or copper used by Grove, as the negative pole. To prevent disintegration of the carbon pole by the nitric acid electrolyte, Bunsen treated the carbon, a mixture of coal and coke, with intense heat. He formed a battery from forty-four subunits to produce the strength of 1171.3 candles, and used about one pound of zinc per hour. Like Grove's battery (see Grove entry), Bunsen's emitted noxious fumes of nitrogen dioxide. In 1842, for this achievement Bunsen was elected to the Chemical Society of London.

Early in 1851, he accepted a professorship at the University of Bresla, where he began to use electrochemical techniques to isolate pure metals in quantities sufficient for determining their physical and chemical properties. He pressed magnesium into wire and used it as a light source in his subsequent photochemical experiments. Commercial manufacture of magnesium was also undertaken and the element came into general use as a brilliant illuminating agent. In 1855, Bunsen innovated a gas burner with a smokeless flame for his laboratory experiments at Heidelberg, today known as the Bunsen burner.

During the next forty years, the scientific world held Bunsen in high esteem. He never married; his teaching and research consumed most of his time, and he traveled widely, either alone or with friends. He also had a reputation as a fun person to be around, full of laughter, but not too careful about his personal appearance. Another professor's wife once said that she would like to kiss him, but she would have to wash him first! He was a person who had a great reputation for warmheartedness, and enjoying jokes and fun. His students admired him greatly. He told a great many anecdotes.[12] Robert Bunsen died August 16, 1899, at the age of 88.

NOTES

11. *Enumeratio ac descriptio hygrometrorum quae sunt inde a saussurii temporibus proposita.*
12. These were published after his death in a short book called *Bunseniana* (1904).

••

Burbank, Jeanne B.
(1915–2002)
X-ray analysis of batteries

Jeanne Beadle Burbank was born in Philadelphia, Pennsylvania, on May 8, 1915, the eldest of three children, to John Bookwalter Beadle, civil engineer, and Isabelle (Peacock) Beadle, personal secretary in the U.S. government. Jeanne's father graduated from Columbia University with a B.S. in Mining and Metallurgy.

John Bookwalter worked as a civil engineer for the U.S. Reclamation Service and later for Brock and Weymouth in Philadelphia. He helped explore and map many parts of the West that had not yet been mapped, and he published many articles on aerial photography and mapping.

Jeanne spent most of her childhood in Washington, D.C. She received a B.A. degree in chemistry from the American University. She married Robert Clowe Burbank on July 1, 1936. She and Robert moved to Philadelphia, where they both worked at Peacock Laboratories (bought out by Libby-Owens-Ford Glass Co. in 1940) as chemists while earning M.S. degrees in chemistry at the University of Pennsylvania.

Her daughter, Carey Burbank Friesen, recalls: "Jeanne and Robert were at a concert when the music was stopped for an announcement—something that was never done. It was announced that Pearl Harbor had been attacked. She was just starting to think that she might be pregnant. What a world to bring a child into! When my Mother came home from the hospital with me as a newborn, my father was sent home for a month of bed rest. Something was wrong with his blood."[13]

Jeanne Burbank had one child, Carey Lea, before being widowed on September 21, 1946, four years later. Robert died from cancer of the lymph (Hodgkins' Disease). After being widowed, Jeanne moved back to Washington, D.C., where she worked as a research chemist for the Naval Research Laboratory (NRL), specializing in the microstructure of lead acid submarine batteries.

In 1949, she co-authored a report on "Phosphate Coatings on Steel," then in 1952, "Positive-grid Corrosion in the Lead-acid Cell: Corrosion Rates of Tin Alloys and the Effect of Acid Concentration on Corrosion" (J.J. Lander, J.B. Burbank, Naval Research Laboratory) and "Subgrain Structure in Lead and Lead-antimony Alloys."

In 1958, she received her first patent for a battery grid and plate (U.S. 2,821,565 A). In 1966, she received the Battery Division Research Award from NRL.

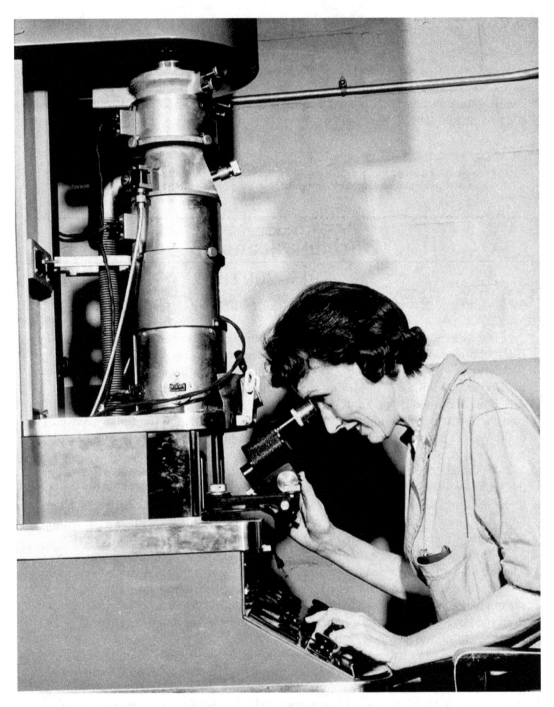

Jeanne Burbank at work at the Naval Research Laboratory, Washington D.C. (courtesy Carey Lea [Burbank] Friesen).

During the 1960s, Burbank and her colleague Charles P. Wales developed the electrolytic cell for X-ray diffraction studies of electrodes, such as silver, to provide analysis for the battery companies such as Gates and Johnson Controls. Among other things, Burbank was a leader in the difficult analysis of the entirely different roles played by the two polymorphs of lead dioxide in the battery operation. One markedly increased the physical stability of PbO_2, while the other was the principal source of reactive energy. Significant groups in the U.S. and Germany were struggling with this question, which influenced both battery design and the processing of materials in manufacture.

The cooperative work resulted in a better understanding of the crystallographic structure of active materials. Her colleague, Albert C. "Al" Simon, of Arlington, Virginia, did parallel studies with the very latest technology from a scanning electron microscope.

In 1967 Burbank and Wales received the NRL Battery Division Research Award for their pioneering work. In 1969, she received the sixth annual William Blum Award from the National Capital Section of the Electrochemical Society, and in 1970, she received the first Frank Booth Award for outstanding technical merit at the International Power Sources Symposium held at Brighton, England. Much of her work concerned submarine batteries, and she was able to study these batteries under working conditions on the USS *Nautilus* (SSN-571), the first nuclear submarine. Carey Friesen relates: "She visited the *Nautilus* while it was docked and was able to see what the conditions were for 'her' batteries. She replicated the battery conditions and set-up at NRL. She was so pleased when NRL gave her her own building which gave her the space to set up the configuration of 'her' batteries."[14]

Jeanne Burbank had many hobbies: drawing and painting in oils, archaeology and studying Native American peoples. She was always interested in minerals and crystals, which she had learned so much about in her work, and she had a wonderful mineral collection.

John Devitt recalls: "Jeanne was able, in spite of many obstacles, not the least being the fact the professional women in her field were almost unheard of, to accomplish much in research in electrochemistry. She was a lady in all the best ways, beautiful personality. Looked great in a lab coat, she could have been a model."[15] Carey Friesen adds: "I'm not sure she would have liked this last statement. She always said she was one of the 'Battery Boys.' I think she felt that her gender had nothing to do with her accomplishments. She was an original believer in equal rights for women."[16]

Jeanne Burbank published over 35 articles in professional journals, and received numerous awards for her work and publications. Several of these were published in four co-authored papers in the Journal of the Electrochemical Society and Electrochemical *Acta*.

Jeanne Burbank retired to Tucson, Arizona, in 1971, where she took up painting in oils and did volunteer work for conferences at the University of Arizona and also volunteer work for the League of Women Voters. Carey Friesen recalls: "She was able to live on several acres in her beloved Sonoran desert, and had a house full of her oil paintings of the desert and also of Native Americans. One of her best is a painting of Ishi, the Last of his Tribe. She was studying the Oglala Lakota language when she started failing."[17]

In 1986 she and her sister, Joan Beadle Gailar, moved to Scottsdale, Arizona. Soon after her sister's death in 1997, Jeanne moved to Life Care Center of Paradise Valley of Phoenix, Arizona. She died on March 2, 2002, aged 86.

NOTES

13. Email from Carey Lea (Burbank) Friesen on November 12, 2014.
14. Ibid.
15. Email from John Devitt.
16. Email from Carey Lea (Burbank) Friesen on November 12, 2014.
17. Ibid.

Burgess, Charles Frederick
(1873–1945)
Improving the dry cell

Charles Frederick Burgess was born on June 5, 1873, in Oshkosh, Winnebago, Wisconsin, the son of Frederick and Anna A. (Heckman) Burgess.[18] After obtaining his B.S. at the University of Wisconsin in 1895, he entered its faculty as instructor and assistant professor of electrical engineering. Inspired by teachers such as Professors D.C. Jackson and Louis A. Kahlenberg, Burgess took up a study of physical chemistry and electrochemistry while teaching, obtaining his EE in 1898. He became assistant professor of electrical engineering in 1898, professor of applied electrochemistry in 1902, and professor of chemical engineering in 1904. Of an inventive turn of mind, he developed several new processes in electrolysis, and in 1904 was made investigator of electrolytic iron alloys for the Carnegie Institute, Washington, D.C. That year, he was a member of the International Jury of Awards at the St. Louis Exposition.

Going out to prove that research could provide its own endowment, Burgess was one of the first to organize a private chemical laboratory for industrial researches: Northern Chemical Engineering Laboratories. In 1907, the French Battery Company of Madison, Wisconsin, asked him and his three assistants to analyze some of its products. Burgess helped the start-up manufacturer produce a better electric dry battery. Soon he bought 100 shares of French stock, was elected to its board and took over the engineering department.

In 1908, Burgess wrote to his father: "Perhaps you are wondering about that battery business I took up last November. Well, I found it in worse shape than I expected and it has been a hard struggle. The company had never made a cent—in fact, had lost over $50,000 ... they were making the poorest battery on the market. While we are not out of the woods, things have materially improved ... at the present time I believe we are making the best battery in the country. We are making about five times as many batteries per day as we were last December."[19]

In 1908 he was elected president of the American Electrochemical Society. In March 1910, with James Aston, Burgess co-authored a report, "the Strength of the Alloys of Nickel and Copper with Electrolytic Iron" (*Bulletin of the University of Wisconsin*, No. 346: Engineering Sciences, Volume 6, No. 2, pages 37–80). In 1911 he received the Octave Chanute Medal from the Western Society of Engineers for his outstanding work on the corrosion of iron in concrete.

Throughout this time, Burgess had also been developing a flashlight, which had been invented in 1900 but was written off by many as nothing more than an impractical gadget. He devoted a great deal of time to finding just the right formula for a flashlight battery. In 1910, French contracted with Burgess to sell the flashlight batteries he was producing in his own laboratories. This was the first year French made a profit. In 1913, he resigned Wisconsin University's College of Engineering. He then enlarged his business and built up a personnel of over 2,000 employees. Following a series of experiments and investigations with woods and other forest products, he set up the Wood Conversion Company, Cloquet, Minnesota, for converting sawmill wastes into insulating and building materials, which are marketed under the trade names of "Balsam Wool" and "NuWood."

Also that year, American Eveready, which controlled 90 percent of the market, attempted to run all of its competitors out of business by claiming patent infringement on a manganese oxide battery component. Ironically, Burgess developed a new material that was so superior that even American Eveready ended up licensing it.

On the outbreak of World War I in 1914, the French Battery Company received a military contract to produce one million 6-inch batteries for use in field telephones. That same year, batteries produced in Burgess's lab were assembled into jackets at the French plant to be sold under the name "Fleur-de-Lis." Burgess-produced flashlights called "French Flashers" also became popular around this time. These developments led to a doubling in sales for both flashlight and 6-inch batteries.

On a disastrous note, a fire occurred in 1915 in the heart of the production season, posing a serious setback for both French and Burgess, who by then had moved his battery-manufacturing operation to a newly built French plant. The blaze destroyed the facility, and relationships were never the same after it was reconstructed.

In 1916, Burgess parted ways with French Battery Company, authorizing the manufacturer to produce flashlights under the patents he then held. The following year, he set up Burgess Dry Cell Ltd., and became chairman of the board of directors of Burgess Part Co. These combined companies did an annual business aggregating more than $10,000,000.

Burgess would take out over 60 patents. Among these: "certain new and useful Improvements in the manufacture of dry cells, yielding oxygen to lessen polarization." The material used was high-grade pyrolusite ore obtained from Russia, analyzing about 5 percent MnO and less than 1 percent of iron, and before using has usually been ground to a 20-mesh size or finer of this material.

In the inter-war years, the Burgess Battery Company became an important manufacturer of dry cell batteries for flashlights, radios, and many wide-ranging technical developments: dry batteries, the microswitch, acoustical silencing products, measuring instruments and methods for noise control, the utilization of wood wastes, development of new clay products, building materials and other applications. It eventually became part of Mallory Battery, now known as Duracell (see Ruben entry).

Burgess contributed much to chemical and electrochemical literature on the corrosion of metals, electric furnace phenomena and on electric batteries. He was a member of the American Electrochemical Society (president 1907–08); the American Chemical Society; the Western Society of Engineers; the Society of Chemical Industry; the Royal Institution of Great Britain; the Beta Theta Pi, Tau Beta Pi, and Alpha Chi Sigma fraternities; the Union League and University Clubs of Chicago; and the Chemists Club of New York City.

Dissatisfied with taxes in Wisconsin, in 1926 Burgess moved himself and his enterprises out of the state. The Burgess Battery Company went to Freeport, Illinois. Burgess Laboratories was reincorporated under Delaware laws. In 1932 he was elected honorary member of the Electrochemical Society. He titled his Perkin Medal address "Research: For Pleasure or for Gold." It dealt largely with the commercial research with which he was concerned and apparently occasioned the inclusion of the reference to gold.

In 1928, Burgess purchased the 104-acre Little Bokeelia Island in southwest Florida. His wife Ida had suffered an illness which had left her unsuited to the harsh Wisconsin winters. He built a sprawling Spanish-style villa, complete with laboratory, landscaped gardens, and a swimming pool. His researches included corrosion, the warm salt waters of the Gulf of Mexico conveniently serving as one of the corroding mediums. He also concerned himself with reforestation of waste Florida lands, study of various forms of vegetation, and growing new types of plants and trees. One of his guests was Tom Edison (see Edison entry). Charles F. Burgess died of heart failure on February 13, 1945, in Chicago, Illinois.

NOTES

18. "Burgess, Charles Frederick 1873–1945." Wisconsin Historical Society.
19. Kenneth D. Rubel, *"The RAYOVAC Story, The First 75 Years."* Rayovac, 1981.

••

Cairns, Elton James
(1932–)
Lithium sulfur battery

Elton James Cairns was born in Chicago, Illinois, on November 7, 1932. Attending South Shore High School, he was inspired by his chemistry and physics teachers. At Michigan Technological University he received B.S. degrees in chemistry and in chemical engineering, graduating summa cum laude at the top of his class. For graduate school, he attended the University of California, Berkeley, receiving a PhD in chemical engineering in 1959. His PhD research dealt with chemical kinetics and transport processes in packed and fluidized beds.

Elton Cairns, professor of chemical engineering at the University of California, Berkeley (courtesy Elton Cairns).

Cairns married shortly after graduate school, and has a daughter. His hobbies have included stamp collecting, raising tropical fish, tennis, gardening, music, and computers.

In 1959, Cairns joined the General Electric Research Laboratory in Schenectady, New York. He conducted research on ion-exchange membrane fuel cells, electrocatalysis, surface chemistry, the anodic oxidation of hydrocarbons and other organic fuels, molten salts, thermodynamics, and concentrated aqueous electrolytes (fluorides and carbonates). He and co-worker David Douglas developed the first metal bipolar plates and the first membrane-electrode assemblies (MEAs) for proton exchange membrane (PEM) fuel cells. The first fuel cells used in the space program were built by General Electric, based on the work of the GE team. For this, in 1963, he was awarded the Electrochemical Society's Francis Mills Turner Award.[20]

In 1966, Cairns joined Argonne National Laboratory as Group Leader of Liquid Metals and Molten Salts Research Group. He conducted research on the electrochemistry of molten salt cells including Li/S, thermodynamics, phase equilibria, and Raman spectroscopy. For this he received the IR-100 Award. In 1968, with H.A. Liebhafsky he co-authored the book *Fuel Cells and Fuel Batteries*.[21] He became section head for R&D of Li/S and related cells in 1970. He was elected a fellow, American Institute of Chemists.

In 1973, he joined General Motors Research Labs as assistant head of the electrochemistry department, responsible for R&D on fuel cells, high temperature cells including LiAl/FeS2. He was responsible for the development of a Zn/NiOOH battery for electric Chevettes and electric Chevy Luv Trucks. The field tests were successful, but the EV project was discontinued when the price of oil dropped in the late 1970s.

In 1978, Cairns returned to his alma mater, where he became professor of chemical engineering at the University of California, Berkeley, and associate laboratory director of Lawrence Berkeley National Laboratory. He was also head of the energy and environment division of Lawrence Berkeley National Laboratory. His research at Berkeley included photothermal deflection spectroscopy for in situ study of electrode reactions, studies of the zinc electrode, oxygen reduction in strong aqueous electrolytes, the electrochemistry of aqueous polysulfides, lithium-ion cells, the lithium-sulfur cell and the application of X-ray absorption spectroscopy and NMR to the study of battery and fuel-cell electrode reactions. In 1979, Cairns received the Croft Memorial Award, University of Missouri, followed by the Centennial Scholar Medal and Award, Case–Western Reserve University (1980). From 1999 to 2000 he was president of the International Society of Electrochemistry.

His teaching at UC Berkeley included electrochemical engineering, energy conversion and storage, transport phenomena, process design, and the chemical engineering laboratory course. His outside professional activities included editing scientific journals. He was an editor of the *Journal of the Electrochemical Society* from 1973 to 1990, and *Electrochimica Acta* from 1987 to 2004. He organized scientific symposia, serving on professional society and NAS committees, and in elected offices including president of the Electrochemical Society and president of the International Society of Electrochemistry. He also enjoys serving as a consultant, and as an expert witness in court cases, being particularly fascinated by patent infringement cases. He has authored or co-authored over 270 technical papers and over 20 patents.

In 2003, Cairns became division president, Berkeley Chapter of Sigma Xi, whose main objective is to encourage and reward scientific research in the community.

In November 2013, Cairns, now 81 years old, and a Faculty Senior Scientist at Lawrence Lab, with co-workers Min-Kyu Song (Molecular Foundry, Berkeley Lab), Yuegang Zhang (Suzhou Institute of Nano-Tech and Nano-Bionics, Chinese Academy of Sciences) announced their innovation of an advanced lithium-sulfur (Li/S) cell that can provide more than twice the Wh/kg of a Li ion battery, and has already shown that it can do 1,500 charge cycles without significant deterioration.[22]

They had synthesized these cells using graphene oxide—a treated version of the very thin carbon layers whose discoverers at the University of Manchester won the Nobel Prize in physics in 2010. Cairns and co-workers figured out what was causing the deterioration (complex sulfur chemistry) and then used a graphene-based sandwich to stop it from happening. And for good measure they also improved the electrolyte, using an ionic liquid, and made several other improvements to the cathode. Experts who have looked at this indicate that these lithium sulfur graphene batteries could enable electric vehicles with a range of more than 300 miles on a single charge. The research was funded in part by the U.S. Department of Energy's Office of Science, Basic Energy Sciences, and a University of California Proof of Concept Award.

Cairns recently stated, "We are now entering the phase of technology transfer to industry under sponsorship form a battery company, with the intent of commercializing the Li/S cell for a wide range of applications."

To relax, Elton Cairns enjoys increasing his large digital music collection, gardening, home repairs, and home electronics. He also very much enjoys being with his two stepsons and their families living nearby.

Source: Information supplied to the author by Elton Cairns, January 2015 and 2016.

Notes

20. Ion Exchange Membrane Fuel Battery, E.J. Cairns and D.L. Douglas, U.S. 3,134,696 (May 26, 1964).

21. H.A. Liebhafsky and E.J. Cairns: *Fuel Cells and Fuel Batteries: A Guide to their Research and Development* (New York: John Wiley and Sons, 1968).

22. Min-Kyu Song, Yuegang Zhang, and Elton J. Cairns: *A Long-Life, High-Rate Lithium/Sulfur Cell: A Multifaceted Approach to Enhancing Cell Performance* (Nano Lett., 2013), 13 (12), pp. 5891–5899. Copyright © 2013 American Chemical Society.

••

Callan, Nicholas Joseph
(1799–1864)
Callan's Coil and the world's largest battery

In 1824, a young Irish priest called Nicholas Joseph Callan may have been in Rome to study divinity at the Sapienza University. But he also took a keen interest in the ground-breaking work carried out during the past forty years by Luigi Galvani and Alessandro Volta on electricity. It was an interest he would pursue during the next 40 years of his life.

Callan was born on December 27, 1799, at Darver in the Parish of Dromiskin, between Drogheda and Dundalk, Ireland. His was a well-to-do family of farmers, malt-sters and bakers, and Nicholas was the fifth child in a family of seven. From the start, his education was inside the Catholic Church: altar boy and Mass server, then starting his priesthood at Navan seminary, and then in 1816 to Saint Patrick's Ecclesiastical College, Maynooth, near Dublin. And it was here that he was initiated into the marvels of magnetism by Dr. Cornelius Denvir, then professor of natural and experimental philosophy.

On his return from Italy in 1826, Callan replaced his former tutor at Maynooth College, where he was to spend the rest of his life, most often in his basement laboratory—when, that is, he was not teaching his students.

Helped by funding from family and friends, the Irish priest began to work on the idea of a device for producing high voltage currents. He built his first one in 1836. Taking a horseshoe-shaped iron bar, he wound it with thin insulated wire and then wound thick insulated wire over the windings of the thinner wire. He thus discovered that, when a current sent by battery through a "primary" coil was interrupted, a high voltage current was produced in an unconnected "secondary" coil (a large number of turns of fine wire).

Callan's Coil also used an interrupter that consisted of a rocking wire that repeatedly dipped into a small cup of mercury. Because of the action of the interrupter, which could make and break the current going into the coil, Callan called his device the "repeater."

Arguably this device was the world's first transformer.

Callan had induced a high voltage in the second wire starting with a low voltage in the adjacent first wire. And the faster he interrupted the current, the bigger the spark.

In 1837, he produced his giant induction machine: using the escapement mechanism from a grandfather clock as his repeater in the primary coil to interrupt the current 20 times a second, it generated 15-inch sparks, an estimated 600,000 volts and the largest *artificial* lightning bolt yet seen!

The following year, this intrepid Irish priest stumbled on the principle of the self-exciting dynamo (ten years after and in ignorance of the work of another priest, Ányos Jedlik; see Jedlik entry). Simply by moving his electromagnet in the Earth's magnetic field, Callan found he could produce electricity without a battery.

He even managed to adapt a motor to drive a small trolley around his laboratory, which led him to proposing that electromagnetic locomotives could be used on the new railways, instead of steam. In 1838, he was designing an engine to propel a carriage and load at eight miles per hour and had hopes of using them to electrify the railway line from Dublin to Dun Laoghaire (formerly Kingstown). But gradually he realized that magnetic action was powerful only at short distances, and how large magnets interfere with each other. Batteries of small electros are complicated and harder to manage than a steam engine giving the same power. He noted too that the galvanic battery needed to produce notable power was both expensive and troublesome. After trials on a large scale, Callan had to admit defeat.

Callan next progressed to connecting up ever larger numbers of batteries.

One of them consisted of 280 cells, but the units were of the conventional type with standard four-inch zinc plates. In the presence of 300 students, he carried out some striking experiments with this battery. To test the magnetic effect, he had a novel tug-of-war between a team of students and one of his electromagnets. When the current was sent through the set of primary coils, all the efforts of robust students failed to dislodge the

Nicholas Callan, priest and scientist (Saint Patrick's College, Maynooth).

keeper from the magnet. But then the professor played a little trick. He cut the current as the team was making a mighty heave: the magnet was no longer active and the members all fell in a heap on the floor, much to the amusement and applause of the onlookers!

He then progressed to connecting 577 cells with a combined area of zinc of some 9m2. It was at least twice as large as that constructed at the École Polytechnique on Napoleon's orders (see Davy entry), and was therefore "probably the world's largest battery." To charge it, he required fourteen gallons of nitric and sixteen gallons of sulfuric acid. In March 1848, before an awestruck audience, he demonstrated the powers of his battery. A very large turkey was instantly electrocuted when placed in the electric circuit (see Frankling entry). A five-inch arc of blinding light was obtained between copper and brass terminals. Carbon arcs burned away too rapidly for the length of arc to be determined. At this stage, several porous pots burst, and some copper leads fell off their zincs through combustion of the solder.

With the need to produce reliable batteries for his researches in electromagnetism, Callan had developed what came to be known as "the Maynooth Battery," developing a single fluid cell the following year. Previous batteries had used expensive gold or platinum, or unsatisfactory carbon, for one of their plates and zinc for the other. Father Callan found he could use inexpensive cast iron instead of platinum or carbon. In the Maynooth battery, the outer casing was of cast iron, treated with an anti-corrosive tin-lead mix, and the zinc plate was immersed in a porous pot. But he then found that he could make a simple and useful battery by dispensing with the porous pot and the two fluids, using a single solution.

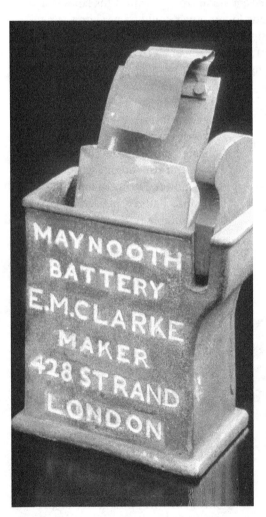

The outer casing of the battery was cast iron. In his damp basement laboratory, when the iron began to rust, Callan investigated a method of preventing this. It was for the principle of galvanization that he was granted the patent in 1853 by Her Majesty Queen Victoria.

The Maynooth Battery was put into commercial production by Edward Marmaduke Clarke at the Battersea Iron Works, and sold from his Adelaide Gallery of Practical Science, 428, The Strand, London.

Callan also experimented with various forms of electric lighting, from arc lights to limelight. By electrolyzing acidulated water he produced hydrogen and oxygen, which gave him an oxyhydrogen torch with which he heated up a block of lime, producing an intensely brilliant light. He hoped that this would

The Maynooth Battery (Saint Patrick's College, Maynooth).

serve for lighthouse beacons, but practical difficulties militated against its use. Hydrogen and oxygen, after all, can form a highly explosive mixture; Callan described one occasion on which an explosion shattered the vessel in which the gases were contained.

Since there were no instruments yet to measure current or voltage, Callan assessed his batteries by the weight they could lift when connected to an electromagnet. His best effort lifted two tons. When Callan reported this in the *Annals of Electricity*, an incredulous London professor made a pilgrimage to Maynooth to witness the spectacle for himself!

For his researches, he purchased vast amounts of mercury, great sheets of copper and zinc, literally miles of copper and iron wire, porous pots and glass containers by the gross, platinum foil, brass and iron and coke in rod and sheet and plate, insulating materials in bulk. At times the science hall must have looked like a factory. He was generous to fellow scientists in various parts of the world, in Ireland, England, and as far away as India, sending them induction coils and electro motors he had personally constructed, with the help of local Maynooth blacksmiths.

It is related how one morning while saying Mass, the priest-scientist found himself using his fingernail to trace diagrams of electro motors on the altar cloth and was shocked to discover that scientific research had taken such a hold on his mind. A simple tale roundly states that as a penance for having spent so much of his time in the physics laboratory, Callan was enjoined by his confessor to devote his leisure hours in future to translating St. Alphonsus Maria Liguori's *Marion Devotion*.

Another yarn relates how Callan once visited the 3rd Earl of Rosse at Birr Castle and asked to see his giant telescope. For some reason, the curious priest was refused. When the Earl later visited Maynooth to inspect Callan's induction coil, Callan was reported to have sent this message to the earl waiting at the college gate: "With Dr. Callan's compliments, and if Lord Rosse would return to Birr, he can see the Callan Coil through his Great Telescope."

The Reverend Callan was said to have used his students as human electrometers in his experiments, asking them to take electric shocks from his coil and then measuring its voltage by their reactions. Fortunately there were no fatalities, but he did manage to render one student, who later became Archbishop of Dublin, unconscious. After this mishap, he limited himself to electrocuting turkeys!

In one letter dated February 21, 1855, one of Callan's students, Lawrence Johnson, wrote: "We have a priest here from Co. Louth, Dr. Callan, the Professor of Science, and many are afraid he will blow up the College. Yesterday in St. Joseph's Grounds we heard an explosion that was like the end of the world. It is believed his health will not hold out, and many say he should be given a good rest." Then on April 9 of the same year, Lawrence writes: "Dr. Callan is still experimenting night and day with gases and metals. In fact there is no knowing where he will stop if his health does not fail. In the Physic [sic] Hall today before the whole class he had his Box hopping by itself all over the floor. But he is a very holy priest."

Nicholas Callan, holy priest and pioneer scientist, died from natural causes at Maynooth on January 10, 1864.

As sometimes happens, Callan's invention of the induction coil was for a long time attributed to a German instrument-maker called Heinrich Ruhmkorff. Callan was largely forgotten by the wider world of science mainly because Maynooth was a theological university and science had a low status on the curriculum. But in 1936 a Professor McLaughlin published his researches into Callan's publications and proved that Callan had indeed invented the induction coil. The need for recognition of Callan was for many years a cause célèbre among the Irish scientific and engineering fraternity. The definitive paper on Callan by the Reverend T.M. Casey was published in the *Proceeding of the Institute of Electrical Engineers* in December 1985.

As part of the Millennium Celebrations, the *Irish Post* launched a "Discovery" series of postage stamps to celebrate major scientific achievements. Included in this series is a stamp commemorating the Reverend Nicholas Callan. Others featured in the series include Galileo, Einstein, Marie Curie and Thomas Edison.

In September 2006, a bronze plaque honoring Callan's work was set up in the foyer of the Electronic Engineering and Bio-Sciences Building at the National University of Ireland, Maynooth. It was unveiled by the President of the IEEE.

The National Science Museum at Saint Patrick's College, Maynooth, holds a remarkable collection of old scientific instruments, including many items salvaged from Father Callan's original laboratory.

Sources: From an article by the author, published in *Batteries International*, Winter 2007, based on information supplied by Dr. Niall McKeith, Radiological Protection Officer at the Dept. of Experimental Physics, Maynooth, Ireland.

....

Chapin, Daryl M.
(1906–1995)
Calvin Souther Fuller
(1902–1994)
Gerald Leondus Pearson
(1905–1987)
The solar battery

It sometimes happens that scientists from entirely different research backgrounds come together to form the catalyst behind a great invention. This time their names were Chapin, Pearson and Fuller, all three middle-aged scientists employed by Bell Laboratories, Murray Hill, New Jersey.

Daryl M. Chapin was an engineer. Following his master's degree at Washington University in 1929, he started off at Bell Labs by investigating magnetic materials. During World War II, he was evaluating underwater acoustics. Following three years of work on magnetic recording, he had turned his attention to special projects such as magnetic measurement, simulated speech, miniaturization, and pulse code transmission.

Gerald L. Pearson was a physicist. Following his master's degree at Stanford University in 1929, he was immediately hired by Bell Labs and began to research noise in resistors, vacuum tubes and carbon microphones. Having worked on military projects during World War II, in 1945 when science groups at Bell were reorganized, Pearson was

Chapin, Pearson and Fuller, co-inventors of the solar battery in 1954 (courtesy Alcatel-Lucent USA, Inc.).

put into a lab dedicated to studying solid state physics. From now on he concentrated on semiconductor research. In this field he had been concerned with thermistors, transistors and silicon reflectors.

Calvin S. Fuller was a chemist. Following a PhD at the University of Chicago, he joined Bell in 1930 and began by researching organic insulating material. Several years later, Fuller had turned his full attention to studies of plastics and synthetic rubber, including investigations of the molecular nature of polymers and the development of plastics and rubber for telephone and associated apparatus. From 1948, Fuller had been concentrating on semiconductor research and the development of semiconductor devices.

In early 1953, Daryl Chapin was trying to develop a source of power for telephone systems in remote humid locations, where dry cell batteries degrade too quickly. He had investigated several alternative energy sources, and settled on solar power as one of the most promising. He tried selenium solar cells, but found them too inefficient. He was unable to surpass a minimal level, 1 percent or so, of efficiency.

However, in another part of the Bell Labs, Professors Pearson and Fuller were working on a separate project: that of controlling the properties of semiconductors by introducing impurities. Fuller gave Pearson a piece of silicon containing gallium impurities. Pearson dipped it in lithium, creating a p-n junction. Pearson then hooked up an ammeter to the piece of silicon and shined a light on it. The ammeter jumped significantly, to their surprise. Pearson, who was aware of Chapin's work, went and told his friend not to waste any more time on selenium solar cells, and Chapin immediately switched to silicon.

The three then worked for several months on improving the properties of their silicon solar cells. One problem was the difficulty in making good electrical contacts with the silicon cells. Another problem was that at room temperature, lithium migrated through the silicon over time, moving the p-n junction farther away from the incoming sunlight. To solve that problem, they tried different impurities, and eventually settled on arsenic and boron, which created a p-n junction that stayed near the surface. They also found they were able to make good electrical contacts with the boron-arsenic silicon cells. Fuller devised a special furnace and a melting process to get rid of the impurities in silicon.

After making some other improvements to the design, they linked together several solar cells to create what they called a "solar battery."

Many years later, Fuller's oldest son, Robert W. Fuller, would recall:

In 1954, I was home on vacation from college to visit my parents. That night my father came home with something that looked like a quarter with wires sticking out of it. This was a device that connected to a small electric windmill that stood on the table. He shined a bright flashlight on the quarter-like object, which was actually a silicon solar cell, and the blades of the windmill started turning. It was so exciting to see the flashlight power the tiny windmill. While this device looked like a quarter to anyone else, it was actually the world's first silicon solar battery—a device that later become known as the silicon solar cell."

A historic press release reads:

News from Bell Telephone Laboratories: For Release at 6pm, Sunday, April 25, 1954: A solar battery—the first successful device to convert useful amounts of the sun's energy directly and efficiently into electricity—was demonstrated today at Bell Telephone Laboratories.

Scientists there, with an amazingly simple-looking apparatus made of strips of silicon, showed how the sun's rays could be used to power the transmission of voices over telephone wires. The Bell solar battery also used energy from the sun to power a transistor radio carrying both speech and music. Bell Laboratories reported that it was able to achieve a 6 percent efficiency in converting sunlight directly into electricity. This compares favorably with the efficiency of steam and gasoline engines, in contrast with other photoelectric devices which have never been rated higher than 1 percent....

A demonstration of the revolutionary new solar energy battery will be given by Bell Laboratories at the annual meeting of the National Academy of Sciences in Washington, D.C., Monday, April 26.

Following this demonstration, the *New York Times* wrote that the silicon solar cell "may mark the beginning of a new era, leading eventually to the realization of one of mankind's most cherished dreams–the harnessing of the almost limitless energy of the sun for the uses of civilization."

On Monday, May 3, 1954, *Time Magazine* published:

Turning the sun's energy directly into electricity has long been a goal of scientists. In Washington last week, the Bell Telephone Laboratories demonstrated a solar battery which can convert sunlight into usable electric current without costly intermediate steps. The Bell Solar Battery resembles a miniature xylophone. It is made of wafer-thin strips of specially treated silicon, linked in series. Silicon is a

Americus, Georgia, 1955: Bell technician fits solar panel (courtesy Alcatel-Lucent USA, Inc.).

semiconductor, i.e., under certain conditions it can be made to carry electricity.... The battery is far more efficient than other photoelectric devices (e.g., the cells used in light meters), produces enough electricity—50 watts per square yard of exposed surface—to power small radio transmitters, record players, etc."

Soon after, the solar three published a paper in the *Journal of Applied Physics*. It was titled "A New Silicon p-n Junction Photocell for Converting Solar Radiation into Electrical Power."

AT&T's film unit now made a 13-minute documentary about the "Bell Solar Battery." While shooting at Murray Hill took only six days, the script had been in preparation, undergoing various revisions, for several months. The three inventors—Chapin, Fuller and Pearson—were each photographed in typical laboratory locations as they talked briefly about their work.

By July 4, 1955, *Time Magazine* had more to report:

> When Bell Telephone Laboratories announced its silicon solar battery, it fired the imaginations of the science fictionists, and the solar system was soon abuzz with solar-powered space ships. Trimming their silicon sails to catch the sunlight, spacemen used the electricity generated by the batteries to push themselves from planet to planet. More practical imaginations were fired too. Last week National Fabricated Products Inc., a Chicago electronics manufacturer, announced that it has had more than 500 inquiries about the silicon batteries which it has just started making commercially under license from Bell Lab's parent company, Western Electric. Inquiries have come from industrial laboratories all over the world, including India. Most customers ask for a dozen or so ($25 each), and seldom say what they hope to use them for.
>
> N.F.P.'s version of the battery is a thin, blackish wafer about the size of a half dollar, enclosed in protective glass. It has two electric terminals like any other battery, and when it is exposed to bright sunlight it generates about half a volt. A square yard of the batteries would light a 100-watt lamp or run an electric fan. A few acres would give enough power for a fair-sized town.

Daryl Chapin and his colleagues must now prove that, although work was still in the laboratory stage, actual use of the solar battery in the telephone business was a strong possibility. If only they could show that silicon solar batteries might be used as power supplies for low-powered mobile equipment, as a sun-powered battery charger which could be used at amplifier stations along a rural telephone system.

That first demonstration was not to take place until the autumn. The site chosen was the rural town of Americus, Georgia. There it was that on October 4, 1955, County Commission Chairman George L. Mathews made the world's first solar-powered telephone call, in the 28th District, near Bethel Baptist Church. It is not known whom he phoned or what was said.

In 1957, Chapin, Pearson and Fuller were awarded U.S. Patent No. 2,780,765 for a "Solar Energy Converting Apparatus."

During the next three years, Bell scientists continued to improve the solar battery, increasing its efficiency from 6 percent to 11 percent. The team responsible included K.D. Smith, E.J. Stansbury, C.J. Frosch and D.F. Ciccolella. Another company, Hoffman Electronics, was also working on more efficient panels.

Very soon, the U.S. Department of Defense realized an extremely valuable application of this device as it deployed self-sufficient power to vehicles and satellites in space. So it was that the earliest significant application of solar cells was as a back-up power source to the *Vanguard I* satellite launched on March 17, 1958. The initial 1.4 kg spherical *Vanguard* satellites were built at the NRL, and contained as their payload seven mercury cell batteries in a hermetically sealed container, two tracking radio transmitters, a temperature-sensitive crystal, and six clusters of solar cells on the surface of the sphere. The latter allowed *Vanguard I* to continue transmitting for over a year after its chemical battery was exhausted. The successful operation of solar cells on this mission was duplicated in many other Soviet and American satellites; for example, in 1962, *Telstar*, the first communications satellite, was powered by 3,600 solar batteries. Seven years later, Bell scientists adapted solar principles to translate electronic data into light energy. This led to the charge-coupled device, or CCD, now used in digital cameras and the Internet.

As for the three pioneers:

With a total of 33 patents to his name, Fuller eventually retired to Vero Beach, Florida, although he spent his time traveling around the United States in a Silver Stream Camper with his wife. He died aged 92.

As early as 1958, Pearson had returned to Stanford University, where he set up a solid-state electronics program, which put his old university in the forefront of the universities in this field. He continued researching into his 79th year.

In 1959, Chapin simplified the solar-cell making process. It became a widely used science experiment for advanced high school students, who used Chapin's accompanying textbook *Energy from the Sun*. The afternoon of his death in January 1995, aged 88, in Naples, Florida, Chapin was working with a friend on a new board game for the blind.

On May 2, 2008, posthumously, the three were elected to the U.S. National Inventors Hall of Fame for their invention of the "Silicon Solar Cell."

Sources: From an article by the author, published in *Batteries International*, Summer 2012, from information supplied by Alcatel-Lucent USA, Inc. Archives.

••

Clark, Josiah Latimer
(1822–1898)
Clark Standard Cell

Joseph Latimer Clark was born on March 10, 1822, in Great Marlow, Buckinghamshire, England. The third son of Josiah Clark, grocer, Joseph studied chemistry at an early age, gaining practical experience of the chemical manufacturing industry in a large Dublin establishment. From 1848, with the boom in the construction of railways, Clark began working in his elder brother Edwin's civil engineering practice and became assistant engineer at the Menai Strait Bridge. Two years later, when Edwin was appointed engineer to the Electric and International Telegraph Company, Joseph again acted as his assistant, and subsequently succeeded him as chief engineer. He held this post until the various telegraphic systems were nationalized in 1870. During this time he filed 150 patents, in different countries, for a variety of improvements concerning telegraph cables. In 1871 Clark took a large part in founding the Society of Telegraph Engineers and Electricians (later renamed the Institution of Electrical Engineers). He devoted much of his leisure to astronomy and photography, inventing a camera for taking stereoscopic pictures with a single lens.

Latimer Clark paid much attention to the subject of precise electrical measurement. In 1873 he read a paper before the Royal Society, *A Standard Battery of Constant Electromotive Force*, describing a constant battery on which he had been supervising experiments since 1867. This wet-chemical cell produced a highly stable voltage. Clark's original cell was set up in a glass jar in a similar way to a gravity Daniell cell. The copper cathode was replaced by a pool of mercury at the bottom of the jar. Above this was the mercurous sulfate paste and, above that, the zinc sulfate solution. A short zinc rod was dipped into the zinc sulfate solution. The zinc rod was supported by a cork with two holes—one for the zinc rod and the other for a glass tube reaching to the bottom of the cell. A platinum wire, fused into the glass tube, made contact with the mercury pool. When complete, the cell was sealed with a layer of marine glue.

It had a large temperature coefficient of -0.00115 V/°C, and suffered from cracking where the platinum connections entered the glass envelope. This was caused by the platinum alloying with the zinc amalgam. In spite of its problems, it was reproducible, and became the first commercially successful standard cell. Lord Rayleigh investigated a form of Clark cell in 1885 that became known as the Board of Trade cell. In 1893, the output of the Clark cell at 15 C was defined by the International Electrical Congress as 1.434 volts, and this definition became law in the United States in 1894.

••

Coetzer, Johan
(1941–)
The sodium–iron chloride Zebra battery

World War II: Hitler had decided to bring the UK to its knees by destroying it with a hailstorm of V rockets. As the particularly lethal V-2 rocket required a reliable battery, a Dr. Georg Otto Erb developed the molten-salt battery, which used the heat of the rocket to keep the salt liquid during its mission…

Thirty years later: 1974. The Arab countries imposed an embargo against the United States, Western countries and Japan for their support of Israel. The price of oil jumped from $3 to $12 a barrel. This triggered a worldwide quest for alternative energy sources and improved batteries for energy storage.

One of those scientists who were to make a major contribution to battery technology was a South African called Johan Coetzer.

Coetzer was born on February 4, 1941, in Bloemfontein, South Africa, where he matriculated in 1958. He attended the University of Pretoria, South Africa, where he received the B.S. degree with distinction in chemistry in 1962. He continued his studies at this university and obtained the M.S. degree with distinction in chemistry in 1964.

In 1963 he married Renée du Plessis, who gave him three children, a girl and two boys. In 1965 he accepted a predoctoral assistantship at Indiana University. During this period he developed a great interest in the structure and properties of materials, which is also evident from the title of his PhD dissertation: "Gas Phase Molecular Structure Studies of 1,6- Methano 1,3,5,7,9—Cyclo-decapentaene and Cyclo-propanone by Means of Electrondiffraction." He received the PhD in 1968.

Following his return to South Africa in 1968, Coetzer joined the X-ray crystallography division of the Council for Scientific and Industrial Research (CSIR) in Pretoria. The work involved the study of molecular structures of single crystal materials by means of X-ray methods. Amongst others, a fully automatic 4-circle X-ray diffractometer was available for this work. He published a number of scientific articles, covering a variety of solid state materials.

In 1973 he was obliged to interrupt his research career to spend time on the family sugar cane farm at Pongola in the Natal province. It was while he was out there that the

Johan Coetzer of South Africa (*Batteries International*).

worldwide oil crisis hit. Inevitably the CSIR strongly encouraged future projects to only concentrate on applied research. Energy conservation became a high priority.

The farming business, although rewarding in its own right, lacked the challenge and intellectual stimulation of the research world.

Returning to the CSIR, Coetzer decided to investigate the structure-electrochemical properties of silver iodide-amine iodide solid electrolytes that showed anomalously high Ag^+-ion conductivity at room temperature.

This project heralded the start of a twenty-year period when CSIR and South Africa would make major contributions to advancing international battery science and technology.

The discovery of the Na^+-ion conducting solid electrolyte, "β-Al_2O_3," by Weber and Kummer at Ford Motor Company in 1967 had opened the door to the possibility of developing a non-aqueous, high energy and high temperature (350 °C) sodium-sulphur (Na/S) battery to replace lead-acid and nickel-cadmium batteries, particularly for electric vehicles and stationary energy storage. By 1975, development of this system was well underway in the USA and Europe.

At the same time, another high-temperature battery, based on a lithium aluminum-iron sulphide ($LiAl/FeS_2$) electrochemical couple and a molten salt (LiCl, KCl) electrolyte, was under development at Argonne National Laboratory in the USA.

Would the ultimate answer to energy storage lie in high temperature sodium—or in lithium-based batteries?

In 1975, Johan Coetzer was joined by Michael Thackeray (see Thackeray entry), already with a B.S. (Honors) and M.S. in chemistry at the University of Cape Town. While

Thackeray used the silver iodide project for his PhD thesis, Coetzer turned his attention to more practical technologies.

Because molten sodium and sulfur are highly reactive and combine violently if the ceramic "β-Al$_2$O$_3$" solid electrolyte in Na/S cells ruptures, and because molten sulfur is highly corrosive, Coetzer proposed the idea of using the pores within zeolitic structures to immobilize and contain the sulfur in a solid electrode matrix, thereby enhancing safety and minimizing corrosion. This concept was first evaluated in high temperature LiAl/LiCl, KCl/Zeolite-sulfur cells using Argonne's cell configuration.

This study prompted Coetzer to consider alternative electrodes for Argonne's technology and his thinking moved away from FeS$_2$ and zeolite-sulfur to iron chloride electrodes, the initial studies being conducted on chlorinated iron carbides, "Fe$_x$CCl$_y$" and, subsequently, simply iron dichloride, FeCl$_2$.

The early battery work and the ideas being generated at CSIR did not go unnoticed. In 1976, Coetzer elicited the interest of industry and, in particular, Roger Wedlake of De Beers who, recognizing the future potential of electric vehicles, persuaded senior management at De Beers and Anglo American Corporation to invest in CSIR's battery initiatives along with the South African Inventions Development Corporation (SAIDCOR) that was affiliated to CSIR.

In 1977, a formal agreement between CSIR, SAIDCOR, De Beers and Anglo American was signed. Significant progress was made and, within two years, several key patents had been filed internationally; potential partners abroad were identified to help drive CSIR's battery technologies forward.

In 1979, visits were made to Argonne National Laboratory, USA, and to the Atomic Energy Research Establishment (AERE) at Harwell, UK, where the Li/FeS$_x$ and Na/S technologies, respectively, were in advanced stages of development. Argonne declined the offer to collaborate, ostensibly because of the political sensitivities in South Africa at the time.

On the other hand, Ron Dell and Roger Bones, who had participated with British Rail in the development of Na/S batteries, and sensing the technological and safety limitations of the Na/S system, welcomed the South African delegation in anticipation of developing an alternative system. A huge advantage of the early collaboration with AERE was that it gave CSIR scientists immediate access to sodium-sulfur technology that enabled the evaluation of CSIR's zeolite-sulfur and iron-chloride electrodes in the sophisticated sodium-sulfur battery configuration.

The apartheid problems of South Africa and the international boycotts against the country made it difficult for CSIR/De Beers/Anglo American to operate openly with Harwell and Beta R&D. For this reason, the collaboration was undertaken without public exposure.

Dell and Bones code-named the project "Zebra" for "*Ze*olite *B*attery *R*esearch in *A*frica."

As Coetzer explains: "Perhaps a fitting description of the Zebra can be the following: a unique and robust creature that is equally at home in the dry, scorching plains of Central Africa where the temperatures can reach over 40°C in summer, as in the desolate, cold mountains of the Southern Cape where sub-zero temperatures are common during the winter months—and then it has a mighty good kick too!"

Because the zeolite-sulfur electrode was solid, a molten salt NaAlCl$_4$ electrolyte (m.p=155 °C) was added to the electrode compartment to enable rapid Na$^+$-ion diffusion between the zeolite-sulfur and sodium electrodes via the solid "β-Al_2O_3" electrolyte. The early results on Na/Zeolite-sulfur cells were not promising, largely because the zeolite component added considerable extra weight to the system, thereby yielding lower energy per unit mass compared to the pure Na/S battery.

Fortunately, the sodium-sulfur battery configuration was also suitable for evaluating the iron chloride electrodes being developed by Coetzer and his team for the Argonne-type high temperature lithium battery. In the sodium cell configuration, the reaction is simply:

$$2\,Na + FeCl_2 \rightarrow 2\,NaCl + Fe$$

It was Roy Galloway at CSIR who first realized and demonstrated that, unlike LiAl/FeS$_x$, LiAl/FeCl$_2$ and Na/S cells that are assembled in the charged state with highly reactive LiAl and Na negative electrodes (anodes), CSIR's sodium-iron chloride cells could be assembled in the discharged state using a simple mixture of table salt (NaCl) and iron metal powders in the positive electrode (cathode), thereby circumventing the difficulty and hazards of handling LiAl alloy or metallic sodium. Galloway also showed that the Na/NiCl$_2$ electrochemical couple offered a slightly higher cell voltage (2.58 V) and was more stable than the Na/FeCl$_2$ couple (2.35 V) to electrochemical cycling, making it the preferred system.

Despite the demise of CSIR's Na/Zeolite-sulfur technology, the name "Zebra" persisted and is still in use today to describe sodium-metal chloride batteries, although the acronym was later changed to represent "Zero Emission Battery Research Activity."

Significant progress was made by CSIR and Harwell in the early 1980s in demonstrating the feasibility of sodium/metal chloride battery technology. In 1982, recognizing the need to scale up the production and expedite the evaluation of Zebra batteries, Anglo American acquired facilities in Derby, UK, and established the company Beta R&D to manufacture "β-Al_2O_3" tubes, cells and batteries under the management of Jim Sudworth, a pioneer of Na/S technology from British Rail (see Sudworth entry). By 1984, a multi kWh Zebra battery had been built and demonstrated in an electric test vehicle.

In 1986, CSIR divested from the Zebra project, with most of the CSIR team joining Anglo American and moving to new facilities Zebra Power Systems Pty. Ltd. outside Pretoria. Johan Coetzer was appointed MD and later a director of the holding company, Dynamic Power Systems, which formed part of the Anglo American Industrial Corporation (AMIC).

The first car tested at Zebra Power Systems was a converted Suzuki minibus powered by a locally assembled 40kWh battery consisting of all-iron Zebra electrodes.

The following year, Coetzer was awarded the gold medal of the South African Academy of Science and Arts for his pioneering contribution to battery technology. At the same time, he was running a small farm nearby.

Over the next ten to 15 years, in a joint effort between Zebra Power Systems, Harwell, Beta R&D and Daimler-Benz, Germany, outstanding progress was made in optimizing Zebra battery technology. For example, to increase the power to energy ratio of the cell, in 1991, Coetzer and Tony Meintjes developed a cell with a convoluted beta alumina tube which both increased the surface area and reduced the thickness of the positive electrode. This became known as the monolith cell.

Such innovations were, of course, tested out in electric vehicles in all weather climates. Of particular note was that the technology was successfully used in Mercedes buses to transport athletes within the Olympic Village at the 1992 Games in Barcelona.

By 1998 AAB had taken the development of the Zebra battery to the point where it was ready to be put into production. The pilot lines in Derby and Berlin were producing batteries at the rate of up to twenty per month, the electric vehicles were performing very well, and the customers were pressing for a commitment for volume production.

Sadly, after 20 years of technological success, both Anglo American and Daimler-Benz decided to withdraw from further development of the Zebra battery, evidently because of the lack of a worldwide electric vehicle infrastructure that would sustain the technology.

Enter Carlo Bianco, the owner of MES, a major supplier of components for the automotive market. Bianco had established MES-DEA to produce components such as motors, drive systems and brake systems for electric vehicles and had purchased several Zebra batteries for powering prototype electric vehicles. In 1999, when the opportunity arose to purchase the Zebra battery technology, he decided to build a new plant for the volume production of Zebra batteries in Stabio, where ev battery manufacture continues to this day.

Johan Coetzer remained involved with the program at Beta R&D in Derby until 2001 as a part time consultant.

In 2002 he left the battery scene to concentrate on his farming activities, which had continued in parallel over the years. Apart from the sugar farm in Pongola, in partnership with his sons, Coetzer bought two further farms, namely, a cattle and a game farm in the Northern Province where a cattle feedlot and the breeding of several species of game were carried out. On the cattle farm a small project used embryo-implantation to produce thoroughbred calves of the Boran beef race.

The sugar farm covered approximately 150 hectares of planted cane fields irrigated by means of electrically driven water pumps from the Pongola River and utilizing an extensive network of overhead water sprinklers.

Of Coetzer's other interests, according to former colleague Roy Galloway, "Johan is a very keen Springbok rugby supporter and his idea of heaven is to watch his favourite club team, the Blue Bulls, play at Loftus Versveldt on a sunny highveldt winter afternoon in Pretoria with a packet of biltong in his hand."

The contributions made by Johan Coetzer and his colleagues to advancing battery technology were recognized at the opening ceremony of the Innovation Hub in Pretoria in 2005.

Sources: From an article by the author, published in *Batteries International* Autumn 2010, based on information supplied by Johan Coetzer, Michael M. Thackeray, Roy Galloway, Annette Joubert (CSIR Archives).

Conway, Brian Evans
(1927–2005)
Supercapacitor

Brian Evans Conway was born in Farnborough, Southern England, on January 26, 1927. He attended Imperial College London, where he became part of an elite group of ten researchers led by electrochemist John Bockris, who supervised them for their PhDs.

The principal subjects studied were electrode kinetics and very high temperature chemistry. During this time, Bockris and Conway attended discussions at the Faraday Society, where they met a famous group of Russian electrochemists, including B. Kabanov (see Kabanov entry).

Having obtained his PhD in 1949, Conway joined the Chester Beatty Cancer Research Institute, University of London, as a research associate with J.A.V. Butler, an eminent electrochemist. His research with Butler, whom he admired and respected greatly as a gentleman and scholar, concerned in part the influence of electrochemically generated free radicals and ionizing radiation for treating certain cancers.

In 1954, Conway moved to the University of Pennsylvania to join his former PhD supervisor, John Bockris, who had taken up a position there in the previous year and convinced Brian to try his hand in the "New World."

He stayed until 1956, at which time he was persuaded by chemical kinetics pioneer Professor Keith Laidler to apply for a faculty position at the then two-year-old Department of Chemistry of the University of Ottawa. Conway would remain there for the next 49 years. He was promoted to the rank of full professor in 1962, then four years later chairman of the department.

Conway proved to be a "complete" electrochemist in that he worked on nearly all aspects of electrochemistry: the electrified interface, ion solvation, adsorption, electrode kinetics, oxide film formation, electrocatalysis, rechargeable batteries, and electrochemical capacitors.

Between 1975 and 1980, Conway carried out extensive fundamental and development work on the ruthenium oxide type of electrochemical capacitor. In 1991 he coined the term "supercapacitor" as the explanation for increased capacitance by surface redox reactions with faradaic charge transfer between electrodes and ions.[23]

From 1983 to 1985, Brian Conway was a Killam Senior Research Fellow and the Natural Sciences and Engineering Research Council (NSERC)—Alcan Professor of Electrochemistry from 1987 to 1992.

Conway's work in applied electrochemistry has allowed the development of rechargeable, compact batteries and supercapacitors for cellular phones. In the early 2000s, Axion developed their e3 Supercell, a low cost battery-supercapacitor hybrid that uses the same cases, materials, internal components and manufacturing equipment as conventional lead-acid batteries; it offers faster recharge rates, higher power output and longer cycle-life.[24] During this time, they collaborated with Brian Conway, the East Penn Manufacturing Company, and Sandia National Laboratories, an independent testing facility owned by the U.S. Department of Energy and managed by Lockheed Martin Corporation.

Brian Conway died on July 9, 2005. Less than one year later, in May 2006, Axion Power International Inc. successfully manufactured its first commercial prototype e3 Supercells on a conventional lead acid battery production line.

Conway published over 260 scientific research articles, and was a senior editor of two series, *Comprehensive Treatise of Electrochemistry* and *Modern Aspects of Electrochemistry*. He also wrote about electrochemical data, electrode processes and ionic hydration in chemistry and biophysics.

Known as the "dean of electrochemistry in Canada," amongst his most prestigious honors and awards: Fellow of the Royal Society of Canada (1968), the Chemical Institute of Canada Medal (1975), the American Chemical Society Kendall Award in Surface Chemistry (1984), the Electrochemical Society Henry Linford Medal (1984), the Olin Palladium

Medal and Award of the Electrochemical Society (1989), the Galvani Medal of the Italian Chemical Society (1991), and Fellow of the Electrochemical Society of America (1995).

NOTES

23. B.E. Conway, "Transition from 'Supercapacitor' to 'Battery' Behavior in Electrochemical Energy Storage," *Journal of the Electrochemical Society* 138 (6) (May 1991): pp. 1539–1548.
24. U.S. Patent (No. 7,006,346) 2006: Positive Electrode of an Electric Double Layer Capacity Technology.

• •

Cooper, John Frederick
(1946–)

*Refuelable metal-air batteries
and direct carbon conversion cells*

John F. Cooper was born in Ohio in 1946. He was inspired to pursue a career in chemistry by his grandfather and his father (prolific inventors of materials for dirigibles and inflatable seacraft, and for advanced jet aircraft, respectively).

During the summers of 1964 to 1967, Cooper began his career as a laboratory researcher in electrochemistry at Rockwell Science Center (Thousand Oaks, California). He obtained his chemistry B.A. at Pomona College (1968). He chose to work in the field of electrochemistry at the University of California, Berkeley, after considering the character and work of his future PhD thesis adviser, Prof. Charles W. Tobias (see Tobias entry), one of the originators of electrochemical engineering field. Cooper's thesis concerned periodic phenomena during anodic dissolution of metals.[25] It was published in 1980.[26]

From 1974 to 1979, Cooper was the principal investigator for the Energy and Resources Program at the Lawrence Livermore National Laboratory (LLNL), Livermore, California. He first investigated lithium-water-air batteries for mobile and transportable power.

From 1980 to 1983, Cooper was national program leader, Department of Energy, Aluminum Air Battery Program, conducted in cooperation with four corporate partners: Lockheed Missiles and Space Co., Alcoa, Reynolds Aluminum and Diamond Shamrock. The objective was that such a battery would weigh only one-sixth as much as standard lead-acid batteries and occupy one-third the space, yet might cost less per mile to operate.

That program advanced to the stage where it was fully transferred to industry, but the battery did not see commercial development in autos because worldwide petroleum supplies remained ample and relatively cheap, and because of the battery's chief drawback: aluminum corrosion. The technology instead evolved into batteries for emergency power reserve units, submarine propulsion, and forklift trucks.

From 1984 to 1989, as research and technology leader, Laser Materials and Processes, Laser Directorate, Cooper worked with Chemist Mary F. Singleton and a team of chemical and mechanical engineers. They developed techniques for rapid and low-cost growth of potassium dihydrogen phosphate single crystals for use as non-linear optical devices in the LLNL Laser Programs. He also developed a thermally stable Bridgman furnace (amplitude $\pm$ 0.1 C/ at 2000 C) for growth of garnet crystals for solid state lasers.

From 1992 Cooper was scientific capability leader, leading a team of chemists and engineers on the Energy, Manufacturing, and Transportation Technologies (EMATT) program. In 1993, he invented and patented a novel cell for consuming 1-mm zinc pellets to generate power for electric vehicles, and a novel technique for recovering zinc pellets from battery products. The cell made use of cross-gap bridging phenomena of large particles to sustain an expanded bed anode. This resulted in continuous discharge and full zinc consumption.

In February 1995, Cooper and his colleagues tested their battery by installing it in an electric bus on loan from the Santa Barbara Municipal Transit District. This road test established the potential of the battery to give electric vehicles some of the attractive features of gas-driven cars: 400-km range (250 miles) between refueling (a ten-minute operation) and highway-safe acceleration. Refueling was accomplished by replacing spent electrolyte with fresh electrolyte containing recycled zinc pellets. The demonstration cleared the way for discussions with a host of interested commercial partners for further development.

With the new millennium approaching, Cooper, as deputy materials program leader, Chemistry and Materials Directorate, LLNL, developed new techniques to eliminate the hazardous organic components in mixed wastes containing nuclear, by means of chemical oxidation using peroxydisulfate radical. The same process was adapted for the destruction of chemical warfare agents and decontamination of equipment.

His primary research concerned development of carbon-air fuel cells and batteries, ultimately concluding that CO_2 evolution combined with high voltages provide for discharge efficiency of 70–80 percent of theoretical. These devices react to atmospheric oxygen and elemental carbon (particles or dense slabs) in a chemically invariant electrolyte of mixed alkali carbonates at 650–750 C. (The work is unrelated to the coal battery of William Jacques, in which the sodium hydroxide electrolyte was consumed as part of the cell reaction (see Jacques entry).

In 1998, Cooper and his colleagues at LLNL assembled and operated the first laboratory carbon-air cells combining cathodes of Molten Carbonate Fuel Cell (MCFC) provenance, porous alumina separator, and a coarse bed of elemental carbon derived from fossil or renewable biomass resources. They showed the cell to be capable of operating efficiency above 70 percent HHV, and that it sustained the net reaction, $C + O_2 = CO_2$. Work with Cherepy et al. in C/air cells reported that rates were determined not by purity but by a measure of atomic-level disorder in the carbon microcrystalline domain.

Work at LLNL followed studies by V. Hauser (1964; Oregon State University), R. Weaver and L. Nanis (1981, SRI), and D. Vutetakis (1986, Ohio State University), who determined independently that CO_2 evolved at high rates under moderate conditions of carbon anode polarization—a precondition for high efficiency conversion. This contradicted early 20th century reports concluding that useful rates could be obtained only at high temperatures with the evolution of CO as anode product (resulting in <50 percent total efficiency).

After 2006, work discontinued in the U.S. but thrived abroad, with hundreds of publications in China (five universities worked in parallel on DCFC), Australia, Japan, Korea, the UK, the European Union, Russia, and others.[27] An *ab initio* model developed by Y. Li (University of Tianjin, China) established that a pure CO_2 product and efficient discharge are possible and depend on the size of the graphite micro-crystal; the model was grounded in experimental data from graphite polarization in molten carbonate half-cells.[28,29]

With J. Robert Selman (Illinois Institute of Technology, Chicago), Cooper then analyzed scores of published anode polarization curves and their dependence on electrolyte flow and specific area to conclude that disordered carbon anodes could achieve sufficient polarization for CO2 and high efficiency discharge in C/air cells by effecting a change in reaction location from the porous interior to the exterior surface of the anode (*International Journal of Hydrogen Energy* 37 19319 [2012]).[30] The paper received international recognition as an innovation in the field of energy conversion. Cooper and Selman subsequently published work that further supported this interpretation from published voltage transients. It was determined that Li's criterion for polarization resulting in 4-electron/mole oxidation could be met by voltage increases associated with supersaturated CO2 levels in micro-pores. A review of work 1998–2008 emphasizing differences between carbon conversion cells operating near equilibrium and under nonequilibrium conditions was recently published by Hemmes, Cooper and Selman.

At time of writing (January 2015), a laboratory prototype is under construction by Direct Energy, Inc. (Montana) for off-grid charging of digital electronic devices (cell phones, computers, TVs, etc.), thermoelectric refrigerators, and LED lighting. The system uses blocks of dense carbon (e.g., charcoal; baked coke) to deliver 5.1 VDC at 6 W for months on a single charge, using dense anodes in a cell design tested at LLNL with dense anodes. The current issue is obtaining very low cost materials of construction. The work is intended to foster an emergent world capability for efficient generation of power from biomass and/or fossil resources in accordance with diverse regional needs, economies and resources.

John Cooper is author of 150 publications (40+ reviewed journal articles and book chapters), 25+ issued patents (50+ invention records filed with University of California; 11 are in the area of carbon conversion cells). Cooper plans to continue to foster international recognition of the prospects for efficient electrochemical conversion of carbon from fossil or renewable biomass resources as an alternative to inefficient and polluting combustion, through scientific research and technical communications.

John F. Cooper is married and has two children. Outside activities include sea kayaking and amateur astronomy.

Notes

25. John F. Cooper, "Periodic Phenomena during the Anodic Dissolution of Copper" (PhD Thesis, University of California, Berkeley, California, 1975).

26. J.F. Cooper, R.H. Muller and C.W. Tobias, "Periodic phenomena during anodic dissolution of copper at high current densities," *J. Electrochem. Soc.* 127(8) 1 (1980).

27. John F. Cooper, 2007. "Direct Conversion of Coal-derived Carbon in Fuel Cells," Chapter 10 in *Recent Trends in Fuel Cell Science and Technology*, 248–266. New York, NY: Springer.

28. John F. Cooper, N. Cherepy, et al., "Direct Carbon Conversion: Application to the Efficient Conversion of Fossil Fuels to Electricity" (Invited paper, Fall Meeting of the Electrochemical Society, Symposium on Electrochemistry and Global Warming, Phoenix, Oct. 2000; pub. Electrochemical Society, April 2001).

29. N. Cherepy, K. Fiet, R. Krueger, A. Jankowski and J.F. Cooper, "Direct Conversion of Carbon in a Molten Salt Fuel Cell," *J. Electrochem. Soc.*, 152(1) A80, Jan. 2005.

30. J.F. Cooper and J. Robert Selman, *Int. J. Hydrogen Energy* 37 19319 (2012).

••

Daniell, John Frederic
(1790–1845)
The constant cell

John Frederic Daniell was born March 12, 1790, in London. His father was a wealthy lawyer. Following a childhood education at home, including Latin and Greek, Daniell

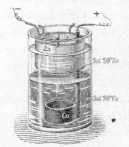

Pile Daniell. — Comme la pile Bunsen, la pile Daniell (fig. 15), qui est employée en galvanoplastie à cause de la constance du courant, est à deux liquides semblablement disposés ; le vase extérieur contient le zinc et de l'eau acidulée, et dans le vase poreux, on place le cuivre et une dissolution de sulfate de cuivre.

Pile Callaud. — La pile Daniell a subi de nombreuses modifications ; la pile Callaud (fig. 16 et 17) en est un exemple. On supprime ici le vase poreux et on profite de la densité de la dissolution du sulfate de cuivre, qui est plus lourde que l'eau ; elle reste, par suite, au fond lorsqu'on verse doucement l'eau qui surnage. Le cylindre Zn est suspendu à la surface tandis qu'une couronne de cuivre Cu repose au fond du vase.

FIG. 15. — Pile Daniell.

Piles thermo-électriques. — Disons un mot seulement de l'électricité provoquée par une élévation ou un abaissement de température. La pile

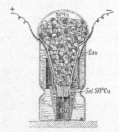

FIG. 16. — Pile Callaud ordinaire.   FIG. 17. — Pile Callaud nouveau modèle.

thermo-électrique ou *pyroélectrique* est ainsi nommée par opposition aux piles ci-dessus décrites et appelées *hydro-électriques* ; elle a pour origine l'expérience que

fit le physicien Seebeck, de Berlin, en 1821. Il recourba en crochet une lame de cuivre et en souda les deux extrémités à un bâton de bismuth. En chauffant une des soudures (fig. 18), il constata la présence d'un courant allant de la soudure chaude à la soudure froide à travers le cuivre.

On se rend facilement compte de la disposition des piles thermo-électriques (fig. 19, 21), par la simple inspection de la figure 20, qui se rapporte à la pile de Melloni : deux barreaux de métaux différents sont soudés ensemble ; si l'on chauffe

FIG. 18. — Expérience de Seebeck.

cette soudure, un courant traverse le fil de cuivre qui unit les barreaux. Nobili

The Daniell battery was more reliable (Musée EDF Electropolis, Mulhouse).

went to work for a relative who owned a sugar refinery and resin factory, where he was able to improve the technology being used. In his spare time, he attended lectures at a medical school in Windmill Street, London, delivered by William Thomas Brande, professor of chemistry, Royal Institution.

The young man soon established a reputation for meteorological experiments carried out at a laboratory in his father's house, Lincoln's Inn Fields, London, and in which he accumulated a substantial collection of rocks and minerals.

In 1813, aged only 23, John Daniell was appointed professor of physics at the University of Edinburgh. The following year, he was elected a fellow of the Royal Institution, London, largely due to the support of patrons including William Brande, George Pearson, physician, and Samuel Lysons, antiquary and vice-president of the Royal Society. In 1815, with his friend and mentor Brande, Daniell went on a geological tour of the British Isles. Returning, they published *A Descriptive Catalogue of the British Specimens deposited in the Geological Collection of the Royal Institution*.

In 1816 during a second tour, this time of France, Germany, and Switzerland, Daniell became more and more interested in meteorology. His meteorological observations began in earnest in 1820 when he developed a new device, the dew-point hygrometer. His research into the atmosphere of hothouses led to him standardizing meteorological observations throughout the British Empire.

Appointed a director of Imperial Continental Gas Company, Daniell developed a new process for manufacturing gas by dissolving resin in turpentine and distilling gas from the solution. He then went on a tour of France and Germany to promote gas lighting. Alongside this, he helped to establish the Society for the Diffusion of Useful Knowledge. Resigning from the gas company, he concentrated on his researches, developing a version of the pyrometer in 1830. The following year he was appointed professor of chemistry at the newly founded King's College, London. His lectures at the college were extremely popular, watched by many other noted British scientists, and reflected his flair for demonstration, allied to meticulous habits of observation and experiment.

Among those who counted themselves as his friends was Michael Faraday, who introduced Daniell to electrochemistry and then challenged him to improve the reliability of the voltaic battery.

Daniell began experiments in this direction in 1835 and soon achieved remarkable results. In 1836, he invented a primary cell in which hydrogen was eliminated in the generation of electricity. Placing a copper plate at the bottom of a glass jar, he then poured copper sulfate solution over the plate to half-fill the jar. Then a zinc plate was hung in the jar and a zinc sulfate solution was very carefully added. Copper sulfate is denser than zinc sulfate, so the zinc sulfate "floats" on top of the copper sulfate.

Daniell had solved the problem of polarization. His cell was the first battery that produced a constant reliable source of electrical current over a long period of time. He reported this in his seminal work: *On Voltaic Combinations*.[34] The Daniell cell provided a reliable supply of electricity necessary for the rapid growth of the Anglo-American telegraph network during the 1830s and '40s.

In 1835 Daniell, aged forty-five, obtained a job as chemistry teacher at the East India Company's Military Seminary at Addiscombe, Surrey. The following year he was appointed a member of the committee of the Royal Society on behalf of the Admiralty to standardize meteorological observations throughout the British Empire. He was awarded the coveted Copley Medal. In 1839, he became foreign secretary of the Royal

Society and served on the committee of the Admiralty Commission on protecting ships from lightning. In 1840, he was invited to deliver the Royal Institution Christmas Lecture on *The First Principles of Franklinic Electricity*. In 1842 he was awarded an honorary doctorate of civil law by the University of Oxford and also the Royal Medal.

John Daniell died suddenly of apoplexy in London on March 13, 1845, the day after his birthday, while attending a meeting of the council of the Royal Society. He was 55.

NOTE

34. J. Daniell, *On Voltaic Combinations*, Philosophical Transactions of the Royal Society of London (1776–1886). 1836–01–01. 126:107–124.

● ●

Davy, Humphry
(1778–1829)
The "Great Battery"

Humphry Davy was born on December 17, 1778, in Penzance, Cornwall, England. The son of a woodcarver, he was educated in Penzance and in Truro. His father died in 1794, leaving Davy and his mother to pay off debts from lost earnings in speculative investments. To do this, Humphry became an apprentice to Dr. John Borlase, a surgeon-apothecary. Aged 19, he took up chemistry and found work with an eminent English physician and scientific writer, Thomas Beddoes, as an assistant at the latter's Medical Pneumatic Institution in Bristol. There he experimented with various new gases. In 1799 he published the results of his work in *Researches, Chemical and Philosophical, chiefly concerning Nitrous Oxide and its Respiration*.[35] This made his reputation and the following year he was hired as an assistant lecturer in chemistry at the Royal Institution in London. There he was a great success, with his lectures soon becoming a draw for fashionable London society.

At the same time, he began to experiment with the chemical effects of electricity. Davy soon recognized that the voltaic pile produces electricity via chemical reactions at the metal solution interfaces: hydrogen is evolved on the "positive" copper disc and zinc is consumed at the "negative" disc. He gave warning that Volta's work was "an alarm bell to experimenters all over Europe." His prediction was soon to be verified.

He soon found that when he passed electrical current through some substances, these

Sir Humphry Davy of the Royal Institution, London (Musée EDF Electropolis, Mulhouse).

substances decomposed. Indeed, this recognition of the relationship between chemical and electrical effects prompted Davy to coin the word "electrochemical," from which sprang the science of "electrochemistry." Davy began to wonder whether electrolysis could also separate other substances into their elements.

He urged the Royal Institution to enlarge and re-equip the basement laboratory and an adjacent theater "for those who attend to the experiments of research." The laboratory, as improved in 1803 and 1804, was said to be equal to any in the country and was one of the best in Europe.

In 1806 Davy published his lecture *On Some Chemical Agencies of* Electricity,[36] for which he received the Napoleon Prize from the Institut de France in 1807. The following year he discovered that the alkalis and alkaline earths are compound substances formed by oxygen united with metallic bases.

By 1808, Davy had a battery built at the Royal Institution composed of one hundred double plates of copper and zinc, each six inches square. After several years of experimentation and lecture demonstrations, this battery was losing its power. Various attempts were made at the RI to provide more effective galvanic combinations with minimum financial outlay. However, when Davy read a further paper on electrochemical researches to the Royal Society, a note was included on the state of the batteries in which he conceded that the apparatus was quite worn out.

To finance a new and more powerful battery, an appeal was organized under RI auspices, but it quickly became known as "Davy's subscription."

Meanwhile, over in France, with whom Britain was currently at war, the Emperor Napoleon, when told about Davy's progress, demanded why such discoveries had not been made in France. He was informed by the scientist Claude Berthollet that, to date, they had not had a voltaic pile powerful enough. The emperor at once commanded that one be built in Paris, and that no expense be spared.

From March 1808, work began to build such a battery. Supervising progress were two chemists, Joseph Gay-Lussac and Louis Thénard, both 30 years old. The Dumotiez brothers, engineers to the Royal Academy of Sciences, were contracted to provide 600 copper and zinc couples which once connected would make up a voltaic pile covering 54 square meters. It was set up in the grounds of the École Polytechnique at Boncour on the Montagne Sainte Genevieve, a hill on the left bank of the Seine. The total cost of the apparatus worked out at just under 20,000 francs. On June 21, 1808, Gay-Lussac and Thénard isolated the element boron, beating Humphrey Davy to it by just nine days.[37]

When news of this French battery reached London, Davy at once appealed to patriotism to fund his new battery. The response to it provides a rough measure of Davy's esteem and popularity. In November 1809, in his fourth Bakerian lecture to the Royal Society, Davy referred to "a fund of upwards of £1,000" (today's equivalent of £100,000) having been raised by subscription. In April 1812, Davy was knighted by the Prince Regent and three days later married a rich widow called Jane Apreece.

Work began on assembling the battery, to be composed of 2,000 cells and taking up 889 sq. ft. (82.591m^2), almost the entire area of the RI basement. In this, Davy was assisted by 22-year-old Michael Faraday, who had sent the pioneer electrochemist a large bound selection of his notes on his lectures. Davy took Faraday on as his assistant due to a temporary blindness he had contracted after an explosion in his laboratory the previous year.

By 1813 the "Great Battery" was ready for testing. Courageously, Davy connected two rods of charcoal, each about one inch long, to the leads of the Great Battery and

FIG. 28. — HUMPHRY DAVY FAIT L'EXPÉRIENCE DE L'ARC VOLTAÏQUE ÉCLAIRANT, DANS SON COURS DE CHIMIE A L'EXPOSITION DE LONDRES.

The basement of the Royal Institution, the 2000-cell "Great Battery" (Musée EDF Electropolis, Mulhouse).

brought them close to one another. A spark jumped the gap, igniting the ends of the rods to "whiteness." As Davy drew the rods apart to a distance of about four inches, the electric arc continued to bridge the space, filling the cellar with brilliant light. In subsequent experiments, materials that he placed in the arc—diamond, sapphire, quartz, magnesium, lime, platina, plumbago, charcoal—either fused, melted or were vaporized.

Thanks to these two RI batteries, Davy is now acknowledged as the discoverer of potassium (1807), sodium (1807), barium (1808), calcium (1808) and magnesium (1808).

At the end of 1813, Davy, with his assistant Faraday, set off on a two-year trip to Europe to study volcanic action. They visited Paris—even though Britain and France were at war—where Davy collected the medal awarded to him by Napoleon!

Upon their return to England, Davy was called upon to study coal mine explosions, responsible for the deaths of hundreds of miners each year. In less than three months, he invented the miner's safety lamp, also called the Davy lamp. It would burn safely even if there was an explosive mixture of methane and air present in a mine. Davy was made a baronet in 1818 and from 1820 was president of the Royal Society.

But in 1827 he suffered a stroke, said to have been caused by the many gasses that he had inhaled over the years. He returned to a youthful hobby, poetry, and produced *Consolations in Travel, or the Last Days of a Philosopher*, an immensely popular, somewhat freeform compendium of poetry, thoughts on science and philosophy.

In 1829 he made his home in Rome but then suffered a heart attack and later died on May 29, 1829, in Geneva, Switzerland. He was 49 years old.

His book, *Consolations in Travel*, published posthumously, became a staple of both scientific and family libraries for several decades afterward.[38]

> Oh, most magnificent and noble Nature!
> Have I not worshipped thee with such a love
> As never mortal man before displayed?
> Adored thee in thy majesty of visible creation,
> And searched into thy hidden and mysterious ways
> As Poet, as Philosopher, as Sage?[39]

Davy was almost certainly the chemist whom Mary Shelley had in mind when she described the teacher of Victor Frankenstein. His assistant, Michael Faraday, went on to establish an even more prestigious reputation than Davy.

NOTES

35. Humphry Davy, *Researches, Chemical and Philosophical; Chiefly Concerning Nitrous Oxide, or Dephlo-gisticated Nitrous Air, and Its Respiration* (Bristol: Biggs and Cottle, 1800).

36. *The Collected Works of Sir Humphry Davy*, ed. John Davy (London: Smith, Elder and Co., 1839), V, 1–57.

37. Jean Paul Barbier, "Bonaparte et les savants. De la pile de Volta a la grande pile de l'Ecole Polytechnique (1800–1812)," *Bulletin d'Histoire de l'Electricité*, No. 34, 1999.

38. Davy, *Consolations in Travel, or The Last Days of a Philosopher* (London: John Murray, 1830).

39. Davy, a late fragment, probably written when he knew he was dying, in *Fragmentary Remains* (1858).

••

Devitt, John Lawrence
(1925–)
The sealed lead-acid battery

John Lawrence Devitt was born on September 27, 1925, in Denver, Colorado. His father, also born in Denver, was a very prominent orthodontist, who had financed his course at dental school by working as a streetcar conductor. His very intelligent mother, secretary to the Denver Public Schools Superintendent, could play anything on the piano "by ear."

Devitt decided to become an electrical engineer in 3rd grade. By then he was making his own electromagnets, inspired by his mother's high-school physics book by Robert A. Milliken and Henry G. Gale.

Living near the Rocky Mountains, Devitt also became a keen mountaineer, cross-country skier and hiker. He joined the Colorado Mountain Club in 1946.

Devitt has recalled, "By the late 1940s, I was in graduate school at the University of Colorado (CU), Boulder, and studying advanced electrical engineering. As I was also a musician, I was leading the CU jazz band (music school, but the really good players were engineering students!). I was to send the written Dixieland charts (Music) when we were finished with them to a fellow named Harry Sparkes Jr. in New Jersey. Harry was a friend of the man who had written these charts. Soon after this, I met up with him and his father, Harry Sparkes Sr., in New York."

Sparkes Sr. agreed to read young Devitt's degree-winning master's thesis: an ingenious timing system for the Pikes Peak annual auto races. Sparkes also happened to be vice-president of the AMF Corporation.

Devitt continues:

> In 1950, when the time came for Sparkes to pick a chief engineer for his forthcoming battery factory in Colorado Springs, he tagged me. The objective was silver-oxide/zinc batteries for air-to-air Navy missiles. At that time no one had come up with a reliable solution. So it was up to us.
>
> I was always the homework type, so I found articles in the Electrochemical Society publications by the Army Signal Corps guys, who had done it. By then my direct boss was Sam Auchincloss, another AMF Vice-President. He had been General MacArthur's assistant Signal Officer in the Pacific during WW2 and knew the folks at the U.S. Army Signal Corps Laboratories in Ft. Monmouth who had done the successful work. Sam and I went there, picked up the good recipes, and the rest, as they say, was history.

John Devitt, inventor of the sealed lead-acid battery, jazzman and mountaineer (Devitt Collection).

Between 1943 and 1955, Devitt had been on the U.S. Naval Reserve. He would only ever hold the rank of lieutenant because the Navy preferred that he concentrate on battery development.

In 1955, not wishing to follow the AMF factory relocation to North Carolina, Devitt remained in Denver, where he originated a new battery organization which became the Power Systems Division of Whittaker Corporation. The Whittaker batteries, dry during storage, were filled very rapidly with electrolyte by a self-contained mechanism, activating the battery, which then provided all needed electrical power to the electronic and mechanical systems. The factory was the principal source of batteries for the main electric power of the Minuteman, Polaris and Poseidon ICBM missiles. Devitt created and managed engineering and manufacture of these.

"But before long," Devitt continues, "I became bored with the bureaucratic nonsense connected with Defence procurement and decided to go into civilian stuff."

In the early 1960s, he worked as chief engineer of the Metron Instrument Co., Denver, developing electronic measuring devices and optical equipment.

Gates is the largest manufacturer of rubber belts and hoses in the world. In the 1960s, it was privately owned by the Gates family; Charlie Gates was CEO, and he ran the company his way. That included an unusual willingness to experiment with new types of products and even completely diverse enterprises. The local Denver grapevine one day yielded the news that Gates was interested in going into the battery business. Devitt grasped the opportunity.

On April 13, 1965, John Devitt, a forty-year-old electrical engineer, submitted a nine-page memorandum to George Jenkins, VP Research of Gates. It was titled "Lead-Acid Sealed Cells." Briefly, Devitt's proposal recommended the development of a cell which would perform in a manner similar to that of the sealed nickel-cadmium batteries then being sold. The proposed cell would provide high-rate discharge capability and thus would employ a spirally-wound electrode configuration. Importantly, it would use less expensive materials.

One object of his pre–Gates civilian battery investigations had been sealed nickel-cadmium cells, which he had heard described at the autumn 1960 meeting of the Electrochemical Society. Another object of his earlier, preliminary work was to find, if available, more-or-less maintenance-free lead-acid batteries. The only ones then worth studying were those made by Sonnenschein in Germany and, at that time, imported by Globe Union. These were called "gel cells" because of the siliceous addition to the acid, which turned it into a stiff jelly and kept it from running out of the battery when it was in a spillable position.

Devitt explains:

> In 1965 the sealed, spirally-wound nickel cadmium cells referred to earlier operated successfully because they employed oxygen recombination at the negative electrode during the inevitable overcharging which occurs. This feature had been recognized by many lead-acid researchers as a desirable way to improve battery usefulness, but none of them had been able to accomplish it to a useful degree. Our main obstacle was the conflict between providing enough reactive acid in the cell while allowing oxygen gas, generated at the positive electrode, to pass directly through a gas space to recombine at the negative surface. Put simply, the separator between the electrodes could not be wet and dry at the same time! At first, we had no idea what combination of new ideas would solve this riddle....

In 1967, Devitt and his twelve-strong team, in particular Dr. Donald McClelland, began work on the research and development of small cylindrical lead-acid cells containing spirally-wound electrodes. The first "Gates D-Cell" was shown to a meeting of the Board of Management by November 10 the same year.

Four years later, in mid–1971, the resulting products were offered for sale by Gates Energy Products: one cell equivalent in size to the conventional manganese dioxide D-cell, and another, the "X-cell," having twice the capacity.

These cells were the first to use a separator material consisting of microfiber glass paper, now generally termed "absorbent glass mat" (AGM). This material, the last of scores of tries using diverse separator materials, has the remarkable ability to absorb enough acid to carry out its stoichiometric role in the classic lead-acid reaction equation, yet remain slightly unsaturated to the extent permitting direct passage of oxygen to the damp negative plate surface. (The alkaline electrolyte in a nickel cadmium cell has no quantitative role in reactions within that cell.) Oxygen recombination in a lead-acid cell can go on indefinitely, limited only by heat dissipation and lead corrosion. Devitt: "For us, this was The Eureka moment!"

A number of technical developments were incorporated including substantial compression of the plate-separator assembly. This greatly lengthened the service life of these first "valve-regulated" cells. Although the pressure-relief check valve used in these cells is crucially important, the valve does not "regulate" the cell. This designation for these batteries, now well embedded in practice, is unfortunate. The valve prevents oxygen (air) from entering the cell, and also provides some pressure rise, enhancing reaction kinetics.

In the following years, many sizes of rectangular batteries using the principles described have been manufactured throughout the world. Based on his development, over a hundred battery plants throughout the world produce VRLA batteries for UPS, traction, automobile, telecommunication, and HEV applications.

Devitt:

George Saul and I were at the annual Army Signal Corps meeting in Atlantic City in about 1971 and we had several of the then saleable D-cells (they were flying out of the pilot plant). George was a sensational salesman I had picked up from GE. We took a D-cell—the one with two Amp tabs protruding from the top, exactly as still sold now, and showed it to the guys in the Eveready hospitality suite. (First time they had even heard of it.) Then we did what has become the famous paper clip trick: Straighten out an ordinary paper clip and then (with covered fingers) set it on top of the two terminals. It quickly glows bright-red hot and melts. We knew that the short-circuit current of the cell was over 100 AMPERES!! This was at least an order of magnitude greater than Eveready could do. There were many questions.

In 1972, when Devitt left Gates to go freelance, there were about 80 people in the battery development team, including the considerable number in the pilot factory making cells for sale.

Since then, Devitt has operated a consulting engineering business which emphasizes laboratory development of new products as well as general consulting work in America, Europe and Asia.

Some completed projects include: the first maintenance-free batteries for the General Battery Corporation; lead-chloride plates including initial production machines; making lead acid cells and batteries equivalent to about 100 automotive batteries (all R&D); low-cost fluoborate battery for automatic fire alarm; automatic surgical soap dispenser; battery-testing laboratory; assisting managers in S. Korea and Taiwan; studies of bipolar batteries, etc.

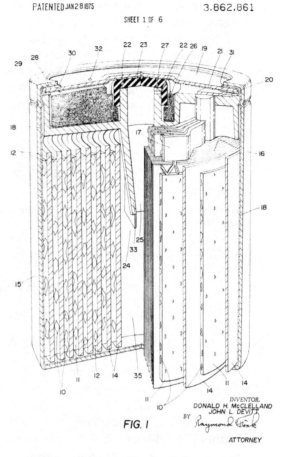

PATENTED JAN 28 1975

SHEET 1 OF 6

3.862,861

INVENTOR.
DONALD H. McCLELLAND
JOHN L. DEVITT
BY
Raymond Fink
ATTORNEY

FIG. I

The Devitt patent (Devitt Collection).

Devitt is also author of 4 scientific publications and holder of 8 patents. The most important is the Devitt-McClelland patent (U.S. 3,862,861) of January 1975, which controlled VRLA intellectual property until its expiration in 1992.

In 1986 he received the Research Award of the Electrochemical Society for the VRLA battery with closed oxygen cycle. In 1999 he received the Gaston Planté Medal from the Bulgarian Academy of Sciences, for the same achievement. In September 2007, Devitt was awarded the International Lead Award in Shanghai. This was most certainly based on the realization that the Gates work produced the largest single boost to total lead sales of any invention in the 20th century. This is an enormous claim, but when one looks for competition to it, one fails.

In his long life, John Devitt has played as much as he has worked: "A close second love is jazz music. I now play regular clarinet, bass same, and soprano, alto and tenor saxes. Well enough to get regular gigs. Music is the very last thing I will give up, maybe about 20 years from now!"

R. David Prengaman (see Prengaman entry) recalls, "At an AABC meeting in Nice, France, several years ago we had a delightful dinner on the roof of the hotel. John serenaded the attendees with his saxophone as we enjoyed the sun and sea in the twilight. It was magical."

Devitt continues: "My third love, other than Jeane, my wonderful lady of 20 years, is mountain climbing. This has included all fifty-four the 14,000 ft peaks in Colorado, as well as 53 years guiding and teaching others up and down such peaks as far away as the Matterhorn, Mont Blanc, etc." In recent years he has not done much climbing over 12,000 ft.

Aged 90, Devitt continues part-time consulting, primarily in projects aimed at simplified manufacture of high performance VRLA batteries for the coming new generations of conventionally powered automobiles.

Sources: From an article by the author, published in *Batteries International*, Spring 2011, based on information emailed by John Devitt.

....

Dicks, Andrew Leslie
(1948–)
Internal reforming for high-temperature fuel cells

Andrew Dicks was born on April 20, 1948, at Wigston, Leicestershire, England. The son of a manager in the wholesale food business, he became interested in science from an early age. At Guthlaxton Grammar School, Wigston, bored with the standard science lessons, Andrew and his friends, as a challenge, repeated Foucault's experiment to measure the speed of light. His teachers encouraged him to continue his studies of physics and chemistry, and from 1966, Dicks read industrial chemistry at Loughborough University, obtaining a B.S. and then a PhD in 1981 for work on the steam reforming of hydrocarbons, using heterogeneous catalysis.

Dicks recalls, "I was inspired by the Christmas lectures, and particularly those of Sir George Porter in a series called '*The Laws of Disorder*' which were my first introduction to thermodynamics. I have always been interested in concepts rather than detailed analysis, and physical chemistry seemed to attract me more than other branches of chemistry. I took an interest in electrochemistry as an undergraduate."

In 1971 he joined the UK Gas Council laboratories at Solihull (later to become British Gas, and then BG PLC), as an experimental scientist, where he worked with a team investigating the development of coal gasification and catalytic gas processing systems, gaining an in-depth knowledge of a large utility industry.

Dicks was able to resume his undergraduate interest in electrochemistry in 1985, when he was given the opportunity to lead a new research group into high-temperature fuel cells within British Gas. Over the following 15 years his research team collaborated with many of the leading international fuel cell developers, e.g., in two major collaborations supported by the European Commission. He also led collaborations between the UK, the USA and Canada, including chairmanship of a major development of PEM fuel cells funded by BG, NSERC (Canada) and Ballard Power Systems.

His research team at BG focused on molten carbonate (MCFC) and solid oxide fuel cell (SOFC) technologies, specializing in internal reforming of natural gas. They developed the reforming catalyst that is now used in some commercial systems, and helped to design high temperature fuel cell networks. These fuel cells operate at high temperatures (600–1000°C) and pressures up to 10 bars. Such conditions working with natural gas pose significant safety hazards, especially with the MCFC, as it contains corrosive molten alkali metal carbonates at temperatures of around 650°C. Simply building the apparatus to study the materials was a challenge because of the operating pressure and temperature, and the need for accurate control of the reaction conditions.

Dicks: "We designed most of the measuring equipment—this was the late 1980s when small computers had not developed to the extent they have now. We had to write all of our own measurement and data logging software, and most of the computer models we developed for fuel cell systems were carried out on a mainframe computer that took hours to run programs. It is so much easier to carry out these experiments now."

Andrew Dicks, British fuel cell innovator (Dicks Collection).

Dicks was a member of the UK Department of Trade and Industry Fuel Cell Advisory Panel, and the EPSRC College of Engineering. In 1991 he was awarded the Henry Jones (London) Medal of the Institution of Gas Engineers for his work on high-temperature fuel cells.

In 2000, with James Larminie, Dicks co-authored the 428-page seminal *Fuel Cell Systems Explained*, since translated into both Japanese and Chinese. The third edition is in preparation.

The following year, Dicks moved to Australia to take up a research fellowship in nanomaterials at the University of Queensland. Here, Dicks continued his interest in materials for solid oxide fuel cells, PEM fuel cells, and materials for fuel processing. In projects that involved fabricating new nanoscale catalyst materials, he collaborated with Ceramic Fuel Cells Ltd. of Melbourne, with the Gas Technology Institute of Chicago, and with other research groups such as the Plasma Physics group led by Professor Rod Boswell at the Australian National University. He was also supported by the Australian Research Council. He supervised several PhD and master's students at the university and taught in the undergraduate chemical engineering course.

In 2004 he became chairman of the hydrogen division of the Australian Institute of Energy, and has contributed to developing a national interest in hydrogen energy systems and technologies, including the National Hydrogen Technology Roadmap published in 2008. In the same year he chaired the World Hydrogen Energy Conference held in Brisbane and he married Cheryl Lennox.

From 2006 to 2009, Andrew Dicks was director of the National Hydrogen Materials Alliance, a CSIRO-supported network of 12 university research groups and ANSTO. He is now the president of the Australian Association for Hydrogen Energy. He has been a visiting lecturer at several universities in the UK, the USA and Canada and has supervised or mentored over 20 postgraduate students during his career in the UK and Australia.

In 2011, Dicks joined the Brisbane-based engineering consultancy, LC Energy, to provide a liaison role with Queensland University of Technology in overseeing a LC/QUT project in advanced fuel processing for fuel cells supported by the Queensland government. He also took part in a collaboration between QUT and the National Physical Laboratory India investigating low-Pt electrodes in PEM fuel cells.

Andrew Dicks has written several book chapters on aspects of fuel cells and hydrogen energy, ten patents, conference papers and over 60 peer-reviewed research articles. He serves on the editorial boards of the *Journal of Power Sources* and the *International Journal of Hydrogen Energy*.

Andrew is an accomplished pianist, organist and choral director. He was a member of the City of Birmingham Symphony Chorus from 1984 to 2000, during the period when Sir Simon Rattle was chief conductor of the orchestra, and with the chorus has performed in concert halls throughout Europe, the USA and Canada. He is planning to spend more time enjoying, performing and listening to music. He is involved in two new startup companies and enjoys mentoring young scientists and engineers.

Dicks: "I have been privileged to be in a very talented team in the UK that developed significant patented innovations in fuel cell system design, process integration, and catalysts. Some of these innovations are now incorporated in commercial systems."

Source: Information supplied by Andrew Dicks to the author in February 2015.

....

Drumm, James J.
(1897–1974)
The traction battery

James Joseph Drumm was born in 1897, the son of an RIC (Royal Irish Constabulary) constable based at Dundrum, Company Down, Ireland. He received his primary education at the National School, where his mother taught, and his secondary education at St. Macartan's College, Monaghan, where he won a County Council Scholarship. In 1914 he entered the Chemistry School of University College, Dublin, under the late Professor Hugh Ryan, and graduated with an Honors B.S. Degree in 1917. In the following year, while the Irish Civil War was raging outside, he obtained his M.S. degree.

He spent three years working with the "Continuous Reaction Company," a chemical company in England, before returning to Ireland in 1922 to work as a research and production chemist with Fine Chemicals Ltd. at 40 Mary Street, in what had just become the Irish Free State. His first invention, in Dublin, was fine quality soap. Then he worked to keep peas green after they were canned.

In 1925, after attending a lecture about hydrogen ions where the quinhydrone electrode was discussed, Drumm suggested that the quinhydrone electrode could be used in a cell to produce current. He experimented with various substituted quinhydrones and found that, though the cell could be charged and discharged rapidly, the battery life was short because of the intractable tars produced by the oxidation of the quinhydrone. Drumm then abandoned this type of cell and turned his attention to the alkaline cell. He was working in the Experimental Physics Laboratory under Professor John J. Nolan, head of the department and also adviser to the Ministry of Industry and Commerce with regard to Drumm's researches.

The government at that time had invested heavily in the Shannon Hydroelectric Scheme developed by the late Dr. Thomas J. McLaughlin. It was capable of supplying abundant electrical power, and to offset the taunt of "white elephant" from the opposition party, the government was anxious to get customers for the surplus supply. Industries capable of utilizing electricity were not numerous, and so electrification of the railways seemed to offer a solution to the problem. However, the relatively small bulk of traffic and the scattered population would have made it impossible to justify the initial cost of a "live third rail" or an overhead cable system. Consequently a suitable battery system would be ideal.

In theory, a battery capable of rapid discharge can also be rapidly charged, for the changes involved in discharge are roughly the reverse of those involved in charging. To construct such a commercially viable cell was the problem which Drumm undertook and solved so brilliantly. From 1926 to 1931 he worked unremittingly at his research, which eventually produced the Drumm Traction Battery, and in 1931 he was awarded the degree of D.S. by the National University of Ireland for his researches.

His invention was first made public in 1927 and attracted widespread interest, not just in Ireland, but across Europe and in the U.S. In 1928 Drumm and a small group of Dublin businessmen formed Celia Ltd., a small firm intended to finance Drumm's research. The government of the day, through the then minister of industry and commerce, Paddy McGilligan, was enthusiastic and promptly allocated development funds. The government invested £5,000 in the development of the battery, and subsequently a further £30,000 to the GSR (Great Southern Railways), as the most likely beneficiary of this new technology. The railway gave assistance in the form of space in Inchicore works to develop the initial batteries and fit them to a trial vehicle. A Great Southern Railways permanent way inspection car was fitted out with 60 nickel-zinc rechargeable battery cells, each the size of a one-gallon (4.5 liters) drum, wired in sequence. The cathodes, based on the Jungner model (see Jungner entry), were manufactured for Drumm at the NIFE factory at Redditch. From this point onwards, Celia Ltd. essentially became a government enterprise.

The initial tests were held during August 1929, between Kingsbridge and Hazlehatch, County Kildare. The train could get up to 50 mph (80 kmh) in just 50 seconds. Extensive testing followed, including at UCD. The longest test run was from Kingsbridge to Portarlington and back, all on a single charge.

By early December 1931, the first Drumm train, with 13.5 tons of batteries fitted underneath it, was ready, capable of carrying 140 passengers. This newspaper reported: "The Drumm train proved itself no longer a pre-vision of the future, but rather a concrete achievement."

In February 1932 the Drumm all-accumulator-driven train was charged at Inchicore and went on a test run to Portarlington and back—a total distance of 80 miles (130 km)—on the single charge. This was repeated several times, and a few days later the railcar went into regular service on the 13-mile (20-km) Dublin-Bray line and was operated for 180 to 230 miles (290 to 370 km) per day. The battery was charged at Amiens Street Station (Connolly Station) and at Bray. The distance is about 14 miles (22 km).

In 1934, Drumm took out U.S. Patent no. 1,955,115 for his storage battery.

By that year, plans were even afoot to use the Drumm batteries in electric trucks, and the wild claim was made that the life of such batteries was ten years, as against only three years for lead-acids.

The Drumm Battery railcar operated successfully on the Dublin to Bray section of the line with occasional runs to Greystones, some five miles farther on, from 1932 to 1948. As passenger numbers increased, two pairs of power units were joined under the control of one driver, and later a specially wired coach was put between the two trains, bringing its capacity up to 400 passengers. By 1939, four Drumm railcars had been built, but it became impossible to secure orders and raw material once war was declared in 1939. The Drumm Battery Company folded the following year. The outbreak of the war made the Drumm trains invaluable, as coal for steam engines was in short supply and inferior.

By the summer of 1944, when electricity was in short supply, the Drumm train had been withdrawn from regular use. In the Dáil that summer, Industry and Commerce Minister Seán Lemass was noncommittal as to whether the trains would ever be used again. After all, it hadn't been developed under a Fianna Fáil government.

The last Drumm train ran on July 12, 1949; most of the coaches were converted to ordinary railway working, and no relics were preserved of the pioneering train.

With the war over, it was decided in 1949 to scrap the Drumm railcars at a time when the promise of diesel locomotives pointed to the end of the steam era. The Drumm railcars, minus their batteries, were sometimes used as ordinary coaches.

Throughout his career, James Drumm continued his involvement with science and industry. He was a member of the Industrial Research Council from its foundation in 1934, a member of the Senate of the National University of Ireland, and in 1935 was appointed vice-president of the Federation of Irish Industries. He was the first to import stainless steel into Ireland. He was a member of the Board of the Emergency Scientific Research Bureau and a member of the NUI Senate from 1935 to 1959. He died in Dublin in 1974.

....

Edison, Thomas Alva
(1847–1931)
The nickel iron battery

Although Tom Edison is better known for his invention of the phonograph, the motion picture camera, and a long-lasting, practical electric light bulb, he also turned his mind and his team at Menlo Park, New Jersey, to improving the storage battery.

His curiosity was aroused from the 1880s following the arrival of the first automobiles. At the time, the gasoline engine was still unreliable, and steam and electric cars were selling in larger numbers. One problem with electric autos was that the lead-acid batteries that they used were extremely heavy. Another was that the acid corroded the lead inside the battery, shortening its useable life.

Edison, in his forties, began looking for a way to make batteries lighter, more reliable, and at least three times more powerful so that they could become the basis of a successful electric car. In September 1889, he created the Primary Battery Division of the Edison Manufacturing Company to develop these batteries.

Edison and his team of assistants conducted tests of all sorts of metals and other materials, looking for those that would work best in batteries. Everything that had been published on the subject of non-acid batteries was reviewed, then abstracted, including all applicable French, German, British and American patents going back to the start of the nineteenth century.

In June 1899, Edison ordered stocks of zinc, copper and copper oxide for his West Orange laboratory, and for the next thirteen months the laboratory notebooks were filled with experiments with the CuO-KOH-Zn system. The tests numbered in the thousands and lasted until he finally declared his battery finished. The battery consisted of a cathode made of nickel and an anode made of iron,

Thomas Edison examines his battery (U.S. Dept. of the Interior, National Park Service, Thomas Edison National Historical Park).

bathed in a potassium hydroxide alkaline solution. True to character, Edison announced the new battery with great fanfare and made bold claims about its performance. He claimed his nickel-iron design to be "far superior to batteries using lead plates and acid."

Manufacturers and users of electric vehicles, which now included many urban delivery and transport trucks, began buying the Edison battery, including companies such as Detroit Electric and Baker Electric. Edison also obtained several patents: U.S. Patent 678,722/1901, U.S. Patent 692,507/1902, and German patent No. 157,290/1901.

Then reports about battery failures started coming out. Many of the batteries began to leak, and others lost much of their power too quickly. The new nickel-graphite conductors were failing. Engineers who tested the batteries found that while lightweight, the new alkaline battery did not significantly outperform an ordinary lead-acid battery.

Edison shut down the factory immediately, and between 1905 and 1908, the whole battery was redesigned. Although the improved battery used more expensive materials, it had better performance and more power. Edison had found that layering nickel hydrate and pure nickel flake gave the best performance. The flake was obtained by dipping copper cylinders in a copper bath, leaving a coating of copper. The process was repeated

Edison stands beside the record-setting electric car (U.S. Dept. of the Interior, National Park Service, Thomas Edison National Historical Park).

until each cylinder was coated with 125 layers of copper alternating with 125 layers of nickel. By 1910, battery production was again underway at a new factory near the West Orange, New Jersey, laboratory, where 3,000 storage cells could be manufactured during each 10-hour day.

In 1910, "Maud," a Bailey electric automobile equipped with the new battery and driven by Captain George W. Langdon, completed a thousand-mile endurance run from New England to New Hampshire. During this marathon, he made seven of the eight-mile climbs up Mount Washington, being prevented from continuing to the very top by rain, hail, and heavy winds.

However, it was too late for the electric car. Edison's friend Henry Ford had introduced the lightweight, inexpensive Model T in 1909, which helped make the gasoline engine the standard for the automobile. The largest remaining market for the batteries was in special commercial vehicles, such as the small trucks and cars used in cities for deliveries, or inside factories to move materials around. Even here, however, Edison's battery was somewhat less powerful than conventional lead-acid batteries.

Around 1912, gasoline automobiles would begin to use batteries to run their starters, but Edison's battery was not suitable for this use because its voltage was too low. Its best feature was its reliability, which made it popular in other applications, such as providing backup power for railroad crossing signals, or to provide power for the headlamps used in mines. While it did not fulfill Edison's dream of powering the automobile, at least it was profitable, and it became one of his biggest moneymakers in later years. When Tom Edison died on October 18, 1931, electric automobiles had become a thing of the past.

Eighty years later, from those original units, Edison's battery was upgraded by Stanford University researchers; Edison had used carbon as his conductive element—but to improve its performance, the Stanford team used graphene, a sheet of carbon just one atom thick. They grew nanocrystals of iron oxide onto graphene, and nanocrystals of nickel hydroxide onto carbon nanotubes. This approach helped the scientists increase the charging rate of the battery by nearly 1,000 times. The prototype battery was only powerful enough to operate a flashlight, but the team hoped that one day it would be used to power modern electric vehicles—or at least as a "power boost" source.

"Hopefully we can give the nickel-iron battery a new life," said Hongjie Dai, a professor of chemistry at Stanford.

••

Faure, Camille Alphonse
(1840–1898)
Rechargeable secondary lead-acid battery

Camille Alphonse Faure was born on May 21, 1840, in Vizille, southeastern France. Since he was passionate for chemistry from his childhood, the studious boy's parents sent him to the École des Arts et Metiers (School of Arts and Trades) at Aix, where he did brilliantly. In 1859, aged 19, he designed a modified form of the Grove-Bunsen nitric acid battery which was sold by the Elliott Brothers firm of London. He obtained a job as a draftsman first with Peyruque-Cousin in Toulon and then with J. Chrétien in Paris. Part of this involved his visiting London in 1862, where he joined the crowds walking around the Great Exhibition. Returning to Paris, he published a report about the latest machine tools. Having learned English at the Philotechnical Association in Paris, on Chrétien's recommendation, Faure returned to London in 1866, where he worked for Debergue & Company, major English manufacturers of machine tools, and was sent to Russia on a commercial mission.

From 1874 until about 1880, Faure worked as a chemist at the new factory of the Cotton Powder Company at Uplees, Faversham, Kent, England. There, together with the factory

Camille Faure, the Frenchman who invented the rechargeable secondary lead-acid battery while in Kent, England (Mary Evans Picture Library).

manager, George Trench, Faure took out patents for tonite, a new high explosive (1874), and an improved dynamite detonator (1878).

Following a visit to the Paris Exposition of 1878, Faure had the idea for his secondary battery. As superintending engineer, the Frenchman also had the leisure for his own experiments as well as a laboratory in which to carry them out. The Faversham factory had plentiful stocks of the two basic materials for battery manufacture—sulfuric acid and lead.

Assisted by patent attorney Dominique-Antoine Casalonga, Faure's key patent was taken out on October 20, 1880, No. 139,358: "Improvements to galvanic batteries and their application to electric locomotives," which he modified several times in January 1881 and October 1881.

Lead plates were coated with a paste of lead oxides, sulfuric acid and water, which was then cured by being gently warmed in a humid atmosphere. The curing process caused the paste to change to a mixture of lead sulfates which adhered to the lead plate. During charging the cured paste was converted into electrochemically active material (the "active mass") and gave a substantial increase in capacity compared with Planté's battery.

Faure's singular innovation was to use such reversible chemical reactions of its elements permitting the "secondary" cell to be recharged and used again, and again.

One of the very first to make use of Faure's battery was the Paris inventor Gustave Trouvé (see Trouvé entry), who in April 1881 used these batteries to test out the world's first electric tricycle. An English Coventry-Rotary tricycle was modified: its two smaller wheels were each driven by a little 5kg (12 lb.) motor; a Faure battery of six accumulators gave the current; the weight of the vehicle was increased to 160kg (353 lb.), and it gave a speed of 12 km/h (7.5 mph). "Behind the seat and sitting on the axle, a rough, newly fashioned wooden box contained six secondary batteries. These accumulators were quite similar to those of Mr. Gaston Planté and actuated the motors."

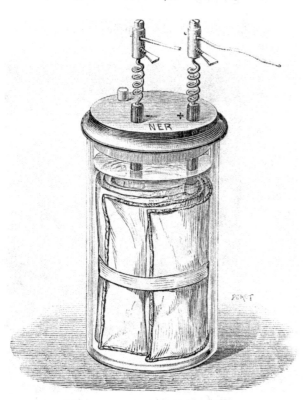

Camille Faure's battery could be used again and again (Musée EDF Electropolis, Mulhouse).

Encouraged and sponsored by M.J. Chrétien, Camille Faure and his brother Jules teamed up with Nicolas Raffard, an engineer working for the company "La Force et La Lumière." Raffard and his colleague Edmond Julien were looking for a battery powerful enough for the prototype electric streetcar they were constructing for the Paris General Omnibus Company. Faure's battery was an answer to

By the 1890s, batteries were used more and more in the home (Musée EDF Electropolis, Mulhouse).

prayer. An array of 225 Faure cells, weighing over two tons, were screwed down under the car's seats. This cumbersome car had "steerable" front axles which allowed it to be run off the rails for short distances. They were unable to demonstrate it at the 1881 Electric Exhibition in Paris because a delay in repairing the dynamo. But the following year, additional tests were operated with the number of battery cells increased to 375. On one trip the car ran from the workshops to Versailles and back without the batteries being recharged.

Even before electric traction had "proved itself," business treachery was interfering. While Simon Phillipart and Faure were over in England setting up an English company, Volckmar and Phillipart Jr. abused the trust placed in them by trying to sell off certain patent rights without the approval of the directors.

While Simon Phillipart set up the English Faure Co. with Sir William Thompson as consultant, and with manufacture to begin in Liverpool as of April 1882, Volckmar and Phillipart soon joined forces with Mr. John S. Sellon of the Anglo-America Brush Co., who had obtained provisional protection for a pasted type plate, differing from that of Camille Faure's in that the active material was pasted into a grid instead of being held by a felt wrapping to the surface of a plain roughed lead plate. The weakness of Faure's design had been that the red lead applied to the lead plates was so friable that with vibration it would lose its grip and fall to the bottom of the battery container, electrically shorting the positive and negative plates.

John Sellon also acquired from J.W. Swan, the English light bulb inventor, a method

s sociétés d'électricité, et ensuite parce que le ser-
ce en augmentant exigerait des stations de charge
ms toute la ville
e Londres.
La première
ation de charge
été établie à
uxon street,
ambeth. Le cou-
nt alternatif est
urni par la
London Elec-
ic supply Cor-
oration ». à
400 volts et à
a fréquence de
5 périodes par
econde. On a
nstallé deux
ransformateurs,
rmés chacun
'un moteur à
ourants alterna-
ifs Thomson-
louston, action-
ant directement
me dynamo à
ourants conti-
ns de 75 kilo-
atts du même

La transformation de l'énergie électrique de haute
tension à courants alternatifs en basse tension à courants continus se
fait avec un ren-
dement de 86
pour 100.
La figure 3
donne une vue du
dépôt des voitu-
res, et la figure 4
une vue de la
salle de charge.
Les coffres d'ac-
cumulateurs ont
été retirés de
dessous les voitu-
res, posés sur des
chariots et ame-
nés le long du
mur pour la
charge. Le prix
de vente de l'éner-
gie électrique est
de $0^{fr},1575$ le ki-
lowatt-heure.
Avec une charge
complète, la voi-
ture peut faire un
trajet de 80 km;
la dépense est

Fig. 3. — Dépôt des voitures.

constructeur. La figure 2 donne une vue d'en-
emble de l'installation des deux transformateurs.

de $2^{fr}.50$. Notre confrère *the Electrical Review*
parle des essais déjà faits et dit que ces premières voi-

Fig. 4. — La salle de charge des accumulateurs.

tures ont fort bien fonctionné dans les rues de Londres,
Attendons-nous donc à voir ce service se développer,
et à trouver aussi dans Paris des fiacres électriques

parmi les fiacres automobiles qu'on nous promet
depuis déjà quelque temps.   J. LAFFARGUE.

Recharging electric vehicles, 1897 (Musée EDF Electropolis, Mulhouse).

of keying the active material by punching holes in the plates, so providing a battery purchase for the red lead. Their Electrical Power Storage Company (EPS) was formed in March 1882 to manufacture the Swan-Sellon-Volckmar accumulator.

At first, the British Faure Co. tried to discredit the EPS Co., claiming infringement of patent rights developed by "discharged employees." The fledgling battery industry already seemed to be in trouble before it had even got underway. In May 1882, the Faure Co. abandoned its threat of litigation and patent rights were given by the Faure Co. to the EPS Co. through a mutual exchange of shares. By 1883 no fewer than eleven concerns were engaged in the manufacture of Faure accumulators. These ranged from "La Force et La Lumière" of Paris; Faure Electric Accumulator Company of London; Force & Power Co. of New York; the French Metropolitan Electric Carriage Co.; EPS of London; India and Oriental Electric Power Storage Company—and even the Australasian Electric Light and Power Storage Co. Following litigation, a new American company, the Electric Accumulator Co. of New York, was established.

As for Camille Faure, aged 41, he now pursued other challenges. In 1883 he set up a trial factory at Saint-Brice-sous-Forêt, in the Ile-de-France region, for the manufacture of aluminum using an electric kiln. By 1886 he had invested 200,000 francs into research and development of the project.

In September 1886 he came to the USA, called by a powerful American company ramified by the EPS of London. He returned to Paris, one month after the opening of the 1889 Universal Expo. He exhibited one of his batteries and was given the gold medal.

But Faure, the chemist, was more interested in manufacture of low-cost aluminum, the mass production of nitrate for agriculture, and in particular that of chlorine. He took out patents for the treatment of alkaline chlorides by electrolysis and in electrical batteries for alkaline salts.

During the 1890s, Faure was fully involved in a whole range of inventions, primarily the development of internal combustion engines for automobiles and motorcycles, including motor vehicle steering systems, but also the use of cyanate as fertilizer, and a device for sterilizing water in living apartments, by using either permanganate of potassium or an electric jet to submit the tap water to an intense centrifugal force. He also envisaged building a factory using the hydroelectric power from the gorges of the Dauphiné Alps to use an electric furnace to manufacture a new improved lower cost nitrate fertilizer.

Camille Faure died suddenly on September 14, 1898, at his home in Paris, aged only 57. Some diagnosed the cause as the long-term results of lead poisoning. Behind him he left his widow, Amalia Maria Francesca Bandinelli, and a 7-year-old son, Camille Jules, who was later killed in the Great War.

••

Feder, David O.
(1924–2011)
The round cell

David O. Feder was born in 1924 and raised in Yonkers, New York. A World War II veteran, he attended Havemayer Hall at Columbia University, where he obtained his B.S. in chemical engineering in 1946, his M.S. in 1948 and his PhD in 1959. By this time, since 1954, Feder was already employed at Bell Laboratories. His responsibilities included electron tube materials and processing; selection and evaluating materials for use in the first orbital communication satellite, Telstar. Feder became the head of the Battery Development Department, which channeled his life activities in that field.

In 1962, David married Denise; they would have four children. In the late 1960s, Feder recruited Louis D. Babusci, who had previously worked on sealed nickel-cadmium cells, and with the Bell staff they developed a cylindrical cell for a stationary reserve lead-acid battery to provide backup power in Bell Telephone System's central offices. The extensive laboratory test and evaluation data suggested that this design should significantly extend the expected life and reduce maintenance in telephone float service vs. conventional designs available. For this in 1969, they were granted U.S. Patent 3,434,883, and what came to be known as "The Round Cell" or "Bell Cell" went into production from 1974.

In the 1980s, Feder became an advocate for battery standards and was appointed as the task force leader to coordinate the activities of three groups that produced the IEEE standards documents covering the manufacturing, testing, acceptance and measurement equipment for batteries. He formed his own company, Electrochemical Energy Storage Systems, Inc. He authored and co-authored many papers still guiding the industry. For example, there is his paper "The never ending pursuit of float voltage uniformity in stationary reserve battery plants," which he presented in 1994 at the International Telecommunications Energy Conference in Vancouver. In 2004 he was inducted into the Battcon Hall of Fame, where his plaque is inscribed: "In recognition of being honored by the Battcon Committee for your outstanding leadership and contributions to the stationary battery industry."

He was a member of the Electrochemical Society; Intellec; and honor societies such as Sigma Xi (Cornell University); Tau Beta Pi (UC Berkley) and Phi Lambda Upsilon (Illinois).

Towards the end of his life, David Feder, who lived in Sag Harbor Village, became involved with protecting the Peconic Bay, which lies between the north and south forks of Eastern Long Island. He died on November 15, 2011, aged 87.

•••

Franklin, Benjamin
(1706–1790)
Coiner of the word "battery"

In 1749, Benjamin Franklin, 43 years old, a successfully retired printer and member of the Pennsylvania Assembly, heard that a Dutch scientist, Pieter van Musschenbroek of Leiden (Leyden) (see Musschenbroek entry), had recently found a way to store static electricity in a special tube called a Leyden jar, a panel of glass coated with metal on each surface. These jars were charged with a static generator and discharged by touching metal to their electrode.

As a hobby, Franklin ordered a batch of the tubes and set up a laboratory in his house. He began to carry out extensive investigations of both water-filled and foil Leyden jars, which led him to conclude that the charge was stored in the glass, not in the water. To demonstrate this, he dissected a jar after it had been charged and showed that little charge could be found on the metal plates, and therefore it must be in the dielectric.

Among his experiments was a bold idea to kill and to roast a turkey using electricity. Franklin decided that linking the jars together in what he termed a "battery" would give a stronger discharge. Up to that time a battery had meant "a group of two or more similar objects functioning together," as in an artillery battery, so it seemed appropriate to adapt the word.

That summer, Franklin had spent his spare time from the Assembly, electrocuting chickens and turkeys in his back yard. To his disappointment, most shocks knocked the birds unconscious, which startled Franklin when they kept appearing to rise from the dead.

Finally Franklin felt he was ready. On December 23, 1750, he wrote, "A turkey is to be killed for our dinner by the electrical shock and roasted by the electrical jack [spit] before a fire kindled by the electrified bottle, when the healths of all the famous electricians in England, Holland, France and Germany are to be drank [*sic*] in electrified bumpers [tumblers]."

A crowd gathered, the turkey was contained, and Franklin readied the lethal charge. He later described what happened in a letter to his brother: "I have lately made an experiment in electricity that I desire never to repeat. Two nights ago, being about to kill a turkey by the shock from two large glass jars ... I inadvertently took the whole through my own arms and body...." He describes the sensation as "a universal blow throughout the body" and says it was "some minutes" before he could collect his thoughts. He did not hear a crack, "tho' bystanders said it was a loud one.... Do not make [this] more public, for I am ashamed to have been guilty of so notorious a blunder." But eventually he found the right battery power and killed a 10-lb. (4 kg.) bird, noting that "the birds kill'd in this manner eat uncommonly tender."

In 1751, Franklin released his book *Experiments and Observations on Electricity....* Published by Edward Cave of London, it became one of the most widely reprinted scientific books of the time. The principles he set forth in the book formed the basis for modern electrical theory. For example, Franklin assigned a positive sign (+) for a gain in electricity and a negative sign (–) for a loss of electricity. This, in turn, led him to the idea that charge is conserved, that is, electricity can be moved around without loss, and the overall amount of negative charge must balance the amount of positive charge.

In the book's appendix, someone added all the embarrassing details

Fig. 249 – Franklin

Benjamin Franklin of Philadelphia (Musée EDF Electropolis, Mulhouse).

of Franklin's party failure. The book fell into the hands of some savvy French chefs, who realized Franklin had accidentally discovered a way to tenderize meat: a strong electrical charge inhibits the effects of rigor mortis, making meat softer!

Almost recklessly, Franklin continued to experiment. In his book, Franklin had proposed an experiment with conductive rods to attract lightning to a Leyden jar, an early form of capacitor. Franklin realized the dangers of using conductive rods and instead used a kite. The increased height allowed him to stay on the ground and the kite was less likely to electrocute him.

According to the legend, during the thunderstorm, Franklin kept the string of the kite dry at his end to insulate him while the rest of the string was allowed to get wet in the rain to provide conductivity. A key was attached to the string and connected to a Leyden jar, which Franklin assumed would accumulate electricity from the lightning. The kite wasn't struck by visible lightning (had it done so, Franklin would almost certainly have been killed) but Franklin did notice that the strings of the kite were repelling each other and deduced that the Leyden jar was being charged. Franklin reportedly received a mild shock by moving his hand near the key afterwards, because as he had estimated, lightning had negatively charged the key and the Leyden jar, proving the electric nature of lightning.

Fearing that the test would fail, or that he would be ridiculed, Franklin only took his son William to witness the experiment, and then published the accounts of the test in the third person.

He also noted that conductors with a sharp rather than a smooth point could discharge silently, and at a far greater distance. He surmised that this could help protect buildings from lightning by attaching "upright Rods of Iron, made sharp as a Needle and gilt to prevent Rusting, and from the Foot of those Rods a Wire down the outside of the Building into the Ground.... Would not these pointed Rods probably draw the Electrical Fire silently out of a Cloud before it came nigh enough to strike, and thereby secure us from that most sudden and terrible Mischief!"

Following a series of experiments on Franklin's own house, lightning rods were installed on the Academy of Philadelphia (later the University of Pennsylvania) and the Pennsylvania State House (later Independence Hall) in 1752.

In recognition of his work with electricity, Franklin received the Royal Society's Copley Medal in 1753. He died on April 17, 1790, aged 84.

Today a single electrochemical cell, e.g., a dry cell, is commonly called a battery. The cgs unit of electric charge has been named after him: one franklin (Fr) is equal to one statcoulomb.

· ·

Furukawa, Jun
(1957–)

Developing the Ni-Cd battery, Ni-MH battery and UltraBattery^{TM}

Jun Furukawa was born in Japan on April 14, 1957. His father Kiyoji Furukawa was employed at the Bank of America in Yokohama, while his mother Chieko and two aunts

were fervent Catholics, and so the entire family was raised in the Catholic faith, somewhat
uncommon in Japan. Indeed, during the
1970s, Jun was educated at the Eiko Gakuen,
a prestigious Catholic preparatory and high
school in Kamakura City in the Kanagawa
Prefecture. Although many Eiko Gakuen graduates enter Japan's top universities, Jun Furukawa's all-consuming passion for tennis led
to his neglecting his studies, entailing his
entering the chemistry department at Ao-
yama Gakuin University's Faculty of Science
and Engineering in April 1976.

Furukawa recalls:

In my University days, I spent too much of my time
doing part-time jobs, which led to my having trouble graduating without doing another year. However, an encounter with Professor Osamu Matsumoto, in charge of graduation work through my
senior year, completely changed my attitude. He is a
prominent scholar for his studies into electrochemistry and plasma-chemistry, and also known for his
educational enthusiasm and sternness. In order to
get a passing grade in my graduation work, I could
hardly take time off through my senior year and

**Jun Furukawa of the Furukawa Battery Co.
Ltd. (Furukawa Collection).**

needed to devote all my time to researching. My work paid off, and on Professor Matsumoto's recommendation, I obtained a job in the R&D department of the Furukawa Battery Co., Ltd. by recommendation of Professor Matsumoto.

It should be explained that Jun is not in any way related to the family who ran this company.

In spring 1980, the first task for this 23-year-old graduate was the research and development of lead-acid batteries for electric buses of the Kyoto Municipal Transportation
Bureau. Once achieved, the following year, he was engaged in the research and development of a method of manufacturing a Pb-Ca-Sn alloy strip for lead-acid batteries through
continuous cast rolling, determining its aging characteristics and its application to batteries.

On May 9, 1982, Jun Furukawa married Ranko Miyoshi, at his regular church, the
Yamate Sacred Heart Cathedral in Yokohama. They would have a son Yuki and a daughter
Saki.

In April 1983, Furukawa was assigned to the Space Technology Department, where
he was involved in the fabrication of a flight model in the development of the space Ni-
Cd battery (commissioned by National Space Development Agency of Japan (NASDA))
and in its qualification tests at NASDA's Tsukuba Space Center. The developed batteries
were loaded on satellites MOS-1, ETS-5, etc.

Just over one year later, he was engaged in the R&D of a ceramic seal terminal by
the Active Metal method (Ti-Ni alloy) for space alkaline batteries such as Ni-Cd and Ni-
H2 (commissioned by NASDA). This was a joint development with Toshiba's Metallic
Material Division and, afterward, put into practical use by Toshiba.

The next challenge was to occupy three years of his investigative mind: the

Kyoto electric buses (Furukawa Collection).

development of the space high-capacity Ni-Cd battery (commissioned by NASDA) and the research and performance improvement of a Ni slurry-sintered plaque for Ni-Cd batteries, as well as the development of manufacturing processes and equipment. The results: "Our achievements were applied to consumer batteries and are still used."

From April 1988 to March 1993, Jun Furukawa, now based at his company's R&D center in Iwaki city, Fukushima prefecture, led a Ni-MH Battery Development Group. Having innovated a mischmetal-Ni hydrogen storage battery, with its negative electrode being a modification of spherical nickel hydroxide, a positive electrode, and a separator, the Japanese team developed sealed Ni-MH batteries integrating these components and processes for manufacturing electrodes and batteries. Having succeeded in putting small consumer Ni-MH batteries into production, Furukawa was transferred to a commercialization team.

During the same period, Furukawa and his associates had co-developed Laves-phase alloy with Professor Wakao at Tokai University's Faculty of Science. He also had to deal with the response to domestic and international problems concerning intellectual property rights.

From April 1993 to March 1999, Jun Furukawa stayed with nickel metal hydride:

As a development director for performance improvement of Ni-MH batteries, I had been working to improve the positive and negative electrodes and the battery structure, and successfully achieved, for example, an increase in the capacity of double A-sized batteries by about 30% from 1100 to 1400mAh. However, we decided to withdraw from the business because competitors had increased the production and Li-ion batteries, made smaller and lighter than Ni-MH, had led to price drop.

It was bitter for me to withdraw from the Ni-MH battery business in which I had been engaged for 11 years from April 1988 to March 1999. We had launched the development of new Ni-MH batteries in 1988 and I was in charge of the development. SANYO, Matsushita (now Panasonic), and TOSHIBA had already started their development nearly 5 years earlier, but we also managed to commercialize our products 2 years after the commercialization by these three leading companies.

During our development, we spent a lot of time avoiding infringement of these leading company's patents, but we could not bypass all of their patents and had to enter into licensing agreements. Payment of these licensing fees resulted in imposing a heavy burden on our business. For a while after the commercialization, our Ni-MH battery business had been successfully growing and, at one time, we produced four million batteries per month to achieve a share of nearly 10%. Our business then focused on moving into the black, which was not long before the Big Three, SANYO, Matsushita, and TOSHIBA, boosted their production several times. In addition, Li-ion batteries began to be produced on a commercial basis. This resulted in the market price of Ni-MH batteries dropping to almost half and hence our business becoming unprofitable rapidly.

In March 1999, the Japanese electrochemist and his team finally had to withdraw from the Ni-MH battery business with a big deficit. As it turns out, Jun Furukawa was a creator of their Ni-MH batteries and, at the same time, a witness who saw the end of their Ni-MH battery business. They managed to avoid bankruptcy but took years to recover from this damage. With the growth in demand for Li-ion batteries, all battery manufacturers except SANYO and Matsushita were forced to withdraw from their Ni-MH battery businesses around the time of Furukawa's withdrawal.

While most of researchers and developers who had been engaged in their Ni-MH battery businesses moved into the research and development of Li-ion batteries, Furukawa was charged with the research and development of lead-acid batteries, which were at the opposite extreme of state-of-the-art Li-ion batteries, though one of their key businesses. The next few years until 2006 saw the Japanese battery innovator turn his mind to the challenge of the day: VRLA.

He was assigned to Technology Development Department and appointed the leader of MV Team and Iwaki Development Center's 2nd Group. The challenge was 36V valve-regulated lead-acid batteries for next-generation 42V-system automobiles, which meant examining positive and negative electrodes, battery structure, evaluation test methods, and heat dissipation mechanisms. "With a view to enhancing the high-temperature durability, we had also co-researched and developed Pb-Ca-Sn-Ba alloy for positive electrode substrates with Toho Zinc, Co., Ltd., and successfully achieved 1.5 times longer life than before and put it into practical use."

Next in this glittering chain of research achievements, Furukawa concentrated on strengthening mechanisms for Pb-Ca-Sn-Ba alloy (collaborative with the Iwaki Meisei University), as well as a method of suppressing sulfation of lead-acid batteries and BCM, a lead-acid battery and supercapacitor module.

Since 2004, in collaboration with the CSIRO, Australia, Jun Furukawa has been part of the team promoting the UltraBattery™.

He explains:

Mr. Shoji Shiga, an executive director and R&D general manager in the Furukawa Battery at that time, had negotiated with CSIRO to buy a license concerning elementary technologies of UltraBattery™ in 2005.

CSIRO's Dr. Lan T. Lam [see Lam entry] and I had started our collaborative development and completed a prototype UltraBattery™ FTZ12-UB with a size of lead-acid battery for motorcycles in mid–2006, just a little more than one and a half year into the collaboration. We then participated in the ALABC's in-vehicle test project on a Honda HEV 'INSIGHT.' The in-vehicle test had started at the end 2006 and gone smoothly to achieve our original target of 50,000 miles in just a half year. We had continued the test with a doubled target of 100,000 miles and also achieved this target in January 2008. This was the first time in the history of lead-acid storage batteries.

In 2008 Furukawa licensed UltraBattery™ to East Penn Manufacturing Co., Inc., one of the best lead-acid storage battery companies in U.S. During this period, Jun was appointed the leader of 1st and 2nd Groups, Technology Development Department in April 2006 and, afterwards, of Development Department 1 in 2009. He recalls, "In March

2009, I and Dr. Lam won 2009 Technical Development Award of the Electrochemical Society of Japan for our "Development of the UltraBattery™."

Now 55 years old, Jun and his wife Ranko live in Iwaki City, Fukushima prefecture. In March 2011, Fukushima made world headlines because of the huge Tohoku earthquake, tsunami and nuclear power plant accident. "Our R&D centre is only 30 miles from the nuclear power plants," he notes.

In 2012, Jun assumed the position of general manager of Corporate Planning & Strategy Division, UltraBattery™ Commercialization Department at his company. In April 2013, sales of the UltraBattery™ were finally launched onto the aftermarket for automobiles, as well as for renewable energy storage applications. In November the Ultra-Battery™ was adopted for new cars to the Honda Odyssey minivan which went on sale at that time. In addition, Furukawa has received a lot of inquiries for UltraBattery™ from new car manufacturers.

In March 2014, Jun submitted a thesis to the Iwaki Meisei University, and received the degree of doctor of science and engineering. The subject of his thesis is "Study on the Application of Ba-Added Pb-Ca-Sn Alloy to Positive Grids of the Automobile Capacitor-Hybrid Type Lead-Acid Battery." That June he was nominated as a candidate for the Gaston Planté Medal. Although he did not receive the medal, "I was honored to be nominated for such a famous prize."

In June 2014, Jun's past performance in the research and development of battery technology was assessed by the Furukawa Company, who promoted him to board member and honored him with the position of senior fellow.

The Furukawas continue to worship at the Catholic church in Iwaki City. Jun is still a member of the Iwaki Veteran Tennis Club and Iwaki Chuou Tennis Club; after 42 years, he plays every Saturday and Sunday for about 3 hours. It obviously gives him the fitness needed to continue the remarkable strides he has already made for battery technology during the past half century.

Sources: From an article by the author, published in *Batteries International*, Spring 2012, based on information supplied by Jun Furukawa.

....

Garche, Jürgen Werner
(1944–)

Model of the dynamic stability of PbO$_2$ electrodes in lead-acid batteries

Jürgen Garche was born on February 23, 1944, in Cottbus, Brandenburg, Germany. His father was an office clerk and later a teacher. Jürgen spent his primary and secondary education in his home town. His interest for chemistry goes back to inspiring chemistry lessons in his 7th class.

In 1962 Garche started a professional training as laboratory chemist at Mineralöl-werke Lützkendorf, near Leuna. He interrupted this training after only one year to begin to read chemistry at Dresden University of Technology (TU Dresden). In doing so, he became the first university student in his family. By 1966 he was involved with electro-

Jürgen Garche in front of a ZSW 2 kW PEMFC test rig (Garche Collection).

chemistry through his participation in an industrial 3 kW FC forklift truck project directed by electrochemist Prof. Kurt Schwabe, rector of TUD and director of the Institute of Physical Chemistry and Electrochemistry. This institute had developed from the Elektrochemische Laboratorium founded in 1900 by Fritz Foerster (1866–1931) at then Technische Hochschule Dresden (TH Dresden) as the first academic electrochemical institute in Germany.

Although Jürgen Garche's interest was related to applied electrochemistry, Kurt Schwabe persuaded him to do his PhD work in theoretical electrochemistry. So he submitted his doctoral thesis in 1970 on "Thermodynamics of Concentrated Electrolytes."

During this period, Jürgen was enjoying sports, both as a middle distance runner and in basketball; he also became a lifeguard. In 1975, he married Ursula Weiss, a doctor; they have a son, Stefan.

As was common in East Germany at that time, Jürgen continued to work at his alma mater, where he was promoted to assistant lecturer, eventually supervising Prof. Klaus Wiesener's applied electrochemistry R&D group "Galvanic Elements," specializing in batteries and fuel cells. Garche's special interest was focused on interface reactions between Pb-grid and PbO_2 active mass in the positive lead-acid battery (LAB) electrode. This positive electrode is thermodynamically instable and in fact already a lead-acid battery system.

In his Habilitation in 1982 (TU Dresden), Garche described a model of the dynamic stability of PbO$_2$ electrodes in LABs, which is also published in *Journal of Power Sources* 30 (1990): 47–54. This model explains the passivation and self-discharge behavior of PbO$_2$ electrodes. Furthermore, Garche established a model of Pb corrosion which explained the influence of the active mass and polarization conditions (*Journal of Power Sources* 53 (1995): 85–92).

Until 1990 he was a lecturer for technical electrochemistry at TU Dresden. During this time he had extended work stay elsewhere, with Prof. Heinz Gerischer at the Fritz-Haber-Institut in Berlin, related to photo-electrochemistry.

After German reunification in 1990, Garche moved to Ulm to join the recently founded Electrochemical Energy Storage and Energy Conversion Division of the Center for Solar Energy and Hydrogen Research (ZSW) a nonprofit R&D institute, established by Professor Wolfgang Witschel. Here he requalified at Ulm University, where in 1991 he was appointed as privatdozent for electrochemistry, then two years later as extraordinary professor for electrochemistry. Four years later he took over from Witschel, expanding ZSW into an internationally well-known institute, employing nearly 100 co-workers, with only 20 percent government financial support.

Highlights at that time were the development of a high rate, long-life and safe polymer 2V Li-ion battery (*J. Electrochem. Soc*, 151 (2004): A2138), which could be used to replace the lead-acid cell; basic work in catalysts and membranes field long-life direct methanol fuel cells (DMFC); and especially R&D in the field of the proton exchange membrane fuel cells (PEMFC). The latter started with basic research in cooperation with Ulm University, going via cell and stack development all the way to PEMFC system integration at first for stationary residential house energy supply and later also for EVs.

As a consequence of this development driven by fuel cell system integration, in 2004 Garche, together with the Ulm Public Utility, initiated the start of a spinoff company, Ulmer Brennstoffzellen-Manufaktur GmbH, UBzM (Ulm Fuel Cell Manufactory), which designs, manufactures and sells mainly complete PEMFC systems up to 2 kW.

Furthermore, he was appointed as guest professor at the Shandong University in Jinan (China) in 2001 and as visiting professor at the Dalian Institute of Chemical Physics.

An area of special concern for Jürgen Garche was always education and training, particularly in fuel cells, which as a young technology needs well-trained specialists but not only academics. In 2003 he founded the Fuel Cell Education and Training Center in Ulm (WBZU) with large seminar rooms and laboratories for practical experiments. The WBZU is a nonprofit registered society with about 50 members, including such important concerns as Daimler AG and Robert Bosch GmbH.

As a member of the executive board of the advisory council of the European Hydrogen and Fuel Cell Technology Platform (HFP), Garche has made a strong impact on the development of the FC and H2 technology in Europe, especially also in the field of education and training. He was the chairman of the initiative group education and training in the framework of the European Hydrogen and Fuel Cell Technology Platform (HFP). Furthermore, he is the chairman of the Education and Training Task Force of the International Partnership for the Hydrogen Economy (IPHE).

In Germany for almost 20 years, Garche rendered great service to the formation of an informal fuel cell and hydrogen alliance, which was the precursor of the German National Organization H2 and Fuel Cell Technology (NOW GmbH), where he is now the deputy chairman of the advisory board.

Jürgen Garche has published several books (see Bibliography) and about 300 papers on electrochemical energy conversion, mainly batteries, fuel cells and electrochemical capacitors. He is the inventor, or a co-inventor, of 10 patents. He is member of the editorial boards of the *Journal of Power Sources, Fuel Cells—From Fundamentals to Systems* and *The International Journal of Hydrogen Economy.*

He has received several important honors for his contributions to electrochemical energy conversion: the First Prize of the Academy of Science of Czechoslovakia and the German Democratic Republic for work on the oxygen electrode in 1985; the German Gas Industry's Award for residential fuel cells in 2000; and the Christian-Friedrich-Schönbein Gold Medal of the European Fuel Cell Forum for his work on PEMFCs in 2003. Furthermore, in 2014 he was listed in "the World's most influential scientific minds" by Thomas Reuters (USA).

Since his retirement from ZSW in 2004, Jürgen Garche has remained active as consultant for both the national (Fuel Cell and Battery Consulting Ulm, FCBAT Ulm) and international industry and institutes and for the German Ministry for Transportation and Digital Infrastructure (BMVI). To relax he enjoys reading books, listening to classical music, biking and trekking. But his main hobby remains electrochemistry, involving reading scientific papers, helping to supervise doctorates, but above all writing books about batteries and fuel cells.

Source: Information provided by Jürgen Garche in February 2015.

••

Gassner, Carl
(1839–1882)
Austrian inventor of the dry cell battery

A street scene in the mid–1880s: At No. 16 Betzelgasse, a small lane in the old part of Mainz, Germany, a confirmed bachelor—an ear and eye specialist by the name of Herr Doktor Carl Gassner—was banging on his doorbell with disgust. The annoyance? His battery-powered doorbell was not working again. The wet Leclanché battery in its glass container, kept in the toilet, had dried out again. No battery-power, no doorbell. To refill it, the doctor, in his 40s, must each time climb onto the toilet seat to reach the glass cylinder.

Fortunately the large house at No. 16 Betzelgasse was equipped with a private laboratory where Gassner, trained like his father as a doctor, could experiment. As no women were allowed in the house, Gassner could make chemical smells to his heart's content.

Eventually, he found the answer to his problem. Replace the liquid with a porous bonding agent, namely plaster, and add water-absorbing ammonium chloride so that the energizing agent remained damp: in other words, a dry cell.

The doorbell worked so well after that before long others heard about the optician's wonder battery. One businessman after another asked him to make them a dry battery. To try to stop the growing demand, Gassner decided to ask for one gold mark for each battery he supplied. This did not deter the stream of requests.

Finally, he decided to register a patent, first in Germany (No. 37758 dated April 8,

Dry battery publicity poster (Musée EDF Electropolis, Mulhouse).

1886). Foreign patents followed: Austro-Hungary, Belgium, France and England—also in 1886. The following year, the U.S. patent was granted.

The company, Carl Gigot in Frankfurt, took over production and exclusive sale of the Gassner dry cell unit. The German postal service ordered 100,000 batteries and tested them for use in phones. "From a quantity of dry elements, which have been tested for their usefulness just as much by consulting engineers in the telegraphs as in the practical microphone business, Dr. Gassner in Mainz has designed a dry battery which has proved itself the best up until now," read a report in 1893.

Production could not keep pace with the quickly growing volume of inquiries. The post and rail administrations and also private commerce and transport companies ordered the Gassner dry cells.

Testament to its popularity and utility were almost universal. "The Gassner dry cell in the microphone business of the town phone system has in the last five years also universally pleased; its efficiency as a microphone element has been flawless, there has been no cause for difficulties in use. In comparison with the wet elements, it has shown its worth, especially through a greater security in use…. An overwhelming number of batteries installed in 1893 are still in use" (1899 report by the State Postal Administration).

Meanwhile the occupant of No. 16 Betzelgasse, who had merely asked for one gold mark for each dry cell sold, became a millionaire several times over. He soon belonged to the then 100 highest taxed individuals in the town of Mainz. This enabled him to fill his house with works of art, but wealth did not affect his eccentric lifestyle. He dined every day at the nearby "Sonnen-Bier" Gasthaus for 80 pfennigs. He bought sausage at "Judenstrauss" because it was five pfennigs cheaper than the neighboring "Falk." He often wore short Wellington boots under long trousers. A nature lover, he let his back garden grow wild, which also saved the expense of a gardener.

Nor did he convert to electric lighting, because apparently the gas lamp reminded him fondly of his youth. It was for him a symbol of the sovereignty of man, which had not yet served to spark the mass consumption of the "switch."

Nor did he own a telephone. Nor even a typewriter, preferring to write letters by hand using carbon copy paper. This did not stop the secretary of his barrister friend taking pity on him and mostly typing out his pieces of work in her office.

Millions of letters from all over the world arrived asking for his wonder batteries. At first he used them to build up a fine stamp collection. But eventually he had had about enough, even of the postman's visits, and for a long time, factory accounts and receipts for money were not dealt with.

Then one day, with typical eccentricity, Carl Gassner refused all his rights to the Frankfurt business. The production of his patent dry batteries ceased. After the factory closed down, Gassner had peace at last. This did him good, for now he had enough time for his expensive collections, which filled the house from top to bottom.

From time to time he would sell off his current collection and begin collecting in a new field. At one time it was antique ceramics, then again late Roman coins or brooches or additionally Rococo porcelain, always something special, which caught his attention completely for the month. One splendid item in his collection was the famous "Eagle Brooch," a late Roman clasp with a golden eagle which was found at the time in the area of Mainz. Without giving it a second thought he paid 20,000 gold marks for the brooch and later sold it to the American millionaire Pierpont Morgan, who for his part gave it as a present to Kaiser Wilhelm, when the latter honored him with hospitality in Kiel.

Carl also collected the oil pictures and aquarelles of Casper Schneider, an 18th century Mainz painter, also known for his unconventional behavior.

Gassner also experimented with celluloid-roll based photography. At the age of 81 he got the idea of testing by his own experience whether man could live only on soured milk. For weeks only soured milk was brought into the house, to the joy of the dairy, but to the anger of the doctors who not long after had to operate on a stomach ulcer that the diet had conjured up in his body.

He died on January 1942, aged 87. He was spared the painful knowledge of his house and artworks being bombed to destruction later that year.

Sources: From an article by the author, published in *Batteries International*, Summer 2008, based on information supplied by Carl Christoph Gassner.

••

Goodenough, John Bannister
(1922–)
Father of the lithium-ion cell

John Bannister Goodenough was born of U.S. parents in Jena, Germany, on July 25, 1922. At that time, his father, Erwin R. Goodenough, was at Lincoln College, Oxford, writing a philosophy doctorate on the Church Fathers. The family returned to New Haven, Connecticut, in 1923, where his father had been appointed assistant professor of the history of religion at Yale University. John was the second son; he went away to Groton School at the age of 12. To keep fit, the teenage Goodenough enjoyed playing individual and team sports of all kinds, and in the summer of 1939 he kayaked from the lakes of Finland down the Ivalo River in the north to Kirkenes in Norway, where his Finnish companion had to return home to prepare for the Russian invasion. After 10 days' walking in the Jotunheimen Mountains of Norway, his six German companions were called home to serve the ambitions of Hitler, who had already moved into Poland.

After Pearl Harbor, he volunteered for service, but was not called up until January of 1943. This gave him time to complete his undergraduate degree in mathematics. He had entered Yale as a freshman with a background in Latin and Greek and little idea of what he would do after the war was over. He had taken an introductory course in chemistry during his freshman year as the science requirement for a liberal arts degree, but he had no thought of a career in science. Goodenough later recalls, "As a young man in search of a calling for my life, I became fascinated by the philosophy of science while struggling to come to terms with a spiritual awakening. While reading Whitehead one night, I decided that if I were ever to come back from the war and if I were to have the opportunity to go back to graduate school, I should study Physics."

During hostilities, as an Army Air Force meteorologist, Goodenough dispatched tactical aircraft across the Atlantic Ocean:

In 1946, while I was still stationed on the tiny island of Terceira in the Azores awaiting my turn to go home, a telegram arrived telling me to report back to Washington in 48 hours. In Washington I was informed that I had been selected to study Physics or Mathematics at the University of Chicago or Northwestern University. My spirit recalled my earlier resolve, so from Washington I went immediately to the University of Chicago to register as a graduate student in Physics. When I arrived, the registration officer, Professor Simpson, said to me, 'I don't understand you veterans. Don't you know that anyone who has ever done anything interesting in physics had already done it by the time he was your age; and you want to begin?'

In 1946, Goodenough married a history graduate student at Chicago named Irene Wiseman. In the decades to come, the couple were to enjoy travel, mountain walking, and meeting scientists and Christians from many countries; invitations every year to lecture abroad would introduce them to Western and Eastern Europe, Russia, India and Nepal, the Middle East, North Africa, Australia, Mexico, and Argentina.

By 1952, still at the University of Chicago, Goodenough had completed his PhD under the supervision of Clarence Zener. This included taking two courses from Enrico Fermi: quantum mechanics and nuclear physics. In 1952, he joined the group at MIT Lincoln Laboratory charged with the development of a ferrimagnetic ceramic to enable the first random-access memory (RAM) for the digital computer.

John Goodenough, an American who co-pioneered the lithium-ion cell in Oxford, England (Goodenough Collection).

Goodenough recalls: "The air defense of this country depended on having a large digital computer, and the computer had no memory! The rolled alloy tapes first tried did not switch fast enough. Although the Europeans who had developed ferrimagnetic spinels were convinced that it would be impossible to obtain the required squarish B-H hysteresis loop in a polycrystalline ceramic, the magnetic-core RAM was delivered within three years of my arrival with a read/rewrite cycle time of less than the required 6 microseconds."

In the course of this work, Goodenough showed how cooperative orbital ordering gives rise to crystal distortions, and he used this ordering to articulate the rules for the sign of the spin-spin magnetic interactions in solids. These rules have subsequently provided a true guide to the design as well as the interpretation of the magnetic properties of solids; they are known as the Goodenough-Kanamori rules, and they inspired the title of Goodenough's first book, *Magnetism and the Chemical Bond* (Interscience-Wiley, 1963).

Since his proposals in the early 1970s to work on energy materials were assigned to the National Energy Laboratories because the Three-Mile Island incident had halted development in the USA of nuclear-power plants, Goodenough looked elsewhere.

In the early 1970s, the first energy crisis alerted the international community to its vulnerability to dependence on foreign oil and the search began for alternative energy.

In the early 1970s, chemists in France and Germany had pioneered investigations of room-temperature reversible lithium insertion into layered transition-metal (M) sulfides and selenides MS_2 and MSe_2, which led to the suggestion that a rechargeable lithium-MS_2 battery would be feasible since lithium (Li) non-rechargeable (primary) batteries were known; they have an organic electrolyte for transporting Li^+ ions inside the battery. In 1976, a rechargeable room-temperature Li-TiS_2 battery cell was demonstrated; it had an acceptable rate of charge and discharge and offered an energy density higher than can be achieved with conventional batteries that have an aqueous electrolyte transporting H^+ ions. However, the Li anode was not replated smoothly on recharge, but developed dendrites that grew across the flammable organic electrolyte on repeated recharge to give an internal short-circuit with disastrous consequences. This effort was, therefore, abruptly abandoned.

It was at this point that John Goodenough accepted a position of professor and head of the Inorganic Chemistry Laboratory at Oxford University, England. He had been contemplating a move to the Ariya Mehr University in Iran to establish an energy institute there when a letter arrived inviting him to apply for the position at Oxford.

Goodenough: "My wife did not hesitate to recommend that I put my name in nomination; and I thought, 'If the people at Oxford have that much imagination, then perhaps that is what I should do.' I was duly elected, and in 1976 I took up the post at Oxford."[40]

Goodenough had been working as a research scientist at MIT's Lincoln Laboratory, where he had been part of an interdisciplinary team that developed the first random-access memory (RAM) for the digital computer. Goodenough's contribution was to the development of the ferrimagnetic, ceramic memory element, a contribution that put him in charge of a ceramics laboratory, and that gave him a decade in which to explore the magnetic, transport, and structural properties of transition-metal compounds.

"The move to England recognized me as a chemist and enabled me to learn some electrochemistry," he would later recall in his typically modest manner. After moving to Oxford, Goodenough recognized that the layered sulfides would not give the voltage needed to compete with batteries using a conventional aqueous electrolyte, but that an oxide would provide a significantly higher voltage. From previous work, he knew that layered oxides analogous to the layered sulfides would not be stable, but that discharged $LiMO_2$ oxides could have the same structural architecture as discharged $LiTiS_2$. Goodenough assigned a visiting physicist from Japan, Koichi Mizushima, the task of working with Goodenough's postdoc, Philip Wiseman, and a student, Philip J. Jones, to explore how much Li could be extracted reversibly from layered $LiMO_2$ cathodes, and with M = Co and Ni he found he could extract electrochemically over 50 percent of the Li at a voltage of ca 4.0 V versus a lithium anode, nearly double that for the sulfides, before the oxides began to evolve oxygen. Their groundbreaking findings with $Li_{1-x}CoO_2$ were published in 1980.[41]

The report concluded with the statement, "Further characteristics of the intrinsic and extrinsic properties of this new system are being made." However, when John went to patent his cathodes, no battery company in England, Europe, or the U.S. was interested in assembling a battery with a discharged cathode, so he gave the patent to the AERE Harwell Laboratory. Nevertheless, with his postdoc Peter G. Bruce, now a professor in St. Andrews, Scotland, and a new student, M.G.S.K. Thomas, Goodenough continued work at the Inorganic Chemistry Laboratory, South Parks Road, to demonstrate that the Li^+-ion mobility in $Li_{1-x}CoO_2$ is even higher than that in the sulfide cathode $LiTiS_2$. This finding meant that a $Li_{1-x}CoO_2$ cathode would provide the needed voltages and rates that would usher in the "wireless revolution."

Meanwhile, Rachid Yazami in Switzerland, exploring Li insertion into graphite, reported that a discharged graphite anode did not have a problem with dendrites if the carbon/$LiCoO_2$ cells were not charged too rapidly, and Akira Yoshino in Japan then assembled the discharged cell carbon/$LiCoO_2$ to demonstrate the Li-ion battery that was licensed to the SONY Corp., which marketed with it the first cell telephone. Today, almost everyone from five years old upwards has an application of this battery in his or her pockets.

Michael Thackeray (see Thackeray entry) was working on the Zebra battery, a modification of the sodium-sulfur battery, in South Africa when he read the article in the *Materials Research Bulletin*. He immediately applied for a sabbatical to work with Goodenough in Oxford. Thackeray stated that he had been inserting Li reversibly into magnetite, the ferrimagnetic spinel Fe_3O_4 used by Greek sailors in an early version of the compass. He wished to replace cobalt (Co), which is expensive and toxic, with iron (Fe), which is abundant and benign. The spinels $A[B_2]O_4$ contain a 3-dimensional framework of $BO_{6/3}$ octahedra sharing edges; in the layered $LiMO_2$ oxides they form 2-dimensional layers. The A atoms of a spinel occupy interstitial tetrahedral sites that are bridged by empty, face-sharing octahedra, and Goodenough realized from his earlier work on spinel memory elements that the Li inserted into $Fe[Fe_2]O_4$ was entering and displacing that interstitial A-site Fe into the bridging interstitial octahedral sites to create a rock-salt structure with the $[Fe_2]O_4$ framework remaining intact. Bill David, now at the Rutherford Laboratory, had just joined Goodenough's group from the Clarendon with a PhD involving structural analysis, so he and Thackeray demonstrated that Goodenough's hypothesis was correct. Meanwhile, Goodenough told Thackeray to investigate the electrochemical reversible insertion of Li into the spinel $Li[Mn_2]O_4$; it gave a voltage of 3.0 V versus lithium. Manganese (Mn) is also abundant and benign. On his return to South Africa, Thackeray showed his students that extraction of Li from $Li[Mn_2]O_4$ gives a voltage of 4.0 V versus lithium. A modification of the $Li_{1-x}[Mn_2]O_4$ spinel cathode is now used by the Nissan Corp. to power their Leaf electric car.

Goodenough recalls: "With the approach of mandatory retirement in England in 1986, I was delighted with an invitation from the University of Texas at Austin to occupy the Virginia H. Cockrell Centennial Chair in Engineering." From then on, as a member of the ME and ECE Departments, Goodenough helped to establish the Texas Materials Institute. With the help of now Professor Arumugan Manthiram, who had come with him from England as a postdoc in 1986, and of Professor Jianshi Zhou, who came to him in 1987 as a PhD student, Goodenough has been able to establish a laboratory that includes in one group solid state chemistry, structural characterization, electrochemistry, and a variety of physical measurements as a function of temperature and pressure.

This organization has enabled him to return to studies of the unusual physical properties imparted by orbital order, structural transformations, and the lattice instabilities encountered at the crossover from localized to itinerant electronic behavior. Some of this is summarized in his volume *Localized to Itinerant Electronic Transitions in Perovskite Oxides* (Springer-Verlag, 2001). He has also continued to develop solid electrolyte and electrode materials for the Li-ion battery and the solid oxide fuel cell (see his book with K. Huang, *Solid Oxide Fuel Cell Technology: Principles, Performance, and Operations*, Woodhead Publishing Ltd., 2009). The olivine cathode $Li_{1-x}FePO_4$ he developed in Texas is now being used for power tools and in a large battery being constructed in Quebec for the storage of electrical energy generated by a wind farm there.

In 2001, John received the Japan Prize for his discoveries of the materials critical to the development of lightweight rechargeable batteries.

John Goodenough is a member of the National Academy of Engineering, the French Academy of Sciences, the Real Academia de Ciencias Exactas, Físicas y Naturales of

Spain, and the Royal Society of the United Kingdom. He has authored more than 750 articles, 90 book chapters and reviews, and five books, including two seminal works, *Magnetism and the Chemical Bond* (1963) and *Les oxydes des métaux de transition* (1973). Dr. Goodenough is co-recipient of the 2009 Enrico Fermi Award. This presidential award is one of the oldest and most prestigious given by the U.S. government and carries an honorarium of $375,000. He shares the honor with Dr. Siegfried S. Hecker, professor at the Management of Science and Engineering Department of Stanford University.

Among his many publications is a very personal one: *Witness to Grace*,[42] in which John describes how his intellectual journey has also included "a religious quest for meaning in what or whom I would choose to serve with my life." *Witness to Grace* also chronicles a struggle to find a calling to a career in the science of the solid state, a career that brought together physics, chemistry, and engineering. The author leaves to the reader the decision as to what was the result of chance and what was the leading of the "Spirit of Love."

The RSC John B. Goodenough Award (previously advertised as the Materials Chemistry Forum Lifetime Award) was established in 2008. The award is to recognize exceptional and sustained contributions to the area of materials chemistry.

On November 30, 2010, the latest presentation of a Royal Society of Chemistry (RSC) National Chemical Landmark plaque took place in the Inorganic Chemistry Laboratory of the University of Oxford. The plaque reads: "Inorganic Chemistry Laboratory where, in 1980, John B. Goodenough with Koichi Mizushima, Philip C. Jones, and Philip J. Wiseman identified the cathode material that enabled the development of the rechargeable lithium-ion battery. This breakthrough ushered in the age of portable electronic devices."

At the ceremony, greetings were received in the form of a pre-recorded speech by Goodenough from his laboratory in the USA. Present at the ceremony itself were Drs. Mizushima, Wiseman, and Jones.

In July 2012, John celebrated his 90th birthday. He received the National Medal of Science (2012). In 2014, he received the Charles Stark Draper Prize of the National Academy of Engineering (2014) together with Yoshino, Yazami, and Nishi.

He has remained active with a full schedule leading graduate students and postdocs in continued research on transition-metal oxides and lithium-ion battery design and production. His jovial demeanor, keen wit and wonderful laugh have made him a favorite of students and faculty alike.

Goodenough notes: "Our work on rechargeable batteries and reversible intermediate-temperature fuel cells for weaning the world from dependence on fossil fuels remain a work in progress."

Notes

40. Interview with John Goodenough in 2012, edited by assistant Melissa Truitt-Green of the University of Texas, and Linda Webb of ICL.
41. *The Materials Research Bulletin* 15 (1980): 783–789.
42. "*Witness to Grace*" (Publish America, 2008).

Grätzel, Michael
(1944–)
Dye-sensitized solar cell

Michael Grätzel was born May 11, 1944, in Dorfchemnitz, Saxony, Germany. He went to school first in Dresden and then in Mersburg beside Lake Konstanz after his family fled from communist East Germany. He graduated in chemistry in 1968 from the Free University of Berlin, obtaining his PhD summa cum laude in 1971.

Grätzel relates: "I was interested in chemistry as a pillar of natural science. I was curious to learn more about the chemical processes that sustain life on earth, in particular photosynthesis and respiration. I was also intrigued by the notion of entropy and how entropy can be used to quantify disorder and describe spontaneous (natural) transformation."

From 1969 to 1972, Grätzel worked as a research associate at the Hahn-Meitner Institute in Berlin. He used radiation chemistry to study the reaction dynamics of nitrogen-oxygen compounds which are now known under the name of NOX and play a key role in environmental pollution. From 1972 to 1974 he was postdoctoral fellow at the Radiation Laboratory, University of Notre Dame, Indiana. His research focused on photo-induced electron transfer reactions in surfactant micelles, which are the simplest model systems for biological membranes.

Grätzel returned to the Hahn-Meitner Institute in Berlin where, from 1974 to 1976, he was a member of the scientific staff and received his teaching qualification (Habilitation) in physical chemistry in 1976 from the Free University of Berlin.

The following year he was appointed associate professor of physical chemistry at the Ecole Polytechnique Fédérale de Lausanne, becoming full professor in 1981.

Here he began to research colloidal semiconductor systems, today known as quantum dots. "I had followed with great interest the work of Professor Heinz Gerischer in Berlin and Professor Akira Fujishima and Kenichi Honda in Tokyo, who illuminated semiconductor electrodes to produce electric power or hydrogen from sunlight."

Michael also met and married Dr. Carole K. Clark, who grew up in Texas and received a PhD in physical chemistry from Rice Univer-

Michael Grätzel holding a DSSC outside the Ecole Polytechnique Fédérale de Lausanne (© Alain Herzog/ EPFL).

sity in Houston. They would have three children, Chauncey, Aimie and Liliane Caroline.

During the next two decades, Grätzel was one of those who pioneered research on energy and electron transfer reactions in mesoscopic-materials and their optoelectronic applications. In the 1980s he discovered a process for the low-temperature methanation of carbon dioxide.

From 1985, based on fundamental studies of the mechanisms and the dynamics of interfacial electron transfer processes in nanodispersed systems, Grätzel became interested in the promising pathway of molecular photovoltaics. In 1988, he made a presentation at the International Solar Energy Conversion Conference held at Northwestern University in Evanston, Illinois.

Brian O'Regan (PhD, Washington University) of the Water Chemistry Program at University of Wisconsin, Madison, was inspired by Grätzel's lecture and approached him after his talk. He suggested that they employ the colloidal TiO2 membrane that he had developed for water filtration together with other colleagues in the group of his supervisor Professor Mark Anderson.

Later that year O'Regan joined Grätzel for a couple of weeks at the Calvin laboratory of the University of California, Berkeley, where he was spending a six-month sabbatical. "We started collaborating on the photo-electrochemical properties of colloidal TiO2 electrodes. He subsequently joined my group in Switzerland. In 1991, we published together in Nature the first paper on dye-sensitized solar cells based on nanocrystalline TiO2 films." The efficiency at that time had reached close to 7 percent.

Together they discovered a nanostructured junction dye-sensitized solar cell (DSSC, DSC or DYSC). This was consecrated by a series of patents in 1988 and revealed by several publications at the beginning of the '90s. It made an exceptional impact.

In short, DSSC mimics the ability of plants to capture photons of light and turn them into electricity. This is achieved by using special dyes to capture the energy in light at different wavelengths, just like chlorophyll pigments in plants. As compared to conventional silicon solar cells, "Grätzel cells" have the ability to capture ambient diffuse daylight and weaker sunlight. They can also be integrated into liquids and gels, hence allowing solar cells to be tinted and installed on window panels.

Over the past two decades, conversion efficiencies have reached 16 percent and excellent stability has been attained, rendering the DSC a credible alternative to conventional p-n junction photovoltaic converters. For tandem devices, such as the DSC coupled to thin film solid-state PV cells, efficiencies exceeding 17 percent have been reached. This higher efficiency has been achieved by using new pigments as light harvesters, in particular metal perovskites.

Grätzel's work on the development of ionic liquids was a crucial step to achieve stable DSC operation to pass the internationally accepted tests for outdoor operation. Also organic donor-acceptor dyes such as indoline sensitizers show great potential for large-scale applications. The record efficiency is held by molecularly engineered porphyrin dyes, which exhibit a beautiful green color, rendering them very attractive for building integrate DSC panels such as the façade at the new Swisstech Congress center in Lausanne.

Mass production of DSSC began in 2009. The company called itself G24 Power and the product was called the GCell, both in homage to Grätzel. Based in Newport, South Wales, UK, a 89,000 sq. meter (9,5799e+5ft^2) factory utilizes a roll-to-roll manufacturing process giving a capacity to produce more than 160,000 feet (500,000 meters) of light-weight flexible large GCell modules per year. These are employed, for example, in back-packs to provide power for portable electronics such as computers, phones, iPads, etc. G24 is supported by their R&D laboratory at EPFL, Switzerland, plus a product development and integration team in Dongguan, China. Sony has developed DSC panels for car battery charging. The production is presently scaled up at SICCAS in Shanghai, China.

Just one example of the world's first major application of (DSSC) was launched in May 2012 with Logitech's light-powered Wireless Solar Keyboard Folio for the iPad 2 and iPad 3. The slim-line design folio provides lightweight portability and durable front and back protection for the iPad. It also boasts the added functionality of a Bluetooth® solar keyboard powered by a G24 solar cell.

While O'Regan is currently a research lecturer at Imperial College, London, Grätzel is still a professor at the École Polytechnique Fédérale de Lausanne, where he directs the Laboratory of Photonics and Interfaces. He is author of over 1300 publications and two books, and inventor or co-inventor of over 60 patents. He has been the Mary Upton Visiting Professor at Cornell University and a Distinguished Visiting Professor at the National University of Singapore. He was an Invited Professor at the University of California, Berkeley, the École Normale Supérieure de Cachan (Paris) and Delft University of Technology. His work has been cited over 144,000 times (h-index 175) making him one of the 10 most highly cited chemists in the world. He was a frequent guest scientist at the National Renewable Energy Laboratory (NREL) in Golden, Colorado, and was a fellow of the Japanese Society for the Promotion of Science.

Grätzel has received honorary doctorates from 10 European and Asian universities. He is an elected member of the German Academy of Science, a Max Planck Fellow, and an honorary fellow of the Royal Society of Chemistry (UK). He is also an honorary member of the Bulgarian Academy of Science, the Société Vaudoise de Sciences Naturelles, and the Israeli Chemical Society. In 2009 he was named Distinguished Honorary Professor by the Chinese Academy of Science (Changchun) and the Huazhong University of Science and Technology. He is the winner of the Harvey Prize (2007), the Balzan Prize (2009), and the Millennium Technology Prize (2010).

In 2011, the Wuhan National Lab for Optoelectronics (WNLO) launched the Michael Grätzel Center for Mesoscopic Solar Cells to promote DSSC's development in China. Grätzel was made honorary director of the Center. In 2012 he received the Albert Einstein World Award of Science (2012).

Michael Grätzel has many interests and hobbies. "First of all, I enjoy sports, in particular hiking and skiing in the mountains. In Lausanne we are blessed with a beautiful environment, which offers many other options including swimming or sailing on Lake Geneva. I use my bicycle to go to work throughout the year. I also love music. Listening to concerts and operas as well as playing the piano and singing in a Gregorian chant choir relaxes me."

Leisure aside, Michael Grätzel is planning to continue his research on mesoscopic photosystems for the generation of fuels and electricity from sunlight.

Sources: Communication to the author November 8, 2014; Brian O'Regan and Michael Grätzel (1991). "A low-cost, high-efficiency solar cell based on dye-sensitized colloidal TiO2 films." *Nature* 1991 353 (6346): 737.

Greatbatch, Wilson
(1919–2011)
Long-life battery-powered pacemaker

Wilson Greatbatch was born on September 6, 1919, in Buffalo, New York. The only child of Walter Greatbatch, a construction contractor who had immigrated from England, and his wife Charlotte, the boy was named after U.S. President Woodrow Wilson. He attended public grade school at West Seneca High School in West Seneca, joined the sea scouts, and obtained his amateur radio license at the age of 16.

He entered military service and served during World War II, becoming an aviation chief radioman before receiving an honorable discharge in 1945. As a chief petty officer, he also taught in the Navy's radar school—an extension of his childhood hobby. After the war, he attended Cornell University on the GI Bill, graduating with a BEE in electrical engineering in 1950; he received a master's degree from the University of Buffalo in 1957. Wilson loved fiddling with objects and this would lead to other great things.

In 1945, he married Eleanor Wright; they would have three children and live in an 1845 converted schoolhouse about 15 miles east of Buffalo. One of Eleanor's skills was making Wilson's trademark bow ties!

During the early 1960s when Greatbatch stumbled on a way of making a pacemaker, he was not the first. The first artificial vacuum-tube pacemaker, developed in Toronto in 1950, was not only external but powered from an AC wall socket, so carrying the potential hazard of electrocution of the patient by inducing ventricular fibrillation!

Eight years later, at Stockholm's Karolinska Institute, engineer and former cardiologist Rune Elmqvist and thoracic surgeon Åke Senning secretly carried out the first clinical implantation of a pacemaker into 43-year-old Arne Larsson. Larsson was a perfect candidate for this kind of operation. He was suffering from cardiac arrhythmia which had worsened as a result of a viral infection. His heart was beating at just 28 beats a minute, well under half the rate of a healthy heart. Larsson was constantly losing consciousness and had to be revived 20 to 30 times a day. There was little hope of a cure. However, his wife Else-Marie refused to accept her husband's impending fate. She read about Senning's and Elmqvist's work on an implantable pacemaker and became convinced that this would be her husband's salvation—although up to then the developers had only experimented with animals and there was no device suitable for the human body. It worked. But only just. For lack of time Elmqvist and Senning coated the components of this first device with epoxy resin in a simple plastic cup. Two electrodes connected to the pacemaker provided the energy to stimulate the heart. The device failed after three hours. A second device was then urgently implanted which lasted for two days. "Guinea pig" Larsson went on to receive 26 different pacemakers during his lifetime! He died in 2001, at the age of 86, outliving the inventor as well as the surgeon.

The first battery they used was a rechargeable nickel-cadmium battery. The cell voltage was 1.25 V with a capacity of 190 mAh. It was recharged by an induction coil from the outside. The major problems were twofold, the first being its very short lifetime. The second was to place the responsibility for recharging in the hands of patients—never seen as good medical practice.

Clearly the best solution would be to use longer-life primary or non-rechargeable

batteries. By this time, Wilson Greatbatch had returned to Buffalo to teach as
an assistant professor of electrical engineering at the University of Buffalo while
he earned his master's degree. He also
worked for the nearby Chronic Disease
Research Institute. By that time, around
1956, commercial silicon transistors had
become available for U.S. for $90 each,
and Greatbatch, working for a doctor at
the institute, was designing a circuit to
help record fast heart sounds. By mis-
take, he grabbed the wrong resistor from
a box and plugged it into the circuit he
was making. The circuit pulsed for 1.8
milliseconds and then stopped for 1 second and then repeated. Greatbatch recognized the lub-dub rhythm. It was then
he realized his invention could be used
as a pacemaker.

Greatbatch met William C. Chardack, chief of surgery at Buffalo's Veterans Administration Hospital. Chardack
predicted such an implantable pacemaker would save 10,000 lives a year.

**Wilson Greatbatch, whose pacemaker battery
has prolonged millions of lives (courtesy Anne
Greatbatch Maciariello).**

Three weeks later, on May 7, 1958,
Greatbatch brought what would become
the world's first implantable cardiac pacemaker, made with two Texas Instruments transistors, to Chardack's hospital. There Chardack and another surgeon, Andrew Gage,
exposed the heart of a dog, to which Greatbatch touched the two pacemaker wires. The
device took control of the heartbeat. The team stared in near disbelief.

Spending two years refining his device in a rented area of the former Wurlitzer
Organ Factory in North Tonawanda, New York, in April 1960 Greatbatch made his first
human implant. The 77-year-old male patient lived for a further 18 months. Greatbatch's
innovation was to use the primary cell mercury zinc battery. A patent for the implantable
pacemaker was filed in 1960 and granted in 1962 (U.S. Patent 3,057,356–Medical cardiac
pacemaker).

The Chardack-Greatbatch pacemaker used Mallory mercuric oxide-zinc cells (see
Ruben entry) for its energy source, driving a two-transistor, transformer-coupled blocking
oscillator circuit, all encapsulated in epoxy resin, then coupled to electrodes placed into
the myocardium of the patient's heart. This patented innovation led the Medtronic company of Minneapolis to commence the manufacture and further development of artificial
cardiac pacemakers.

Although ARCO developed isotope-powered pacemakers, by 1971 Wilson Greatbatch and his colleague Ralph Mead had come up with his second breakthrough: the
WG1 lithium-iodine-polyvinyl pyridine cell.

In 1968, Catalyst Research Corporation of Baltimore, Maryland, had developed and patented a lithium battery cell (USA patent 4,049,890). The cell used two elements at near ends of the electrochemical scale, causing a high voltage of 2.8V and an energy density near the physical maximum. Unfortunately, it had an internal impedance which limited its current load to under 0.1 mA and was thus considered useless.

In 1970 Greatbatch, having founded his own company, introduced the developed WG1 cell to pacemaker developers in 1971, but was met with limited enthusiasm. On July 9 of 1974, Manuel A. Villafaña and Anthony Adducci, founders of Cardiac Pacemakers, Inc., in St. Paul, Minnesota, manufactured the world's first pacemaker with a lithium anode and a lithium-iodide electrolyte solid-state battery. The lithium-iodide cell manufactured by Greatbatch is now the standard cell for pacemakers, having the energy density, low self-discharge, small size and reliability needed.

Worldwide, around three million people currently benefit from Greatbatch's discovery, with an additional 600,000 being implanted every year.

In 1983 the National Society of Professional Engineers selected the pacemaker as one of the greatest contributions to society of the previous 50 years. In 1998 Greatbatch was inducted into the National Inventors' Hall of Fame in Akron, Ohio, alongside his hero Thomas Edison. This was followed, in 2001, by the granting of the highest honor from the National Academy of Engineering, shared with his peer Earl Bakken, who invented the external pacemaker.

Referring to himself as a "humble tinkerer," Wilson Greatbatch was responsible for more than 320 inventions, and he received more than 150 patents. In his latter years, most of the millions that Greatbatch earned were ploughed back into research or donated to education and charities. He turned his passion towards the environment, AIDs research and educating the future generation. He even invented a solar-powered canoe, which he took on a 160-mile voyage on the Finger Lakes in New York on his 72nd birthday.

He challenged the scientists to break the world's dependence on fossil fuels, which he believed will be exhausted by 2050. One of his proposed solutions was the use of nuclear fusion, using an isotope of helium found in lunar soil, suggesting, "There is more He-3 energy on the Moon than we have ever had in the form of fossil fuels on Earth. All we have to do is to go there and get it."

Wilson Greatbatch died on September 27, 2011, at the Oxford Village assisted living center in Canterbury Woods, a suburb of Buffalo, New York. He was 92.

In his memoir, *The Making of the Pacemaker: Celebrating a Lifesaving Invention*, published in 2000, he wrote: "To ask for a successful experiment, for professional stature, for financial reward or for peer approval, is asking to be paid for what should be an act of love."

Sources: "Wilson Greatbatch." Inventor profile. National Inventors Hall of Fame; USA Patent 3,057,356–Medical cardiac pacemaker.

••

Green, Martin Andrew
(1948–)
Buried contact solar cell

Martin Andrew Green was born in Brisbane, Australia, on July 20, 1948. Neither of his parents had attended high school. As a young boy at Coorparoo State Primary School

Martin Green holds a Solarex multicrystalline Si panel fabricated in Sydney circa 1990. The system in the background is the first PV system connected to the electricity grid in New South Wales in 1994 (Green Collection).

he was more interested in playing rugby than in schoolwork. At Brisbane State High School, he took study more seriously. A physics teacher who conducted experiments about electricity particularly inspired him. In his final year exams, Green became Dux of the School and received the Lilley Medal for topping Queensland's 1965 Senior Matriculation Examination. By this time had become interested in microelectronics, tailoring his studies accordingly. As he matured, he would become increasingly disillusioned with this choice.

Green began studying electrical engineering at the University of Queensland in 1966. He was already intrigued by the physics of materials such as silicon in semiconductors, and was reinforced by a traveling scholarship that allowed him to visit microelectronics companies in Sydney and Melbourne. In 1971, winning a Commonwealth Scholarship, Green completed his PhD at McMaster University in Canada in engineering physics, studying the properties of a semiconductor device structure that became the foundation of his subsequent research.

Before leaving for Canada, Green married Judy Smith on July 4, 1970, then working for a stockbroker, but later for the Australian Olympics Committee. After completion of his studies, he was offered a position at the University of New South Wales in Sydney, returning to Australia in 1974. The couple took up residence in Sydney's eastern suburbs, close to the beaches, where they have lived ever since.

At the university, Green started a group to work on the development of silicon solar cells. His initial work, which soon started making international impact, was based on using the device structures he had studied during his PhD to improve the voltage output of silicon solar cells. He introduced a postgraduate course on silicon solar cells.

During the contemporaneous oil embargoes, a large USA solar program was launched at still-unequaled funding levels. Scientists believed 20 percent of the sun's energy was the most a cell could ever change into electricity. According to the laws of physics, the remaining energy would have to be reflected, or lost as heat. Green worked out that if a particular loss of energy in the cell was avoided, it might eventually be possible, in theory, to make a cell that changed 30 percent of the sun's energy into electricity.

On a very modest budget, using equipment rescued from the scrap heap, Green's small team started making progress. In 1983, they made the first silicon cell to convert electricity to sunlight with more than 18 percent efficiency (18 percent of the incident sunlight energy converted to electricity). In 1985, they increased this to 20 percent, the photovoltaic "4-minute mile," using a cell structure that used the same type of expensive processing as in microelectronics.

In 1983, Martin also started working with Stuart Wenham. Wenham, who had been working as a scientist for Australia's first silicon solar cell manufacturer, was attracted to Sydney by Green's work. Green and Wenham invented a new type of cell, called the "buried contact solar cell," to allow cells of 20 percent efficiency to be produced inexpensively for commercial use.

Like earlier cells, it was made by slicing a block of solid silicon into "wafers," but in this cell the wafer has metal contacts "buried" into it, rather than sitting on top of it. This increases the amount of electricity the cell produces. In 1984, they filed the patent application: "Buried Contact Solar Cell" (Australian Patent 570,309; U.S. Patents 4,726,850 and 4,748,130).

In 1986, this became the second cell to exceed 20 percent efficiency. This work was later recognized by their being awarded the CSIRO External Medal for "outstanding research achievement of commercial significance" and contributed to their being awarded the 1999 Australia prize for "distinguished research in experimental physics."

In 1985, BP Solar became the first licensee of this new technology. It was used in production from 1992–2006, accumulating over U.S. $1 billion in sales. The technology demonstrated a significant performance advantage over existing technology, producing the first 14 percent efficient commercial solar panels. The technology's advantages were dramatically demonstrated in the 1993 Sunrayce, a solar car race for U.S. universities. To keep costs down, race rules stipulated that teams must use inexpensive commercial cells but could choose from any manufacturer worldwide. Nine of the first 10 cars to finish used BP's cells (including all top 5). Rules for the next race were altered by restricting entrants to U.S.–made cells to broaden the supply base.

Many researchers entering the field have learned about photovoltaics from Green's textbook *Solar Cells: Operating Principles, Technology and System Application* (Prentice-Hall, 1982), probably the field's most widely used publication, introducing many current researchers to photovoltaics. The book also includes a section on energy storage that describes the operation of the Fe-Cr redox battery, in which Green had become interested during a visit to NASA-Lewis. With NASA's assistance, Green's thesis student built an Fe-Cr redox battery at UNSW for further evaluation. Dr. Maria Skyllas-Kazacos (see Skyllas-Kazacos entry) and her team, also at UNSW, soon converted this into the first vanadium redox battery. The textbook was the first of six books and a chain of over 500 scientific papers with Green being identified as a 2014 Highly Cited Researcher (ranked among the top 1 percent most cited researchers in his subject field for years of publication between 2002 and 2012).

In 1989, Green and co-workers reported a new type of solar cell, the PERC cell (Passivated Emitter and Rear Cell). This became the first silicon cell to demonstrate energy conversion efficiency above 23 percent. The key design feature involves making rear contact through holes in a rear insulating layer, simultaneously improving both the optical and electrical properties of the cell. Ongoing refinements to the PERC cell resulted in steadily improved performance, widening their unbeaten lead on the rest of the world. In 2008, Green's team reported the first silicon solar cell to achieve the milestone of 25 percent efficiency, as subsequently published in the journal *Progress in Photovoltaics*.

The whole photovoltaic industry is presently moving en masse to incorporate PERC cell technology into production. Installed PERC production capacity was estimated by market research company NPD Solarbuzz to be 2.5 gigawatts in August 2014, and growing quickly. This capacity would produce product valued at over U.S. $4 billion at the system level. The same company anticipated that PERC could account for the majority of installed manufacturing capacity by 2018.

The World Solar Challenge is a race for solar-powered cars, run over 3021 kilometers between Darwin and Adelaide, Australia. From 1990 to 1999, every car but one that won the race used a cell invented at UNSW (see Rand entry). Licensed technology has also been used in other high-profile applications including the *Solar Sailor*, a solar-powered passenger catamaran that plies Sydney harbor; on the Sydney town hall; and on the Wharf Theatre in Sydney, where Cate Blanchette was CEO from 2008–2013.

The awards continued to acknowledge Green's achievement: the 1988 Award for Outstanding Achievement in Energy Research (Australian Industry Confederation); the joint award of the 1992 CSIRO External Medal and 1999 Australia Prize (highest Australian government scientific award). International awards include the 1995 IEEE Ebers Award for "sustained technical leadership in the field of silicon photovoltaic solar energy conversion," the highest international recognition for electron device research, awarded previously exclusively for work in the USA, Europe or Japan; the 1999 Australia Prize; the 2002 Right Livelihood Award (also known as the Alternative Nobel Prize); the 2004 World Technology Award for Energy; the 2007 SolarWorld Einstein Award; the 2009 ENI Award for "Renewable and Non-Conventional Energy"; and the 2014 James Cook Medal.

Green also served on the board of the Sydney-based CSG Solar, as research director and as honorary president, Guodian New Energy Research Institute, Beijing (Guodian is one of China's "big 5" power companies). His portrait was painted by Giles Alexander with fellow scientist Ross Garnaut for the Archibald Prize 2010. The painting was a finalist, losing to a portrait of Tim Minchin. He is also a Scientia Professor at UNSW and Director of the Australian National Energy Agency-supported Centre for Advanced Photovoltaics.

In May 2013, Green was named director of the UNSW–based Australia-U.S. Institute for Advanced Photovoltaics, an historic international research initiative, and in the same year was inducted into the Fellowship of the Royal Society. Scientists arrived from around the world to study this course and work with Green. One scientist, Shi Zhengrong, became a billionaire by founding Suntech Power, formerly the world's biggest manufacturer of silicon solar cells. Other students hold, or have held, key positions in all leading manufacturers, including Trina, Yingli, Hanwha, JA Solar, SunPower, SolarWorld, Jinko, Canadian Solar, CSUN, LG Electronics and Samsung.

Continuing in his mission, Green provoked interest in third-generation solar cells, through another of his books, *Third-generation Photovoltaics: Advanced Solar Energy Conversion*. This argues that photovoltaics must continue to evolve to ever-increasing conversion efficiency. In November 2014, Green and co-workers succeeded in converting over 40 percent of the sunlight hitting a solar system into electricity, the highest efficiency yet reported, using third-generation concepts. The world-beating efficiency was achieved in outdoor tests in Sydney, before being independently confirmed by the National Renewable Energy Laboratory (NREL) at their outdoor test facility in the United States. The work was funded by the Australian Renewable Energy Agency (ARENA) and supported by the Australia–U.S. Institute for Advanced Photovoltaics (AUSIAPV).

Martin Green continues to enjoy living and working in Sydney while having the opportunity to travel worldwide to meet with colleagues involved in the ever-expanding solar industry. His hobbies include swimming, running, and writing. For many years, he and wife Judy have organized the Sunday jog at Bronte Surf Club, where they are honorary members.

His current interest is in combining other semiconductor material on top of silicon to improve efficiency, to perhaps beyond 50 percent.

Source: information provided by Martin Green to the author in January 2015.

....

Grey, Clare P.
(1965–)
Nuclear Magnetic Resonance Spectroscopy

Clare P. Grey was born on March 17, 1965, in Middlesborough, Northern England, moving to the Netherlands two years later. She was educated in the Netherlands and then at the British School of Brussels (1972–1979). Her family returned to the UK in 1979 where she completed her secondary education at St. Albans Girls' School. Her father and maternal grandfather were both chemists, working in the chemical industry and as a teacher, respectively, providing early inspiration.

In 1983, Grey obtained an Open Scholarship at Christ Church College, University of Oxford, to study Chemistry. Her final year "Part II" research project was performed under the direction of Prof. Anthony K. Cheetham in the Chemical Crystallography Laboratory at Oxford, her work on paramagnetic shift probes in high-resolution solid-state nuclear leading to a paper in *Nature* and to First Class Honors in Chemistry in 1987. Cheetham, a leading solid-state chemist, and an expert in neutron diffraction and structure solution with synchrotron methods, was starting to explore how the use of a relatively new technique, high-resolution solid state NMR spectroscopy, could be used to solve problems in solid state chemistry. Grey devoted her research efforts from the beginning, first as a Part II, and then as DPhil student, to solid-state NMR studies of a wide variety of materials; she used a CXP200 Bruker spectrometer housed in the laboratory of the local NMR expert, Dr. (now Prof.) Christopher M. Dobson of the Inorganic Chemistry

Laboratory. Dobson had worked on paramagnetic molecules in solution NMR spectroscopy and so Grey benefited from many interactions with him and his group. She obtained her DPhil. in 1991 with the thesis title: "^{119}Sn and ^{89}Y MAS NMR Study of Rare-Earth Pyrochlores."

She spent a Royal Society postdoctoral year at the University of Nijmegen in the laboratory of Prof. W.S. Veeman, where she changed directions, focusing on NMR method development, working on new experiments for quadrupolar nuclei. She then spent two years as a visiting scientist at DuPont Central Research and Development in Wilmington, Delaware. Working with Dr. Alexander J. Vega, she applied in-depth NMR studies to molecular sieves and to inorganic-organic composites. She co-authored two influential papers, "Rotational Echo ^{14}N/^{13}C/^{1}H Triple-Resonance Solid-State Nuclear-Magnetic-Resonance: A Probe of ^{13}C-^{14}N Inter-Nuclear Distances" and "Determination of the Quadrupole Coupling-Constant of the Invisible Aluminum Spins in Zeolite HY with 1H/27Al TRAPDOR NMR," which described new NMR experiments for measuring distances between atoms in the solid state and for probing local environments for ions in the solid state which were previously very difficult to detect.

In 1994 Clare Grey joined the faculty at SUNY Stony Brook University as an assistant professor, winning a National Science Foundation National Young Investigator award. By 2001 she was promoted to full professor; in 2009 her major research activities moved to the UK and she became the Geoffrey Moorhouse Gibson Professor at the Department of Chemistry, University of Cambridge. She started as the head of the Inorganic Sector, becoming the head of the Materials Research Interest Group in 2010.

Over the past 20 years, Clare Grey's wide interests in solid-state NMR innovation focused on a variety of subjects within material science. Initially she was more concerned with structural features, later becoming more and more fascinated by dynamical aspects in the context of mobility within porous solids, and ionic transport in ceramics. She met Dr. Bill Bowden, a scientist from Duracell, at a (Gordon) conference in 1996 and this interaction (and the exchange of battery materials), coupled with off-court conversations with her squash partners (from nearby Brookhaven National Laboratory) kick-started her research program in lithium ion batteries. Notably she was able to use some of the methodologies and insight from her D.Phil. work on paramagnetic materials to make insightful contributions to examine paramagnetic battery materials.

Today, her papers belong to the most detailed studies of cathode materials in rechargeable batteries during electrochemical cycling that are presently available in literature. Her major focus is on Li-ion batteries. She showed, together with her research group, that NMR is a superb and unique tool for exploring and understanding cathode materials in batteries under working conditions. It allows the skilled designer to optimize electrodes for high power and for high capacity conditions, also in rechargeable battery systems. She has coupled her NMR studies with other detailed structural studies that make use of synchrotron and neutron diffraction, using relevant theoretical methods (for example, density functional theory, or DFT) to compute experimental observables, structures and energetics for the processes that she studies. "We have developed NMR methodology to monitor structural changes that occur during the operation of a battery. These in-situ NMR studies allow us, for example, to capture metastable phases, to follow reactions between the electrolyte and the electrode materials and to investigate the effect of rapid charging and cycling of the battery."

Clare Grey has to a large extent created, by her own contributions, a flourishing new field of NMR with a great potential for future beneficial discoveries and applications. In her studies, Grey is taking advantage of all conceivable NMR nuclei, including ^{1}H, ^{2}H, ^{6}Li, ^{7}Li, ^{13}C, ^{14}N, ^{17}O, ^{19}F, ^{29}Si, ^{31}P, ^{119}Sn, and more. She is applying her methodology to the so-called "beyond lithium" technologies, including lithium air, lithium sulphur, and Na and Mg batteries.

She has published over 300 technical papers and has received a necklace of honors for her findings. In 2008 she was made Vaughan Lecturer; in 2010 won the Royal Society of Chemistry John Jeyes Award; in 2011 won the Kavli Medal and was elected Fellow of the Royal Society; in 2012 received an honorary PhD "Docteur Honoris Causa" from the University of Orleans; in 2013 won the Günther Laukien prize; in 2014 the Davy Medal; in 2015 the Arfvedson-Schlenk Award for her work involving lithium.

Her recent investigations were focused on the field of lithium ion batteries (LiBs), where she uses in-situ ^{6}Li/^{7}Li solid state NMR spectroscopy to investigate the mechanisms of lithium insertion and extraction during battery charge/discharge. She studies the effects of local structure and electronic properties on LiB performance and she identifies nano-sized or amorphous phases which are formed on lithium incorporation.

These investigations are especially useful for the development of high-capacity conversion-type electrode materials, which may lead to the next generation of high energy lithium batteries required for electric power train technologies, e.g., for long-range e-mobility.

> Our work has underpinned the understanding and development of new electrode materials—from high energy density silicon anodes to lithium-excess nickel manganite cathodes. We are now aiming to obtain higher resolution NMR spectra (to obtain more detailed structural details) while cycling a battery. To track surface changes with increasing sensitivity to examine electrolyte degradation processes in real time.

Source: Information provided by Clare P. Grey, October 2015.

··

Grove, William Robert
(1811–1896)
The "gas voltaic battery" or first fuel cell

William Robert Grove was born on July 11, 1811, in Swansea in South Wales, the only child of John, a magistrate and deputy lieutenant of Glamorgan, and his wife, Anne née Bevan. His early education was in the hands of private tutors, before he attended Brasenose College, Oxford, to study classics, though his scientific interests may have been cultivated by mathematician Baden Powell. Otherwise, his taste for science has no clear origin, though his circle in Swansea was broadly educated. He graduated in 1832.

In 1835 he was called to the Bar by Lincoln's Inn, but ill health, which had probably kept him out of the clutches of public school, kept him out of active legal practice throughout the 1830s.

In 1829 at the Royal Institution, Grove had met Emma Maria Powles. Marrying in 1837, the couple embarked on a tour of the Continent for their honeymoon. This sabbatical offered Groves an opportunity to pursue his scientific interests and resulted in his first scientific paper suggesting a novel form of electric cell.

In a letter dated October 1838 but published in the December 1838 edition of *The London and Edinburgh Philosophical Magazine and Journal of Science*, William Grove wrote about the development of his first crude fuel cells: "As it seems probable that at no very distant period voltaic electricity may become useful as a means of locomotion, the arrangement of the batteries so as to produce the greatest power in the smallest space, becomes important." Grove also announced his invention to the Académie des Sciences in Paris.

His cell consisted of a zinc anode dipped in sulfuric acid and a platinum cathode dipped in nitric acid, separated by porous earthenware. The Grove cell provided a high current and nearly twice the voltage of the Daniell cell, which soon made it the favored cell of the American telegraph networks for a time. However, it gave off poisonous nitric oxide fumes when operated. The voltage also dropped sharply as the charge diminished, which became a liability as telegraph networks grew more complex. Platinum was also very expensive.

In 1840 Grove invented the first incandescent electric light, useful in mines, which was later perfected by Thomas Edison (see Edison entry). Later that year he gave another account of his development at the British Association for the Advancement of Science, meeting in Birmingham, where it aroused the interest of Michael Faraday. On Faraday's invitation Grove presented his discoveries at the prestigious Royal Institution Friday Discourse on March 13, 1840.

Grove's presentation made his reputation, and he was soon proposed for fellowship of the Royal Society by such distinguished men as William Thomas Brande, William Snow Harris and Charles Wheatstone. Grove also attracted the attention of John Peter Gassiot, a relationship that resulted in Grove's becoming the first professor of experimental philosophy at the London Institution in 1841. Grove's inaugural lecture in 1842 was the first announcement of what Grove called the correlation of physical forces, or in modern terms, the conservation of energy.

In 1842, Grove developed the first fuel cell, which he called the gas voltaic battery. It produced electrical energy by combining hydrogen and oxygen, and he described it using his correlation theory. In developing the cell and showing that steam could be disassociated into oxygen and hydrogen, and the process reversed, he was the first person to demonstrate the thermal dissociation of molecules into their constituent atoms. He gave the first demonstration of this effect privately to Faraday, Gassiot and Edward William Brayley, his scientific editor. His work also led him to early insights into the nature of ionization.

During the late 1840s Grove became disenchanted by the debasement of science by monetary greed. In 1846 he resigned his London professorship and returned to the Bar. His legal career prospered instead. He was a Queen's Commissioner by the mid-1850s and ended his career at last as a judge in the Court of Common Pleas. He sat on Royal Commissions (on sewers and on patents). In 1871 he was knighted. He became a judge of the Queen's Bench in 1880 and Privy Councillor in 1887. He died on August 1, 1896.

Hare, Robert
(1781–1858)
The "galvanic deflagrator"

Robert Hare was born in Philadelphia on January 17, 1781. He was the son of Robert Hare, Sr., a major Philadelphia brewer, and Margaret Willing, niece of Thomas Willing, the political leader and president of the Bank of North America. Hare demonstrated an interest in science from an early age. As a young man, he attended the Academy of the University of Pennsylvania. Possessed of an innate mechanical aptitude, Hare developed a passion for chemistry while attending the lectures of James Woodhouse.

Aged 19, Hare and Edward Daniel Clarke of Oxford constructed and tested out an oxy-hydrogen blowpipe.

Hare was a professor at the University of Pennsylvania between 1810 and 1812 and between 1818 and 1847.

In 1820, having found a way of obtaining a corresponding amount of surface and its resultant power with a single roll of metal, Hare developed what he called a "galvanic deflagrator." This was a type of voltaic battery in which a large sheet of copper having several hundred square feet of surface and a similar one of zinc, separated by a piece of felt or cloth saturated with acidulated water, were then rolled up or interleaved in the form of a cylinder.

With one of Hare's deflagrators, in 1823, Benjamin Silliman, professor of chemistry and natural philosophy at Yale, first demonstrated the volatilization and fusion of carbon, a result then considered so extraordinary that it was a considerable time before it was fully credited. It was with these batteries that the first application of voltaic electricity to blasting under water was made in 1831 in experiments conducted under Robert Hare's direction.

As an instructor, Hare was at his best with advanced students but was generally appreciated for his dramatic demonstrations of chemical principles, often employing apparatus he had developed himself. His *Compendium of the Course of Chemical Instruction* (1828) went through at least four editions before 1840.

Later in life Hare converted to Spiritualism and wrote several books that made him very famous in the United States as a Spiritualist. In 1854 he published a book titled *Experimental Investigation of the Spirit Manifestations*. His work was criticized by his fellow scientists but was warmly welcomed with enthusiasm by the Spiritualists. He died four years later.

Haring, Howard Egbert
(1898–1965)
The lead-calcium alloy storage battery

Howard Egbert Haring was born on August 27, 1898, in Pennsylvania. He attended Franklin and Marshall College, Princetown University, and was awarded his B.S. in 1916. He joined the American Chemical Society in 1917.

In 1927, working at the U.S. Bureau of Standards in Washington, D.C., Haring, aged 32, and his colleague Barrows, developed a process for the electrodeposition of chromium from chromic acid baths, whereby the United States Bureau of Engraving and Printing would save hundreds of thousands of dollars in its printing of currency and postage. Two years later, he was recruited to work at Bell Telephone Laboratories, Murray Hill, New Jersey, where he became part of a team researching into lead alloys.

They found that the lead-antimony alloys almost universally employed in storage cell construction were far from ideal for the purpose from the electrochemical standpoint. In the course of normal operation of the existing cell, antimony was leached out of the positive electrode, passed through the solution and deposited on the negative, where it promoted "local action" and self-discharge. They also demonstrated that stibine was generated in perceptible amounts by the existing battery on overcharge. To replace this, Haring and co-workers developed the lead-calcium alloy storage battery. For this in 1936 they were granted U.S. Patent 2,042,840 concerning "Superiorities of lead-calcium alloys for storage battery construction."

In 1945, towards the end of World War II, Haring, in charge of Bell Research Labs, and co-workers developed the "sea-water" battery for the U.S. Navy. It was capable of a high-power output per unit of weight and volume when immersed in sea water. Previous batteries ordinarily operated for a relatively short period of time before they were substantially discharged, usually for not more than 10 minutes. With appropriate changes in construction, batteries could give lower power outputs for much longer periods of time. The sea-water battery was particularly adapted for the propulsion of naval torpedoes.

Postwar, Haring became involved with research in silver chlorides and also developed a device to demonstrate theoretical principles underlying electrochemical action. In January 1952, he published his findings, "The Mechanism of Electrolytic Rectification," in the *Journal of the Electrochemical Society*. This device became known as the Haring cell.

During the 1950s, he was investigating the characteristics of semiconductor devices. Howard Haring died of a heart attack on November 12, 1965, aged only 67.

• •

Hatazawa, Tsuyonobu
(1962–)
Biofuel cell

Tsuyonobu Hatazawa was born in Japan on August 5, 1962, at Nagoya Aichi, Japan. He was the first son of Minoru Hatazawa, who was the first son of a temple carpenter in Akita prefecture. His mother, Noriko Hatazawa, was the second daughter of a temple master of Heart Sutra in the same prefecture. Although Tsuyonobu Hatazawa was born while his father was working at the temple in Aichi, soon after, Minoru Hatazawa was nominated as a general manager of one the state's house-building projects. So the whole family moved to Tokyo.

During his first six years, Tsuyonobu Hatazawa's favorite toys were his drawing board, slide rule and ruling pen. Aged only six, he had a hobby of dismantling and reassembling the watches of his adult relatives. This activity was not always 100 percent successful and would upset his parents. By ten years old, he was able to design and build his own radio set. Apart from such interests, Tsuyonobu was quite a normal boy who liked running, cycling and baseball.

In his first year at junior high school, his summer vacation report was "Difference of current characteristics in low-frequency amplification transistor versus the high-frequency amplification transistor; measurement and decomposition observation." He recalls: "Unfortunately this report was not published but I hope it has been stored in my school. Around this time, I began to think about what key technology was changing the world. I talked a lot to myself: 'Is it my Walkman? No. Circuit board? No. Even this transistor? Maybe not.' My answer was 'the material which enables the transistor to work.' This is the reason why I decided to study material science."[43]

Tsuyonobu Hatazawa obtained his B.A. at Sophia University in Chiyoda, Tokyo, in 1985. From 1986 to 1992, he worked at the Sekisui Chemical Co. Ltd., where he carried out applied electronics laboratory research into optical films and polymer materials for the IT company, NEC and basic research into organic EL (red) materials.

In June 1988, Tsuyonobu married Misako Hatazawa. They have two children.

From 1992 until 1994, Hatazawa was a visiting scientist at Professor Royce Murray's Laboratory at the University of North Carolina at Chapel Hill. Here he worked on the synthesis and analysis of ionic conductive polymer metal MV. He also invented a measurement system for isolating ionic and electric conductivity. In 1996 he received an award at EuroDisplay96 SID (the Society for Information Display) for his back-lighting method for LCD display.

In 1997, Hatazawa became the R&D Manager at the Sony Corporation, Kanagawa, as successor of Dr. Yoshio Nishi, who, with John Goodenough (see Goodenough entry), is the co-inventor of the lithium ion battery and 2014 winner of Charles Stark Draper Prize. Hatazawa himself next innovated the polymer gel electrolyte and lithium-ion polymer battery. For this new industry incubation, he later received the Technical Development Award of the Electrochemical Society of Japan (Tanahashi Award) in March 2008.

From 2005 to 2010, Hatazawa worked on the Bio Fuel Cell with the Energy Device research group at Sony's Advanced Materials Lab. In this he was supported by Professor Kenji Kano's laboratory at the Division of Applied Life Sciences, Kyoto University.

Inspired by power generation in living organisms, Hatazawa and fellow researchers such as Hideki Sakai and Yuichi Tokita developed a bio-battery that could generate electricity from glucose using enzymes as catalysts. Until then, the energy output from biofuel cells had been too low for practical applications. Electron transfer in a biofuel cell can be slow, so Hatazawa used a naphthoquinone derivative—known as an electron transfer mediator—to shuttle electrons between the electrodes and enzymes. This

Tsuyonobu Hatazawa, inventor of the lithium-ion polymer battery and biofuel cell (courtesy Hatazawa).

increased both the current density—a measure of the rate of an electrochemical reaction—and the power output.

To increase the current density further, Hatazawa packed the mediator and enzymes onto a carbon-fiber anode. The large surface area and porosity of the electrode avoided disruption to glucose transport and maintained enzyme activity. They used a similar design to optimize the cathode so it supplied oxygen efficiently to the fuel cell.

When the researchers stacked four of the cells together, they achieved a power output of 100 milliwatts—enough to run an mp3 player with speakers or a small remote-controlled car.

The research results on the high-power glucose-oxygen biofuel cell presented by Sony were accepted as an academic paper for the 234th American Chemical Society National Meeting & Exposition in Boston. The presentation took place on August 22, 2007.

In 2009, Hatazawa et al. were granted Patent No. 20090047567 for "A biofuel cell with a structure in which a cathode and an anode are opposed to each other with an electrolyte layer provided there between, at least one of the cathode and the anode including an electrode on which at least one enzyme and at least one electron mediator are immobilized."

From 2009 to 2012, Hatazawa and his team at Sony's Battery R&D Lab developed an energy server system, using $LiFePO_4$ cathode technology which was installed in Tohoku University, Miyagi, Japan.

They then progressed to binder technology developed for a high performance (650Wl/L) LCO-graphite cell, using Si-anode technology, electrolyte for high voltage, advanced polymer battery.

In August 2013, Tsuyonobu Hatazawa left Sony to become chief technology officer, in charge of 40 scientists and engineers, at Nexeon Japan and Nexeon Ltd., a battery materials and licensing company developing silicon anodes for the next generation of lithium-ion battery. Nexeon has a fully automated and instrumented pilot plant in operation and has filed a sequence of patents covering a unique solution to the well-known cycle-life problem with silicon.

Hatazawa now divides his time between Nexeon's Oxfordshire and Tokyo offices. He has been the recipient of many prestigious awards, and holds some 83 Japanese and foreign patents.

To relax at his home in Machida-shi, Tsuyonobu plays jazz and blues on one of his 10 Fender Stratocaster electric guitars. "I started playing electric guitar when I was 13 years old. My favorite one is a black 1962 model."[44]

NOTES

43. Communication sent to the author on November 28, 2014.
44. Ibid.

• •

Hellesen, Frederik Louis Wilhelm
(1836–1892)
Danish dry cell battery pioneer

Wilhelm Hellesen was born on February 2, 1836, at Kalundborg, Denmark. Although the family business was in butter, Hellesen was also particularly interested in physics and chemistry. By 1876, aged 40, he had begun to investigate a new type of battery, carrying out experiments in the coach house of his residence in Frederiksberg. Before long, isolated research in his spare time soon became so demanding that in 1885, he sold his business to be able to devote full time to the project.

By 1887 Hellesen had produced his version of the dry cell, based on Leclanché's unit (see Leclanché entry). Into a zinc container he placed carbon rods surrounded by a mixture of brown stone and graphite. Instead of liquid there was a paste of ammonium chloride. The paste was held by adding starch. Finally, the whole was sealed with pitch.

Unknown to Hellesen, Carl Gassner of Mainz was developing almost exactly the same type of battery (see Gassner entry).

In November 1888, Hellesen took out a German patent for his battery (No. 48,448). This was followed during 1889 and 1890 by patents in France, Belgium, the British Empire, Switzerland, the Austro-Hungarian Empire and the USA (U.S. 439,151). By this time Hellesen had been joined by a young electrochemist called Valdemar Ludvigsen.

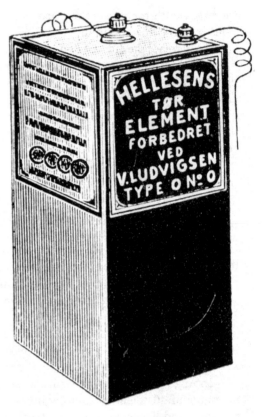

The Hellesen dry cell battery (c. 1900) (Danmarks Tekniske Museum).

Starting in 1889 with a delivery of batteries to the Copenhagen Telephone Company, during the next four years W. Hellesen & Co. delivered about 7,000 batteries.

Sadly, Hellesen died on December 22, 1892. After his death, his widow changed the name of the company to "W. Hellesen's Enke" (enke = widow). In 1895, Valdemar Ludvigsen discovered that the addition of zinc chloride made an even more durable battery. In 1897 the widow's company manufactured one thousand small battery flashlights; they were ready for sale just before Christmas and became a sensation. Several types of battery were manufactured at the plant at No. 14 Åboulevarden.

From January 1899, with Ludvigsen admitted as a partner, the company name was changed to "W. Hellesen's Widow & V. Ludvigsen." When widow Hellesen left the business in 1906, V. Ludvigsen became the sole owner.

By 1900 the company had established itself both at home and abroad with a solid battery. It had a virtual monopoly in the domestic market and had started a comprehensive export abroad, which by 1910 included 60 different countries. The batteries were marketed as quality products that were better than other comparable units on the market, and at the Universal Exhibition in Paris in 1900, the company was awarded a gold medal. Already in 1890, the patent rights for Germany and Austria-Hungary had been handed over to the German company Siemens & Halske, and in England to Siemens Brothers, who established factories in London, Berlin and Vienna. The laboratory in Copenhagen collaborated with laboratories in London and Berlin on the further development of the batteries.

Jache, Otto
(1915–1993)
Innovator of the gel-filled battery

The year 1910 saw the foundation of a factory "Akkumulatoren Fabrik, Aktienge-sellchaft" by Dr. Theodor Sonnenschein, former student of Max Planck in Berlin. Its specialty: starter batteries. Five years later, Otto Jache was born in the southeast Berlin suburb of Treptow. His father had been killed the year before fighting for the Kaiser, so he was brought up by his mother Gertrud. At school he was particularly encouraged by his chemistry teacher and from then on chemistry became his first love.

Jache did not have any scientific training. He was a chemical engineering technician, first working for C. Lorenz, AG, and then at the Edeleanu petroleum refinery in Berlin.

The young Jache appears to have had a great sense of humor. One night when he was out with friends, they threw some NJ3 (nitrogen triiodide) into Berlin's Landwehr-kanal then stood back to watch the multi-colored "Bengal Fire" display! They also developed a lotion that when stepped on, went off like a gun!

During World War II, he served as a soldier in France and in Finland. In September 1944, when Finland signed an armistice with the Soviet Union, he realized that, unless he wanted to be taken prisoner by the Soviets, he had to escape, via Norway. During this marathon, he was accompanied by a Norwegian woman, Reidum Ingrid Karlsen, who had to leave her native country because she had collaborated with the Germans. She became his wife.

Immediate postwar Germany faced an impossible task of regaining its place in the industrial world. One could no longer select places to work and live in. With the Soviets occupying the Berlin-Marienfelde suburb where the Sonnenschein factory had been based, they decided to confiscate some of the equipment as reparation payment. But not all of it. Clemens Jonen, brother-in-law of the founder, the late Theodor Sonnenschein, managed to save some material. After a considerable search, he came across the possibility of setting up a new factory at Büdingen in Hessen and moving his staff there, including "Chemoteckniker" Otto Jache.

Since 1936 Büdingen had been a garrison town for the Third Reich, with the local Thier-garten area used as a training field. From 1946, while occupying U.S. armored divisions continued to use the training area, Sonnenschein acquired a number of the buildings, which they were to occupy until 2008.

Jache's first job at Büdingen was to cast lead grids for pasting together into positive and negative plates. For small batteries, there could be

Otto Jache of Sonneschein (Jache Collection, *Batteries International*).

as many as 12 plates. To transport quantities of these around, with his fellow workers, Jache designed and built electric trolleys to replace the horse-drawn ones.

In terms of living quarters, everyone at Sonnenschein had to make do with what was available. Some staff took up residence in the former local hunting lodge of the Ysenburg princes. During the next thirty years, Otto and Reidum Jache's home was a converted former ammunition depot, just 200 meters from the factory. It was here that their three children grew up. This proximity to his laboratory would mean that Otto could often work into the night as he did not have far to get home. Social contacts were rare, and although invited, he did not join the skittles club formed by his colleagues.

After the death of Clemens Jonen in 1957, Dr. Christian Schwarz-Schilling, the husband of Sonnenschein's daughter Marie-Luise, joined the company. There were about 250 employees and he was looking for an outlet to expand. Until then the company had been making wet lead-acid batteries for radios, and also for photo-flash devices with charge-indicators using balls of different specific weights. Such batteries were tilt-proof but only operated when upright.

Encouraged by Schwarz-Schilling, Otto Jache now formed a team to research dryfit batteries, which could be used in transistor radios and photoflash units, etc. They found that lead-calcium (PbCa) gave a cleaner step from charging to H2-emission and avoided the formation of poisonous SbH3. Silica immobilized the electrolyte. Oxidation of the negative plates by air was hampered by a valve, integrated in the cover.

The first "dryfit" gel batteries were 2-cell 1Ah, Type 2Ax2, delivered in October 1958. As they came to be accepted, these dryfits were used in telecommunications for gliders and even "environmentally important" applications like golf carts and toilets for cats!

One of Jache's close colleagues, Günter Piske, has recalled, "When I finally joined Sonnenschein in Feb[ruary] 1959, I found many of these batteries inadequate. So we had to

The Sonnenschein stand at the 1960 Hannover Industrial Exhibition (Jache Collection, *Batteries International*).

tackle a sequence of technical problems such as the filling method, charging, and a reliable regulating valve."

In 1965 the first "dryfit" license contract was established with Globe Union.

Several years before, Jache's wife Reidum had left him and gone to live in the USA. In 1968, Jache married again, and his new wife Sigrid bore him two sons. The electrochemist found great relaxation in gardening, particularly growing flowers.

In 1978 came the appearance of the larger gel-filled cells for industrial batteries of from 24 up to 120 volts. These were to remain in production until 1984.

Jache was to remain innovative for the rest of his life. Against in the 1970s, he filed another patent application: "The present invention relates to the leak-proof bonding of components of an electrical storage battery, and particularly to the leak-proof bonding of storage battery components made of thermoplastic material either to other components made of substantially the same material of to current-carrying components made of metal such as lead."

Four years later, he was applying for a patent for "a precursor for an electrical storage lead battery which can be converted into an operative storage battery by the mere addition of a sulphuric acid electrolyte."

In 1989, aged 74, he was filing for a "Method for the production of a lead accumulator with a thixotrophic gel as an electrolyte that consists essentially of sulphuric acid and a gel former, comprising the steps of impregnating the pores of active material in the electrodes and the pores of the separators."

For many years he was a consultant for lead-acid separators Grace GmbH in Hamburg. Otto Jache died on January 10, 1993, aged 78.

Sources: From an article by the author published in *Batteries International*, Autumn 2009, based on information supplied by Helmut Schnierle, Günter Piske, Frank Jache, and also Kristin M. Wohlleben of J. Addams & Partners, Inc.

• •

Jacques, William W.
(1855–1932)
Coal battery

William W. Jacques was born at Haverill, Massachusetts, on August 30, 1855. In 1876, aged twenty-one, Jacques graduated the physics course of at the Massachusetts Institute of Technology, going on to obtain his PhD from Johns Hopkins University, Baltimore, Maryland, in 1879. Known as a brilliant young inventor, Jacques became the first PhD to join Dr. Alexander Graham Bell at his telephone company in Boston, Massachusetts. There he was part of a team that developed several useful telephone components.

In October 1887, Jacques, living in Newton, Massachusetts, and his colleague Lowell Briggs, contracted with Thomas Edison, for the rights to manufacture and market "talking dolls." This was a 22-inch children's toy doll invented by Edison in 1877. The doll featured a removable phonograph that played nursery rhymes. Although it had spent several years in experimentation and development, the Edison Talking Doll was a dismal failure, and was only marketed for a few short weeks in early 1890.

On Labor Day 1891, Jacques and little daughter Louise had taken a ride in an open carriage through the streets of Florence, Italy, when they were stoned by a mob of anti–American socialists. Although injured, they escaped with their lives.[45]

Returning to his home in Newton, Jacques turned to the problem of making a source of electric power that was more efficient than existing steam engines. He developed an electrochemical generator that he hoped would convert coal directly into electricity: a coal battery. The apparatus consisted of 100 cells arranged in series and placed on top of a furnace that kept the electrolyte temperature between 400 and 500 degrees C. The output was measured as 16 amps at 90 volts. He obtained a Canadian patent in this type of fuel cell in 1897.

Initially, Jacques claimed 82 percent efficiency for his carbon battery, but critics soon pointed out that he had failed to account for the heat energy used in the furnace and the energy used to drive an air pump. The most important losses, however, were associated with the resistance of the electrolyte and the voltage losses on the cathode. The result was an efficiency of only 23 percent. This modest efficiency fell short of the improving efficiency of concurrent steam plants. Several subsequent researchers have stated that Jacques's was the last notable attempt to derive electricity directly from coal without first extracting and purifying the carbon.

The primary shortcoming of Jacques's battery is that caustic was consumed along with carbon, according to the net reaction, $C + 2NaOH + O_2 = Na_2CO_3 + H_2O$, 1.4 V. The NaOH (or KOH) are many times more expensive than the coal. Still, the cells demonstrated the high power achievable by the carbon/caustic-melt electrode. Some (e.g., Ostwald) suggested that the cell reaction involved oxidation of hydrogen generated by chemical reduction of caustic by carbon. Because the electrolyte was progressively consumed to form higher-melting carbonates, Jacques's devices are not considered to be fuel cells.[46]

Work was revived by SARA, Inc. (Cypress, California) in the early 2000s using modern cell designs and cathode materials together with synthesized carbon fuel rods, but again failed to achieve commercial success because of the consumption of expensive NaOH and/or KOH and problems with electrode disintegration.[47] (Today, major efforts are underway outside of the U.S. for development of an unrelated fuel cell using carbon derived from fossil or renewable biomass resources and reacted in a mixed carbonate electrolyte cell with a different net reaction: $C + O_2 = CO_2$, 1.23 V.)

In 1900, Jacques acquired a summer home at Chester, on the shores of Nova Scotia, Canada, then part of the British Empire. During the next thirty-three years, he and his family would come here. During World War I, he spent considerable time working on a submarine detecting device for the British government.

In 1905, Jacques, a member of the American Academy of Science, donated a sum of one thousand dollars per annum for the next five years to the Massachusetts Institute of Technology for the purchase of laboratory equipment. Jacques died at his summer home in Chester on July 25, 1932. He was 77 years old.

NOTES

45. "The Newton Graphic," Friday, July 31, 1891.

46. H.A. Liebhafsky and E.J. Cairns, *Fuel Cells and Fuel Batteries: A Guide to their Research and Development* (New York: John Wiley and Sons, 1968).

47. Zacevic, Strahinja; Edward Patton, Parviz Parhami, 2003, "Electrochemistry of Direct Carbon Fuel Cell Based on Metal Hydroxide Electrolyte," DOE Direct Carbon Fuel Cell Workshop, NETL, Pittsburgh, PA; July 30; proceedings on line, http://www.netl.doe.gov/.

Jedlik, Ányos
(1800–1895)
The monk of the self-excited dynamo

In 1827, a young Benedictine monk called Ányos Stefan Jedlik began experimenting with an electromagnetic rotating device he called a "lightning magnetic self-rotor."

"What if," he wrote in Latin, "by any chance, a considerable electric flow before making real use of it were led through the coils placed around the magnetic poles? If this made the strength of the poles stronger, then the electric flow would also be made stronger whereby the poles would also be made stronger which, again, would give stronger flow and so on until a certain limit."

As one side of his coil passed in front of the north pole, crossing the line of force, current was thus induced. As the frame rotated further, the current diminished; then, arriving at the front of the south pole, it rose again but flowed in the opposite direction. Young Jedlik's frame was connected to a commutator so that the current always flowed in the same direction in the external circuit. The wires powering the electromagnet protruded into two small semicircular mercury cups on either side of the shaft. This provided the required commutation as the wires picked up the current from alternate cups as the shaft rotated.

As his rotor seemed to have no practical application, and as commercial concerns were not part of the Benedictine way of life, Brother Stefan put it to one side. Indeed, he would not speak about his revolutionary invention for another thirty years. After all, his main mission was as a Benedictine teacher.

Jedlik was not the first man in Holy Orders to involve himself in things electrical. Ampère was a Franciscan Tertiary, Pastor Bohnenberger built several electrostatic machines, and an Irish priest, Father Nicholas Callan, invented the induction coil (see Callan entry).

Ányos Jedlik was born on January 11, 1800, in Szimö in the Hungarian city of Komarom. After attending Nagyszombat and Pozsony high schools, in 1817 the teenage Jedlik became a Benedictine, and from then on continued his studies in schools belonging to this order.

From 1831 Brother Stefan taught physics at the Royal Academy of Pozsony, then from 1840 he was the professor of the department of physics and mechanics at the University of Pest.

Ányos Jedlik (photograph collection, Pannonhalma Archabbey).

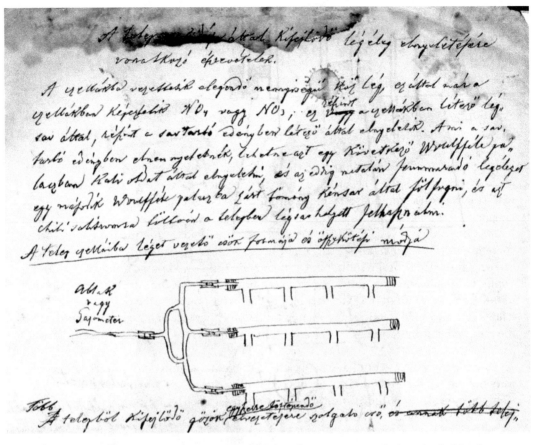

Jedlik's drawing of a battery (photograph collection, Pannonhalma Archabbey).

At the time all lectures were given in Latin, so he never taught in the Slovak language. He personally spoke a little Slovak. Once when he traveled through Moravia he spoke with the people in Slovak.

Despite this, in the early 1840s Jedlik was planning to compile a more comprehensive work on natural science, a book of university standards with Hungarian technical terms as well. Unfortunately, only the first part of the book appeared in printed form, having the following complete title: *The basics of natural science, Ányos Jedlik, member of the Benedictine order at Pannonhalma, professor of natural science at the University of Pest.* In the preface Jedlik announced that if his effort "receives some appreciation from the readers," he would be "enormously inspired" to elaborate and publish the "science of weightless bodies as well."

In 1846 he became dean of the faculty of arts. The following year he began to prepare a manuscript about the theory of heat. It was to take him four years and is in the Hungarian language (not Latin). Foreign words are avoided, although—as an explanation—Latin expressions are given in parentheses. This period of the Hungarian scientific language did not last long. Károly Nedtvich, in his work titled *The Basics of Chemistry*, written in 1854, already returned to the use of Latin and Greek words.

In 1853, Jedlik invented a dividing machine which could produce not only straight-line optical gratings but also so-called circular gratings having 2,093 lines per mm. The latter was a plane spiral of constant pitch which, to a good approximation, could be viewed as a uniform-density sequence of concentric circles. Jedlik designed and built an automatic indexing machine, and made it adaptable for electromotor drive two years later. The color effect of the gratings produced by the Jedlik machine was superior to that of any previous apparatus and was, therefore, sought for even abroad. His machine was later perfected by his student and fellow Benedictine, Gergely Palatin.

But what of his self-excited dynamo—preceding the famed inventions of men like Siemens, Varley and Wheatstone? Jedlik even built another motor based on similar principles—just to supply electric currents strong enough for his lecture demonstrations.

He planned and built "an electric battery consisting of 8 Leyden flasks from which—if the charged flasks are connected together according to the principle of voltaic cells—some 2 feet long discharge lightning sparks can be obtained."

To achieve this, he grouped his Leyden jars in parallel and charged them with the electrostatic machine, following which he disconnected them from the charging unit and aligned them so that the tension of the jars should be added. He built two instruments according to this theory, which he published in 1863, the year he was rector at his university. This instrument produced with four Leyden jars nearly four times the charging voltage. The two instruments differed from each other only by the mechanical realization of switch-over. With the voltage produced by them, he succeeded in sparking over the distance of 2 feet, which was the longest for that time.

The importance of this work lies in the theory of switch-over referred to above, because it is used with very little modification in today's impulse-generators of more than one million volts.

Jedlik perfected his apparatus by replacing the Leyden jars with smaller, high-voltage capacitors, constructed of glass tubes. Jedliks's tube-capacitor thus had four times the capacity of his Leyden jars.

Jedlik was encouraged to make his invention public. He even sent his work to Poggendorf in Berlin, but his paper was never published. Poggendorf patronized him in a letter stating that his invention was not a novelty, and that even he himself had constructed such a device. This incident negatively influenced Jedlik, who was a reticent person, and contributed to his reluctance to publish further accounts of his work. This was probably the reason why many of his inventions remained unknown until others reinvented them and published the results.

Another example of Jedlik's genius is evidenced by an interferometer using a pair of mirrors to determine the wavelength of light. The device—reinvented some 20 years later—became known worldwide as the Michelson interferometer. These machines might easily have been forgotten had not the Hungarian Benedictine made a description of them while making an inventory of the items in his university!

Since 1858, Jedlik had also been a corresponding and also normal member of the Hungarian Academy of Sciences, and in 1873 became an honorary member. That year, at the World Exhibition of Vienna, Jedlik exhibited his high-voltage generators incorporating his tube-capacitors and was awarded the Medal of Progress.

In 1878, he designed and built a mechanical analog computer.

Then the year after, he retired from the university, aged 79, to spend the next sixteen years of his long life in complete seclusion at the Priory of Györ, improving his beloved generators.

He died on December 13, 1895. Today the Anyos Jedlik Laboratory in Budapest is a multidisciplinary science-education-technology center for bio and sensor computing, telepresence and language technologies: a fitting tribute to his pioneering genius.

Source: *Batteries International*, Autumn 2007, based on information received from Friar Wolfgang Mayer, the Benedictine Priory of Györ, Hungary.

....

Jungner, Ernst Waldemar
(1869–1924)
The nickel cadmium battery

Ernst Waldemar Jungner was born on June 19, 1869, in Västergötland Province. His parents, Jonas Jungner and Josefina Blomberg, were ministers in the Vilske-Kleva congregation, Skaraborg. In 1869, the year he was born, failed harvests caused famine throughout Sweden, which affected Jungner's health. He also contracted measles and scarlet fever. He attended Skara upper secondary school, and studied chemistry, mathematics, astronomy, botany, geology and Latin at Uppsala University. Throughout his years at school, he loved to read books about the great inventors and was inspired by the famous Swedish physicist and chemist, Svante Arrhenius. Sadly, Ernst's father Jonas Jungner died when the boy was 13 years old. He went on to carry out further studies at the Royal Institute of Technology (KTH) in Stockholm.

Before hydroelectricity arrived in Sweden, this Scandinavian country was heavily dependent on paraffin in winter. This proved to be a dangerous fire hazard. In 1880, 19-year-old Waldemar Jungner thought he had the solution. He constructed a fire alarm system consisting of thermocouples connected in series, with every second soldered joint thermally insulated. When heated, this apparatus activated a relay device and a signal was produced. In principle this *Pyrofonen* worked very well, but soon complaints were made concerning the source of current for the signal unit, which consisted of dry batteries. This is said to be the origin of Jungner's future laborious experiments to create a source of current with properties superior to those of the dry battery and the lead accumulator.

Jungner, in an interview in 1915, gave another explanation for his interest in electric accumulators. "When as a student I travelled to Uppsala in the spring of 1890, my train passed a river swollen from the spring flood. I began to ponder the possibilities of utilizing all this energy. Would it not be possible to develop a low weight, portable source of power, which could be charged via water power and then used for propulsion of trains, and so on? I considered that the only storage battery known at this time, the lead-acid battery, was unacceptable for various reasons."

Whichever the inspiration, after graduating from Uppsala University and conducting additional studies at the Stockholm College of Technology, Jungner, residing in Skara, in Sweden's Västra Götaland County, started systematically to investigate the possibilities of constructing a storage battery with better properties than the lead-acid system. Enter what he called "the unchangeable electrolyte." He soon became convinced that an electrolyte which did not change its composition during charge and discharge would offer greater advantage than an electrolyte that took part in the electrochemical reactions (with a change of its concentration), as does the sulfuric acid in lead-acid cells. Among other things, the amount of electrolyte could in this way be kept to a minimum—an advantage from point of view of weight.

As early as 1893 he was quite aware that an *alkaline* electrolyte would make it possible to introduce inactive supporting materials with considerably better mechanical properties than the lead used up to that time.

In his preliminary experiments Jungner mixed different metal oxides with graphite, added dilute potassium hydroxide, and pressed the mass in cloth bags. The cloth bags shrank in the alkali and exerted a certain pressure on the active material. As conductors, Jungner used rods of copper or graphite. Subsequently the bags were replaced by narrow folded pockets of thin perforated copper sheet, and in a modification of this design the mass was pressed between two perforated metal sheets of wire mesh, which were sewn together. He patented this, aged just 28, in 1897.

While investigating the metals or metal compounds that might be used in the alkaline accumulator-to-be, Jungner made extensive experiments. By means of the previously mentioned pocket constructions, he tested every conceivable combination and established, as the experiments went on, a more and more electromotive series.

As a sideline to this work, Jungner devised a modification of the Lalande-Chaperon cell in which the positive plate was made of copper oxide in the usual manner and the negative plate of zinc. Jungner used a gelatinized electrolyte, and he intended that the zinc electrode, after discharge, should be replaced by a new one in a simple way. In order to turn this idea to profitable account, he formed the Aktiebolaget Torrackumulator (Dry Accumulator Company). A battery of this construction, propelling a boat, was shown at the Stockholm Exhibition in 1897. Owing to difficulties with the zinc electrode, the activity of the company was soon discontinued.

An important element still needed by Jungner was the inactive metal support for the positive electrode. In connection with the previously mentioned electrode experiments, Jungner had noticed that none of the metals tested was resistant to anodic oxidation in an alkaline electrolyte. This detail nearly put a definite stop to the progress of his work on the alkaline storage battery. Jungner decided, however, to make a comprehensive investigation including every available material, and during the winter of 1897–98 he started tests involving the influence of anodic oxidation of metals in alkaline solution. He found that three months of anodic polarization caused a more or less severe attack on platinum as well as silver, bismuth, cadmium, and iron. Nickel alone retrained its smooth surface and its weight. Jungner extended his experiments also to nickel-plated metals and found that even a very thin layer of nickel was sufficient to protect every metal with a smooth surface from electrolytic attack. In nickel, Jungner thus found his supporting metal and, thanks to this discovery, his ideas took a great step towards a practical realization.

Waldemar Jungner was modest and very unobtrusive. He avoided public appearances, parties and banquets and preferred to be surrounded only by his closest friends. His working habits were strange: he preferred to work at night, especially when his inventions were in critical phases. Despite this, with a fine baritone voice, he was also a member of the famous O.D. (Orphsi Dränger) choir and traveled with them for concerts in various European towns.

During his search for the ideal alkaline storage battery, Jungner also made experiments with couples of silver oxide-iron and silver oxide-copper. A silver oxide-copper prototype was tested in the summer of 1899 by Professor Svante Arrhenius, who obtained energy of not less than 40 Wh/kg from this system; the potential, however, was low, only 0.6–0.8 V. Even before these experiments, Jungner had worked with cadmium as an active material in negative electrodes, but that work had not been encouraging. In these preliminary experiments he had used a mixture of cadmium and graphite, which he pressed into pockets mentioned earlier, but such electrodes had poor efficiency. After unremitting experimental work, he succeeded, however, in producing a porous cadmium metal with acceptable mechanical and electrical properties by a chemical electrolytic method. This material, in combination with silver oxide, gave a cell with an energy content of about 40 Wh/kg and a voltage of about 1.1V. The silver systems were thus capable of storing large amounts of energy per unit of weight.

Jungner built batteries of the silver-cadmium type to supply the motive power for motor cars, and these batteries were tested in Stockholm in 1900 with satisfactory results. After each charge it was possible to drive 140–150 km. However, the silver was considered too expensive in this connection and cadmium too rare.

On March 11, 1899, Jungner, presented his fundamental ideas concerning alkaline accumulators in Swedish Patent 11132. The same year he also patented a method for producing silver electrodes and a way to make the previously mentioned porous cadmium electrodes for use in alkaline cells. On January 22, 1907, Jungner took out a Swedish patent in which the reactions of the systems of nickel-iron and nickel-cadmium were given.

In the spring of 1900 the Ackumulator Aktiebolaget Jungner was formed to exploit Jungner's storage battery ideas. This company manufactured and tested the previously mentioned silver-copper and silver-cadmium batteries and the first nickel-iron batteries. At his side, Jungner had the innovative engineer K.L. Berg, formerly of the Swedish General Electric Co., who worked on the mechanical design of the cells and converted them into hardware. This was a daunting prospect—with very little money, before the invention of oxyacetylene welding, with no reliable separator and no reliable steel plating. Because of the inability to nickel-plate onto steel ribbon, a pure nickel ribbon had to be used to enclose the positive material. Their first attempts to perforate this ribbon were made on Mrs. Berg's sewing machine in the family kitchen!

Jungner himself was strongly concerned with batteries for various traction purposes, which is indicated by his statement: "The objective of my work has essentially been the development of a means of assistance for communication and transportation."

But as if the technical challenges were not enough, the newly founded company soon was involved in a lengthy patent suit against Thomas A. Edison (see Edison entry), who was also actively working in this field. It is difficult to reconstruct the actual timetables of work leading to the alkaline battery inventions of Jungner and Edison, but briefly, Jungner had a Swedish patent valid from January 22, 1901, and Edison had a German patent valid from February 6, 1901. Undoubtedly there was a period of independent overlapping research. Jungner Accumulator and Edison competed on the world market and also engaged in patent suits for the next few years. The patent suits took a great deal of Jungner's time and money, and when his laboratory and factory at Kneippbaden outside Norrköping were destroyed by fire in the fall of 1905, the financial difficulties were too great for him; the company had to transfer its resources and debts to a new company, Nya Ackumulator AB Jungner, with other shareholders.

At this point Jungner left the direct management of the company, but continued his association as a consultant on a retainer. Axel Estelle became managing director and chief chemist, with Berg continuing to look after production. The company was at first entirely directed towards the manufacture of nickel-iron batteries sold primarily for traction use. Flat, vertically mounted pockets of nickel-plated iron sheet were used for both the positive and the negative plates, and as separation between the electrodes, perforated hard rubber sheets were used. Estelle, who had been working with Jungner earlier, patented in 1909 a method for electrolytic co-precipitation of iron and cadmium sponge from a sulfate solution. Jungner's name has been associated with the nickel-cadmium cells, although the Jungner cells from the very beginning bore the trademark NIFE, which, of course, is based on the chemical symbols for nickel and iron.

In spite of the technical progress mentioned, Nya Ackumulator AB Jungner soon got into financial difficulties, and in 1910 the company was put into compulsory liquidation. In the same year the Svenska Ackumulator AB Jungner was formed, and under the management of Robert Ameln, Jungner's ideas were made profitable by the introduction of several modifications of methods and constructions. Cells manufactured after 1910 had flat, horizontally placed perforated pockets for both the positive and negative electrodes. In 1918, Svenska Ackumulator AB Jungner started a subsidiary in the UK under the name Batteries Ltd. using the brand name NIFE, and operating at Hunt End, Redditch, on a site that had been previously occupied by the Royal Enfield Cycle Company.

After he had left the management of the storage battery company, Jungner devoted himself mainly to other inventions. The great problem of converting fuel energy directly into electric energy was of special interest to him. As early as 1907 he took out some patents on fuel cells of different types in which, among other substances, carbon, hydrogen and sulfur dioxide were mentioned as fuels. In 1917 he patented a cell, for which he had great hopes, especially for solving the problem of lighting in the countryside. The positive electrode consisted of a porous body of carbon containing a small amount of copper oxide; the electrolyte was alkaline, and the negative consisted of zinc. The cell attracted considerable attention at that time; however, the production and distribution of electrical energy went on along quite different lines.

Among Jungner's other work, his method for simultaneous production of alkali and cement, presented in 1912, is notable. An amusing coincidence is that during a period of their lives both Jungner and Edison, the great names in the alkaline accumulator field, were occupied with the production of cement.

Jungner's last research work, involving the extraction of radium from Swedish rocks, was interrupted by illness and was never concluded.

Not until near the end of his life did Jungner's merits obtain public recognition. He was elected a member of the Swedish Academy of Science and Engineering in 1922, and in 1924 he was presented with the Oscar Carlson Award by the Swedish Chemical Society. He died of pneumonia on August 30, 1924, in Kneippbaden, at the age of 55.

It was said of Jungner that, like so many geniuses, he often lost interest when the practical development stage was reached.

In the years which followed, the materials for such a chemical-couple battery were expensive compared to other battery types available, and its use was limited to special applications. On the mission to rescue Umberto Nobile and his companions on the North Pole expedition in 1928, several batteries were dropped from an airplane to supply electricity to the radio of the expedition. Only the Jungner NiFe battery worked. In 1932, the active materials were deposited inside a porous nickel-plated electrode, and in 1947 research began on a sealed nickel-cadmium battery.

At present, Ni-Cd battery production at Oskarshamn is in the control of the French company SAFT, who have retained the name NIFE as an important brand name.

Sources: From an article published in *Batteries International*, Spring/Summer 2010, based on information supplied by Leif Olsson (Oskarshamn) and Kjell Åkerström (Norrköping Museum).

••

Kabanov, Boris Nikolaevich
(1904–1988)
Silver-zinc batteries

Boris Nikolaevich Kabanov graduated from the chemistry faculty, Moscow State University, in 1930. As a student, he was laboratory assistant in a chemical bacteriology laboratory at a factory. Having graduated, he worked for ten years as scientific-staff member at the Karpov Institute of Physical Chemistry. From 1940 to 1958, he was head of the Laboratory of Electrode Processes, in the Department of Electrochemistry headed by Alexander Frumkin, at the Institute of Physical Chemistry, the USSR Academy of Sciences.

In 1958, Kabanov moved his laboratory to the Institute of Electrochemistry, Academy of Sciences of the USSR, set up by Frumkin, where he headed the Laboratory of Electrode Processes in Chemical Power Sources, which was later named Laboratory of Electrochemistry of Metals and Semiconductors.

By his character and convictions, Boris Nikolaevich inclined to fundamental science. However, the situation forced him to develop problems aimed at solving practically orientated tasks, e.g., design and modification of power sources, development of methods for electrochemical machining metals, etc.

During the war years Kabanov provided useful guidance to factories manufacturing power sources and invented several simplified methods for metal corrosion protection for defense factories. When solving application problems, Kabanov conceived and implemented them so perfectly that many of his findings became cornerstones of modern electrochemistry.

In his first fundamental work, Kabanov explored a solid/liquid/gas three-phase boundary at an electrode surface. He studied effects of forces emerging at such an interface on the behavior of gas bubbles and, in collaboration with Frumkin, he developed a quantitative theory for the balance of forces at the boundary. The equation, derived for linking acting forces to the contact angle between a bubble and the electrode surface, became known as the Frumkin–Kabanov equation. The results of those studies are widely used for interpreting mechanisms of flotation, electrolytic degreasing of metals, phenomena caused by the bubble formation at boiler walls, etc. The method for the contact angle measuring, developed in those studies, opened the way for determining the potential of zero charge (PZC) of solid electrodes. Progress in the electrode kinetics and theory of metal corrosion demonstrated that PZC is an important electrochemical constant. Kabanov paid much attention to this problem: his laboratory determined values of PZC for many a metal.

In the mid–1950s, Kabanov turned to an exceedingly pressing problem of processes in silver–zinc batteries. At that time, the silver–zinc battery was thought of as a very promising power source in need of rapid development. This challenge coincided with the foundation of the Institute of Electrochemistry. Processes involving silver and zinc electrodes were studied.

B.N. Kabanov's brilliant scientific intuition played a part in the discovery of electrochemical incorporation of metals into solid electrodes at potentials much more positive than equilibrium potentials of these metals.

Electrochemical incorporation was Kabanov's favorite brainchild and the most important result of the last three decades of his scientific work. Undoubtedly, he believed the advances in this field to be the major achievement of his life, and not only because it cost him enormous effort to demolish popular opinion, but also because he was the first to fully appraise the importance of electrochemical incorporation of alkali metals for the progress of electrochemistry and managed to convert many electrochemists to his point of view.

Kabanov continued to research many fundamental areas of electrochemistry, including the analysis of various interfacial processes at solid and liquid electrodes, anodic dissolution and passivation of metals, corrosion, electrochemical machining, and electrode reactions in chemical power sources. He studied the phenomenon of electrochemical incorporation of alkaline metals forming chemical compounds with cathode materials via a single-stage electrochemical reaction. This phenomenon, understood presently in the framework of the insertion electrochemistry concepts, is sometimes considered as having both distinctive and common features with respect to underpotential deposition and intercalation processes. Kabanov contributed also to the determination of zero-charge potential (point of zero charge) of various solid electrodes, and the analysis of hydrogen overvoltage at very high current densities.

Kabanov always supported novel scientific trends in his laboratory: the electrochemistry of semiconductors, photoelectrochemistry, and so on.

Kabanov was an excellent experimenter. He would invent experimental procedures, design electrochemical cells, and adapt electrical instruments, sometimes changing their design.

Kabanov had never taught or lectured; however, his educational activity was quite extensive. In the 1940s and 1950s, the principal textbooks on the electrochemistry were those he edited. He contributed the appendix "Electrode Processes and Electrical Double Layer Structure" to S. Glasstone's monograph *An Introduction to Electrochemistry* (New York, 1947), translated into Russian in 1951. In it, Kabanov presented for the first time current views on the link between the electrical double layer structure and electrochemical kinetics. A year later, the well-known *Kinetika elektrodnykh protsessov* (*Electrode Kinetics*), edited by A.N. Frumkin, was published, for which Kabanov wrote the introduction and three chapters. His book *The Electrochemistry of Metals and the Absorption*, published in 1966, attracted considerable attention among electrochemists. Under Kabanov's guidance, over thirty students obtained their degrees.

For his service to science and engineering, B.N. Kabanov was bestowed with orders and medals of the USSR. He died on August 12, 1988, in Nikolina Gora, Moscow.

The most striking feature of Kabanov's character was probably benevolence, which was felt by anyone at first contact. It is remarkable that he was at the same time a man of principle and strictness in both scientific and everyday activities.

Source: *Russian Journal of Electrochemistry* 40, No. 12 (2004): pp. 1227–1229.

Kelley, Kurtis C.
(1952–)
Lead-acid carbon-foam battery

Kurtis Chad Kelley was born on March 23, 1952, in a small farming community of central Illinois, the fifth son of a German mother and Irish father. He has one younger sister. His father was a civil engineer and his mother was an accountant. As a boy, he worked summers as a farmhand and attended school from fall to spring. After graduating from high school, he worked various jobs, making steel, bottling whiskey, canning pumpkins, and working farms while he attended his first few semesters of college. He generally found college uninspiring and moved on to tour North America. He left college finally settle down for a couple of years as the grounds supervisor for a winery near Seattle, Washington, where his first son was born in the winery's caretaker's cottage. Shortly after, Kurt moved on to the San Francisco area in California, where he worked as a carpenter and drove a moving van.

In 1978, Kurt's grandfather died, leaving him enough cash to pay for a semester's tuition at Arizona State University, where the work of Prof. James E. Canright in paleobotany caught his interest. Kurt and his 2-year-old son moved immediately to Arizona, where he was registered as a botany student. The study of paleobotany and the re-creation of past events from minuscule fossilized remnants fascinated him so much that he expanded his studies into chemistry and geology. Each day he worked in a local machine shop between classes, and after putting his young son to bed, spent the late evenings studying. Raising a child, working, and going to school soon left Kurt short of cash for tuition, but after he informed the school that he would need to leave and work, the college of botany kindly waived his tuition for the following semesters so he could continue his study. He loaded up his coursework to the maximum every semester and graduated with a B.S. in botany with minors in both chemistry and geology in just two and half years. Kurt immediately sought out another famous paleobotanist, Prof. Aureal T. Cross at Michigan State University, and started graduate school there the following semester. A year later, his second son was born and his father died.

In addition to his fascination with the chemistry and evolution of Earth's past, the physics of it all became a great puzzle to solve, and he began studying the mechanical and electrical properties of all the materials involved.

Kurt worked as a research assistant, drafting geologic maps and working on various projects for organizations exploring and mapping fossil fuels and geologic formations around the globe. His intent was to get a full-time job in oil exploration after getting his degree, and Kurt put off job offers with oil companies until his degree was locked in. Unfortunately, with oil prices dropping to $10/barrel in the mid–'80s, exploration for new resources stopped worldwide and Kurt joined thousands of other exploration geologists looking for new careers. He returned to his earlier roots and worked carpentry full time.

But then in 1988, Kurt was presented with an offer to join Caterpillar's World Research Center in Peoria, Illinois. He enjoyed carpentry and didn't know how his background might fit into a huge engineering firm like Caterpillar, but a regular paycheck and benefits seemed attractive, and he accepted a research chemistry position a few months later.

Kurtis Kelley holds the key electrode for his carbon foam battery (Kelley Collection).

Much to his surprise, he had no trouble understanding engineers: metallurgy, ceramics, polymers, plasmas, stresses, strains, and complex environments were all common to the study of Earth's evolution over billions of years. The similarities between engineering and all the other sciences he'd been studying staggered him and he now considers that the only major difference is the language each discipline uses. At the time, it never occurred to Kurt that he would ever become known for work on lead-acid batteries.

Indeed, the director of research at Caterpillar, Charles Grawey, who hired him, wanted him to continue to think like a paleobotanist rather than an engineer and encouraged nontraditional approaches to solving engineering problems. Kurt was not the first Kelley to work for Caterpillar: his father had been the assistant director of research and was up to the directorship just before he died.

During his tenure at Caterpillar, Kurt was involved with hundreds of programs and his access to the resources of Caterpillars R&D facilities expanded his own knowledge base considerably. He developed the first Solid State Motor (SSM) suitable for operating in an engine environment. When the world record for an SSM was just 10 million cycles at room temperature, Kurt's team succeeded in developing a production unit capable of over 6.5 billion cycles operating at temperatures between -40 and 120 centigrade. Among other uses, that design is in use operating the fuel injectors in many of the advanced diesel engines today. Kurt also guided the research efforts that produced coatings for eye surgery tools, high temperature thread lockers, evaporator coil coatings that increase the heat exchange rate, shock-wave apparatus that strips paint from metal surfaces without chemicals, and coatings that allow engines to run in extreme conditions with low quality fuels.

As one example, Caterpillar, who makes heavy earth-moving equipment, found that their vehicles were plagued with battery failures. Batteries had to work in environments of extreme hot and cold temperatures, tremendous vibrations, and long periods of down time when the batteries weren't used, and current lead acid technology wasn't always up to the task. Kurt was asked to build a better battery.

Kelley, who had never worked with batteries before, started by taking batteries apart and found that the lead plates in these batteries were often failing due to corrosion on the positive plate and sulfation on the negative plate. Most of the other battery issues seemed to involve simple mechanics, so he focused on developing a materials solution that would be more comfortable in the electrochemical environment. Carbon was a key. Cheap, plentiful, and tolerant of the lead-acid environment, certain types of carbon looked like a pathway to improving the battery. His first success came from coating the positive electrodes with a specific PVD carbon coating process that resulted in a huge reduction in intergranular corrosion. The process, however, was expensive and very sensitive to process parameters, making it an unlikely candidate for keeping costs down. He was walking down the hallway one day and saw a group of his co-workers examining some graphite foam that they were investigating for use in radiators. To Kurt, it looked more like an ideal structure for a battery electrode.

The first graphite electrodes failed quickly and Kurt was informed by industry battery experts that the problem was oxidation. Being skeptical of such offhand claims, Kurt took a closer look and found no oxidation was evident, but that ion intercalation between the graphene layers had physically weakened the structure so much that it had simply fallen apart. Intercalation now became the issue to tackle before he could go further. The simple solution was to physically restrain the graphite foam structure from expanding and block the entrance of ions. Because the type of foam that Kurt was using at the time was strongly anisotropic, restraint was only needed in one direction.

In 2000, he had a new electrode assembled with a simple plastic frame around it and suddenly the life of the electrode jumped from 30 minutes to 200 hours. The next step was laminating two thin sheets of foam to each other with a thin plastic film between. This battery operated for over a year as a lab curiosity, until he finally put it on display at a Caterpillar innovation fair. The small, strange-looking carbon foam battery in a glass beaker received enough attention for Caterpillar to consider doing something with it. In 2002, the company decided that, while it did not fit in with Caterpillar's core business, it was worthy of investment.

In 2003, Caterpillar, along with the State of Illinois, invested all of the battery intellectual property and $900K seed funding into a new start-up company, Firefly Energy, in exchange for an 80 percent stake in the company. The name Firefly was chosen with heavy use of a thesaurus and cross-referencing to available Web domain names. The unusual attributes of the battery, such as "energy efficient," "lightweight," etc., were searched in a thesaurus and the various tangents followed. A list of words was compiled and the most common were compared with available Web domains and finally trademarks. "Firefly" became the trademark of the energy product and research, and firefly-energy.com became the Web domain.

Kurt left Caterpillar and along with two other seasoned entrepreneurs, and took the helm of Firefly Energy in May 2003.

Of the 8 Firefly patents, the key one was U.S. 6,979,513 March 12, 2004, and December 27, 2005, 10,798,875: Battery including carbon foam current collector. A battery having a current collector constructed of carbon foam. The carbon foam includes a network of pores into which a chemically active material is disposed to create either a positive or negative plate for the battery. The carbon foam resists corrosion and exhibits a large amount of surface area. The invention includes a method for making the disclosed carbon foam current collector used in the battery. To date (2015) this patent has been granted in the U.S., Russia, China, South Korea, and Canada.

The first carbon foam plates were built with graphite and had no metallic lead in them. Foam plates used on the positive and the negative plates were traditional. Foam was laminated with plastic and all busswork was woven bundles of carbon fibers. Graphite cost was a problem and Firefly had limited time and funding to get to product. The decision was made to focus on a product using foam in the negative only to get something into production. Kurt assigned a team to specifically study carbon chemistry and production methods in order to get the cost down. Over the years of development, the cost dropped from $15 per cu. inch to less than $0.15 per cu. inch, more than two orders of magnitude. Now the cost of a carbon electrode was competitive with lead, but with higher efficiency.

The first real production battery began assembly in 2006 and was designed for an electric lawnmower. The key features were its ability to cycle 1300 times at 100 percent DOD and its insensitivity to being left discharged for months without sulfation damage.

The U.S. economic troubles resulted in Firefly Energy's declaring bankruptcy in 2010. While this was a caustic blow to the stellar technology team, the technology was purchased six months later and emerged as Firefly International.

As of January 2015, Firefly International Energy has been manufacturing its innovative Group 31 batteries on a small scale from the Peoria, Illinois, location and supplying them to a select few customers. Kurt is now a private consultant. He troubleshoots for various companies around the world with apparatus design problems or battery storage issues, and continues to do some consulting for Firefly. He is author of 30 U.S. patents and co-author in over one hundred.

Today Kurt resides in Midcoast Maine with his wife and children, working out of his home office and traveling the world to consult in person. To relax, he enjoys fishing, reading, exploring new ideas, and maintaining his 9-acre homestead.

Source: Information supplied to the author in January 2015.

••

Kirchhof, Charles F.
(1811–1882)
Earliest patent for storage battery

Charles F. Kirchhof was born in Weimar in Saxony on March 31, 1811. Weimar was considered the toy center of Germany. Kirchhof entered college to become a surgeon, but was unnerved by the sight of blood, so he switched over to engineering. After graduation he moved to Chemnitz, Germany, where he went into business building weaving looms and special machinery. He married Eugenia Amalia Andestone Dietze.

A member of the revolutionists during the Rebellion of 1848, Kirchhof made speeches against the Saxon government in Dresden. He was subsequently arrested, sent to prison, and sentenced to death for treason. A sympathetic local burgermeister helped him and several other prisoners to escape. A political refugee, he immigrated to New York City in 1850.

Two years later, the German émigré, recalling the toys made in his native town, set up the Kirchhof Patent Company. During the next twelve years, Kirchhof took out a dozen patents: magnetic telegraph, 1856; sleigh bell, 1863; magnetic telegraph, 1865; design for pending wheel (yoyo), 1867; candle-holder (Christmas tree), 1867; toy air gun, 1868; candle-holder (Christmas tree), 1875; candle-holder (Christmas tree), 1877; candle-holder (Christmas tree), 1881, with a counterweight at the bottom to help the candle stand upright.

Alongside these in 1861, he took out arguably the first official patent for a secondary battery improvement: "Generating Electric Current" (battery), 1861; "Improved method of integrating inconstant electric currents," U.S. 31546 A.

This consisted of metal plates coated with mercury and immersed in acidulated water or in solutions of sulphate of copper. Kirchhof describes another consisting of plates of metal coated with peroxide of lead and spongy lead, by electrodeposition in a solution of nitrate and acetate of lead. He describes using lead plates coated with mercury, and says: "Electricity from any source may be stored up, as, for instance, connecting these forms of batteries between a lightning rod and the earth to obtain atmospheric electricity, or with a rubber of a frictional machine, or with a magneto electrical machine."

Never fully developing his innovation, Charles Kirchhof died on October 12, 1882.

König, Wilhelm
(fl. 1930s; dates unknown)
The "Baghdad Battery"

Little is known about Wilhelm König, except that he was a house painter by profession with an interest in natural science. In 1930, he went out to join the German Oriental Society's archeological dig at Uruk Warka in southern Iraq. At the end of that year, when A. Nöldeke, head of the excavations, was offered the post of director of the Baghdader Antikenverwaltung (the Baghdad Antiquities Administration) in Iraq, König became his technical assistant. By 1934, he was appointed head of its laboratory.

Among the artifacts König examined were twelve curious clay jars recently unearthed during excavations of a Parthian settlement at the site of the hill Khujut Rabuah near Baghdad (the ancient Ctesiphon). Before the precision technique of carbon dating, the jar was estimated to come from the mid-third century BCE to the early third century CE.

The jar measured 5½ inches (15 cm) high and 3 inches (7 cm) across. It contained a cylinder of sheet copper soldered with a 60:40 lead/tin alloy, capped with a crimped-in copper disk and sealed with bitumen or asphalt, with a further insulating layer of asphalt on top. This held in place an iron rod suspended in the center of the cylinder, which showed signs of acid corrosion, with an asphalt plug held in place by a copper sheet rolled into a tube.

Early tests revealed that an acidic agent, such as vinegar or wine, had been present. König came to the extraordinary possibility that such jars had been galvanic cells (batteries) perhaps used for electroplating gold onto silver objects. He also examined copper utensils from ancient Sumer, which appeared to have been electroplated with silver. This would have predated such technology by thousands of years. Since then, many experimental copies have shown that such a design is indeed capable of providing a charge of about one volt using lemon juice or vinegar as an electrolyte.

In 1936, König published his unorthodox conclusions in the journal *Forschungen und Fortschritte* (*Research and Progress*) in an article titled "Ein galvanisches Element aus der Partherzeit?" ("A galvanic element from the Parthian period?").[48]

In February 1939, as a result of blood poisoning, he was forced to return to Europe. The following year he wrote up his findings in a book, *The Lost Paradise: Nine Years in Iraq*.[49]

But soon the world was at war, and his discovery was forgotten. So was he.

It has since been argued that the jar is not Parthian. Skilled warriors, the Parthians were not noted for their scientific achievements. It is more likely that it came from the Sassanian period (circa 225–640 CE), which marks the end of the ancient and the beginning of the more scientific medieval era. Furthermore, although König believed that there is evidence for Mesopotamian electroplating of silvered copper vessels, this is no longer thought to be the case. The items in question are now believed to have been fire-gilded, using mercury.

Some of the original twelve "Baghdad Batteries" can be seen at the National Museum of Iraq, which is currently closed due to the 2003 looting which saw nearly half its collection stolen.

Notes

48. Wilhelm König, "Ein galvanisches Element aus der Partherzeit?" ("A galvanic element from the Parthian period?"), *Forschungen und Fortschritte* (*Research and Progress*) 14 (1936): p. 8.
49. Wilhelm König, *Im verlorenen Paradies. Neun Jahre Irak* (Rudolf M Rohrer, Baden bei Wien u.a., 1940), 184 pp.

• •

Kordesch, Karl V.
(1922–2011)
The Alkaline Primary Battery Cell

Karl V. Kordesch was born on March 22, 1922, in Vienna. He studied chemistry and physics at the University of Vienna. In 1941 Kordesch was conscripted into the German armed forces, interrupting his studies at the University of Vienna. In 1944, he was wounded while serving in Russia. In 1945, he was released from military service at the end of World War II, having attained the rank of lieutenant battery leader. The following year he married Erna Böhm and returned to the University of Vienna to complete his studies.

Earning his doctoral degree in 1948, he began to work at the university's Chemical Institute. In 1949, Kordesch accepted a part-time consulting position for Wiener Isolier-rohr, Batterie, und Metallwarenfabrik, a battery manufacturer located in Vienna while continuing to work at the University of Vienna.

In 1953, he was recruited as a member of Operation Paperclip, which took leading scientists from Europe and moved them to the United States. From 1953 to 1955 Kordesch was a scientific staff member of the U.S. Signal Corps, Fort Monmouth, New Jersey, where his management of its battery section resulted in several patents assigned to the U.S. government.

Kordesch then moved to Lakewood and began working in Cleveland for National Carbon. The company eventually became part of Union Carbide Corporation and his laboratory moved to Parma. From 1955 at Union Carbide. he started out as a scientist, then group leader, then department head, and finally corporate research fellow in the fields of manganese oxide batteries and fuel cells. During this time Kordesch filed 22 patents.

As one example, in 1957, Karl Kordesch, Paul A. Marsal and Lewis Urry (see Urry entry) filed U.S. patent 2,960,558 for the alkaline dry cell battery, which eventually became the D-sized Eveready Energizer battery. It was granted in 1960.

Karl Kordesch (Karl and Erna Kordesch Papers, Oregon State University, Special Collections and Archives).

Another fundamental contribution that changed the battery world was Kordesch's creation of the thin carbon fuel cell electrode. He presented a fuel cell demonstration at the Brussels World Fair in 1958, using a suitcase with a hydrogen-oxygen fuel cell. His development of thin electrodes for fuel cells came soon thereafter. He was awarded the Wilhelm Exner Medal from the Austrian Association of Small and Middle-Sized Enterprises.

In 1967 Kordesch built a fuel cell/NiCad battery hybrid electric motorcycle. The motorcycle was featured in television commercials for the program *21st Century*, hosted by Walter Cronkite. Kordesch relished telling people how he had to join the actors' union to ride in the commercials! It was fitted with a hydrazine fuel cell, capable of 200 miles to the U.S. gallon. Kordesch ran up over 300 miles on the motorcycle.

In 1970 Kordesch fitted his own

The hydrogen-fueled automobile designed and built by Karl Kordesch, 1970 (Karl and Erna Kordesch Papers, Oregon State University, Special Collections and Archives).

Austin A40 automobile with a hydrogen fuel cell (ammonia being too hard to come by), and used the adapted vehicle as his personal transportation for over three years. The fuel cell was installed in the trunk of the car and hydrogen tanks on the roof, leaving room for 4 passengers in the 4-door car. It had a driving range of 180 miles (300 km). Thus, he was the first person in the world to have produced and driven a practical fuel cell/battery electric automobile. His fuel cell design provided the basis for the 40 kWh alkaline hydrogen-oxygen fuel cell used in the General Motors Electrovan.

In 1977, Kordesch took early retirement from Union Carbide and was offered the position as full professor to the chair of electrochemistry at the Technical University Vienna, Austria, or head of the Institute of Inorganic Technology and Analytic Chemistry at the Technical University of Graz in Austria. He accepted the latter position and remained as director of the Institute until 1992.

Julio Oliveira, a former Graz student, has recalled, "He inspired me with his relentless optimism and passion. He used to say, 'I work with electrochemistry, and my hobby is electrochemistry.' He would listen carefully to any idea of his students no matter how young or inexperienced."

During this period, Kordesch directed work on electrochemical systems under contracts with Varta Batteries in Germany and other European battery manufacturers. He also headed the Austrian Government Scientific Program, managing a 1984–89 joint five-year program with eight different participating Austrian universities and industrial groups covering fuel cell systems, zinc-bromine batteries, bipolar batteries, catalysts, environmental studies, among others.

From 1981 to 1983 Kordesch was also general secretary of the International Society of Electrochemistry (ISE). In 1986, he received the Technology Award of the U.S.-Electrochemical Society (Vittorio De Nora Gold Medal). In 1990 he received the Austria State Energy Prize and the Ernst Schroedinger Prize. In 1991 he was awarded the Frank M. Booth Prize of the Royal Society of Great Britain. In 1992 he was awarded the Auer V. Welsbach Medal.

In 1986 Kordesch was a co-founder of Batteries Technologies Incorporated (BTI) in Toronto, Canada, and became the senior vice-president of Research & Development. Twenty patents were granted to him and assigned to BTI on rechargeable alkaline manganese dioxide (RAM) batteries (small batteries for flashlights and small appliances, not competitive with AES's lead cobalt batteries). BTI has licensees in the USA (Rayovac), in Korea (Young Poong), Malaysia and Austria (Grand Battery Inc.), and in Germany (Battery Innovation Group).

In 1988, he formed Kordesch & Associates, Inc., as a consulting company in Canada, serving BTI and others. Between 1988 and 1993, he participated in the European Space Agency (ESA) program developing an alkaline matrix fuel cell for the manned space vehicles Hermes under contracts between the Technical University of Graz, Dornier and Siemens.

In 1990 Kordesch received an honorary doctorate from the Technical University of Vienna. He wrote several books on batteries, electric vehicles and fuel cells, the latest being *Fuel Cells and their Application* published by Verlagsgesellschaft mbH (VCH) in Germany, Switzerland, UK, USA, Canada and Japan in 1996, and has written over 200 technical publications. In 1992 he became professor emeritus with that institute with an office, laboratory and staff at his disposal.

In 1997 he joined Apollo Energy Systems, Inc., in Fort Lauderdale, Florida, as vice-president in charge of fuel cell development. He was tasked with the continued development of fuel cells, and with the technology transfer of the Apollo Fuel Cell Program from the Technical University of Graz in Austria (TUG) to Fort Lauderdale, Florida. The program was started in 1997 and completed near the end of 2001. The Apollo Fuel Cell represented a considerable improvement over Kordesch's previous fuel cells. The new electrodes develop over 100 percent more power than the previous ones.

On March 22, 2002, Karl Kordesch celebrated his 80th birthday, still active 12 hours a day. He was gratified to see the electric car and the hybrid-electric make a comeback in his last years. He was 40 years early with the electric hybrid vehicles that he enjoyed building and driving. His son Albert recalled, "He knew things would finally move to electric cars. He was ahead of the curve."

In 2009, Karl Kordesch was recognized by the American Chemical Society for fifty years of service. He died in died in Eugene, Oregon, in 2011, aged 88. In total, he had filed 150 patents, as well as producing numerous books and over 200 publications, all on the topic of batteries and fuel cells.

Lam, Lan Trieu
(1953–)
UltraBattery™

Lan Trieu Lam was born on February 20, 1953, in Chau Doc, Vietnam, and grew up during the hostilities of the Second Indochina War. His father, Thoai Vuong, was a businessman, and his mother, Nga Lam, a housekeeper. He has five brothers and four sisters, but he became the only scientist in the family. His father wanted him to study medicine, but Lam did not follow his wish; he still feels uncomfortable and nervous at the sight of blood, even during a blood test. Furthermore, during high school, Lam always obtained very high marks for physics, chemistry, and mathematics, and low marks for other subjects like literature, history, and geography.

After graduating from Van Hoc High School, Lam went to Japan in 1972 as an overseas student. He obtained his bachelor of engineering (1977) and master of engineering (1979) degrees at Yokohama National University, Japan, conducting research in chemical solutions for silver polishing and electroplating of lead. In 1982, he obtained his doctor of engineering degree at Tokyo Institute of Technology, in the field of pulse plating, focusing on the diffusion control, nucleation of growth and preferred orientation of silver, zinc and nickel during pulsed current plating.

In Japan, Lam met Phuong Lan Vo, another Vietnamese overseas student reading economics. They were married on March 21, 1977, and had one son, Vu Hien Lam, and one daughter, Tu Anh Lam.

In 1983, Lam joined Toshin Industrial Co., Ltd., as chief of the Research and Development Laboratory and during the next six years was responsible for the research and development of a quick metal recovery machine to recover gold and silver from rinse water and used plating solution, a reel-to-reel gold spot plating machine for a connector used in computers, and a semi-automation gold spot plating machine for can-type transistors used in automobiles.

In 1988, Lam joined David Rand (see Rand entry) at the CSIRO's Battery Research Group division as research leader for a succession of projects: technology for improved battery manufacture (GNB Australia); tin-dioxide coated glass-flakes/spheres for enhanced battery performance (Monsanto Chemical Co, USA, and Owens Corning Fiberglas Corporation, USA); minor elements in lead for batteries (Pasminco Ltd.); orifice pasting of battery plates (Wirtz Manufacturing Co, Inc., USA); fast-charging techniques for electric-vehicle batteries (Advanced Lead-Acid Battery Consortium (ALABC), USA); elucidation of early failure of original equipment automotive batteries (Holden Ltd.); determination of maximum acceptable levels for impurities in lead used in the production of valve-regulated lead-acid batteries on stand-by duty (ALABC, USA); and novel technique (Novel Pulse™ device) to ensure battery reliability in 42-V powernets for new-generation automobiles (ALABC, USA).

In 2002, when David Rand was redeployed by CSIRO to assist with the coordination and advancement of Australian efforts in the development of hydrogen, Lam became the senior principal research scientist in the Energy Storage Theme of CSIRO Energy Technology. By 2003, instigated by David Rand, Lam and colleagues began to develop a highly efficient hybrid battery combining a supercapacitor and a traditional lead-acid battery

The UltraBattery™ team. Left to right: Owen Lim, Chris Phyland, Rosalie Louey (lady), Nigel Haigh, Lan Vu (lady), Lan Lam, David Vella (Lam Collection).

for hybrid electric vehicle and renewable applications. This hybrid, known as the Ultra-Battery™, has been considered as a step-change technology by the Science Review Panels and is covered by thirteen patents.

Lam took up the idea of the UltraBattery™ after his involvement in the development of high-power batteries for two low-emission, hybrid electric cars, ECOmmodore and aXcessaustralia for the CSIRO flagship project (1998–2000) and, more importantly, after understanding the key factors causing the premature failure of lead-acid battery under hybrid electric vehicle applications. The key patent is L.T. Lam, N.P. Haigh, C.G. Phyland, D.A.J. Rand: High performance energy storage devices, Publication Number WO/2005/027255, International Application Number PCT/AU2004/001262. 24 March 2005.

The technology has been licensed to Furukawa Battery Co., Ltd., Japan and East Penn Manufacturing Co., Inc., USA, and is also under licensing negotiation with companies in Europe, China, India, South Africa and Australia. In addition, a spin-off company originally from CSIRO, called Ecoult, has been established and subsequently become a subsidiary of East Penn for marketing the UltraBattery™ and battery management system for renewable-energy applications.

In January 2008, a pack of prototype UltraBattery™ units, constructed by the Furukawa Battery Co., Ltd., in Japan, were fitted to a Honda Insight HEV and successfully completed a 160,000- km (100,000 miles) test run at the Millbrook Proving Ground in the UK.

In 2009, Lam and Jun Furukawa took out a further patent for the UltraBattery™,

CA 2680743. For this, that March, Jun and Lam won the Technical Development Award of the Electrochemical Society of Japan for their "Development of the UltraBattery™."

The U.S. government recognized the importance of the UltraBattery™ and awarded East Penn Manufacturing US$32.5 million towards the development and commercialization of the technology. The grant was announced by President Obama on August 5 as part of U.S. $2.4 billion in funding for 48 advanced battery and electric-drive projects under the American Recovery and Reinvestment Act.

In April 2013, sales of the UltraBattery™ were finally launched onto the aftermarket for automobiles, as well as for renewable energy storage applications. In November, the UltraBattery™ was adopted for new cars to Honda Odyssey which went on sale.

UltraBattery™ technology has also been successfully installed in large-scale solar power plants in New Mexico and on King Island off the coast of Tasmania—the largest renewable energy storage system in Australia. UltraBattery™ storage allows intermittent renewable energy to be smoothly supplied to the electricity grid.

For over twenty years, Lan Trieu Lam has been a key scientific adviser to eight Asian countries (China, Indonesia,

Lan Lam and Jun Furukawa, co-workers (Furukawa Collection).

Japan, Korea, Malaysia, the Philippines, Taiwan, and Thailand). Through his knowledge and teaching/linguistic skills (fluent in three Asian languages), he has enabled CSIRO to forge strong links with the Asian Battery Industry. Since joining CSIRO, he has published 37 papers, 14 patents and 83 industrial reports, has been a keynote speaker at several international conferences and workshops, and has served on the expert panels of both the Asian and the European Battery Conferences.

For his outstanding contributions to his field, Lam has received the following awards: 2000: CSIRO Chairman's Medal (Low-emission Vehicle team); 2005: International Lead Medal; 2008: CSIRO Medal for Research Achievement (UltraBattery™ project); 2009: Technical Development Award of the Electrochemical Society of Japan and Gaston Planté Medal in 2011.

Lan Trieu Lam retired from CSIRO in February 2013. Following his retirement, he continues to enjoy reading, video editing, swimming, gardening, playing with grandchildren and traveling. Beside these activities, he is still working with the Furukawa Battery Co., the East Penn Manufacturing Co., and B.B. Battery Co., Ltd., China, as a technical consultant.

Source: information supplied by Lan Trieu Lam to the author in January 2015.

••

Leclanché, Georges
(1839–1882)
A creator of the dry cell battery

Georges Leclanché was born on October 9, 1839, at Parmain to the north of Paris. His father, Léopold Leclanché, a prominent lawyer and a collaborator of the political revolutionary Ledru-Rollin, was forced to flee the country in June 1849.

A peaceful protest against the first president of the republic, the newly elected Louis-Napoléon, turned nasty. His enemies called it armed insurrection. Three years later Louis-Napoléon staged a coup d'état, re-added Bonaparte to his name, and became king of France and better known as the Emperor Napoléon III.

At the age of nine, Georges Leclanché left his native France for the then calmer shores of England. His first interest in electricity and batteries was thus stimulated by the enormous impact Michael Faraday, the inventor of the electric dynamo and much more, had on the wave of interest in science that swept across Britain in the 1830s and 1840s.

It was only in 1856 that it was considered safe enough for the 17-year-old Leclanché to return to France. He studied metallurgy at the École Centrale des Arts et Manufactures in Paris, graduating four years later as a qualified engineer.

His first job was a crucial one for the eventual development of his battery. Working for the railroad company, Compagnie des Chemins de fer de l'Est, his job was to develop the rudimentary electrical systems used for signaling the length of the 500km (300-mile) line to Strasbourg. The problem for signaling in the formative days of the railways was more than just the ability to communicate in the early days of the Morse code—it was creating the infrastructure needed to transmit signals.

So it was here that Leclanché started his research into batteries. His first experiments looked at exploiting the oxidation properties of copper carbonate. Leclanché's research was interrupted by yet more political trouble in France. In 1863 a crisis emerged when Louis-Napoléon Bonaparte's Second Empire

Leclanché's battery (Musée EDF Electropolis, Mulhouse).

came under threat from legislative elections that threatened to limit his powers. Troops went into the streets.

For the second time in his life Leclanché went into exile. This time he went to Brussels, where he lived close to Victor Hugo, the French playwright and his family. The exile was to last a further seven years until the end of the Second Empire.

Working in his shed, he continued to experiment and improve on his designs, moving from a battery using copper carbonate (which he patented in 1866), to one using manganese. He made his first working battery on January 8, 1866, patented it the following year, and exhibited it as the Exposition Universelle in Paris, where it was awarded a bronze medal.

Until Leclanché, most batteries had been based on Alessandro Volta's 1800 design. The most popular in Leclanché's time was Planté's lead-acid battery (see Planté entry). In 1860 this had been demonstrated using long foil strips, which were wound spirally with intermediate layers of cloth, then immersed in a solution of 10 percent sulfuric acid. This was capable of high power, but was also heavy, and the chemicals were dangerous.

Georges Leclanché, of Belgian origins, worked in Paris (Musée EDF Electropolis, Mulhouse).

Leclanché's cell, called a "wet cell," replaced Planté's lead with zinc and a carbon-manganese dioxide mixture. He also replaced the sulfuric acid with much less toxic ammonium chloride. This meant the cell was lighter; its safety and lightness were considered perfect for use in signaling, requiring occasional short-burst use and little maintenance.

In Leclanché's first battery, open-topped glass jars, about 20cm high, were used to contain the various chemicals. The elements were kept separate using a porous pot, allowing the liquid electrolyte to pass through it. In 1871, the manganese dioxide/carbon mixture was molded into two blocks, held in place around the 4mm-5mm carbon plate by rubber bands. In a later development, the porous pot was replaced by a canvas container, and the zinc rod changed to a cylinder to increase the surface area and lower the internal resistance.

In 1867, only a year after patenting his invention, Leclanché was already so confident of its success that he quit his job to promote the battery.

He was helped both by his father's legal advice, and assistance from a Belgian friend, Charles Mourlon. Mourlon, who helped him industrialize the product, put him in contact with the Belgian telegraph service, and after testing, they adopted the Leclanché battery for their network; the Dutch railways did the same, and a workshop was set up in Brussels to produce the batteries for them.

In 1871 the Mourlon-Leclanché factory was employing five workers, run from the ground floor of a small white-shuttered building in Brussels on Rue d'Aerschot. That year, political events at home allowed him to return to Paris with the establishment of what became known as the Third Republic and the end to the Franco-Prussian war that May.

And in one of the ironic twists of history, this time it was Napoléon III's turn for exile. Captured the September before in the ineptly handled Battle of Sedan against the Prussians, he was deposed in absentia. He died in England three years later.

Leclanché opened a studio at 9, Rue de Laval in Paris and settled down. At this point, love entered his life and in 1873 he married Gabrielle Clémentine-Lannes. Two children followed swiftly—Max-Georges in 1874 and Marianne in 1876.

The year of Marianne's birth was an important one in the breakthrough of the development of his battery. He succeeded in gelifying the electrolyte through the addition of starch. This immediately made the battery easier to transport.

Leclanché formed a partnership with Ernest Barbier, and a new Leclanché-Barbier battery was announced. Fate was on his side this time. It was perfectly timed to coincide with the arrival of the telephone, commercialization of which started in France the following year—as well as the steady boom in rail. Leclanché-Barbier were the only makers of batteries in France.

Around this time his health started to fail. The end came after a long illness, and he died Thursday, September 14, 1882, aged 43.

From 1895, Leclanché's son Max, having gained a doctorate in chemistry, continued researching and improving the battery, replacing what had been a porous ceramic pot with a Hessian bag to hold the powdered coal and manganese dioxide mixture. Meanwhile, Leclanché's brother, Maurice, took over directing the business, until his death in 1923. The company has changed hands and names many times since and is now part of Alcatel.

Leclanché lies buried in the Père-Lachaise cemetery in Paris. Perversely, even in death he was unable to escape the turbulent history of his times. Not far from his grave lies the remains of his father's revolutionary friend Ledru-Rollin, which again is just yards away from the famous Mur des Fédérés, where 147 revolutionary communards were shot just days before his return from Belgium.

....

Lewis, Gilbert Newton
(1875–1946)
Frederick George Keyes
(1885–1976)
Discoverers of the non-chargeable lithium isotope

Gilbert Newton Lewis was born at Weymouth, Massachusetts, on October 23, 1875. He was educated at home by his parents in the style of the English tutoring system. His only public schooling occurred between the ages of 9 to 14 years in Lincoln, Nebraska. At age fourteen, Lewis entered the University of Nebraska but transferred to Harvard College after three years.

In 1899 he was awarded his PhD at age 24 under the supervision of T.W. Richards. Richards trained Lewis in experimental techniques and careful measurements and fostered his interest in thermodynamics. Conflicts with Richards over bonding in atomic and molecular structures caused Lewis to leave Harvard. This ended a two-year period in which he published nothing, the only nonproductive time in his career.

Lewis spent one year in the Philippines as the superintendent of the Bureau of Weights and Measures before joining the faculty at MIT, where he found a group of young, talented physical chemists interested in doing research. This group was brought together by A.A. Noyes, who, like Richards, had received his doctorate under Ostwald at the University of Leipzig. This research center provided an energizing atmosphere where Lewis spent seven productive years, during which he undertook the systematic determination of the electrode potentials of the elements.

Among those he investigated were potassium and lithium. In this he was assisted by a brilliant 28-year-old Canadian, Frederick George Keyes. In 1910, Keyes had invented a method to sterilize milk using ultraviolet rays, thereby discovering that ultraviolet rays kill germs. He was then head-hunted by Noyes to join the MIT team as a research postdoctoral associate. Together with Keyes, they published a four-page paper, "The Potential of the Lithium Electrode," in the *Journal of the American Chemical Society*.[50]

It begins: "The method used in measuring the electrode potentials of sodium and potassium has, with some modifications, proved applicable to the determination of the potential of the lithium electrode...."

Lewis left MIT when he was appointed the chairman of the Department of Chemistry and the dean of the College of Chemistry at University of California, Berkeley, in 1912, positions he held until his sudden death by intoxication in his laboratory on March 23, 1946, ended a remarkable 34-year tenure. Keyes remained at MIT, retiring after 66 years as emeritus professor and lecturer in physics and chemistry.

It would not be until the 1970s that Lewis and Keyes's nonrechargeable lithium battery would be made rechargeable, due to work by John Goodenough and colleagues (see Goodenough entry).

NOTE

50. *Journal of the American Chemical Society* 35 (4) (1919): pp. 340–344.

•••

Monahov, Boris Ivanov
(1954–)
Understanding the nature of alloy additives, etc.

Boris Ivanov Monahov was born on March 24, 1954, in the city of Varna, on Bulgaria's Black Sea Coast. Both his parents were highly respected scientists. Although one grandfather had been a farmer, to say that Boris grew up in a scientific family would be an understatement! For half a century, Boris's father Ivan was one of Bulgaria's most active research geologists, and was one of the founders of the oil and gas industry in that country. He was involved in fieldwork, in academic research at the Institute of Minerals of the Council of Ministers, and in teaching as associate professor at the State University of

Sofia "St. Kliment Ohridski." His contributions were published in over 130 articles, three monographs and couple of general reviews.

Boris's mother Liljana was associate professor in geochemistry at the Institute of Minerals of the Council of Ministers and managed a specialized lab for studying the composition of underground waters as indicator about the probability to find oil or gas in the drilling where the samples come from. She had over 50 articles published. Some parenthood!

Boris's interest in science, analysis and deep understanding was encouraged by both his parents and his teachers at the German Language High School in Sofia. In the 1970s, in Bulgaria, physics (физика) and physicists were considered very special by many educated people.

Boris recalls: "Attending the high school, I had three friends who shared my love of mathematics and physics. Now all they are prominent physicists, two of them in Bulgaria and one in Florida. In the upper high school classes I attended a physics school, organized by the University of Sofia for interested high school students. There we had lectures presented by leading professors, and could get familiar with the base of the mathematical methods used in theoretical physics."

Between 1975 and 1980, Monahov read solid state physics at the State University of Sofia "St. Kliment Ohridski." Towards the end he had an internship at the Institute of metal science of the Bulgarian Academy of Sciences. Boris continues: "This how I met Professor Detchko Pavlov. At that time he and his team were doing electrochemical studies of lead electrodes. This sounded interesting to me. *After long hesitation* he decided to offer me a position in his lab. I regard the twenty-five years spent with Professor Pavlov and his team as improving my education through research rather than work."

Boris Ivanov Monahov (Monahov Collection).

He was also courting his neighbor, a mechanical engineer and scientist called Natasha Arsova. They married in 1981. "Since then, Natasha's help to me in any of my efforts and challenges has been of critical importance."

From 1980 until 2004, Monahov was carrying out fundamental and applied electrochemical research of model lead electrodes, model lead-acid cells and advanced lead-acid batteries. He then specialized in lead-acid battery electrochemistry with Prof. M. Maya at the Politechico di Torino, Italy (1982), and with Prof. Z.A. Rotenberg at the Russian Academy of Sciences in Moscow (1986–87).

Besides his daily 1 to 3 miles of jogging, Boris also enjoyed swimming and basketball. "My complete lack of musical talents was a big disappointment for my mother. Instead I do enjoy photography, mountain tourism and cars."

Eventually, in 1994, he would obtain

his PhD in electrochemistry and electrochemical power sources from the Bulgarian Academy of Sciences (BAS) in Sofia, Bulgaria.

Monahov is very modest: "I didn't make any breakthroughs. For people with breakthroughs, you should read the Nobel committee press releases, or *Forbes* magazine! Under the scientific guidance of Professor Detchko Pavlov I was able to contribute to the new and deeper understanding of some important processes involved in the operation of lead-acid batteries."

Nonetheless, he was able to contribute to what we know about the electrochemical models and understanding about the influence alloy additives of antimony, tin, silver and calcium on the properties of the corrosion layer and of the positive active mass, about the importance of the microstructure, phase composition and hydration of the corrosion layer and the layers formed between it and the positive active mass for the performance of the positive plate, about the processes of oxygen evolution in the positive plate and their dependence on potential, temperature and alloy additives, about the effect the concentration of the sulfuric acid solution (the electrolyte) on the properties of the corrosion layer and the positive active material, about the way oxygen recombines at the negative plate, about the way thermal runaway develops in lead-acid batteries, and how can it be suppressed and avoided.

Of the 60 papers Monahov has published, he selects the following three as important for him:

a) D. Pavlov, B. Monahov, M. Maja and N. Penazzi, "Mechanism of Action of Sn on the Passivation Phenomena in the Lead-Acid Battery Positive Plate (Sn-free Effect)," *J. Electrochemical Soc.* 136 (1989): 27-33;

b) D. Pavlov and B. Monahov, "Mechanism of the Elementary Electrochemical Processes Taking Place During Oxygen Evolution on the Lead Dioxide Electrode," *J. Electrochemical Soc.* 143 (1996): 3616-3629;

c) B. Monahov, D. Pavlov, A. Kirchev and S. Vasilev, "Influence of the pH of the H2SO4 solution on the phase composition of the PbO_2 active mass and of the PbO_2 anodic layer formed during cycling of lead electrodes," *Journal of Power Sources* 113/2 (2003): 281-292.

About his long-term colleague, Professor Pavlov has this to say:

Boris is talented and very intelligent person. He is open-minded, hard-working researcher who always maintains a mature and responsible approach to his tasks and carries out in-depth investigations on different managing levels. All the time he speaks in a friendly manner and spreads contagious enthusiasm. He hardly ever loses his good sense of humour. Boris seems to be ever in high spirits. He knows a lot of jokes and he uses them during work conversations in a very unconstrained manner. When something is done not properly he makes friendly jocular remarks. So working with him is pleasant and joyful. His leadership skills are based on the unique combination of flexibility, consistency in the pursuit of goals and natural empathy.

Monahov might have stayed on in Bulgaria. But then Boris and Natasha's son Alex had diabetes, and they wanted him, then a high school junior, to get better medical care. The USA had a government lottery that allows people who want to live and work in America to receive (= win) a U.S. green card. Natasha won the lottery and obtained a green card, and Boris and Alex received their green cards as part of her good luck. They immigrated to the United States in 2004, settling in Peoria, Illinois. Later, in 2010, they obtained U.S. citizenship.

From November 2004, Boris took up a post as senior electrochemist of the start-up, Firefly Energy Inc., in Peoria. Working with Kurtis Kelley (see Kelley entry), he became involved in designing the negative and positive carbon foam based plates of Firefly's 3D and 3D2 battery plates; creating new cell designs and paste recipes; developing new formation, charge and test profiles; and conducting research on the properties of lead, carbon and lead dioxide electrodes in sulfuric acid solution. He holds 3 patents related to this work: "We, the authors of this patent believe, that one day this method will help battery producers to get higher capacity and longer cycle life of their products in a very inexpensive way, and without changing much the elaborated production technology."

But in March of that year, Firefly Energy filed for bankruptcy. Seven months later, Firefly International Energy Co. acquired assets of Firefly Energy from the bankruptcy estate and resurrected its operations at the same location. Laid off, Boris and Natasha Monahov had moved from Peoria to Durham, North Carolina, where he took up the post of program manager of the Advanced Lead-Acid Battery Consortium, a program of the International Lead Zinc Research Organization (ILZRO) based in North Carolina. The ALABC is a nonprofit international organization with 75 members worldwide: lead metal and lead-acid battery producing companies and industry suppliers.

This is currently the only large international R&D institution whose studies are focused on enhancing the performance of lead-acid batteries in emerging markets like hybrid electric vehicles, energy storage and grid support systems, where the requirements for the batteries are specifically high and regular batteries have issues with performance and durability. The scope of the ALABC program is the enhancement and design optimization of lead-carbon batteries aiming at increasing their market position at traditional and new markets.

Boris Monahov has been honored for his achievements. Already a member of the SAE and the Electrochemical Society, in 2012 he received the Lead-Acid Award of *BEST* magazine for outstanding individual contribution to the lead-acid battery industry. In 2014 he received the International Gaston Planté Medal for fundamental contributions to the development of lead-acid battery science and technology.

When asked about his plans for the future, Monahov, just turned sixty, replies, "I would like to enable more ALABC customers and partners to find out about the benefits of modern lead-acid batteries and contribute for expanding their use for making electric energy and people's cars cleaner and more affordable; find a place to consult some basic electrochemical studies on lead and carbon electrodes."

As for relaxation, he would like to visit, spend some time at and take photos of the highest mountains of Europe.

Source: *Batteries International*, 2014, from information supplied to the author by Boris Monahov.

••

Moseley, Patrick Timothy
(1943–)

*Addition of graphite to the positive
plates of a lead-acid battery*

Patrick Timothy Moseley was born in Iver, Buckinghamshire, on August 23, 1943. During school years, sports, particularly running, was more important to him than science, but when the time came to move on, it was a chemistry teacher who suggested that a university education would be a good idea. In 1962 Moseley went north to read chemistry at Durham University. After graduating in 1965 he remained at Durham as a research student under Dr. Harry Shearer, studying the crystal and molecular structures of organometallic compounds of group II metals. The compounds were all air-sensitive and had to be maintained in atmospheres of dry, oxygen-free nitrogen in sealed glass capillaries to allow single crystal X-ray diffraction data to be collected. The research work involved the recording of diffracted X-ray beams on photographic film and the evaluation of the intensities of each of the beams with the aid of a light box and a graduated scale in a darkened room. Moseley was awarded his PhD in 1968.

In 1968, he moved to the Harwell Laboratory of the UK Atomic Energy Authority, where he would work for the next 23 years, bringing his background of crystal structure and materials chemistry to the study of a variety of materials that find use in energy storage devices (batteries and fuel cells) and in sensors aimed at monitoring the concentration of impurity gases in air.

During this time he met and married Heather Jane Bailey. They would have 4 children.

One brief but important X-ray diffraction investigation in the early 1980s served to establish the reactions on which the sodium–metal-halide (ZEBRA) battery depends (J. Coetzer, *J. Power Sources* 18 (1986): 377). The discharged positive electrode was originally based on a specific class of transition metal compounds known as the intermediate hard metals. This group involves the transition metals (Cr, Mn, Fe, Co, Ni) in combination with certain non-metals such as carbon and boron. The range of discharged electrodes was extended to cover the above five metals in elemental form and it was then shown, with the aid of X-ray powder diffraction (once more in sealed glass capillaries because of air-sensitivity), that the metals became chlorinated in the charged state. This observation led to the first patent application to cover the ZEBRA cell in the form we know today (J. Coetzer, R.C. Galloway, R.J. Bones, D.A. Teagle and P.T. Moseley, U.S. Pat. 4,546,005).

In 1982 Pat Moseley moved on to begin work on lead-acid batteries. This change coincided with one of the periods of interest in deep cycling of batteries for electric vehicle applications, and the work began with a fundamental study of the factors that might limit the capacity available from the active material of the positive plate. The influence of crystal structure, hydrogen content and method of preparation (chemical or electrochemical), were all covered, and it was made clear that crystallinity, and the lack of it, was a key factor affecting utilization.

In 1992 he left Harwell and, with two former Harwell colleagues, founded Capteur Sensors Ltd. to produce a range of new semiconducting oxide gas sensors for monitoring the presence of toxic and/or flammable gasses in air ambients. In 1994 he was awarded a D.Sc. for research publications in materials science, again by Durham University.

In 1995, with Capteur successfully launched in the marketplace, Moseley moved to North Carolina to become manager of electrochemistry at the International Lead Zinc Research Organization and program manager of the Advanced Lead–Acid Battery Consortium (ALABC). ALABC is a global grouping of more than 50 lead-producing and battery-manufacturing companies that pool their research resources in order to enable lead-acid batteries to be able to compete with batteries based on other chemistries. During Moseley's watch the Consortium research program developed the capability to deep-cycle valve-regulated lead-acid batteries, an essential requirement for electric vehicles, and showed that, with an appropriate algorithm, they could be recharged very rapidly, with 80 percent charge returned in 15 minutes.

With the arrival of hybrid electric vehicles around the turn of the century, the required duty cycle altered dramatically, and instead of deep cycling, vehicle batteries were called upon to provide thousands of very short charge and discharge events and to be able to accept charge at extraordinarily high rates. Once more the work of the Consortium was key, and it was shown that the addition of certain forms of carbon to the negative plate would invest the battery with the required performance. In 2005 Moseley became president of the Consortium, and in 2008, he was awarded the Gaston Planté Medal by the Bulgarian Academy of Sciences.

Moseley was one of the editors of the *Journal of Power Sources* from 1989 to 2014, and together with David Rand, was a co-editor of the 5-volume *Encyclopaedia of Electrochemical Power Sources* that was published by Elsevier in 2009. He has published over 150 papers, patents and reviews and several books: *Solid State Gas Sensors* (Adam Hilger, 1987); *Techniques and Mechanisms in Gas Sensing* (Adam Hilger, 1991); *Sensor Materials* (Institute of Physics, 1996); *Valve-regulated Lead-acid Batteries* (Elsevier, 2004), *Towards Sustainable Road Transport* (Elsevier, 2014); and *Electrochemical Energy Storage for Renewable Sources and Grid Balancing* (Elsevier, 2014).

He retired from ILZRO and the ALABC in 2012 but continues working—as a director of Atmospheric Sensors Ltd. in the UK. He continues to enjoy jogging and gardening at his home in Chilton, Oxfordshire.

Source: Information and photo provided by Pat Moseley to the author on January 15, 2015.

··

Musschenbroek, Pieter (Petrus) van (1692–1761)

De Leidsche Flesch (the Leyden jar)

Pieter van Musschenbroek was born on March 14, 1692, in Leiden, Holland, in the Dutch Republic. His father, Johannes van Musschenbroek, was an instrument maker, who, watched by his son, made scientific instruments such as air pumps, microscopes, and telescopes. Pieter attended Latin school until 1708, where he studied Greek, Latin, French, English, High German, Italian, and Spanish. He studied medicine at Leiden University and received his doctorate in 1715.

Two years later, aged 25, van Musschenbroek visited London, where he was very impressed by the lectures of Sir Isaac Newton. Completing his study in philosophy, he obtained the post of professor of mathematics and philosophy at the University of Duisburg, where he worked with Fahrenheit. In 1721, he also became professor of medicine. In 1723, he left his posts in Duisburg and became professor at the University of Utrecht. It was from here that in 1726 he published *Elementa Physica* (1726), the translation and distribution of which spread Isaac Newton's empirical ideas in physics across Europe, and for which he was elected a fellow of the Royal Society. Tragically, in 1732 his first wife Adriana died. In 1738 he remarried Helena Alstorphius, and the following year, they returned to Leiden, where he took up the post at the Theatrum Physicum of that town's university.

As a student at Leiden University, twenty-five years before, Musschenbroek had been fascinated by electrostatics. At that time, transient electrical energy could be generated by friction machines, but there was no way to store it. Determined to rectify this, and knowing that water was a conductor of electricity, Musschenbroek and his lawyer friend, Andreas Cunaeus, filled a glass jar with water and placed a brass rod into it. Then Musschenbroek, while holding the jar with his right hand and the rod with his left hand, had Cunaeus connect it to the friction electrical machine, and then turn its glass globe.

But nothing occurred until Cunaeus placed one end of the wire into the water while Musschenbroek, grounded, was still holding the wire. Musschenbroek received a violent shock. The jar device had accumulated the electricity produced by the static machine and then all at once it discharged it to Musschenbroek.

Pieter van Musschenbroek of Leiden (Musée EDF Electropolis, Mulhouse).

On January 20, 1746, Van Musschenbroek communicated this discovery in Latin to the Paris scientist René Réaumur:

> I would like to tell you about a new but terrible experiment, which I advise you never to try yourself, nor would I, who have experienced it, and survived by the grace of God, do it again for all the kingdom of France. I was engaged in displaying the powers of electricity. An iron tube AB was suspended from blue-silk lines; a globe, rapidly spun and rubbed, was located near A, and communicated its electrical power to AB.
>
> From a point near the other end B a brass wire hung; in my right hand I held the globe D, partly filled with water, into which the wire dipped; with my left hand E I tried to draw the snapping sparks that jump from the iron tube to the finger; thereupon my right hand F was struck with such force that my whole body quivered just like someone hit by lightning. Generally the blow does not break the glass, no matter how strong it is, nor does it knock the hand away [from the phial]; but the arm and the entire body are affected so terribly I can't describe it.
>
> I thought I was done for. But here are some peculiarities. When the globe D is made of English glass, there is no effect, or almost none; German glass must be used. Dutch doesn't work either; D does not have to be a globe, a drinking glass will do…. I've found out so much about electricity that I've reached the point where I understand nothing and can explain nothing….[51]

When translating Musschenbroek's letter from Latin, the scientist-clergyman, l'Abbé Jean-Antoine Nollet, named the invention the "Leyden jar." The name stuck. That year the experiment was repeated at the Royal Academy of Sciences. There another experimentalist, Le Monnier, electrified a row of 200 Carthusian monks in Paris. Each participant was joined to the next by a 25-ft. (7-meter) length of iron wire. With some satisfaction (and probably amusement), the Abbé Nollet noted that all the monks started swearing, contorting or jumping in sharp response to a discharge from a Leyden jar which had been charged from a glass globe design of a generator.

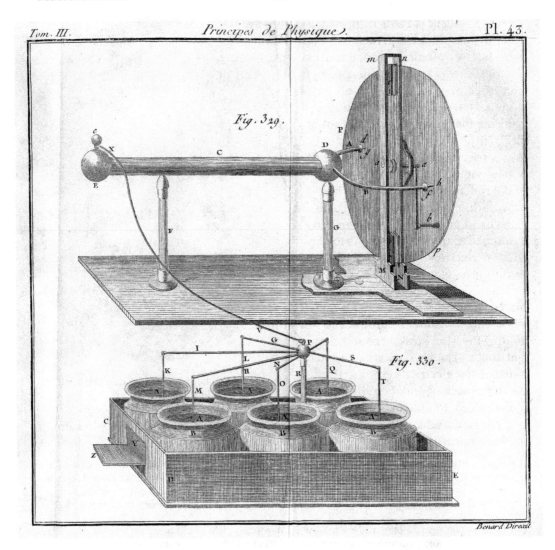

The prototype Leyden jar (Musée EDF Electropolis, Mulhouse).

News of the Leiden experiments also reached London, where they caught the attention of the versatile William Watson, physicist, physician, and botanist. He, too, set about repeating the basic experiments of Van Musschenbroek, improving the Leiden jar by coating its inside and outside with metal foil. In so doing, he observed a pattern of electrical discharge—namely, that a participant, like Cunaeus, tended to feel the shock "in both his arms and across his breast." It suggested that a single "electrical aether" or fluid is transferred, but never created or destroyed, from one body to another only when one has a surplus and the other a deficit of electrical aether.

Scientific curiosity can occur simultaneously and separately in different countries. Soon afterwards, it transpired that a German scientist, Ewald von Kleist, dean of the cathedral at Kammin in the Kingdom of Prussia, had independently constructed a similar device, the Kleisten Jar, in late 1745, shortly before Musschenbroek.

In 1754, van Musschenbroek became an honorary professor at the Imperial Academy of Science in Saint Petersburg. He was also elected a foreign member of the Royal Swedish Academy of Sciences in 1747. He died on September 19, 1761, in Leiden.

The Leyden jar was used to conduct many early experiments in electricity, and its discovery was of fundamental importance in the study of electricity. A famous use of the Leyden jar was Benjamin Franklin's kite experiment, which gave rise to the phrase "capture lightning in a bottle" (see Franklin entry).

NOTE

51. Pieter van Musschenbroek to Réamur (January 20, 1746), in *AS. Proc. verb.*, LXV (1746), 6.

....

Nora, Vittorio de
(1912–2008)
Dimensionally stabilized anode

Vittorio de Nora was born in Altamura, southern Italy, on November 11, 1912. He obtained his basic technical education at Royal Politecnico Institute of Milan in 1929, from which he gained a doctorate in electrochemical engineering with full honors in 1935. Rather than accepting an invitation in 1936 to become a professor of physical chemistry and electrochemistry at the Royal Politecnico Institute, Vittorio decided to carry out research abroad. He spent time doing research at King's College, University of London, and then at the Hochschule of Dresden. Leaving Dresden in 1937, Vittorio de Nora went to the United States, in order to work as a Volta Fellow with Professor Allison Butts at Lehigh University in Bethlehem, Pennsylvania, where the results of his research permitted him to receive a PhD in physical chemistry in just nine months, a feat never since repeated. His subject was the structure and grain size of electro-deposited copper. In 1938 de Nora was awarded a Weston Fellowship by the U.S. ECS and returned to Milan and the Royal Politecnico, where, aged 26, he was named professor of physics and chemistry.

But the Second World War had already begun in Europe and his colleagues and family finally advised de Nora to escape Italy and the Fascists so that his talents would not be commandeered by the Axis powers during the occupation of Italy. It was the Swiss ambassador to Italy who helped him to get to Zurich, in order to prevent his having to work for the Axis. The ambassador had a daughter, Chantal, and one evening while dining with the ambassador and his family before leaving Italy, Vittorio met her and said to himself, "This is the woman I am going to marry," although at the time she was only sixteen years old. Chantal would become Vittorio's wife in 1944.

He left for Switzerland to begin his nonacademic research career in the field of electrometallurgy, in particular electrochemistry, and in this he was able to develop more efficient submarine batteries for the Allied Powers.

In the late 1940s Vittorio joined Nora-Impianti Elettrochimici, the company his brother Oronzio had set up in 1923, as adviser and consultant. The firm started to work on a mercury cell and won a set of basic patents. Mercury cell know-how at the time was the closely guarded property of a few European firms; de Nora snapped up a major part of the U.S. business. By 1952, de Nora's 300-ton chlorine plant for the U.S. Army Chemical Corps was the largest in the world, boasting 232 36,000-amp cells.

Vittorio would probably have been content to continue his private research and work with the brother he revered, had they not been contacted in 1962 by Henri Beer, founder of Magneto-Chemie BV. in the Netherlands. Beer had written letters to the major chlorine producers asking them to consider the use of his patents for a novel chlorine cell anode made of a titanium metal alloy instead of carbon. Oronzio showed the letter to Vittorio, who immediately saw the value of Beer's idea.

When de Nora and Beer met, they instantly liked each other. Beer gave him the details of his invention, which would replace the unpleasant carbon anodes in chloralkali cells with metallic anodes. These would save energy and eliminate the emissions related to burning carbon anodes to make chlorine.

Recognizing the value of Beer's non-carbon anode material, Vittorio improved the invention and added a coating that made it feasible industrially.

Given that the size and shape of this dimensionally stabilized anode do not change during operation, de Nora called their product the Diamond Shamrock. By 1970, the de Nora companies, such as Eltech Systems Corporation, not only developed the bi-polar chlorine cell, but also built plants accounting for one-third of the world's chlorine production. This included the largest chlorine cell yet built (450,000 amp). They also constructed the world's largest water electrolysis plant having heavy water as a by-product.

Despite the financial reward that came with his technical success, Vittorio de Nora continued to actively devote his career to advancing electrochemistry, and with his innovative mind became the author or co-author of several hundred patents linked to the electrochemical industry. These include aluminum production, where he gained more than 70 patents related to an inert anode for aluminum production, as well as a similar number of patents for cell design innovations to facilitate inert anode use and for improvements existing electrode technology.

While Eltech provided the initial R&D facilities for de Nora to pursue his goal, he later formed a private company, Moltech, specifically for R&D in aluminum cell technology, and more specifically for new materials development. As it progressed, Vittorio established a scientific team in purpose-built laboratories in the Swiss Valais, where they not only worked on perfecting the material science, but also developed prototype anodes. Since 1999, they have operated pilot test cells utilizing the de Nora inert anodes.

Throughout his life, Vittorio was a lover of fast vehicles, including a Ferrari Boxer sports car, two BMW motorcycles, an 80 mph speedboat and a private executive jet.

Always an academic at heart, Vittorio displayed research leadership skills that continued to inspire others to pursue their goals. He generously facilitated and encouraged other noteworthy technical achievements by sponsoring research through various endowments and awards. Included among these were his sponsoring of the Ernest B. Yeager Center for Electrochemical Science at Case Western University (see Yeager entry), and the endowment of the ECS Vittorio de Nora Diamond Shamrock Award for distinguished contributions to electrochemical engineering and technology.

Vittorio de Nora's personal devotion to the betterment of global society was also demonstrated in his support and helping to found the International Physicians for the Prevention of Nuclear War, to whose activities he contributed. The group was awarded the Nobel Peace Prize in 1985.

Vittorio had the distinction of being the Society member with the second-longest membership record. Vittorio de Nora was elected an honorary member of ECS in 1982 and became a fellow of the Society in 1992, in recognition of his contributions to science and electrochemical engineering. Case Western University, Lehigh University, and the University of Cincinnati all conferred on him the honorary degree of Doctor of Science.

Vittorio de Nora died on June 29, 2008, aged 95.

Source: Matteo de Nora.

Ogumi, Zempachi
(1945–)
Battery reaction mechanisms

Zempachi Ogumi was born several weeks before the end of World War II, on June 18, 1945, in Tokushima Prefecture, located on Shikoku Island, Japan. He grew up in Osaka. Before he took the entrance examination for Kyoto University, Zempachi's friends and family advised him to choose medical school, but he did simply not like the sight of blood. He therefore chose chemistry at Kyoto University. Out of the 5 chemistry departments in the Faculty of Engineering in Kyoto University, Zempachi selected the Department of Industrial Chemistry because it covered the widest area of chemistry.

At the end of his third year at the department, he decided to do research at the Electrochemistry Laboratory, which was led by Professor Shiro Yoshizawa. But Zempachi was unable to answer the question of "labile" and "inert" in the examination for inorganic chemistry at Professor Yoshizawa's class. Then he wanted to challenge the professor. He was more interested in reactions than materials. This examination was to have the biggest influence on his life's work.

Zempachi Ogumi studied and worked on electrolysis through the earlier half of his academic career. His thesis was titled "A Study of Initiation Mechanism of Electro-polymerization of Acrylamide." While working on this, he examined the electro-oxidation of aniline and phenol, discovering, to his annoyance, the formation of sticky and insulating polymerized films of these monomers on electrodes. He did not then have a perspective on the later boom for conductive polymers on anodes!

After pursuing his undergraduate and graduate studies at Kyoto University, in 1975, Zempachi Ogumi worked for one year as a postdoc with Professor Heinz Gerischer at the Fritz Haber Institute of the Max Planck Foundation in West Berlin, West Germany. From

Zempachi Ogumi of Tokyo, Japan (courtesy Mr. Ogumi).

November 1976, he was hired as a research associate for Prof. Yoshizawa's group at his alma mater, Tokyo University. He was promoted to associate in 1984 and then to professor in 1992.

As a research associate, Zempachi worked on the engineering aspect of organic electrochemistry; he studied the porous electrode, the fluidized bed electrode, and the suspension-circulated electrode. He then became interested in the SPE electrolyzer (solid polymer electrolyte electrolyzer, itself the reverse of PEM FC). He applied this electrode system (the MEA of the present PEM FC) to electro-organic synthesis, aiming at reducing the energy of separation and purification of products after electrolysis. During this work, he studied solubility and diffusion of oxygen and hydrogen in Nafion. However, he found problems with the swelling of Nafion by organic solvent through the work of SPE electrolyzers. By the middle of the 1980s, Ogumi, working with Yoshiharu Uchimoto, arrived at the preparation of a cross-linked Nafion-type membrane by plasma polymerization in order to suppress membrane swelling. In 1990, they published their findings in the *Journal of the Electrochemical Society* (137), 3319.

Utilizing their plasma polymerization technology, Ogumi and Uchimoto also entered the lithium battery community, the field of laboratory leader Professor Takehara. They reported a Li/plasma-polymer electrolyte/TiS2 battery of 20 µm thick ("Chemical Solutions," *The Journal of the Chemical Society* (1989): p. 1673).

After Zempachi Ogumi moved to the laboratory of industrial analysis, he shifted to in-situ analysis of battery reactions. Together with Minoru Inaba, Ogumi challenged in-situ Raman spectroscopy of HOPG edge plane under $Li+$ insertion and extraction (*JES*, 1995 (142), 20). They then initiated in-situ STM work to investigate $Li+$ insertion and reactions of SEI formation at the initial stage of first charge, using HOPG as a model of graphite negative electrode. STM observation clarified that $Li+$ solvated with ethylene carbonate insert at the initial stage of insertion into HOPG and the co-intercalated solvent is reductively decomposed, leading to formation of the stable SEI layer (*Langmuir*, 1996 (12) 1535). He of course extended the STM work to AFM. He also introduced a thermal pyrolytic GC-MS to examine organic entities composing SEI and detected polymerized products formed through ring-opening of ethylene carbonate. He made clear that desolvation of $Li+$ is the rate determining step of $Li+$ insertion into oxide positive electrodes and graphite negative electrodes. He was also interested in phase transformation during charge and discharge of lithium ion batteries. He published stage transformation during $Li+$ intercalation into HOPG (*JES*, 1999 (146), 2443).

Ogumi was also active in fuel cell research. He investigated reaction sites on solid oxide fuel cells (SOFC) using a thin film electrolyte layer prepared by electrochemical vapor deposition method. He also challenged electrolysis in non-equilibrium plasma, i.e., gas-phase electrolysis. He reported preparation of $Ag+$-conductive thin films and Yttria stabilized zirconia thin films using gas-phase electrolysis (*Journal of Applied Physics*, 1992 (72), 1577). He worked on PEM FC with Minoru Inaba. They mainly focused on degradation of MEA. He also challenged anion-exchange-membrane fuel cells (*Journal of Power Sources*, 2005 (150), 27).

Since retiring from the Tokyo University Faculty of Engineering in 2009, Zempachi Ogumi has been working as an adjunct professor of the office of Society-Academia Collaboration for Innovation in the same university. He is also a visiting professor at Waseda University.

Ogumi is also the project leader of the Research and Development Initiative for

Scientific Innovation of New Generation Batteries (RISING), a joint project promoted by the New Energy and Industrial Technology Development Organization (NEDO), aiming at developing novel rechargeable batteries with 5 times as much energy density as those available today. RISING is a Japan-wide project involving 13 universities, 4 research organizations, and 13 enterprises of Japan's leading auto and battery manufacturers, with the main research facilities located in Kyoto University and AIST (National Institute of Advanced Industrial Science and Technology) Kansai Center. In the project he is also leading the group of developing advanced technology for in-situ observation of battery reactions using storage-ring X-ray beam, neutron beam, NMR and other facilities. This project will finish in February 2016, when Ogumi can take a well-deserved retirement.

In 2006, Ogumi initiated ACEPS, the Asian Conference on Electrochemical Power Sources, combining some Asian conferences on electrochemical energy conversion and storage, which is a series of scientific electrochemical power source conferences. He served as the chairman of the Committee of Battery Technology, and the president of the Electrochemical Society of Japan in 2007–2008, and served as the vice-chairman of the Battery Division in 2007–2009. Also, he was also president of the Solid State Ionics Society of Japan in 2004–2006, and the president of IBA in 2010–2012. He has been a regional editor of *Journal of Power Sources* since 1999.

Zempachi Ogumi likes playing sports. He has enjoyed basketball, baseball, badminton, and tennis and now he is enjoying playing golf. He has two daughters, who majored in music and law. His wife, Toyoko, is a professional flutist and teaches some music colleges and high schools.

Source: Information supplied to the author by Zempachi Ogumi, February 2015.

· ·

Ohl, Russell Shoemaker
(1898–1987)
Light-sensitive device using silicon

Russell Shoemaker Ohl was born on January 31, 1898, in Macungie, a suburb of Allentown, Pennsylvania. His father was in the lumber business but was a keen amateur astronomer. Aged only six, Ohl began to learn electricity from his brother, who was a telegraph operator. From Keystone High School, Ohl entered Pennsylvania State University at the age of 16. In his senior year, he took a course in vacuum tubes, used at the time for radio. He didn't quite believe the theories of how radios worked so he built a makeshift radio with his friends in his chemical fraternity, Alpha Chi Sigma. On the first try, they heard signals being broadcast through the air. Ohl was amazed and the radio bug bit him. He was to continue research in radio for the rest of his life.

During World War I, 20-year-old Ohl serviced batteries for the U.S. Army Signal Corps. Postwar, from working in the vacuum tube department of Westinghouse, in June 1927, Ohl found work at Bell Telephone Laboratories, Holmdel, New Jersey. Determined to develop a radio receiver that could handle higher frequencies, Ohl thought crystals might be the answer. Several times the management at Bell Labs tried to shift him into other directions of research, but he always managed to convince them to let him keep working with crystals.

On February 23, 1941, Ohl was examining a crystal with a crack down the middle when he noticed that the amount of electrical current changed when the crystal was held close to an incandescent lamp. By afternoon, Russ Ohl realized that it was light shining on the crystal that caused this small current to begin trickling through it. On March 6, Ohl showed his prize silicon rod to colleagues at Bell Laboratories. With his coal-black crystal attached to a voltmeter, Ohl turned on a flashlight and aimed the silicon at it. The voltmeter instantly jumped up half a volt…. He had discovered what is now known as the P-N Junction.

The patent which Ohl and Bell filed in 1941 for a "Light sensitive device using silicon" was finally granted in 1948 (U.S. Patent 2402662). Ohl later found that super-purifying germanium was the key to making repeatable and usable semiconductor material for diodes. All diodes, including LEDs and laser diodes, are descendants of Ohl's work. By 1954, three scientists at Bell Labs took Ohl's discovery to the point where they had assembled 400 silicon cells into the world's first solar battery (see Chapin entry).

Ohl continued his research into semiconductor crystals, determining how best to grow them and how best to dope them. From 1948 to 1952 he pioneered the bombardment of ions into silicon, developing a semiconducting translating device. In 1955, he was elected a fellow of the Institute of Radio Engineers. Even after his retirement in 1958, Ohl kept on researching and publishing papers about the resistivity response of plants, crystal growth, etc. Russell Ohl died on March 20, 1987, at Cambria, California.

Ovshinsky, Stanford Robert
(1922–2012)
Ovonic Man

Stanford Robert Ovshinsky was born on November 24, 1922, in the industrial town in Akron, Ohio, then at the center of the American rubber industry. His father, Benjamin Ovshinsky, and his mother, Bertha Munitz, were Jewish immigrants from Eastern Europe. With his horse and wagon, and later his truck, Ben Ovshinsky made his living collecting scrap metal from factories and foundries.

Based on his father's example, and on teachings offered by the Akron Workmen's Circle, an organization mainly of Jewish immigrants who believed in social justice, young Stan developed a deep commitment to social values: "I was always in the trenches for peace and for civil rights and civil liberties and for labor organization. I offered my life up to it."

The teenager began work as a tool maker and machinist in various shops affiliated with the rubber industry. While graduating from Buchtel and Hower Vocational high schools in June 1941, he relied on the well-stocked shelves of local public libraries to educate himself.

Excused from military service during the Second World War because of asthma, Ovshinsky and his bride Norma Rifkin moved to Phoenix, Arizona, where he worked in the tool room of a Goodyear aircraft factory in Litchfield.

Returning to Akron just before the war ended, with a love of machinery, he set up his own machine and lathe manufacturing company, Stanford Roberts, in a barn, and registered his first patent (the first of almost 500!) for a new lathe. He named it the Benjamin Center Drive lathe after his father. The design caught the attention of the New Britain Machine Company in Connecticut, who bought the Stanford Roberts Company in 1950 and used the new lathe to solve a crisis in the production of artillery shells during the Korean War.

In 1951, Stan Ovshinsky accepted an offer to move to Detroit and work in the automotive industry as the director of research at the Hupp Motor Company. While spending his free time reading up all he could on computers and the human brain, intelligent machines and cybernetics, he next invented electric power steering. Despite this, Hupp's president was opposed to completing the arrangements with General Motors to utilize the product.

So not long after that, Stan and his younger brother Herb Ovshinsky, a talented mechanical engineer, established a small company called General Automation in a Detroit storefront. There, Stan continued his study of intelligent machines and embarked on early research and development of various energy and information technologies.

Stanford Robert Ovshinsky holds a photovoltaic roll (courtesy Ben Ovshinsky).

At the same time, he began studying neurophysiology and neurological diseases. On the basis of his early writings about nerve impulses and the nature of intelligence, he was invited by Wayne Medical School in June 1955 to participate in pioneering experimental research on the mammalian cerebellum.

These cross-disciplinary researches soon began to pay off. By 1959, Stan had patented, and brother Herb had helped to build, a mechanical model of a nerve cell. They announced it as the Ovitron.

In an attempt to model the learning ability of nerve cells, which Stan recognized as deriving from the plasticity of the cell's membrane, he drew on his knowledge of surfaces and materials to fashion very thin layers of amorphous material, thus pioneering the use of nanostructures. He created these layers by combining elements, especially from the Group 16 elements under oxygen, known as chalcogenides, including sulphur, selenium, and tellurium. Stan would continue to work with chalcogenides for his inventions for decades to come.

On January 1, 1960, Ovshinsky divorced Norma Rifkin and married Iris Miroy Dibner, a highly qualified scientist: she had a B.A. in zoology, an M.S. in biology and a PhD in biochemistry. Together they founded the Energy Conversion Laboratory in Rochester

Hills, Michigan. Their aim was to develop Stan's inventions in the interest of solving societal problems, especially those they identified in the areas of information and energy (eventually pollution and wars over oil).

Continuing to work on his atomically designed chalcogenide materials, which Ovshinsky realized offer unique electronic physical mechanisms, he utilized chain structures, cross links, polymeric concepts, and divalent structural bonding with a huge number of unbounded lone pairs to achieve what is now referred to as the Ovshinsky Effect = "an effect that turns special types of glassy, thin films into semiconductors upon application of low voltage."

Applying this effect, he built new types of electronic and optical switches, including his Ovonic Phase Change Memory and his Threshold Switch. The former would become the basis of his subsequent inventions of rewritable CDs and DVDs and other new computer technologies including his cognitive computer.

Recognizing the significance of their results, Ovshinsky applied for a patent on June 21, 1961, making his first licensing pact on phase-change memory the year after.

In 1964, Stan and Iris changed the laboratory's name to Energy Conversion Devices and moved the company to larger quarters in Troy, Michigan. ECD went on to become a forefront invention and development laboratory whose products have built new industries, many of them aimed at making fossil fuel obsolete.

In 1968, the Ovshinskys held a press conference at which Stan announced that his Ovonics transistor would eventually lead to desktop computers and television sets "hanging like portraits on the wall." The announcement made the front pages and ECD's stock soared.

Within days, however, semiconductor engineers dismissed the idea and ECD's stock price collapsed. Most scientists had never heard of amorphous materials, and some rubbished Ovshinsky as a high school dropout and former machinist with no university qualifications. He was branded a crank.

This may not have helped finances, but it would not stem the pilgrimages continually made to the ECD labs by a galaxy of eminent scientists. One of these, Helmut Fritzsche, a University of Chicago physicist, commented: "There is a mysterious quality in Ovshinsky's persona that attracts people into his sphere, builds lifelong friendships and awakens deep respect and devotion. Meeting him leaves each person with a deep impression of his superior intellect, his self-confidence, his compassion to improve society combined with his certainty that his vision can be realized. His enthusiasm is contagious. In his presence, you feel how exciting it would be to join him in his endeavors."

In time, license fees to ECD began to grow, especially when amorphous silicon was used to make solar cells "by the mile," with an approach that originated from Ovshinsky's non-silver photographic film work. It led to the bold approach of creating the first continuous web photovoltaic machine, designed and built under Stan's direction by Herb Ovshinsky and a small group in the machine division. Generations of machines later resulted in sufficient money to reach Ovshinsky's objective of building a 30-megawatt machine, rather than a 5-megawatt machine. Despite considerable skepticism toward the machine, it is now being cloned very successfully by ECD in new factories at Auburn.

In 1992, the Ovonic Battery Company at Auburn Hills, Michigan, won the race to secure the first contract to develop NiMH batteries for electric vehicles from the U.S. Advanced Battery Consortium, a group which included the automobile manufacturers Chrysler, Ford and General Motors. Their patented battery was lighter, smaller and longer-lasting than conventional batteries. It consisted of special alloys, and specific multicomponent alloy compositions, whose disordered structure enabled the storage of much larger quantities of electricity. Ovonic licensed these batteries to over 50 companies worldwide, who used them in millions of devices such as laptop computers, digital cameras and mobile phones.

But as Stan Ovshinsky stated, "The various special interests like the oil companies weren't very happy about it. They helped GM suppress the first electric cars." However, Ovonics had greater success in Japan, where Toyota launched the first mass-produced hybrid range in 1997.

Ovshinsky's commitment to clean energy also extended to hydrogen-fueled vehicles, a field in which he developed a solid hydrogen storage system based on granular metal hydrides.

In 2006, Iris Ovshinsky, Stan's wife and partner of almost fifty years, died suddenly while swimming. A year later, Ovshinsky retired from ECD but launched a new company with Rosa Young, whom he later married. Rosa, a physicist, had worked at ECD on numerous energy technologies, including a hydrogen-powered hybrid car, and on Ovshinsky's vision of a hydrogen-based economy.

At Ovshinsky Innovation LLC, Stan continued his work on information and energy science, in strong relationships with colleagues and with industrial partners. One example is Ovonyx for developing phase-change semiconductor memory. Ovshinsky Innovation is currently focusing on a new kind of photovoltaic plant based on a new concept promising to lower the cost of photovoltaic energy sources below that of coal. This latter innovation would help realize his long-term goal over the last half-century to make fossil fuels obsolete while, at the same time, providing countless jobs in new industries.

Stanford Ovshinsky, a man who wanted to change the world and its attitude towards sustainable energy, once said, "When I die, I'll die with my boots on." He died October 17, 2012, in Bloomfield Hills, after a long struggle against prostate cancer. He was 89. He was buried privately at the Workmen's Circle Cemetery in Akron, Ohio.

As author of more than 275 scientific papers ranging from neurophysiology to amorphous semiconductors, Stan Ovshinsky has been compared to Einstein. Because of his 500 patents, he is also likened to Tom Edison. In the area of alternatives to fossil fuel, his pioneering work has caused many writers to refer to him as "the modern world's most important energy visionary." In 1999 *Time* magazine declared him "Hero for the Planet," while Ovshinsky and Iris were named "Heroes of Chemistry" by the American Chemical Society in 2000.

Ovshinsky remained modest about his achievements, claiming, "I owe a lot to great scientists who believed in me." Ovshinsky liked to boast that he was "probably the only chief executive that is a union member." His personal motto was: "With the oppressed against the oppressor."

Sources: From an article by the author published in *Batteries International*, Spring 2013, based on information supplied by Benjamin Ovshinsky; BASF.

Pavlov, Detchko
(1930–)
Lead-acid battery development team leader

Detchko Pavlov was born on the September 9, 1930, in Shipka, a small town in central Bulgaria nestling at the foot of rugged Balkan Mountains, 650 meters above sea level. Whilst his paternal grandfather was a farmer of humble origins, his maternal grandfather was a state officer, a very intelligent man with a great sense of humor.

Detchko and his sister attended the local Saints Cyril and Methodius Grammar School in Shipka, where their mother taught mathematics and physics and their father taught in the primary school.

Detchko's sister, who later also became a physics teacher, describes him as "a serious tidy boy, fond of books and very determined in his actions."

In 1946, at the age of sixteen, Detchko moved to the high school in the town of Kazanlak. There a young chemistry teacher taught the students how to work out chemical equations and demonstrated various chemical experiments. For young Pavlov's creative nature, this was an epiphany, which inspired him to decide to study industrial chemistry.

During the next two years, Detchko became the model pupil. For his excellence, he was selected to be the school standard-bearer in his final year.

In 1948, he obtained a place to read chemical engineering at the State Polytechnic in Sofia. By 1953, he had gained a degree in electrochemistry from the Higher Institute of Chemical Technology and Metallurgy in Sofia. Pavlov was then invited to join the department, headed by Professor Stefan Hristov, a pioneer in the application of quantum mechanics to electrochemistry.

In the same department working alongside him as assistant professor was a fine, brown-eyed, shy girl, who had just completed her higher education at the D. Mendeleev Chemical Technical Institute in Moscow. Her name was Svetla Raicheva. Their scientific collaboration grew into a friendship and ultimately, a marriage. Thus, the two scientists created their shared home with a peculiar atmosphere. (Svetla went on to earn her PhD in quantum chemistry and became first an associate professor and then a full professor. She chaired the Department of Physical Chemistry and also became head of the institute.)

In 1961, Detchko obtained a post at the Institute du Radium, Marie and Pierre Curie Laboratory, Paris, France. The laboratory director, Prof. Haisinski, had once worked with Marie Curie. He now directed Pavlov towards research on complex anode processes with practical applications. This specialization deeply influenced the young researcher and opened new horizons for him. (Coincidentally, his private residence today is on Jolio Curie Blvd., in Sofia.)

During that year, he saved money, passed his driver's license exam in Paris, and purchased a second-hand Ford Anglia. Joined by his wife Svetla, he toured Europe on their way back to the People's Republic of Bulgaria.

At the 1960 National Congress of Chemists, Pavlov had reported the results of his research into polarography. Impressed, Academician Kaishev, director of the Physical Chemistry Institute at the *Balgarska akademiya na naukite* (Bulgarian Academy of Sciences, aka BAS), invited Pavlov to join the Department of Electrochemistry. Bulgaria had begun to specialize in the production of electric forklift trucks, and Pavlov was assigned the task of researching in the area of lead-acid batteries. It was then that he began his studies of the processes of lead electrodes in sulfuric acid solutions.

In 1967, Detchko and his colleague Professor Evgeni Budevski established the Central Laboratory of Electrochemical Power Sources (CLEPS), in which he became the head of the Lead-Acid Battery Department (LABD).

During the next half a century, working on the 4th floor of Building 10 on the BAS campus, Pavlov built up a team of 25–28 co-workers to assist him in his meticulous researches into lead-acid batteries and lead electrodes. The team would change, but basically they were the best graduates from the University of Chemical Technology and Metallurgy and the Faculties of Chemistry and Physics of the Sofia State University.

1950s: Detchko Pavlov of the Bulgarian Academy of Sciences (courtesy Detchko Pavlov).

Indeed, through the years, he would become the mentor of fifteen PhD students and of four postdoc students. The doctors he trained in electrochemistry are now working in 7 countries on three continents–Bulgaria, Germany, France, Italy, Finland, the USA, and Algeria.

Detchko Pavlov dislikes appearing in public. He is a modest, charming person with a gentle character and dignified looks, but is also very easy-going. He has never distinguished his work from that of his team, whom he and his late wife always considered as "family."

Following the discovery of rich deposits of lead ores in Southern Bulgaria, in the mid–1960s, this Communist state got the role of supplier of forklift trucks and batteries to the USSR and other eastern bloc countries. Alongside their scientific research, the LABD boffins actively supported the Bulgarian battery industry with new technologies, transfer of knowledge and genuine theoretical modeling.

For example, Pavlov and colleague Vasil Iliev proved that when distinct types of polymers are added to the negative active mass of the battery, its power at low temperatures increases.

Their scientific contribution paid off. The starter batteries produced in the Bulgarian

"Start" factory in Dobritch exhibited the highest powers at negative temperature. With Yugoslavia, Czechoslovakia, East Germany, and Tyumen unable to provide anything comparable, Bulgarian batteries were purchased in large quantities, starting at 300,000 units and subsequently rising to 600,000 units. In return, Bulgaria received 12,000–15,000 automobiles per year from the Zhiguli-Lada factory in the Soviet city of Toliati.

Since then, many times when the lead-acid manufacturing industry has met with a problem that requires scientific interpretation, it has invariably called upon the "Bulgarian School of Pavlov" to undertake the necessary investigation.

Pavlov's efforts have been devoted to the development of lead-acid batteries science. The range of studies has been extremely wide and comprehensive. These include: kinetics of the electrochemical processes; electrochemistry of lead electrodes; semiconductor properties and structure of lead oxides, lead sulfate and basic lead sulfates; processes related to all stages of the technology of battery manufacture including paste mixing, curing, drying, pickling and formation; structures of Pb and PbO_2 active masses; processes taking place inside the battery during its storage, operation and rest; electrochemistry of antimony and tin electrodes; processes of oxygen evolution and its recombination back to water; thermal phenomena in VRLAB and the mechanism of the processes causing thermal run away in VRLAB; and degradation processes and the ways to suppress or avoid them.

The genius of Detchko Pavlov has been in the way he pinpoints scientific problems in every piece of battery production or use, then through extremely in-depth studies, reveals those processes involved by combining various fundamental methods. Having developed mechanisms explaining how and why these processes work, he finally describes these in a such a clear and simple style that not only scholars but any production engineer or qualified user can understand and use it to his practical or theoretical ends. This can range from writing a PhD thesis, to developing a new product or technology, to solving a technical problem or earning an extra dollar.

In consequence, Pavlov et al. have been granted 38 patents, both in Bulgaria and abroad. Detchko also developed lecture courses, "Processes that occur during battery manufacture" and "Essentials of Lead-Acid Batteries," which he has presented in 23 countries worldwide.

Detchko Pavlov's passion is to find out as much as he can about the world in which we live. So in his extensive travels, he would stay an extra day or so to do sightseeing, to take photographs and to get acquainted with the host country and the people.

If he has another passion, it is both classical music and pop music of the 1960s and 1970s.

Running parallel with his researches, Detchko Pavlov recognized the need for an international meeting with a strong focus on battery science and technology, rather than on commercial considerations. In 1977, he was co-chairman of the 28th Meeting of the International Society of Electrochemistry in Varna, Bulgaria, with the theme of "Electrochemical Power Sources." The following year he became a member of the Electrochemical Society, USA, and before very long had organized "Advances in Lead-Acid Batteries" in New Orleans for their 166th Meeting.

Pavlov was awarded a doctor of science degree in 1984. Fully occupied at CLEPS, he simply had not found the time to make a conventional approach. So when he submitted his thesis, the Scientific Council of Physical Chemistry—the "toughest" in Bulgaria—agreed that this was not merely a PhD work, but something much bigger. They awarded him a DSc.

From 1988, he was the motive force behind the outstanding success of the LABAT (Lead Acid Batteries) series of conferences which have since been held every three years. As testimony to their importance, the proceedings of these meetings have been published as Special Issues of the *Journal of Power Sources*. He has also served for many years as a distinguished member of the International Advisory Board of this journal.

He also initiated the decision of the Bulgarian Academy of Sciences to award battery scientists and experts with the Gaston Planté Medal for outstanding contributions. Up to now 14 battery men from 7 countries have received this award.

During the same period, Pavlov et al. were investigating the way in which expanders affected the performance of negative lead-acid battery plates and how they could be improved. This lead to the creation of a new generation of highly efficient organic lignosulfonate expanders produced by Borregaard LignoTech, Norway. The team revealed also the mechanism of the processes taking place in the AGM separator and developed a modified, better AGM with programmable properties.

In the early 1990s, with the Republic of Bulgaria undergoing democratic changes amid rising inflation and falling salaries, Pavlov at once realized that there was a risk that the department he had been building up for over 25 years may fall apart. He introduced what he called "the American approach to science."

Before long he had persuaded international concerns such as Varta Research in Germany, ALABC in the USA, and Oerlikon in Switzerland to offer his department remunerative several-year contracts to develop production technologies. This placed them on a surer financial "world scientific market."

In 1997 he was elected a full member, or academician, of the Bulgarian Academy of Sciences. This is regarded as the highest scientific rank by Eastern European countries. It is only when one Academician dies that a new one can be elected. The same year, Academician Pavlov became advisor and cooperative member of ITE Battery Research Institute, Nagoya, Japan.

Detchko Pavlov has published extensively: more than 220 papers in international scientific journals and conference proceedings which have more than 4300 citations. Often just one of these papers has gone through as many as 16 drafts before he is satisfied. Among his more recent monographs is *Essentials of Lead-Acid Batteries*, compiled and edited by B. Hariprakash, T. Prem Kumar, A.K. Shukla, published by SAEST, Karaikudi, India, 2006.

Pavlov and his collaborators—research scientists Geno Papazov, Stefan Ruevski, Temelaki Rogachev, Boris Monahov, Vasil Iliev, Galia Petkova, Mitko Dimitrov, Veselin Naidenov, Plamen Nikolov, Maria Matrakova and others—have long been enthusiastically studying the processes and phenomena that proceed in lead-acid batteries and suggesting new theoretical concepts and practical ideas. Each paper published by Prof. Pavlov and his team is oriented toward solving a "natural intrigue," as he calls it.

In 2007 Pavlov's life changed. After suffering from an incurable disease for a few months, his wife Svetla moved to the other world. Pavlov managed to overcome his profound sorrow at the loss of his best friend for 50 years and love of his life with hard work.

Elsevier Publishers commissioned Pavlov to write a book on lead-acid batteries. After four years of compiling, writing and self-editing work, Pavlov submitted his manuscript in 2010. The 656 paged book *Lead-Acid Batteries: Science and Technology* was published in 2011. It is well accepted by engineers, technologists, lecturers and students around the world. For the great interest in this book, a Chinese publisher signed a contract with Elsevier to translate it into Chinese.

The endeavor to reduce the concentration of carbon dioxide emissions in the urban atmosphere has lead to the introduction of hybrid electric vehicles, which need batteries with high specific energy, high specific power and high energy efficiency. It had been established that lead-acid batteries with carbon additives demonstrate good values of these parameters. Pavlov and his collaborators disclosed that carbon additives incorporate electrochemically in the negative active mass and charge-discharge processes proceed on both lead and carbon surfaces. In this way, lead-acid batteries with carbon additives to the negative plates become reliable power sources for hybrid electric vehicles.

The value of Acad. Pavlov's contribution has been acknowledged through a series of awards and honors: 1976, the Cyril and Methodius Medal; 1980, the Award of the Federal Ministry of Australia; 1984, the Research Award of the Electrochemical Society; 1986, the National Dimitrov Award for Science; 1994, the Gaston Planté Medal; 1995, the International Cultural Diploma of Honor; 2006, the Marin Drinov Medal with Ribbon—the highest award of the Bulgarian Academy of Sciences; 2010, the ILA Lifetime Award; and the 2013 Pitagor Award for Significant Scientific Contributions of the Ministry of Education and Science of Bulgaria.

Detchko Pavlov was once asked to prepare a very brief CV. He wrote: "Born under the sign of Virgo according to the Christian believers and under the sign of the Horse according to the Eastern ones. In love with discipline, demanding perfect order from the people around him."

Sources: from an article by the author published in *Batteries International*, Winter 2010–2011, from information provided by Detchko Pavlov, Dina Ivanova (IEES), Patrick Moseley and Boris Monahov (Advanced Lead-Acid Battery Consortium).

Peters, Kenneth
(1928–)
Commercializing the VRLA—
the British contribution

Kenneth Peters was born November 20, 1928, in Salford, a suburb of Manchester, England. "My early education was interrupted when I was evacuated to rural parts of Lancashire away from nightly bombings over my native city by the Nazi Luftwaffe."

In the immediate postwar period, chemistry was a high-profile discipline, with researchers and major companies developing new materials such as plastics and new organics, so the chemistry faculties at most universities were very popular. Peters obtained London University (Imperial College) degrees in general science and special chemistry (with honors) in electrochemistry.

He then had to put in the mandatory two years of National Service, spending most of his time at the REME (Royal Electrical and Mechanical Engineers) headquarters in Farnborough developing radar equipment for the Army.

In 1953, shortly after leaving the Army, Ken Peters married Joyce Johnstone, then secretary to the northern editor of *Melody Maker* magazine. They remain happily married after 58 years with three children (their younger daughter died in 2006) and three grandsons, all now in college.

Peters's entry into batteries came in 1953 when, after leaving the Army, he joined the Chloride Electrical Storage Company at their Clifton Junction plant.

As Peters recalls: "In those days the global battery industry was dominated by three major companies. The Electric Storage Battery Company (ESB) with over 70% of the North American market, Akumulatoren Fabriken Aktiengesellschaft (AFA), later renamed Varta, with factories throughout Europe, and Chloride with factories in Britain and in all the former Imperial countries. These companies were almost self-sufficient in materials and components."

The Clifton Junction factory where Peters started work employed over 3,000 workers producing two million car batteries per year, tubular motive power cells, Planté and flat plate stationary cells, as well as submarine, aircraft and signals defense batteries. Smelting, alloy, oxide and separator production took place on the same site, as were expanders and additive preparation. Additionally, Chloride made containers a few miles away. Design and manufacturing technology was closely guarded and supported by a substantial technical team.

As a trainee, Peters worked in all the manufacturing areas:

> There was little automatic equipment and I was involved in installing and operating their first automatic Winkel pasting machines. I joined the Research department which later moved to a new Technical Centre away from the demands of the manufacturing plant and equipped with the most advanced analytical and test facilities.
>
> Our Technical Director was Dr. Montefiore Barak [see Barak entry]. He was very outward looking and instrumental in starting the International Power Source Symposium (IPSS) with the inaugural meeting which I attended in October 1958. It was unique within the industry at that time; companies did not share even limited technical and test data, and it was the principal industry conference for many years.

Peters became involved in a range of programs including the manufacture of electro-deposited plates for torpedo batteries for the UK Admiralty and the development of impregnated cellulose separators. Chloride produced both microporous and sintered PVC separators (Porvic). Cellulose separators were a further cost reduction and were subsequently made at several plants from 1956 until the mid–1970s, when microporous P.E. separators became widely available.

With about 20 chemists, engineers and technicians, a workshop was set up for making experimental designs and their own plate and cell test equipment plus supporting laboratories for physical and chemical analysis. Peters worked as part of a team on the process and product development and assessment of new materials.

During his time off, Ken Peters enjoyed rock climbing and fell-walking (i.e., hiking in the hills). "Great days out with working colleagues in Snowdonia, North Wales, the Lake District and more extensively in Scotland, 'capturing the Monroes,'" he observes.

Back at work, one early and successful job was to assess and qualify lead oxides produced in a new Chloride-designed oxide mill fitted with in-built classifiers and temperature controls, the forerunner of many later installed at numerous factories. Peters recalls, "I learned a lot about the rheology of battery pastes during that work. Maintenance-free car batteries were topical and we studied gassing rates, impurity influences, and developed and patented low antimonial alloys producing ductile thin grids which were could be cast on automatic machines. This was before the widespread use of calcium alloys, a technology adopted initially from ESB who had developed these alloys for Telecom batteries."

Chloride sponsored basic research at several British universities. As industrial supervisor, Peters would visit and contribute to a great many academic journals. Several students subsequently joined the company. "Later, the University of Salford with whom we collaborated awarded me a Master's degree."

Until the late 1950s, all the major battery companies were more or less self-contained in terms of their technology. They did their own development of virtually everything, and up to then, any innovations either design or additives, separators, alloys, containers, etc., were developed in-house and closely guarded. R&D consisted of electrical engineers, material scientists as well as electrochemists and designers.

In 1960, Chloride, ESB and AFA (Varta) signed an unprecedented technical exchange agreement. All three companies employed experienced and well-known electrochemists and researchers. Ken Peters began to have regular meetings with Paul Ruetschi (see Ruetschi entry), Alvin Salkind (see Salkind entry) and David Boden at ESB, and Professor Hans Bode (see Bode entry), Research Director at AFA, with his colleagues Ernst Voss (see Voss entry), and Dietrich Berndt. They would also visit Chloride at Clifton Junction. In 1968 this arrangement was deemed to be unlawful and cooperation stopped.

Initially as research manager, Ken Peters had done work that covered a range of electrochemical systems including alkaline batteries and hydrogen/air fuel cells, work which was presented by a colleague at an IPSS meeting in the 1960s and demonstrated by powering an industrial truck. "At the time," he recalls, "our fuel cell technology was said to be five years from commercialisation. It's still the same."

In 1964 he was appointed head of Lead Acid Development and started a study which was to indirectly lead him to making a major contribution to battery technology. At that time, sealed rechargeable Ni/Cd cells were leak-proof. As they lost no water in service due to recombination of oxygen at the negative plate inhibiting hydrogen evolution, they became popular for portable equipment. Earlier gas recombination devices used expensive and inefficient catalytic systems.

Peters recalls:

> The same recombination approach seemed possible with lead so we started work to study the feasibility. High charging rates with good recombination efficiencies were possible with separator saturation being the main controlling parameter. Subsequently we made several hundred D-sized cells with wound lead electrodes and Porvic separators, the most porous separator available at that time. There were cost benefits over alkaline cells but the output was relatively poor and with no great enthusiasm for this work within the company, it was shelved.
>
> I later presented a performance comparison of three types of D cell (primary Leclanché, alkaline, lead acid) at the IPSS conference in 1971. At the same meeting I was approached by Don McClelland of Gates Rubber Company. I didn't know Don or the company whose principal business was tyres and hoses. Gates apparently had similar ideas some years earlier and had formed a venture group specifically to develop batteries for cordless equipment, nickel/zinc and lead acid being the obvious candidates. McClelland sent me 50 wound, D size lead acid cells which we tested and I reported to my management that they were rather special.

Their highly porous, resilient and compressible glass separators (the main inventive claim of the Devitt & McClelland U.S. Patent 3,862,861, published in 1975) maintained close contact with the plate surfaces and resulted in cells which had high power capability, cycled well and could be charged seemingly forever without water loss. Peters now suggested a similar design approach could be used in Chloride's main industrial and automotive batteries with very beneficial effects. Subsequently the Brit was invited to visit Gates at their Denver head office for discussions with their board of management.

Under John Devitt (see Devitt entry), Gates had put together an experienced team:

both Devitt and McClelland, who had worked on nickel-zinc and silver-zinc cells; Will Bundy, who had spent many years with the National Lead Company; and a young electrochemist named Kathryn Bullock, later to be president of The Electrochemical Society (see Bullock entry).

Peters continues:

It seemed that I was invited to the Gates Board meeting to validate, and possibly explain the claims of their scientists. Their interest in batteries was based on advice given to them by ADL, that small rechargeable wound cells for cordless equipment could conveniently be marketed on garage forecourts alongside their tyres and hoses. I explained the key points and the potential benefits of their patented cell design and subsequently a joint working group was set up to review the situation and consider the way forward. Over the following months we had several meetings.

The Gates team was keen to stick to their wound cell design but their initial manufacturing process was slow, expensive with very high scrap levels. High purity, and expensive, lead, litharge and red lead were used with high density pastes and formation over several days. The separators were high quality glass filter papers purchased from the UK and although they were exploring cheaper U.S. supplies, nothing had been qualified. It was difficult to see how this approach could be used to manufacture the larger batteries needed for industrial and automotive applications in the numbers required and at acceptable cost.

We agreed to follow different approaches. Gates would pursue their wound cell approach for the cordless appliance market whilst we at Chloride would consider how their existing manufacturing plant such as casting and pasting machines could be used to make products with the same beneficial features as the Gates cell.

Once back in Britain, Ken Peters and his team went on to develop a range of telecom and UPS standby batteries using more or less conventional methods:

Plates wrapped in compressed glass microfibre separator were inserted in strong plastic containers fitted with one-way valves. New processes and equipment for acid filling and formation were developed and a source of good quality glass microfibre paper at a reasonable price was found at a small paper mill in Gloucestershire, with whom we had previously worked on the cellulose separator programme. Subsequently this company was acquired by H&V who sent a team to our workshops for extensive discussions on quality standards.

At that time, Telecom and UPS batteries were located in central stations often in large basements near conurbations, open-top cells were common and needed frequent service and maintenance with the atmosphere both noxious and hazardous. Distributed power supplies were being considered. Their new valve regulated cells had appreciably higher volumetric energy density than the existing batteries, power outputs were better and with no water losses or gases evolved they could be located on power racks in offices or where most convenient to the end user.

Our first prototype designs were supplied to British Telecom for trials in the late 1970s and production commenced at the Clifton Junction factory in 1983.

By 1989 BT had installed 500,000 2v/100Ah valve regulated cells in power racks in their System X digital telephone exchanges and were installing them at a rate of 120,000 per year. In 1990 they reported reliability, based on mean time between failure (MTBF), exceeded their target and was very much better than the Planté cells in their central stations.

After 1990, various design changes were made to extend service life. Within a few years, distributed power supplies with similar valve-regulated designs were adopted by Telecom companies everywhere.

Peters notes: "Parallel with the standby battery programme, we were developing valve regulated car batteries with similar beneficial features; leak and spill proof, improved cycling and a much higher cranking performance than equivalent flooded batteries. Also they had a respectable reserve capacity, always difficult to achieve in limited electrolyte designs. They had dual terminals (top and side), multiple hold-downs, a carrying handle and stackable features, all novels at that time, giving suppliers the opportunity to better display and hold a smaller range."

Production of this battery (Torquestarter) started in Brisbane, Australia, in 1984, and was soon followed by manufacture in Tampa (U.S.), Benoni (RSA), and Dagenham (UK). The batteries made in Tampa and Benoni had major quality problems with many early failures and production ceased a year later.

In Australia and the UK, after good early sales, the demand decreased due to the higher cost. Production stopped about three years later. Peters explains:

> Torquestarter was a good battery but benefits to the motorist, who already had a long-lasting maintenance free battery, or the car manufacturer, were dubious, and it was more expensive.
> I twice visited Ford, Detroit, with a marketing team to discuss their use as initial equipment without success. In 2011 similar valve-regulated batteries are now fitted in micro hybrid cars. They provide more freedom for location and improved cycling supporting manufacturers' changes to get better fuel economy and reducing emissions.

In the late 1980s Chloride Group sold off their worldwide battery operations, concentrating on their emergency equipment business.

Since his retirement in 1992, Ken Peters has enjoyed fly fishing in Scotland, landscaping his garden, and following his favorite teams at Lancashire County Cricket Club and Manchester United.

Sources: From an article by the author, published in *Batteries International*, Fall 2011, based on information supplied by Ken Peters.

•••

Pierson, John Ronald
(1936–)
Improvements in the mechanization of battery making

John Ronald Pierson was born in 1936 to second-generation Scandinavian parents Delbert (Swedish) and Dagmar (Danish) Pierson in the industrial city of Racine, Wisconsin. He was the youngest of three children. Growing up in Kringleville, John was always doing experiments using a chemistry set. He would also cast lead soldiers using steel molds. Magnifying glasses and microscopes intrigued him. In 8th grade, John's career paper was on "Chemistry and Chemical Engineering." In high school a teacher who made the subject matter (chemistry) most interesting was named Mr. Rodgers.

Pierson attended public schools in Racine, graduating from Washington Park High School in 1954. The school subsequently inducted him into their exclusive Hall of Fame in 2003. There he was active in the Boy Scout movement, attaining the ultimate rank of Eagle Scout at age 15. He was also an active participant in numerous sports including basketball, football, swimming, baseball, bowling and golf.

John also became an accomplished musician, participating with bands, orchestras, and as a French horn bugler with several renowned drum and bugle corps. It was with the latter that he later met his future wife Celine Schallhorn, who marched with a color guard in many of the same parades and contests around the country.

When he was 17, John enlisted in the Wisconsin Air National Guard, where he would serve on a part-time basis for eight years (sufficient to exempt him from the military draft through college). His unit was an aircraft control and warning squadron, in which John attained the rank of staff sergeant.

He received a B.S. in chemical engineering from the University of Wisconsin–Madison in 1959. Unit operations, inorganic chemistry and electrochemistry were among his favorite subjects at the university. He later completed a management development program (accelerated MBA) at Northeastern University in Boston (1982) and was trained in microscopy and X-ray diffraction analysis at McGronie Research Institute and Illinois Institute of Technology, respectively.

Upon graduation from college, John accepted a position of management trainee/student engineer with Youngstown Sheet and Tube Company of East Chicago, Indiana. The job offered the opportunity to study the various basic steel-making operations from coke plant through rolling mills. The tour, however, was interrupted by the last great strike by the United Steel Workers, which locked employees out of the mills from July to November.

John Pierson and his wife Celine (Pierson Collection).

Pierson recalls: "Despite the interruption, it became clear to me and my recently acquired Milwaukee-born wife that we would prefer to raise our family nearer the Wisconsin homes of our parents. While visiting home for Christmas of 1959 Celine noted a want ad in the *Milwaukee Journal*'s Sunday edition by a company named Globe-Union looking for Chemical Engineers. Without knowing a thing about the Company, its products or history, I applied, was interviewed and received the job offer. I got no increase in compensation but a superior environment to work and live in and most importantly a happy wife."

John would start as a battery process engineer in the Globe Battery Division on March 1, one week after their first daughter was born. The move went smoothly into an upper flat freshly decorated by helpful relatives happy to have them back home.

Globe-Union, a company founded in 1920 with the merger of two battery manufacturers, Globe Battery of Milwaukee and Union Battery of Chicago, was headquartered at 900 E. Keefe Avenue in an industrial area of Milwaukee. The products manufactured there and elsewhere included roller skates, golf clubs, spark plugs, ignition parts, radio components (capacitors, resistors, etc.) and *automotive batteries*. Globe-Union's major customer by far was Sears Roebuck and Co.

Pierson continues: "On the night before my interview at Globe Union I saw an interesting piece of news on the TV (black and white). A large local company, Allis Chalmers, was demonstrating an all-electric tractor powered by a recently developed fuel-cell [see Bacon entry]. When I asked my interviewer (Chief Engineer Tony Sabatino) about fuel cells and the future of lead-acid batteries he answered, 'Don't worry, lead-acid batteries will be around for at least five years'—that was 54 years ago."

When Pierson started, automotive batteries were strictly housed in hard rubber and primarily 6-volt, which was the electrical system of the day. Batteries had relied on individual rubber covers and terminals on each cell, and they had asphalt tops. At that time, there were only about 10 to 12 group sizes offered.

John showed up for his first day of work equipped as a typical engineer with a briefcase, pocket protector and slide rule, and he was handed a copy of *Storage Batteries* by George Wood Vinal. "I was soon warned by fellow engineers to wear clothes that I was not real fond of tomorrow when we do experimental paste mixing to establish mixing curves for a new oxide source."

John became part of a small but talented engineering team that was already working behind closed doors on what would become a major breakthrough in battery assembly technology—the first cast-on strap (COS) machine. A good deal of development effort on the four-station automation device was required prior to rolling it out to the fifteen small branch plants.

A second major development in battery assembly technology, thru-partition welding (HV), followed closely on the heels of the COS. HV stood for high voltage of the product due to low electrical resistance. This technology was also rolled out to the branch plants. Milwaukee at the time benefitted from numerous quality machine shops capable of replicating prototypes built at the Keefe Avenue facility.

A third major development by the engineering team was made possible by material development in the chemical industry—copolymers of propylene and ethylene. This material development, plus German injection molding equipment and complex molds, made possible the first successful thin-walled polypropylene (PP) battery container and cover. The resulting product was translucent, allowing for the viewing of electrolyte levels; it was heat-sealable and decorateable, but most important, the strong thin walls allowed the product designer to increase the number and size of electrodes in a given cube, enhancing product performance. A large, modern injection-molding facility was constructed and equipped in Florence, Kentucky, to provide containers and covers to meet the growing demand.

The combination of these three technical developments (COS, HV, and PP) allowed Globe-Union to offer a unique, differentiated product to its best customer, Sears. At the time, Sears was opening free-standing auto centers and needed a marque product to heavily advertise. In 1967 the DieHard was born.

It is rare indeed in a strictly commodity business such as automotive batteries that a truly differentiated product is developed. The Sears DieHard looked and performed differently from any of its competitors. At approximately the same time American Motors, now part of Chrysler Corporation, became the first vehicle manufacturer to accept polypropylene-contained original equipment batteries.

Until 1962 all Globe-Union factories were supplied with lead oxide in 600-pound drums supplied by companies such as National Lead, Eagle Picher, Bunker Hill and Western Lead. A decision was made to begin vertical integration, including oxide manufacturing on site. The newly commissioned Geneva, Illinois, plant was selected as the guinea pig and two process engineers—John Pierson and Bob Wiethaup—were given the task.

Says Pierson: "After many months of equipment installation, start-up, operator training and learning, our new Barton oxide system was up and running. During the learning period we made frequent calls to consultant Tom Blair for advice and counseling. Barton oxide systems were subsequently installed in three additional plants."

Globe-Union was very successful in protecting its inventions with U.S. and foreign patents, and in 1967 won in a patent infringement suit of its thin-walled polypropylene container patents against Joseph Lucas Ltd. of Birmingham, England. As a result of the litigation, Lucas was required to provide full technology in three areas to Globe-Union— plate-curing chemistry, fast-setting epoxy resin, and ball mill oxide manufacturing. The first two were straightforward and paralleled work already underway at Globe-Union. The third, however, ball mill oxide, provided an opportunity to directly compare a world-class ball mill system and the oxide it produced to that of the Globe Barton systems.

Pierson continues:

I visited the Lucas plant on Foreman's Road in Birmingham in the fall of 1967 to begin the ball mill oxide technology transfer. The large array of Hardinge conical mills, fed with shot cast by TBS made casters with temperature-sensing kiels riding on the load, was impressive. I ordered a shipment of oxide to be delivered to the Keefe Ave facility for evaluation. The battery test results were sufficiently encouraging to warrant that I purchased a small obsolete Lucas mill for more thorough evaluation. Subtle enhancements in plate strength formation efficiency and product performance were attributed to the oxide. Full scale Hardinge mills were subsequently installed in most Globe Union facilites. Modern smaller mills provided by Sovema have more recently become the oxide system of choice.

Being active in the introduction of oxide manufacturing to Globe-Union, Pierson became interested in the chemical and crystallographic characteristics of oxide and the reactions encountered in process of battery plates. He recalls what this involved: "In addition to his chemical process training and natural curiosity I applied microscopy and x-ray diffraction technology to the reaction studies. I noted that plate curing was a particularly uncontrolled process yielding a variety of chemical compound and crystalline structure. So I built the first controlled curing chamber using wooden 2 × 4s and plastic sheeting and supplied it with heated humidified air. Then I revised the plate-stacking procedures leaving spaces between plate stacks. The results were plates of consistent chemistry and crystallography optimized for life and initial performance."

Similar studies of chemical crystallographic changes encountered in battery electrode process have led to optimization of the oxide-making, paste-mixing, curing and formation process. This included a high-rate one-shot formation system using cooling water for temperature control.

In the late 1960s and early 1970s the Ford Motor Company decided to embark on a vertical integration mission and purchased a large old battery factory in Owosso, Michigan, from Autolite. Ford then broke ground on a second state-of-the-art battery factory in Shreveport, Louisiana. The U.S. courts ruled the acquisition violated the antitrust laws and forced Ford to divest themselves of the two facilites and discontinue battery manufacturing.

John and product engineering manager Chuck Wright were commissioned to explore the potential of the Owosso facility. The plant was acquired by Globe-Union, substantially upgraded and eventually closed several decades later. The Shreveport plant was purchased by Gould National Battery Co. (GNB), but several of the pieces of novel equipment had to be replaced with tried-and-true technologies. This plant was also ultimately closed. The Owosso plant acquisition propelled Globe-Union into the original equipment battery business and allowed them to access to Ford's substantial research reports on calcium alloy maintenance-free batteries.

In 1967 Globe-Union's headquarters were relocated from the old Keefe Avenue facility to a newly constructed campus of buildings in suburban Glendale, Wisconsin. These ultramodern facilities were eventually adapted by Johnson Controls as corporate and power solutions (battery) headquarters and have been significantly expanded and upgraded over the past decades. The Keefe Avenue facilities and the specialty battery businesses were eventually sold to C and D Battery Co. and are still in operation.

In the 1970s Globe-Union purchased a vacant facility near their corporate headquarters on Teutonia Avenue in Milwaukee and equipped it as an engineering pilot facility. This facility, with its single casting, pasting, assembly and formation lines along with a mechanical engineering and process engineering lab, was the site for major process and product development programs for several decades. The engineering facility, under the banner "Home of the Unfair Competitive Advantage," was the original manufacturing site for Ford maintenance-free batteries, as well as the new high-powered Group 65 and 33 batteries for Ford diesel-powered automobiles. All new concepts were piloted at the facility, including new grid designs and alloys, plastic/lead combination girds, paste additives and continuous (expanded metal) negative and positive (wrought punched) grids. Such a nearby facility allowed engineers to conduct complex projects without the expense of travel or the interruption of production lines at branch plants.

In conducting experiments aimed at enhancing initial performance and life of batteries, it became apparent to Pierson and his team that many potential improvements were masked by lack of control of paste weights and density of belt-pasted plates. A pasting machine capable of producing consistent plates with the grid centered in the paste became a priority. Winkel belt pasters were the standard of the industry and a search of machine vendors came up blank. One device, the Lund fixed-orifice paster, was in use, but was exclusively available in the U.S. to Gould National Battery Co. A Lund paster located in Australia was purchased and installed in the Keefe Avenue plant.

Pierson was charged with commissioning the machine and evaluating the quality of plates it produced. The grids supplied to the vertical-orifice plate paster were milled to reasonably consistent thickness, and sample quantities of plates were produced. The machine was slow and very selective relative to grid uniformity, but the resulting plates performed uniformly and well.

Pierson: "We decided to charge the Mechanical Engineering team with designing a high speed horizontal flow fixed orifice paster (FOP). Progress in this development program was slow primarily due to variations in cast grid thickness and the initial attempt to roll it out to the plants was unsuccessful due to low productivity. The devices were recalled and after significant re-design of the orifice plates and a focus on enhanced grid quality the FOP, renamed the JCI paster after the new parent company was successfully re-launched. The uniformity and quality of the resulting plates was exceptional."

In the meantime, JCI's product engineers, under the direction of Vince Halsall, Chuck Wright and Pierson, developed a continuous stream of enhanced product features to offer an ever-growing customer base. Developments included: safety vent systems, side and dual termination, computer-modeled grids with central lugs and tapered radial wires, and climatized batteries. The overriding objective was to enhance product performance, extend life and lower cost and weight of the product.

In 1978 Globe-Union became the target of a very hostile takeover by UV Industries of New York. Two "white knights" appeared, offering to protect Globe-Union from the takeover attempt—Square D Corporation, with some manufacturing facilities in Milwaukee, and Milwaukee-based Johnson Controls (JCI). Through strategic moves by its president Fred Brengel, JCI became the successful bidder in the race. JCI sales the year prior to the merger/acquisition were slightly less than Globe-Union's, so it has been called a merger of equals. JCI sold off the Central-Lab Electronics division of Globe-Union, but culturally and financially has strongly supported the battery division since.

Globe-Union had an International Division which marketed equipment and know-how worldwide. Pierson participated with this team as technical advisor, including assignments such as equipping two factories in the former Yugoslavia with up-to-date battery-making technology. He also worked with FEMSA in Spain on updating their technology, as well as facilitating gelled electrolyte (Gel Cell) technology transfer from Sonnenschein (Germany) to Globe-Union.

Two extensive technology exchanges, based on relationships established by Pierson, proved beneficial to all parties. The first such exchange was in 1980 with Matsushita (Terry Kawase), and the second with Varta (Dr. Robert Friedrich). The Matsushita exchange resulted in JCI's gaining access to many automation advances utilized by Matsushita at their vast plant in Hamanako, Japan. The Varta exchange culminated with acquisition of the German auto battery business by JCI.

Pierson: "At the opening reception of 5ELBC in suburban Barcelona, Spain, I was approached as the sole JCI representative by two principals of Amara Raja Battery Company of India. Ram Galla and his son Jay were interested in obtaining technical and financial support for their business. So I invited them to Milwaukee which they accepted and he subsequently visited their facilities in India. JCI agreed to support the company providing technical support and taking an equity position in this now thriving venture."

Pierson spent many weeks during the 1980s negotiating battery specification in Japan with engineers representing car companies interested in starting assembly expansions in the U.S. The relationships built assisted JCI in becoming a source of original equipment batteries to each manufacturer.

Along with other JCI executives, he visited battery plants in Brazil and Argentina to determine the viability of jointly or solely acquiring the facilities. It was determine that Sao Paulo (Brazil) plant would be a good fit, but the Buenos Aries (Argentina) plant and equipment were obsolete. JCI acquired the Brazilian operation. Pierson recalls:

In 1989 our eldest daughter married Francisco Benitez, a Colombian-born U.S. citizen in a ceremony at the Milwaukee courthouse. In 1995 they decided to renew their vows in the Catholic Church in Colombia. Celine and I, with youngest daughter Beth flew to Medellin to participate. Prior to the visit, I had contacted Diego Mejia Castro, Vice President of MAC Battery and an old friend to see if a plant visit would make sense. Diego invited me to visit their plant in Cali and comment on their manufacturing processes and products. Diego and his brother Louis picked me up at the Medellin airport in their single engine airplane with Louis as pilot and Diego in the rear seat, leaving the copilot seat to me. After taxing [sic] to the runway Louis said "Ok John you're the copilot read me the checklist." I looked down at the large laminated checklist with panic—it was entirely in Spanish. Diego saved the day by turning the document over to the English side and the checklist was read. The plant visit went well with some perhaps useful suggestions by me but the highlight of the day was meeting Diego's father, the company's founder for an outdoor lunch at his club.

Pierson visited MAC again as a consultant to comment on plans for a new battery factory. The majority of MAC was acquired by JCI in 2014.

In the mid–1990s, John was one of three board members on a joint venture with the Chinese in Shanghai. The other two JCI representatives were Chairman Art Nenning (finance) and Jerry O'Karma (legal). Many modifications were made to enhance productivity and quality and the overall experience of quarterly meetings was excellent. "My opinions on Chinese culture, work ethic and dining will be the subject of another day."

A good deal of the process and material development that John Pierson participated in was considered confidential trade secrets and therefore not patented, although much of the findings were published in four papers. His name is on about 6 or 8 patents; a couple of the more recent ones are 5,204,610 Long Lived Dual Battery, and 6,265,091 B1 Modular Electric Storage Battery, issued in 1993 and 2001 respectively.

John Pierson has authored or co-authored 29 technical papers on subjects ranging from crystallography of battery-active material and the impact of impurities on battery performance to design of batteries for modern internal combustion engine, hybrid and electric vehicles. His technical findings have been presented at conferences in the United States, Great Britain, Japan, Germany, France, Spain, Poland and Bulgaria. His most recent paper, "Control of Vital Chemical Processes in the Preparation of Lead-Acid Battery Active Materials," was presented at LABAT 2005 in Bulgaria, organized by John's longtime friend, Detchko Pavlov. "My initial visit to beautiful Bulgaria was both successful and exciting though much of the excitement was at the hands of a band of pocket-picking gypsies, during a post-conference tour. I returned to Bulgaria three years later to attend LABAT 2008 without incident."

Pierson served as chairman of the Battery Division of the Electrochemical Society, chairman of the Storage Battery Committee of SAE, and chairman of the Technical Committee of BCI during his career.

In May of 2010 John was one of many long-term JCI management personnel to be honored at the company's 125th anniversary. A festive cocktail party and dinner at the newly expanded and remodeled headquarters marked the event. The following day John and Celine headed for Austin, Texas, and the annual BCI convention. Pierson was awarded the BCI diamond-studded pin for 50 years of service in the battery industry. At the annual quarter-century club breakfast, John's keynote address delivered the message, "Memoirs of a Battery Man," closing with a list of lessons learned.

Since his retirement, John has done some consulting work in countries such as Ecuador, Colombia, Brazil and Mexico, in addition to the U.S. He is an avid fan of the University of Wisconsin Madison basketball and football teams and the Milwaukee Brewers baseball and Green Bay Packer football teams. He also follows the Interstate Battery-sponsored NASCAR racing team.

John's family currently consists of three married daughters, six grandchildren and four great-grandchildren. The entire family, some 21 strong, enjoys being together for week-long spring stays at exotic locations such as Jamaica, the Dominican Republic, Mexico, Costa Rica and Hawaii, as well as annual summer retreats to lake cottages in the Wisconsin north woods.

He still manages to play golf weekly in the Wisconsin Senior Golf Tour during the spring, summer and fall seasons. He also plays 3 to 4 rounds per week while he and his wife winter in Florida (January–March). He much enjoys time with his family, travel, gardening (flowers and vegetables), photography and golf. His education continues with some of the instructors being his grandchildren and great-grandchildren—particularly in the area of electronic communication.

John and Celine, his beautiful wife of 55 years, reside in a home on a one-acre lot in Brookfield, a Milwaukee suburb. Celine is the proud survivor of not one but two bouts with breast cancer and a nearly year-long fight with a debilitating staph infection. All three of his daughters' families live within an easy 30-minute drive of John, making frequent family visits easy.

Looking back, John Pierson comments, "I'm grateful that I had the opportunity to work as part of a talented, supportive team during my 38 years with the company and beyond. I have also been blessed with longstanding relationships established with friends throughout the battery industry—including suppliers, customers, and competitors."

Source: Originally published in *Batteries International*, Fall 2014, from information supplied to the author by John Pierson.

....

Planté, Raymond-Louis-Gaston
(1834–1889)
Inventor of the rechargeable lead-acid battery

Raymond-Louis-Gaston Planté was born on April 22, 1834, in Orthez, France, one of three brothers, each brilliant in his own way. Originating from Orthez in the Pyrenées Atlantiques, Leopold, Gaston and Francis had benefited from the wealth and the love of learning emanating from their scholarly father, Pierre Planté, keen to make his sons succeed—so much so that in 1841, the family moved up to Paris.

The first to shine was brother Francis, a child prodigy pianist, who gained first prize in a contest at the Paris Music Conservatory, aged only 11. From there on Francis Planté would become a famous virtuoso, later known as the "God of the piano." Léopold Planté would later become one of the capital's most eminent barristers.

At 7 years old Gaston was sent to a boarding school, run by the Abbé Poiloup at Vaugirard, thence as a day student to the Lycée Charlemagne, where he obtained his doctorate of philosophy in 1850, aged only 16, and his doctorate of sciences in 1853, aged 19. He continued his brilliant academic career at the Sorbonne University, to the point that Morin, then director-general of the Conservatoire National des Arts et Metiers, named him laboratory assistant in physics under Edmond Becquerel, the man who some twelve years before had discovered the photovoltaic effect, the physics behind the solar cell, in 1839. Planté was described as "a studious man of zeal."

In 1855, Planté, as assistant physics lecturer at the Conservatoire des Arts et Metiers, discovered the fossil of a great flightless bird in a clay pit at Meudon, near Paris. Impressed, the revered French Academy of Sciences decided to name the fossil after the young man *Gastornis parisiensis*—or "Gaston's bird of Paris."

But Planté was as much interested in electricity as in fossils. In 1859, following several years of experimentation, he delivered a report to the Academy of Sciences, in which he announced that he had produced "a secondary battery of great power"—one which could be recharged. Although Sintenden (see Sintenden entry) had observed the effect in 1854, Planté's was the first which could be regularly recharged. To arrive at this, Planté had

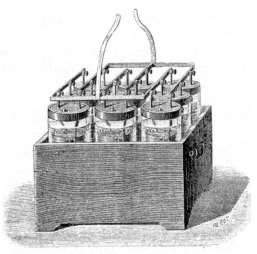

Left: **Raymond-Louis-Gaston Planté.** *Above:* **Planté's battery (Musée EDF Electropolis, Mulhouse).**

experimented with all manner of metals, from tin and silver to gold and platinum. Eventually he settled on lead. His early model had consisted of a spiral roll of two sheets of pure lead separated by a linen cloth, immersed in a glass jar of sulfuric acid solution. But the one he presented was a nine-cell lead-acid battery.

Such an invention obtained for the 26-year-old the post of professor of physics at the Polytechnic Association for the Development of Popular Instruction. During the next six years, Gaston Planté went full out with a series of researches concerning electrolytic deposits: he had been pushed by observations which he had been able to make during his previous work. He had made these researches in the laboratories of the Maison Christofle to which he belonged for some years, at first in his capacity as electrochemist, then administrator.

Further marks of respect for this young physicist came with his being appointed deputy for the inspector general in the French section at the London Universal Exhibition of 1862; jury member at the International Exhibition in Bayonne in 1864; and member of the Admission Committee and of the Reunion of Offices of the 10th Group at the Paris Universal Exhibition of 1867.

By the 1870s, Planté was placing his rechargeable lead-acid battery inside protective boxes and was supervising its adaptation for a whole field of applications, the widest and most unexpected. It was used in medicine to power galvanocaustic and laryngoscopic devices, and others aimed at therapeutic treatment. Gustave Trouvé (see Trouvé entry) worked with him in developing his polyscope, which instead of a light bulb used a fine piece of platinum transformed from red to white and placed inside a little reflector.

Planté's battery also powered miners' electric lamps; the electric brakes of steam trains; for the production of signals at sea or on the coasts; to power electric motors, for electric candlesticks, for electric bells, for arc lighting, for luminous signals, etc. This in itself would again have been enough to make the name of Gaston Planté enter into the history books. But brilliant men tend to move on from challenge to challenge. As a geologist he continued to search, finding some remarkable plant fossils in the Paris basin, which he gave freely to the Natural History Museum.

In 1873 Planté adapted Gramme's machine for recharging his batteries. The two inventors had met at the Breguet Company, which wanted to electrify their machinery. In 1873, at the Vienna Exposition, Planté exhibited a steam engine linked to a pump over a mile (2 km) from there, by the intermediary of two electrical machines, one acting at the start as generator, the other at the other end as receiver. This was the beginning of industrial electricity.

He also began to investigate the differences between *static electricity* and *dynamic electricity* (i.e., from batteries).

On October 29, 1877, he presented to the Academy of Sciences his "rheostat machine," capable of "transforming a given quantity of electrical energy ready to supply the current in a quantity of corresponding electrical effects in static form."

Planté's rheostat machine used a bank of mica capacitors, a clever rotating commutator, and a series of contacts to alternately charge a bank of capacitors in parallel (from a high-voltage battery source), and then connect the capacitors in series. This arrangement multiplied the battery voltage by the number of capacitor stages to obtain *very high voltages*. By rapidly rotating the shaft, a series of high-voltage sparks many centimeters long could rapidly be generated.

At the time, the effects he created using multiples of his accumulators coupled to his rheostatic machine were nothing short of impressive, supplying in the first instants of their discharge an electromotive force from 2,000 to 4,000 volts! As if this were not enough, the big model of the machine had 80 condensers; supplied by a battery of 1600 volts, the tension obtained is close to 100,000 volts!

Planté's apartment, No. 56 Rue Tournelles, close to the Place des Vosges, was not merely a laboratory, and all those who went to visit him, both ordinary people and scientists, left filled with admiration after looking at such a broad display of the marvels of science brought together with such simplicity, austerity and largeness of soul.

And among those curious visitors was the technology-keen Don Pedro II d'Alcantara, Emperor of Brazil. Already his reign in that country had seen the beginnings of industrialization, the first paved roads, the first steam-engined railway, and a submarine telegraphy cable. Indeed, Don Pedro was the first Brazilian to enjoy the use of the newfangled telephone as supplied by Alexander Graham Bell.

During a dinner held by His Serene Majesty, Planté was invited to demonstrate his rheostat machine in front the marveling guests. This resulted in his not only being awarded the Order of the Rose of Brazil, but in receiving financial patronage. In return for this, he dedicated his book *Researches into Electricity*, presented to the Academy of Sciences on February 24, 1879, to the Emperor as a "feeble witness of my profound thanks. You were the first to encourage my work."

With the industrial applications of his battery and his rheostat machine, Gaston Planté could have made a fortune, but for him it was only a source of work. Not only would he never take financial advantage of his discoveries, but he never retained from his income more than was necessary, which for him came down to very little.

An injustice to another revolted him, but for him he pardoned everyone. He never became involved in a discussion on the subject of his theories and let go any criticisms.

"I am delighted whenever one would like to make use of my ideas, because this shows me that one does not always think them bad ones."

He gave the whole of his Lacaze Prize of 10,000 francs, which he had been awarded by the Academy of Sciences, and pushed his generosity to selling his great Ampère medal, in gold, which is considered as an unproductive capital, so as to give the sum to the poor.

In 1880, Planté's father, with whom he had been living, died. Some said the scientist never quite got over the loss of someone who had supported and encouraged him from his infancy.

In the nine years which followed, the inventor-turned-scientist now directed his brilliant questioning mind and piercing eyes towards Nature herself, the great generator. He investigated globular lightning, hailstorms, waterspouts, cyclones, polar auroras—hitherto mysteries that had eluded scientists.

He observed. One night, he was at his property at Meudon when a violent storm broke out over Paris, and from this natural observatory he studied the lightning which appeared. "The most remarkable of all, he said, "is that which was launched from the heavens to the ground describing a curve and which remained visible for an appreciable moment, forming a rosary of brilliant beads."

But he also worked to reproduce these effects in miniature using high-tension electricity. In short, he reduced distances and tamed the elements in his laboratory. The results were awesome! Tesla-like *before* Tesla. Witnesses saw the globe of fire of lightning moving around in a bowl, the varied fires of the polar auroras, water drops, the generation of hail pulverized by electrical discharges, the formation of waterspouts and cyclones, etc.

Nor did Gaston Planté consider our globe be an exception to the planetary rule. Relying on astronomical observations, and still with his rheostat machine, he studied solar spots, the nature of spiral nebulae, even the electrical constitution of the sun itself. He put forward theories about them often very close to those which physicists elaborated later, armed with all of today's knowledge.

Publishing his findings in a second book, *Electrical Phenomena of the Atmosphere*, he summed up his approach in a quotation from Saint Augustine: "*Quaero, Pater, non affirmo*" ("I question, Father, I do not affirm").

Planté was awarded France's highest honor, Chevalier de la Légion d'Honneur, on April 23, 1881, being made an officer four years later. His sponsor, M. Hervé-Mangon, wrote to the French finance minister, "I do not believe I am exaggerating by confirming that M. Planté is one of the greatest inventors of our time."

But inventions, without knowing the side effects, can take their toll on their inventor (see Ritter entry). Gaston Planté was working on terrestrial magnetism when in April 1889 a weakening of his sight, caused by the brilliant discharges of his batteries of accumulators, made him fear blindness. So he began to learn Braille. Sadly, on May 21, a serious congestion struck him down in his garden at Bellevue sous Meudon, and ten minutes later he died. He was only 55 years old.

He had bequeathed his property of Bellevue to the Humanitarian Society of the Friends of Science to be converted into a retirement home for impoverished scientists and set up a biennial monetary prize with the Academy of Sciences to be awarded to the author of a discovery in electricity.

His brother Francis Planté, the famous pianist, lived on to 1934, giving concert recitals until the age of 91. The year before, a developed version of his brother's rheostat machine, a Marx pulse generator assembled at the Ampère Laboratory in Ivry, had supplied shock sparks whose tension reached a then staggering 3 million volts. Its purpose: to simulate the effects of lightning during high voltage and aviation equipment testing.

From the 1950s, a line of deserving electrochemists have received the Prix Gaston Planté, including Henri-Georges André (see André entry). In 1989, on the centenary of his death, the Bulgarian Academy of Sciences took over the Gaston Planté Medal, which is awarded every few years to scientists who have made significant contributions to the development of lead-acid battery technology. The first recipient was Dr. Ernst Voss, Varta Batterie AG, Germany (see Voss entry).

Sources: From an article by the author, published in *Batteries International*, Summer 2007, based on information supplied by Musée EDF Electropolis, Mulhouse, France.

• •

Prengaman, R. David
(1943–)
Alloys for battery grids

Raymond David Prengaman was born in 1943 in Pittsburgh, Pennsylvania. While his father was employed as a machinist for Westinghouse, his grandfather and 5 of his father's brothers also worked there as machinists.

Prengaman recalls: "None of my father's brothers or sisters graduated from college. My father was always interested in math and science and taught himself calculus. I was the oldest of 6 children and have worked all my life to earn enough money. I had a newspaper round, picked berries in the summer to sell in the grocery stores, and worked as a caddy at the local country club. I attended Catholic school where the nuns gave me a wonderful education. My father would take several children to the Carnegie Museum whenever the weather was rainy or cold. After many visits I knew that I wanted to do something in science perhaps in Medicine or engineering."

When he was 14 years old, David Prengaman was selected to attend the Joe Berg science seminars. These involved visits to many company facilities and laboratories in the Pittsburgh area to see scientists or engineers at work. The first factory that they visited was Pittsburgh Steel Company's metallurgical laboratory. At that time the various phases in steel were being correlated with the properties of the steel. When it was David's turn to look into the microscope at the various

R. David Prengaman (RSR Technologies).

steel samples, "It was as though I had looked at them all my life. I knew then that I wanted to be a metallurgical engineer."

He attended the Carnegie Institute of Technology. Its closeness to the family home enabled him to commute to the institute each day, as his father did not have enough money to enable him to live on campus. The research that gained him his B.S. in 1965 was aimed at segregation in alloys and the structures generated during the solidification.

Having loved golf since his childhood, David now played for the Carnegie Institute's golf team. "As University golf team members, we were permitted to miss some classes due to practice or travel for matches with other universities. Most of these matches were on Thursday afternoons when I had a metallography laboratory. The professor was angry that I kept missing his classes, but gave me the opportunity to make up the classes at night. To frustrate me he gave me the most difficult samples to polish and etch including copper and steel with lead in the structure as well as lead and lead tin solder samples. There could be no scratches on the samples or lead pulled out of the samples." This proved the best training, as the young graduate developed polishing and etching techniques that he would take with him through his career in lead that were extremely difficult for others to duplicate.

In 1967, Prengaman obtained his PhD in metallurgy and materials science. His research was into the development of rolling textures in high Cr high Ni stainless steels and the properties and corrosion resistance of these materials. The work was aimed at Ford Motor Company, as they were very interested in stainless steel car bodies, since corrosion of the vehicles was a very serious problem at the time.

Prengaman: "I was going to work for Ford when I graduated with my Master's degree. I passed the PhD. qualifying examination, but had no money and could not live on the Fellowship. The director of research for St. Joe Lead Company, Carl Long convinced me that if I could repeat the things that I was doing with the stainless steels in lead alloys, I would be only one of a kind as opposed to the many researchers at Ford. I accepted the challenge."

Prengaman's work at St. Joe involved the development of rolled lead calcium tin alloys. The rolling process developed structures and rolling textures which made the material very resistant to corrosion. Delco was interested in the new material because they had such severe cracking in their cast lead antimony alloys that they were scrapping as many as ⅓ of their battery grids. The new rolled expanded metal material did not crack and grids could be produced at 10 times the speed. One of the benefits of the change in grid material was the fact that it did not contain antimony, which was not transferred to the negative plate to cause gassing, thus resulting in maintenance-free batteries.

Apart from golf as his main relaxation, David also played in an industrial basketball league against other companies in the area. He also bowled, hunted, and fished.

In 1968, David was introduced to Miss Marilyn Miller by the department secretary, who said that she had the perfect young lady for him. Although resisting for three years, he finally told the secretary that he would ask Marilyn out to dinner, she would hate him, then the secretary could stop bothering him.

"The day before the dinner, I was playing in the basketball league and was hit in the face, breaking my glasses and cutting my face. I had 18 stitches around my eye which was very swollen and had to wear my laboratory safety glasses with sideshields to our first date."

Despite this, they married. They have two children, a son who is a photographer who sells his prints to galleries and calendars, and a daughter who is a chemical engineer and patent attorney.

In 1973, Prengaman moved to Atlanta to join Evans Metal. While he was there, the chief engineer from Delco visited Atlanta to meet with him and the owner of Taracorp. They made a proposal that they would build a lead rolling plant which would supply all 5 Delco factories with strip if Prengaman would operate the plant. He refused because at that time all the metal for the rolled grids came from primary lead and the lead calcium alloy-rolled expanded metal grids would make obsolete the lead antimony alloys which the smelter produced.

Prengaman: "When they turned down the offer from Delco, I was ready to look for another position. Within a week I saw an ad in a trade magazine that RSR, a major battery-recycling company, was looking for a chief engineer. Replying to the ad, I indicated that I was not interested in the Chief engineer's position, but I thought that RSR would be interested in talking to me."

Prengaman was hired to start a R&D group and provide technical assistance to the battery customers. He spent most of the first year working with Delco to build their new rolling and expanding battery grid production lines. The main problem of the lead recycling process at that time was the production of pure lead which could be utilized as an active material in the battery. The impurities were too high and the refining as well as the analytical techniques to remove and analyze the impurities in the lead were not developed.

So Prengaman and his resourceful colleagues set about developing new refining practices to remove the major gassing elements in pure lead, thereby making it suitable for battery oxide. In addition with only AA instruments available at the time, they developed new techniques to analyze these elements in the lead at very low levels. Necessity is the mother of invention. To extract the newly solidified lead strip from the aluminum mold, they adapted the wringer part of an old washing machine because it had rubber rolls which could grip the lead and pull it out of the mold continuously. They called the original casting machine Maytag 1 after the most famous washing machine in the 1960s in the U.S.

By 1975, The RSR team had developed and introduced the first low-antimony maintenance-free battery grid alloy, which could be cast on conventional grid casting equipment without cracking. It is called R275. In the late 1970s, they set up a pilot plant to recycle the active materials in the battery by leaching and electrowinning the lead. This produced pure lead, but improvements made to the smelting process at RSR recycling plants made the process economical.

In the early 1980s the Environmental Protection Agency declared that the slag from the battery recycling was a hazardous waste. So Prengaman et al. developed an improved recycling process using an electric furnace to clean the slag and produce a non-hazardous slag.

By the mid 1980s, Prengaman was part of a team which looked for acquisitions in Europe, primarily battery recycling factories. They would acquire factories in the UK, France, Italy, Germany, Austria, South Africa, and Saudi Arabia in the mid and late 1990s. Prengaman worked to make these factories profitable and environmentally ahead of the regulations.

During the same period, Prengaman went on to develop rolled lead anodes for copper and zinc electrowinning. The anodes were based on the rolled lead calcium tin alloys which he had developed for battery grids. These anodes have become the dominant anodes for copper mines worldwide. About 95 percent of the mines use these anodes for recovery of copper in low-cost operations by RSR and the affiliated companies of the Ecobat group which produce anodes.

In 1992 RSR and Metallgellschaft in Germany formed a group of lead companies which joined together to form the Advanced Lead Acid Battery Consortium. Prengaman: "The Advanced Battery consortium for the California initiative of 2% Electric Vehicles in 5 years did not include lead acid Batteries. I agreed to become the technical director of the consortium and RSR allowed me the time to spend to assure the success of the group."

In the mid–1990s the vehicle profiles changed, with the air now flowing over the vehicle instead of through the front grille. This caused the engine compartment to become very hot and battery life to become much shorter. In 1999 Prengaman developed an alloy called 007, which had silver added to a lead-calcium-tin alloy. The alloy was called 007 because the active material would "Bond" to this grid, compared to other alloys with silver, which had to be specially treated to accept the paste.

Recently, Prengman has developed a new alloy for both Teck Cominco Cast or punched grids as well as rolled-punched grids which will perform very well at elevated temperatures. It is called 009. In addition he has developed a very low-impurity secondary lead which can be substituted for primary lead for use in low water loss wet batteries or VRLA batteries. It is called Supersoft Ultra.

From 1996 to 2014, Prengaman was president of RSR Technologies, Inc., providing research and development services to RSR Corporation, the European and South African Eco-Bat Group, and their customers for battery recycling. RSR Tech has scanned into RSR Tech servers his extensive library on lead and batteries to make these available to Ecobat and RSR Tech researchers and technical personnel.

Alongside his innovative work at RSR, David has chaired a number of committees: the North Texas Chapter of the American Society for Metals; Pb-Zn-Antimony and their Alloys subcommittee of American Society for Testing and Materials; and the Lead-Zinc-Tin Committee of 1994, "Wrought lead-calcium-tin alloys for tubular lead/acid battery grids...."

He has published extensively on the above subjects and has served in various positions in TMS, the Electrochemical Society, Battery Council International, and American Society for Testing and Materials. He was technical chairman of the Advanced Lead Acid Battery Consortium (ALABC), a consortium of virtually all the battery producers and lead producers throughout the world to build improved lead-acid batteries for electric vehicles.

Prengaman has received a galaxy of awards: the Hoffman Memorial Prize; the Distinguished Service Award from the American Society for Metals; the Alpha/Beta Society Award from the battery industry for his work on premature capacity loss in batteries; the Gaston Planté medal; and the International Lead Award.

He has served on the EPD Council as well as its membership and long-range planning committees. He also served as co-editor of the Lead-Zinc '90 proceedings volume.

According to John Devitt, who has known him for many years, "Dave Prengaman is undoubtedly the world's expert on lead metallurgy, plus many other metals. And he is uniquely accessible to all battery folk. He is the pioneer on many of our best alloys, so essential to a really good battery. He never fails to give a good and complete answer."

In the course of this work, Prengaman has published more than 90 technical papers and been granted 15 patents. He has presented seminars in USA, Europe, Asia, South America and Eastern Europe on processes to produce improved lead-acid batteries.

David has continued his love of golf. In 2003, he moved to a house on the Rolling Hills Golf Club course in Arlington, Texas, on which he plays as frequently as possible. "My main problem is that I am afflicted with a condition called Fuch's Distrophy which has slowly robbed me of my sight. For the last five years I have not seen where the golf ball has gone when I hit it. Luckily my colleagues and competitors all watch the golf ball for me when I hit it."

"The Lead Pope's" current challenge is to develop a lead-acid battery which is easy to produce on conventional battery-making equipment, but will also compete with Ni metal hydride and Li-ion batteries for use in HEVs as part of the ALABC programs.

Prengaman: "I think that my most successful invention was the development of the rolled lead calcium tin alloys for positive grids of lead acid batteries. The optimum alloy for positive grids was also the alloy of choice for copper electrowinning anodes. This technology is used throughout the world today to produce positive grids. The same alloy and rolling technique is also used in the new rolled punched battery grids used to reduce grid weight and extend battery life. The next most important was the development of a method to add calcium and aluminum to lead."

••

Rand, David Anthony James
(1942–)
Co-inventor of the UltraBattery™

David Anthony James Rand was born on October 26, 1942, in Haslemere, Surrey, England. He attended Purbrook Infant School in Hampshire (1947–48), Wimborne Junior School in Portsmouth (1949–50) and, finally, the Portsmouth Grammar School (1951–61). On his 11th birthday, his uncle gave him a chemistry set to conduct experiments at home, and Rand succeeded in making his own fireworks. His growing interest in the world of atoms and molecules was boosted by the fact that Portsmouth Grammar's laboratories were very well equipped and there were school outings to scientific meetings. Years later, David was to declare: "My nascent ambition to become a research scientist was strengthened further after listening to a mesmerizing account of the wonders of inorganic chemistry in a youth lecture given by Professor Ronald Nyholm." Interestingly, Nyholm was an Australian—were geographical forces also shaping Rand's destiny?

In October 1961, David was awarded an Open Exhibition by Trinity Hall, a college of the University of Cambridge. He enrolled for the Natural Sciences Tripos. Part I of this course required students to take three experimental subjects. In his second year, therefore, in addition to continuing with chemistry and physics, he elected to study biochemistry. In Part II, however, he abandoned his aspiration of becoming a molecular biologist and decided to major in organic chemistry. It was his intention to carry out postgraduate research into new compounds and materials that would be of benefit to society.

In 1964, David joined the Unilever Research Laboratorium at Vlaardingen in the

Netherlands to undertake a six-week "work experience" project. The objective was to elucidate the mechanism of fat bloom formation in dark chocolate, a process that gives the product an unappetizing appearance. While engaged in this study, entirely unexpectedly, he received an invitation from Dr. J.N. Agar to return to Cambridge and become an electrochemist! In addition, Trinity Hall offered him a research scholarship. His task was to unravel the complex behavior of porous gas-diffusion electrodes in fuel cells, with a view to enhancing their performance. Valuable guidance and encouragement were freely given to Rand not only by Agar himself but also by the latter's close friend, Tom Bacon, who had built his ground-breaking alkaline fuel cell in a nearby facility. And so the die was cast—Rand, having obtained his PhD, was to pursue a career in electrochemical science.

In 1969, Rand and his wife Gwen moved to Melbourne, Australia, where he joined the prestigious electrochemistry team at the Division of Mineral Chemistry, part of the Commonwealth Scientific and Industrial Research Organisation (CSIRO). His initial mission was to develop better electrocatalysts for direct methanol fuel cells. There followed successive research campaigns into novel electrochemical sensors to enhance the beneficiation of mineral sulfide ores, advanced secondary batteries, and hydrogen energy systems.

In 1977, David established the CSIRO's Battery Research Group. In the intervening years, the Group emerged as a world leader in lead-acid battery research. It also expanded the experimental program to encompass alternative batteries and supercapacitors, together with their integration into hybrid energy storage–delivery systems for stationary, mobile and portable applications.

David's early scientific achievements were based on his development and application of methods that allowed the systematic study of the physicochemical properties of lead-acid battery constituents and their influence on battery performance. The work conducted under his direction provided new knowledge about the chemistry of battery constituents during manufacture and service. This, in turn, enabled optimization of processing, control of product quality, increased productivity and diagnosis of manufacturing problems, as well as the explosion of much industry folklore that could inhibit advances in practice. The results have been applied by industry both in Australia and in many other countries.[52]

In 1993, David initiated and assumed the chairmanship of the World Study Group into Premature Capacity Loss of Lead-Acid Batteries. The Group was set up by the Advanced Lead-Acid Battery Consortium (ALABC) to share knowledge, analyze data, reach a universal understanding and seek solutions to the serious limitation to battery performance that was prevalent when using lead-calcium alloys for the grids in valve-regulated ("maintenance-free") cells. A notable contribution towards understanding the phenomenon was made by Rand and his colleagues via the formulation of fast-charging algorithms and the subsequent discovery of the advantageous effect of pulsed-current charging on extending the cycle-life of batteries with grids made from low-antimonial lead or lead-calcium alloys.[53] Between July and December 1994, Rand served as acting manager of the ALABC. The efforts of the "PCL Group" proved successful and caused Patrick Moseley, Rand's successor at ALABC, to declare, "PCL had been defeated!" Accordingly, the valve-regulated lead-acid battery became a reliable and dominant technology in many energy-storage applications.

Two other important commercial outcomes have resulted from the research of Rand

and his colleagues, namely: the Sun-GEL battery for operation in solar-based, remote-area power-supply (RAPS) duties, and the UltraBattery® for hybrid electric vehicles.

SunGEL batteries are designed specifically for solar applications and employ innovative, long-life plates developed by CSIRO. This advance evolved from the field experience that David gained in formulating control methodology to improve the efficiency and endurance of the batteries that were operating in the RAPS facility on Coconut Island (now known as Poruma Island) in the Torres Strait. SunGEL batteries, manufactured by Battery Energy in Sydney, are used widely in remote rural electrification projects and telecommunication systems through-out Australia, as well as overseas in

David Rand of CSIRO, Melbourne, Australia (Rand Collection).

many similar installations. For instance, the battery was the technology of choice for a major solar facility built in the Amazon Basin of Peru. Given CSIRO's international recognition as a center of excellence in RAPS battery technology, the World Health Organization commissioned Rand to set the performance specifications for the batteries required by the solar-powered refrigerators that are employed in the global "cold chain" for the storage and transport of vaccines in a potent state.

Rand and Lan Lam are patentees of the CSIRO UltraBattery®, which is the world's first lead-based hybrid battery–supercapacitor power source for hybrid electric vehicles (HEVs) (L.T. Lam, N.P. Haigh, C.G. Phyland, D.A.J. Rand: High performance energy storage devices, Publication Number WO/2005/027255, International Application Number PCT/AU2004/001262, March 24, 2005).

The design harnesses the best of both technologies to produce a battery that can provide/accept high-rate discharge/charge with a long, low-cost life. A road test of a Honda Insight medium-hybrid, in which the original nickel–metal-hydride (Ni–MH) battery had been replaced by an UltraBattery® of the same voltage (144 V), was continued for 100,000 miles at the Millbrook Proving Ground in the UK. At the end of the test, the battery was still fully functional. In a similar project, a Honda Civic fitted an UltraBattery® pack ran for 150,000 miles on roads in Phoenix, Arizona. During both trials, the cells remained fully balanced without the intervention of any external equalization. Self-balancing of the UltraBattery® has also been observed in stationary energy-storage applications. The technology is under commercial development by Furukawa Battery Co. (Japan), Ltd. (see Furukawa entry), East Penn Manufacturing (USA), and Ecoult (Australia).

In 1987, David formulated the battery regulations for the World Solar Challenge.[54] This is the world's premier race for solar-powered vehicles and is conducted in Australia along the Stuart Highway from Darwin in the north to Adelaide some 3000 km to the south. The event provides an effective means whereby both local and international interests, from all walks of life, can meet to explore and discuss ways to achieve global energy sustainability, particularly in the transportation sector. For instance, it is said that the World Solar Challenge has presented automobile manufacturers—Ford, General Motors, Honda, Nissan, Mitsubishi and Toyota have all competed—with a valuable "live laboratory" for the development of both electric and hybrid electric cars. Rand has served as the chief battery scientist for all thirteen World Solar Challenge events held to date.

David was appointed as an editor of the *Journal of Power Sources* in 1983. He worked closely with Derek Collins, the founding editor, in helping to establish the high editorial standards of the journal at an early stage, and build its reputation. After 30 years of service—mostly as the Asia-Pacific Regional Editor—Rand stepped down from his position in 2014 to join the International Advisory Board.

In 2003, David was redeployed by CSIRO to assist with the coordination and advancement of Australian efforts in the development of hydrogen as the key vector for a sustainable energy society. He was the principal author of a government report on "Australian Hydrogen Activity." This work examined the various technologies for hydrogen generation, distribution, storage and utilization in the total chain required for the implementation of a "hydrogen economy" and, against this backdrop, Australian effort in each core area was evaluated. Internationally, he represented Australia at meetings of the International Partnership for the Hydrogen Economy (IPHE). He also served as the vice-chairman of the 17th World Hydrogen Energy Conference and, together with Dr. Andrew Dicks, was the prime mover in the establishment of the Australian Association for Hydrogen Energy and became its first deputy-president.

David Rand retired from full-time employment in December 2008. As a CSIRO honorary research fellow, however, he strives to continue his energetic participation in the organization of scientific meetings, as well as to remain a persuasive advocate for the advancement of electrochemical power sources as key technology for a sustainable society.

Rand's work has been published in the form of 171 research papers, 189 technical reports, and seven patents. He has also edited 39 volumes on battery and fuel cell topics.

The research conducted by David Rand has been recognized both nationally and internationally by the following awards: the Faraday Medal of the Electrochemistry Group of the Royal Society of Chemistry, UK (1991); elected a fellow of the Australian Academy of Technological Sciences and Engineering, (1998); the UNESCO Gaston Planté Medal, presented by the Bulgarian Academy of Sciences (1996); the CSIRO Chairman's Medal (2000); Doctor of Science, University of Cambridge (2000); the Australian Centenary Medal (2003); the R.H. Stokes Medal of the Royal Australian Chemical Institute (2006); the International Energy Agency Hydrogen Implementing Agreement L'Ange Hia Award (2008); and the CSIRO Medal for Research Achievement (2008). Rand was awarded a Member of the Order of Australia medal in 2012 for his service to science and technological developments in the area of energy storage, particularly rechargeable batteries.

Source: Information supplied to the author by David Rand, early 2015.

Notes

52. D. A. J. Rand, "A journey on the electrochemical road to sustainability," *Journal of Solid State Electrochemistry* (2011) 15: 1579–1622.

53. L.T. Lam, H. Ozgun, O.V. Lim, J.A. Hamilton, L.H. Vu, D.G. Vella, D.A.J. Rand, "Pulsed-current charging of lead-acid batteries—a possible means for overcoming premature capacity loss?," *Journal of Power Sources* (1995) 53: 215-228.

54. D.A.J. Rand, "Solar Cars: Batteries" in: J Garche, C.K. Dyer, P.T. Moseley, Z. Ogumi, D.A.J. Rand, B. Scrosati (eds.), *Encyclopedia of Electrochemical Power Sources*, vol. 1 (Amsterdam: Elsevier, 2009), pp. 276–292.

Renard, Charles
(1847–1905)
Pioneer flow battery

August 9, 1884. A cigar-shaped balloon graced the skies of Paris, hub of 19th-century ballooning experiments, and also the international center of battery development. Although not a first in the history of ballooning, or even that for electrically powered ballooning—the Tissandier brothers had achieved the world's first battery-powered airship flight the previous October—it was the first time a new type of battery took to the skies.

The battery in question was what is now called a flow battery—electrical energy was stored by pumping chlorine from one chamber to another containing zinc, and so generating power to a motor. Its creator was one Charles Renard. His was an extraordinary concept at a time when even the rudiments of electrochemical activity were unformulated.

Louis-Marie-Joseph-Charles Clément Charles Renard was born in Damblain in the Vosges regions of France in November 1847. A clever child, he won a scholarship that eventually led him to graduate with honors from one of the leading polytechnics (France's so-called *"grandes écoles,"* or top universities).

He was only 23 when the Franco-Prussian War broke out in 1870. Given command of a section of the 15th Army Corps on the Loire, he took part in the battles of Artenay, Cercottes and Orléans, and was awarded the Cross of the *Légion d'honneur* for his bravery in leading a counter-defense against the Prussians.

Extraordinarily, during the same period, this brilliant young engineer presented a way to adjust numerical values used in the metrical system for mechanical construction. The interval from one to 10 was divided into five, 10, 20 and 40. The Renard series helped the French army to reduce the number of different balloon ropes kept in its inventory from 425 to 17! (In 1952, the Renard series was adopted in the ISO 3 norm.)

Charles Renard (Musée EDF Electropolis, Mulhouse).

Three years later, and now a lieutenant, Renard of the 3rd Regiment of Engineers started working on flying machines, with what he called a "directional parachute" or *Aéride*. The idea was for a 10-winged glider, without pilot and weighing just 7.5 kg (16 lbs.) to be launched from a balloon to transport messages. It was tested with success in 1873 close to Arras, from one of the towers of the Mont Saint-Eloi abbey.

In 1877, Renard, assisted by captain La Haye, founded the Central Establishment of Military Aérostation in the park of the old Château de Chalais at Meudon outside Paris. First, he modernized the existing equipment. This included the building of a powerful, continuous-circulation hydrogen generator, designed by Charles Renard and built under the supervision of his brother Paul.

At this point enter Arthur Constantin Krebs. Three years younger than Renard, his senior officer, Krebs had also fought against Prussia. Transferred to the workshops of the Chalais-Meudon Aérostation, the innovative Krebs worked for the Renards and de la Haye, resulting in a direct circulation steam generator, called the Renhaye.

Among Krebs's contributions was the development of the engine which would power the airship and the building of an electric boat, the *Ampère*, to measure the resistance of airship models. Early electric motors—in the days before the invention of the internal combustion engine—were the only mechanical form of propulsion available to balloonists.

At the end of 1881 Renard had begun to research the electric generator indispensable for his project. His previous experiments showed he needed to create a generator capable of giving 10hp for two hours, and weighing less than 480 kg. (1,060 lbs.).

Working on the new theory of chemical affinity, Renard retained chlorine and bromine as his anodic couples. For the cathode: magnesium, aluminum, calcium and zinc. After abandoning bromine for safety reasons, and magnesium, aluminum and calcium as being too expensive, the chlorine-zinc couple remained.

The positive electrode retained was a silver-plated leaf of a thickness of one-tenth of a millimeter, the negative being a rod of pure zinc. After a great deal of experimentation he chose as his electrolyte a mix of hydrochloric acid at 11° Baumé and chromic anhydride, likely to release the chlorine.

To avoid excessive overheating during the discharge, a tubular form was created, the container serving as a thermal radiator.

At the start of 1883, the construction of the definitive battery began. It had a specific capacity of 44 kg. (971 lb.) per horsepower. Krebs built the electric motor, a rotor of two crowns of eight electromagnets, supplied on average by eight brushes. The whole weighed 88 kg. (1,941 lb.) for 8.5hp. On the side of the airship gondola, a steering wheel controlled the power of the batteries by pushing the zinc cathodes in and out of the batteries.

And so in 1884 the balloon airship *La France* took to the air at Meudon. It then flew above a farm at Villacoublay, then made a controlled return to Meudon—the world's first closed circuit flight. The flight lasted 23 minutes for a circuit of 8 km (5 miles), giving "*le dirigéable*" (directable) *La France* an impressive speed of 19.8 km/h (12.5 mph).

The following year, Renard, now a colonel, persuaded the French finance minister to invest the then staggering sum of 200,000 francs in the project, including the erection of a hangar necessary for the construction and sheltering of balloons and airships. This would become the cradle and home for *La France*.

La France demonstrated that controlled flight was possible if the airship had a sufficiently powerful lightweight motor. In 1889 it was proudly put on show at the military pavilion in the Place des Invalides, Paris, during the Universal Exhibition that year.

But Renard also realized that lighter-than-air, battery-powered electric-engined dirigibles had their limitations. And for the last 20 years of his life he moved away from electrical research and spent his time creating more efficient engines. In 1902, working with the engineer Léon Levavasseur, he developed a gasoline-fueled aero engine—a revolutionary V8 capable of 80hp.

Renard's last years were not happy ones. He had financial difficulties and grew tired of fighting the inertia within an Army whose enthusiasm for aeronautics was lackluster. He was also a bachelor and his only relaxation was to visit his brother Paul's family and play and compose on the piano.

Then his health deteriorated. Early in 1905 he suffered a bout of flu which lowered his resistance. On April 13, he was found dead in the office of his chalet in the park. He was 58. Although the official diagnosis was a heart attack, rumors circulated—and still persist to this day—that while depressed, Renard had committed suicide. They were never substantiated.

Sources: From an article by the author, published in *Batteries International*, Summer 2007, partly based on information supplied by Musée EDF Electropolis, Mulhouse, France.

●●

Ritter, Johann Wilhelm
(1776–1810)
Extending the Voltaic pile

Johann Wilhelm Ritter was born December 16, 1776, in the little village of Samitz (Zamienice) near Haynau (Chojnów) in Silesia. He was the son of Johann Wilhelm Ritter, a Protestant pastor, and Juliana Friderica, née Decovius. After attending Latin school until the age of fourteen, he was sent to Liegnitz (Legnica) to serve as an apprentice. During the next five years, while learning and practicing the trade, he found ample opportunity to pursue his own studies from chemical texts and independent experiments, often to the neglect of his professional assignments. His yearning for more intellectual stimulation and independence was satisfied in 1795 by a modest inheritance. Thus, at the age of nineteen, Ritter entered the University of Jena in April 1796, to study medicine. Encouraged by Alexander von Humboldt, he soon began independent galvanism studies.

During the period 1797–1804, Ritter engaged in empirical research and writing, mainly on electrochemistry and electrophysiology. In these years he attained recognition and respect throughout Europe. In 1801 the Duke of Gotha and Altenburg, Ernst II, appointed him to his court in Gotha, where Ritter lived in early 1802.

In 1800, shortly after the invention of the voltaic pile, William Nicholson and Anthony Carlisle had discovered that water could be decomposed by electricity. Only a month afterward, Ritter also discovered the same effect, independently. Besides that, he collected and measured the amounts of hydrogen and oxygen produced in the reaction. He also discovered the process of electroplating. In 1802 he built the first electrochemical cell, with 50 copper discs separated by cardboard disks moistened by a salt solution.

Ritter found that his new combination worked as well as the Volta pile to charge Leyden jars, and continued to function equally well for six days. Volta's pile worked only about 15 to 20 minutes before exhausting. Ritter again did not publish his work on the dry pile because he stated that his two months of very concentrated research would take him two years to write.

During the winter semester of 1803–1804, he lectured on galvanism at the University of Jena. A disagreement, however, with university officials about the nature of his future appointment disrupted further association with that institution. Subsequently Ritter sought a new position, and in November 1804 he was called to serve as a full member of the Bavarian Academy of Sciences in Munich. He moved to the new location the following spring with his young wife Johanna and their daughter; they had three more children in Munich.

Ritter decided that the best way to test his theory was on his own physical body; by applying the poles of a voltaic pile to his own hands, eyes, ears, nose and tongue. Ritter applied current to his tongue, where it produced an acidic flavor. Shoving the wires up his nose made him sneeze. Touching them to his eyeballs caused strange colors to swim in his vision. Ritter also applied the current to his genitals.

He continued to push his limits, increasing the current to dangerous levels, forcing himself to endure longer periods of time, and using opium to dull the pain. As a result, his health suffered. Repeated electrocution caused his eyes to grow infected. He endured frequent headaches, muscle spasms, numbness, and stomach cramps. His lungs filled with mucus. He temporarily lost much of the sensation in his tongue. Dizzy spells overcame him, causing him to collapse. A feeling of crushing fatigue, sometimes lasting for weeks, often made it difficult for him to get out of bed. At one time, the current paralyzed his arm for a week. And yet he continued on, boasting, "I have not shrunk from thoroughly assuring myself of the invariability of their results through frequent repetition."

Some of Ritter's researches were acknowledged as important scientific contributions, but he also claimed the discovery of many phenomena that were not confirmed by other researchers. For instance: he reported that the Earth had electric poles that could be detected by the motion of a bimetallic needle; and he claimed that he could produce the electrolysis of water using a series of magnets, instead of Volta's piles.

Ritter had no regular income and never became a university professor. He was unable to provide the needs of his family. Plagued by financial difficulties and suffering from weak health, perhaps aggravated by the galvanic self-tests he had carried out on his own body, he died from pulmonary failure on January 23, 1810, in Munich. He was only 33 years old.

Ruben, Samuel
(1900–1988)
Duracell genius

During the dark days of World War II, the U.S. Army in both North Africa and the Pacific were encountering an alarming problem over the unreliability of the small zinc-carbon batteries which powered their walkie-talkies, mine detectors and other similar equipment. The problem was solved with remarkable swiftness by a shy but brilliant inventor in his small laboratory just outside New York. In later years, a modified and improved version of this battery would become world-famous as the Duracell. The name of the inventor was Samuel Ruben.

Ruben was born July 14, 1900, in Harrison, New Jersey. His father, Louis Ruben, originally a sausage maker and butcher from Kiev, in Ukraine, had emigrated to the USA, settling in his port of entry, Baltimore. Moving to New York City, he met and married Pauline Bauer, who had emigrated from Alsace-Lorraine, France.

Samuel had an older sister, Estelle, and a younger brother, Julius. They were educated in New York City public schools. He started experimenting with electricity and chemistry at the age of 11, became

The first Duracell (courtesy Laurens Ruben).

a licensed ham radio operator and built radio sets with spare parts. He worked to support his family after graduating from high school. He taught himself introductory and advanced chemistry and physics from books in the New York City Public Library.

Though he attended college briefly, he withdrew after a short period of time, as the stress was making him physically ill. He then attended an experimental high school in New York City and completed only a handful of college night classes.

Throughout his life, one of Ruben's great loves was going to concerts and to opera in downtown New York. According to his son Laurens: "When he was young and poor, he was allowed in free to attend the operas by serving as a 'clack,' a person who starts the clapping at appropriate times. Apparently, a number of folks were scattered throughout the 'house' for that purpose. He once told me that he also carried a spear in the march in *Aïda*. To my knowledge, he did not himself sing."

From 1917 to 1921, Ruben worked as a researcher for the Electrochemical Products Company, a Brooklyn start-up that attempted to extract atmospheric nitrogen for wartime munitions via high-frequency electrical discharges. The process never worked and the company floundered, but Ruben earned the respect of project consultant Bergen Davis, a physics professor at Columbia University. Impressed by the young man, Davis allowed him to sit in on colloquia and formal courses at Columbia and to borrow books from his personal library. He also tutored him in the evening and made sure that he did his assignments.

In 1922, Davis persuaded Electrochemical's main investor, patent attorney Malcolm Clephane, to finance a private laboratory for Ruben in lower Manhattan using the equipment from the failed nitrogen project. Clephane would pay Ruben a small stipend and cover all expenses in exchange for fifty percent of any future royalties. For the first three years, Ruben did everything in the laboratory himself—swept the floors, cleaned the beakers, blew the glass. As the business progressed he hired two helpers: Fred D. Williams, Jr., an electrical engineer, and William Sauerbrey, a technician.

"We purposefully keep it small," Ruben once explained. "It's less complicated that way."

In 1924 Ruben married Rena Sylvia Koch of French Alsace origins, whose father had been hired by the Wine Board of California to introduce their wines into New York City restaurants.

Enter Philip Rogers Mallory, whose company since 1916 had supplied tungsten wire filaments to manufacturers of incandescent lamps. In 1924, Ruben sent one of his assistants to Mallory's New Jersey plant to purchase some tungsten wire for an experiment. In this way, Mallory learned of Ruben's solid-state rectifier, a device that converted regular household electric current for use in radios. Before this, radios had been powered by lead-acid storage batteries, which frequently spilled over and ruined carpets and furniture.

Mallory obtained an exclusive license, and incorporated it into a new battery charger. From now on the inventive genius of the one would be coupled to the other's manufacturing muscle. Their partnership would last until 1975 with Mallory's death.

The most important connection between Mallory and Ruben Laboratories was Leon Robbin. Robbin was Ruben's cousin, and after he finished Georgetown Law School in 1922, Ruben employed him part-time as his patent attorney and sales agent. In 1930, Philip Mallory arranged for Robbin to spend his spare time working in Mallory's New York business office; he became a full-time Mallory employee in 1933 and eventually held several high-ranking posts.

In 1930 Ruben Laboratories moved north to New Rochelle, New York, remaining there for the next half century. New Rochelle also became the Ruben family home.

Among the first inventions to emerge from the New Rochelle laboratory was the dry electrolytic capacitor, a small device that stored electricity, making it possible to reduce radically the cost and size of radios. Because early vacuum tubes for radios took so long to heat up, in 1936 Ruben came up with the "7-second vacuum tube" used for tuning, i.e., detecting the radio signal at a certain frequency, or amplifying the detected signal. Following the grid bias cell, Ruben invented a battery which provided constant voltage to the tube to control the flow of electrons. He licensed these to the Arcturus Radio Tube Company and subsequently visited their Harrison, New Jersey, lab "once a week as a consultant at a high fee" for the next two years.

During World War II, the Army Signal Corps turned to the National Inventors Council to help them solve operational problems with unsealed zinc-carbon Leclanché batteries. Because of the corrosive nature of these batteries, operators found that 80 percent of them had spontaneously discharged during storage.

In July 1941, Thomas R. Taylor, staff director of the Department of Commerce's National Inventors Council, asked Ruben for his assistance. Within weeks, Ruben sent prototypes of his "tropical" battery, a small-scaled mercury cell, to the U.S. Army's Signal Corps Laboratories in Fort Monmouth, New Jersey.

Initial tests confirmed that Ruben's mercury button cell in its airtight casing resisted ambient atmospheric effects and had four to five times the capacity of standard zinc-carbon cells. In addition, the new cell had a "flat" discharge profile with a constant output of 1.34 volts. Though tiny and long-lasting, a single cell by itself could not provide enough voltage to power an Army radio. However, by combining seventy-two cells in series, the Signal Corps produced a battery pack powerful enough for use in its mobile communications equipment, including flashlights, mine detectors, and handie-talkies (today's walkie-talkies).

On Ruben's recommendation, in 1943 P.R. Mallory and Co. were given the contract to mass-produce it. Initially, Mallory struggled with material and manpower shortages, and its hastily prepared manufacturing techniques resulted in thousands of failed cells. In an effort to increase production, the Signal Corps arranged for Mallory to sub-license the mercury battery to other U.S. and Allied manufacturers, including Ray-O-Vac, Sprague, Magnavox, and British Eveready.

In this way, peak wartime production was able to reach a million mercury cells a day, and the batteries were successfully used in the harsh climates of wartime theatres like North Africa and the South Pacific.

Given its strategic importance, the mercury cell received a confidential classification from the Patent Office and Samuel Ruben was not allowed to apply for a patent (U.S. 2482514 A) until July 10, 1945, just before the end of the war. Though he was

Sam Ruben in the lab (courtesy Laurens Ruben).

owed approximately $2 million per year in royalties from the Signal Corps, Ruben felt that "it would be unconscionable to receive such large payments for military requirements during wartime." He voluntarily turned over all his patents to the government and canceled his royalty arrangements with his licensees, accepting instead a flat payment of $150,000 per year for the use of his battery and other speculative inventions during the war.

Among those other inventions were low-temperature batteries for operation at 40 to -60° F.

Following the Armistice, perhaps the most tangible sign of Mallory's long-term commitment to Ruben was the decision to relocate its battery operations from Indianapolis to Tarrytown, New York, only 20 miles from Ruben Laboratories in New Rochelle. In his memoirs, Philip Mallory confirmed that this May 1946 move was undertaken explicitly to be "close to the inventor's laboratory."

During the next six years, Ruben and Mallory worked on the cell's design and consistency, including such improvements as a copper outer casing. Though they were used in various applications, the batteries were not listed in Mallory's catalogue until May 1952, a date close to Bell Laboratories' introduction of the transistor.

Suddenly Mallory found itself squarely in the midst of a revolution in electronics. Old, clunky products were soon being miniaturized as transistors and new batteries were incorporated into their design. New consumer applications quickly emerged such as pocket-sized hearing aids in 1952.

The Ruben/Mallory battery drew the attention of inventor Wilson Greatbatch (see Greatbatch entry) and heart surgeon William Chardack. In 1960, they implanted the first clinically successful cardiac pacemaker in a human subject. Powered by ten Mallory mercury cells, the pacemaker operated without incident for eighteen months before it was surgically replaced. Later, in 1971, Greatbatch pioneered the even longer-lasting lithium-iodine battery system that eventually supplanted Mallory's mercury cells. However, Greatbatch later wrote, "We must not forget that it was this [mercury] cell that made pacemaking possible. It was the industry standard and remained so for some 15 years."

Other battery companies joined in. In 1957, Union Carbide introduced its own Energizer button cell in the legendary Hamilton Ventura, the world's first electrically powered wristwatch. Three years later, Mallory cells were powering the Bulova Accutron, the first watch to employ a transistor.

Miniaturization was crucial for space flight, and Mallory mercury cells served on some of the first U.S. satellites. They had also been used during the Korean War.

Though small and powerful, the mercury button cell was expensive to produce. Ruben and Mallory continued to innovate and improve the alkaline manganese battery, making it more compact, durable, and longer lasting than anything before it. At about the same time, Eastman Kodak introduced their Instamatic cameras with a built-in flash unit and their "Super Eight" home movie camera, both of which required more power than zinc carbon cells could provide. The cameras needed alkaline manganese cells but in a new size. Mallory made the new batteries, called the AA, and also licensed the technology to others because the company, at that time, had no consumer distribution.

But it was not merely with the button cell that Sam Ruben can be credited. His dry electrolytic condenser, for example, was found in nearly every radio and television set manufactured for decades and in the starters of most electric motors, with several hundred million condensers produced annually.

In 1963, Mallory unveiled a new and improved Tarrytown Battery Research Center and dedicated the lab to the shy, unassuming Ruben in a public ceremony.

The following year the term "Duracell" was formally introduced as a brand. The name is a portmanteau for "durable cell." It was simpler than the "Mallory Alkaline Manganese Battery."

The year after, Ruben was named Inventor of the Year by George Washington University.

Soon, the consumer market for Duracell batteries rocketed and supplies had to be rationed in the 1970s as manufacturing capacity caught up.

From 1976 to 1984, Ruben was a staff associate at Columbia University, which in 1982 created a chair in electrochemistry at its School of Engineering and Applied Science to honor him and Peter G. Viele, the head of Duracell Inc., who died in that year, and with whom Ruben had worked for many years.

Ruben's relationship with Mallory and Duracell continued well after Philip Mallory's death in 1975 and the company's acquisition in 1978. In 1983—at the age of 83—he contracted with Duracell to investigate "a number of cell systems to be looked at as possible replacements to the present alkaline system."

Although Samuel Ruben never earned a college degree, let alone an engineering certificate or a doctorate, he received many academic honors. He held honorary doctorates from Columbia, Butler University and the Polytechnic Institute. He held the Acheson Medal of the Electrochemical Society (1970) and the Longstreth Medal of the Franklin Institute.

By 1984, when Ruben retired, his laboratories had accumulated over 300 patents and earned him millions of dollars in royalties. Such wealth had enabled him and his wife Rena to enjoy holidays such as Lackawanna Railroad tours to the western United States or on cruises to the Caribbean.

Moving from New Rochelle to Milwaukee, Oregon, despite his great age, Samuel was appointed an adjunct professor of physics at Reed College in Portland. He died on Saturday, July 16, 1988, just two days after his 88th birthday.

Ruben's belief in the importance of teaching is evidenced by his gift of £10,000 in support of the ECS Henry B. Linford Award for Distinguished Teaching. He also financed the Professor Bergen Davis Fellowship, to be awarded to a student in chemical engineering and applied chemistry upon the recommendation of the senior professor in chemical engineering active in electrochemistry research.

Sources: From an article by the author published in *Batteries International*, Summer 2009, based on information supplied by Dr. Laurens Ruben; Eric S. Hintz of the University of Pennsylvania; the Chemical Heritage Foundation; the Electrochemical Society; Columbia University Archives; and Kathryn R Bullock of Coolohm, Inc.

• •

Ruetschi, Paul
(1925–)

Quantitative description of the
pH gradient in the corrosion layer

Paul Ruetschi was born on September 3, 1925, in Regensdorf, a suburb of Zurich, Switzerland. Having graduated from the Teacher's College in Wettingen, he entered the Federal Institute of Technology in Zurich and obtained PhD (Dr. Sc. Nat.) from the Department of Physical Chemistry under Professor Trumpler. He stayed on as assistant, and later spent one year in the research group headed by Professor Paul Delahay at Louisiana State University, Baton Rouge.

Ruetschi: "My first contacts with the science and technology of lead-acid batteries go back 40 years. I was then still at the Federal Institute of Technology in Zurich. A couple of businessmen had approached me to look into new ways of making a lead-acid battery." Ruetschi was awarded the Silver Medal of the Swiss Federal Institute of Technology in 1953.

In 1955, Ruetschi was offered a position at the Electric Storage Battery Company (ESB) in Philadelphia. There, he became manager of electrochemical research. From then on, he was involved in a number of investigations relating to lead-acid batteries. One of his first studies in this field was the development of fuel-cell type auxiliary electrodes, for gas consumption in sealed lead-acid cells. Another area of research was the study of corrosion phenomena and the composition of multilayer corrosion films on lead and lead alloys. In 1957 he was given the Young Author Award of the Electrochemical Society.

During his time in the USA, he served as chairman of the Physical Electrochemistry Division of the Electrochemical Society and was executive committee officer of the Battery Division.

Ruetschi returned to his native Switzerland in 1964 and was appointed technical director at Leclanché SA in Yverdon-les-Bains. Work carried out during his time with Leclanché included a quantitative description of the pH-gradient that exists in corrosion layers. Alkaline primary battery electrolyte and lithium miniature primary batteries with long service life (1976) were also projects.

Paul Ruetschi (Detcho Pavlov).

The major scientific contributions of Paul Ruetschi in the field of lead/acid battery research are as follows:

- Discovery of a-PbO_2 in corrosion films formed on lead and lead alloys at high anodic potentials.
- Disclosure of the individual self-discharge processes in lead-acid batteries, and the stability of lead oxides in H2S04 solution.
- Determination of the composition of the corrosion layer on lead electrodes in H2S04 at various potentials.
- Investigation of ion selectivity and diffusion potentials in such corrosion layers.
- Quantitative description of the pH gradient in the corrosion layer.
- Development of a cation-vacancy model that relates defects in the crystallographic structure of MnO_2 and PbO_2 to their electrochemical activity.
- Various other achievements in the research of HgO, Zn, MnO_2 and Ag20 electrodes.

In 1980 he was awarded the Frank Booth Medal of the International Power Sources Conference Committee. Ruetschi retired at the end of 1992 to work part-time as a consultant for Leclanché SA. In 1993 he was awarded the Gaston Planté medal. He is the author of over 70 scientific publications and over 30 patents. He has been active in many scientific societies.

Source: Information provided by Paul Ruetschi to the author, 2014.

Sadoway, Donald Robert
(1950–)
Liquid metal battery

Donald Robert Sadoway was born in Toronto, Canada, March 7, 1950. His grandparents were immigrants from the Ukraine, which at the time was under Austro-Hungarian rule. When he was born, Donald's parents lived with his grandparents in Toronto. Only Ukrainian was spoken at home and Sadoway didn't speak English until he was three years old.

Sadoway was attracted to chemistry at the Donevan Collegiate Institute in Oshawa, Ontario. He was especially fond of applied inorganic chemistry, which led him to metallurgy and materials science. In the summer of 1971 Sadoway obtained a job as an intern in the research department of Dominion Foundries and Steel Co. in Hamilton, Ontario. Here he worked on uneven wear patterns in rolls in the hot mill where big steel ingots are rolled down to plate.

He did his undergraduate studies in engineering at the University of Toronto. Under the supervision of Professor Spyridon N. Flengas, in 1972, Sadoway obtained his BSc. in engineering science. This was followed by an MSc. in chemical metallurgy in 1973, and a PhD in in extractive metallurgy in 1977. His topic: "Thermodynamic properties of some alkali-metal hexachloroniobates and hexachlorotantalates, and the separation of tantalum from niobium."

That year, he received a NATO postdoctoral fellowship from the National Research Council of Canada and went to MIT to conduct his postdoctoral research under Julian Szekely, professor of materials engineering. With Szekely he learned transport phenomena plus how to think about real world applications of university research. This, coupled with Sadoway's own upbringing in which he observed service to community, led him to choose big problems with the potential for great societal impact.

In January 1998, Don Sadoway became John F. Elliott Professor of Materials Chemistry at MIT, and for the next sixteen years, ending in 2010, using an animated teaching style, he taught Solid State Chemistry to one of the largest classes ever known at MIT. In 2004, Sadoway married Rebecca Rivkyn, a former high school chemistry teacher and modern dancer, now interior designer.

As a researcher, Sadoway focused on environmentally sound ways to extract metals from their ores, as well as the development of more efficient batteries. In August 2006, a team that he led demonstrated the feasibility of extracting iron from its ore through molten oxide electrolysis. MOE produces iron from iron oxide by the action of electric current. Since this process differs from conventional steelmaking—no carbon is used in MOE—no greenhouse gas emissions come from the smelter.

In 2006, Sadoway proposed a liquid metal battery, a very low cost molten salt battery based on magnesium and antimony separated by a salt that could be used in stationary energy storage systems. This consists of a dense positive liquid metal electrode at the bottom of the battery and a lighter liquid metal electrode floating on top. A molten salt electrolyte lies in-between. This material, used in the "sLimcell," has the capability of allowing batteries to offer twice as much power per kilogram as is possible in current lithium ion batteries.

In April of that year, A.M. Mayes, D.R. Sadoway, P.P. Soo and B. Huang were granted U.S. patent no. 7,026,071. Over time, research on their liquid metal battery was funded to the tune of $13.35 million by ARPA-E, Total S.A. and others. Experimental data showed a 69 percent DC-to-DC storage efficiency with good storage capacity and relatively low leakage.

David Bradwell played an instrumental role in advancing the technology while he completed an M.Eng degree, a PhD, and a one-year postdoctoral fellowship. In 2010, Bradwell and Sadoway, along with Luis Ortiz, co-founded the Liquid Metal Battery Corporation with the goal of commercializing the technology. This was soon renamed Ambri—a take on the town in which the company is located: *Cambri*dge.

In 2012, Sadoway was named one of *Time* magazine's "Top 100 Most Influential People in the World" for his continuing work in improved batteries. In January 2013, Sadoway became John F. Elliott Professor of Materials Chemistry at MIT. In June, he was presented with an honorary Doctor of Engineering by the University of Toronto in recognition for his contributions to higher education and sustainable energy.

In February 2014 Ambri won a $250,000 grant from New York State to develop and test a prototype battery with Con Edison. The company, backed by investors including billionaires Bill Gates and Vinod Khosla, planned to install its first two prototypes by early 2015 at a Massachusetts military base and a wind farm in Hawaii. In November, it opened its first manufacturing facility in Marlborough, Massachusetts, and is planning a larger one next year. A setback came when it was discovered that a battery seal, which can withstand the liquid metal battery's high temperatures, had shown disappointing results in tests, thus slowing its commercialization path. By the fall, Ambri was working on testing out new types of seals that could hold up under the high temperatures needed.

One of Ambri's first prototype systems produced in Marlborough will eventually be installed at the Joint Base Cape Cod, where it will enable the base to reduce electricity costs, improve power quality and grid resiliency, and integrate additional onsite renewable generation. That deployment will be funded through the Massachusetts Clean Energy Center's InnovateMass Program.

Donald Sadoway explains: "People would like better batteries but they are wary of making investments. What is required is both a technology push and a market pull. If we can get liquid-metal batteries down to $500 a kilowatt-hour, we'll change the world."

Sources: H. Kim, D.A. Boysen, D.J. Bradwell, B. Chung, K. Jiang, A.A. Tomaszowska, K. Wang, W. Wei, and D.R. Sadoway, "Thermodynamic Properties of Calcium-Bismuth Alloys Determined by Emf Measurements," *Electrochim. Acta* 60 (2012): 154–162; information provided to the author by Donald Sadoway, February 2015.

Salkind, Alvin J.
(1927–2015)

Rechargeable MnO$_2$ systems for both lithium and alkaline electrolytes

Alvin Salkind was born on June 12, 1927, in New York City. His father, also born in New York City, was a descendant of immigrants from the Vilnus area of what was then Russia (now Lithuania) who came to the U.S. about 1888. Alvin's mother Florence Zins was also born in New York City, a descendant of parents who came from Austria in about

Alvin Salkind (courtesy estate of Dr. Alvin J. Salkind).

the same time period. Alvin had an uncle who was a math professor and many engineers as cousins.

His primary school education (5th–8th grades) was in a special wing of a nearby public school in which IQ gifted children were trained. The minimum IQ was 150. Alvin went to the nearest high school, Tilden, where he could walk to school with neighbor children. He then attended the Polytechnic Institute of Brooklyn, New York (now New York University), for his bachelor's, master's and doctoral degrees.

He learned electronic repair in the Eddy program of the U.S. Navy. Most of his graduate studies were part-time while he worked at Usalite, a small manufacturer of dry and special cells, and Sonotone, where he was a senior engineer responsible for nickel-cadmium cell components. In his doctoral training, his major field was chemical engineering and his minor fields were chemistry and X-ray physics. His thesis advisors included Donald Othmer, Paul Bruins, J. Steigman, and I. Fankuchen. Other advisors included Herman Mark and Rudy Marcus.

In 1958, Salkind started employment as head of a research group at the central labs of ESB Inc. (common trade or divisional names included Exide, Rayovac, Grant, Edison, Willard and Yardley), Pennsylvania (near Princeton). While at ESB Inc. he took research management courses at the Penn State University, and as a member of the Industrial Research Institute, he took special research management training at Harvard Business School. He also started teaching graduate courses one night a week, initially at the Poly and later at nearby Rutgers University.

In the 1960s ESB supplied Ernest B. Yeager (see Yeager entry) of Case–Western Reserve University with the catalyzed silver electrodes for his mercury-amalgam fuel cell designs.

In 1965, Alvin married Mary Koenig; they had two children, Susanne and James. At this time, he was a competitive swimmer, sailor and ski instructor.

In 1970 Salkind became president of the Research Lab Corporation and a vice-president of the parent NYSE-listed company. ESB had licensees, technology collaboration agreements, and equity interests throughout the world and at one point owned the Chloride Battery Company in England. The agreements included: the NIFE (Jungner) company in Oskarshamn, Sweden, where S. Uno Falk was the chief engineer on alkaline batteries (see Jungner entry); Varta in Kelkheim, Germany, where Hans Bode was research director (see Bode entry) on lead-acid and dry cells (Voss was also there); Hellesens in Denmark on dry cells; Toshiba in Japan; Century in Australia; Tudor in Spain; Microlite in Brazil; and others. The Chloride agreement included all technology.

In 1974, ESB was acquired by the INCO Company. When the decision was made to close the central lab in 1979, Salkind returned to teaching with two half-time appointments. The first was as a tenured full professor in the Rutgers Medical School, where he was head of a bioengineering division of the department of surgery. Here he developed battery-powered medical implants.

The second was as a professor and later associate dean of the Rutgers School of Engineering. He founded the Rutgers Center for Energy Storage Materials and Engineering, where improved silver-zinc and lead-acid batteries were developed. He also started a consulting engineering company, Alvin J. Salkind Associates, which carried out projects in North America, South America, India, Europe, and Australia.

During the 1970s, Salkind had collaborated with Ernest Yeager (see Yeager entry) in editing 5 books titled *Techniques of Electrochemistry* published by Wiley. Sales of a Russian translation, published by Mir. Total, have approached 20,000. In 1980, Salkind assisted Yeager in starting the Center for Electrochemical Sciences at Case as a part-time visiting professor and executive director of the Center.

After retiring from Rutgers in 2004, Alvin became a part-time faculty member and lecturer at the University of Miami, City University (NYC), and University of Adelaide in Australia, as well as a visiting professor at the Academy of Science (Moscow), Technical University (Graz), the Academies of Science in Belgrade, Serbia, and Zagreb, Croatia, in Japan, and at the Chinese Academy of Science, Jilin. He served as a member of advisory boards of many companies, including ElectroEnergy, PowerGenix, Hittman Labs, Ackrad Labs, Rechargeable Battery Co., Exide-ASEA (Sweden), Inframat, Wonder Battery (France), and HBL (India).

Salkind was the author or editor of 11 other books or proceeding volumes, 120 technical peer-reviewed papers, and over 400 articles. He was the holder of over 2 dozen patents. He was a fellow of the Electrochemical Society, American College of Cardiology, AAAS, AIMBE, and the New Jersey Academy of Medicine. His honors include: Distinguished Alumnus Award (Polytechnic), Case Centennial Scholar Medal, the ITE Award (Japan ECS), Frank Booth Medal (IPPS, UK), and the Edison Patent Award (NJR and D council).

At age 87, Alvin Salkind was organizing an LLC to study advanced energy storage battery systems, especially suited for locations with no grid. Salkind declared, "There are bright and willing people everywhere. Take time to learn from them. The world is a small place and needs preserving." He died on June 9, 2015.

Source: Info supplied to author by A. Salkind in February 2015.

Sampson, Henry Thomas
(1934–)
Gamma electric cell, nuclear battery

Henry T. Sampson, Jr., was born in Jackson, Mississippi, April 22, 1934, the son of Henry T. and Esther Ellis Sampson. He and his younger brother John B. Sampson were the only children. His father was an educator. His mother was from Vicksburg; she earned her M.S. degree in social work and was considered the first African American social worker in Mississippi in that era. She also worked as professor of social work studies at Jackson State University. Henry's family life was a very privileged one for that era.

Sampson, Jr., graduated from Lanier High School in Jackson, Mississippi, in 1951. He then attended Morehouse College in Atlanta before transferring to Purdue University in Indiana, where he became a member of the Omega Psi Phi fraternity. He received a bachelor's degree in science from Purdue University in 1956.

Sampson worked as a research chemical engineer at the U.S. Naval Weapons Center, China Lake, California, from 1956 to 1961 in the area of high-energy solid propellants and case bonding materials for solid rocket motors. He went on to the University of California, Los Angeles, where he graduated with an M.S. degree in engineering in 1961. Sampson was a member of the United States Navy between the years 1962 and 1964. He earned an Atomic Energy Commission honor between 1964 and 1967, receiving an M.S. in nuclear engineering from the University of Illinois Urbana–Champaign in 1965, and in 1967 becoming the first African American to earn a PhD in this discipline.

He then moved on to the Aerospace Corp, El Segundo, California. His titles included project engineer, 1967–81, as director of Mission Development and Operations of the Space Test Program.

On July 6, 1971, he was awarded U.S. patent 3,591,860, with George H. Miley, for a gamma-electrical cell, a device that produces stable high voltage from radiation sources, primarily gamma radiation, with proposed goals of generating auxiliary power from the shielding of a nuclear reactor. Additionally, the patent cites the cell's function as a detector with self power and construction cost advantages over previous detectors. This patent has often led to Sampson's being cited, mistakenly, as the inventor of the cellular phone.

From 1981, Sampson was director of planning and operations directorate of Space Test Program, where he pioneered a study of internal ballistics of solid-fueled rocket motors using high-speed photography.

Later he was awarded the Black Image Award from Aerospace Corporation in 1982. He was awarded the Blacks in Engineering, Applied Science Award and prize for education, by the Los Angeles Council of Black Professional Engineers in 1983.

In addition, Henry Sampson is a noted film historian. He wrote the book *Blacks in Black and White: A Source Book on Black Films*, which examines often overlooked African American film makers from the first half of the 20th century. In addition he authored *The Ghost Walks: A Chronological History of Blacks in Show Business, 1865–1910*. He has produced documentary films on African American film makers. In 2005, he published *Singin' on the Ether Waves: A Chronological History of African Americans in Radio and Television Programming, 1925–1955* (2 vols., Lanham, MD: Scarecrow Press).

Source: Henry T. Sampson and Laura H. Young-Sampson, "The Making of a Nuclear Engineer, Inventor, and

Black Film Historian: Dr. Henry Thomas Sampson, Jr.," *Journal of African American History* 94 (2009): 2, 224–247.

....

Sastry, Ann Marie
(1967–)

Thin-film solid-state lithium battery
and physics-based modeling of batteries

Ann Marie Sastry was born in Peoria, Illinois, on September 8, 1967. Her father, Tony Sastry, was a mathematics professor at Bradley University, and her mother Barbara (Herr) Sastry was a schoolteacher. Sastry spent much of her childhood on the Bradley campus with her father, who immigrated to the United States from India. A precocious child, Sastry learned with pen and pad in her father's office how to write equations in precise, errorless script. Her mother taught her to read very early, and took her along to volunteer activities, imbuing in the child a sense of social activism.

Sastry's talent for mathematics was evident, and she frequently sat in the Bradley classrooms as her father lectured. Occasionally, he called her to the board to work a problem, playfully demonstrating to the undergraduate students in his class that even a child could do calculus. For her part, Sastry thrived under her father's attention and his oft-repeated assertion to her that she could do anything. Her upbringing combined the food, social activities, and customs of her father's Andhra Pradesh origins with her mother's Milwaukee German heritage, and gave Sastry a multicultural perspective decidedly uncommon among those coming of age in a medium-sized Midwestern U.S. city in the 1980s.

Sastry graduated as valedictorian of Richwoods High School class of 1985, maintaining a perfect grade point average and earning a National Merit Scholarship even while working a succession of part-time jobs. She accepted a full-ride Eugene I. DuPont scholarship to attend the University of Delaware, where she graduated *cum laude* in 1989 with multiple awards and honors and a B.S. degree in mechanical engineering. During all four years of her studies at Delaware, Sastry worked in the laboratories of the UD Center for Composite Materials, where she completed an undergraduate thesis on viscoelasticity of polymer composites. Sastry also interned in the summers following her junior and senior years at the DuPont Company's Experimental Station in Wilmington, Delaware, where she carried out research on aerospace composite materials.

It was at the University of Delaware that Sastry met her future husband, Christian Lastoskie, a fellow E.I. DuPont Scholar and chemical engineering graduate. The couple met during their very first weekend on the Newark, Delaware, campus and began a lifetime partnership as research collaborators, husband and wife academicians, and best friends. Sastry and Lastoskie were married in 1989 and they attended graduate school at Cornell University, both as National Science Foundation (NSF) Graduate Fellowship students. They would dedicate many of their scientific works to one another, and to their two children, Katherine Lastoskie (born in 1997) and Peter Lastoskie (born in 2001), maintaining their respective foci in clean energy technology and environmental engineering.

At Cornell, Sastry earned additional honors, including the DuPont Graduate Fellowship. Her dissertation made seminal contributions to the calculation of stress concentrations in damaged composite solids for determining the strength distributions of composite materials. Following the completion of her M.S. and PhD degrees at Cornell, Sastry took a position in 1994 as a senior member of the technical staff at Sandia National Laboratories in Albuquerque, New Mexico. It is at Sandia that Sastry first began working in batteries, writing code for heterogeneous materials in dynamic finite element solvers that led to her first battery research grant from the Department of Energy. Her funded research on the mathematical modeling and design of batteries would continue uninterrupted for more than two decades.

In 1995, Sastry accepted a faculty appointment as an assistant professor in mechanical engineering at the University of Michigan, perennially one of the

Ann Marie Sastry of Sakti3 (Sastry Collection).

top five programs in the U.S. At Michigan, Sastry's impeccable mathematical preparation and her computational expertise produced a constellation of discipline-spanning scholarly contributions over a period of 17 years, which saw her swiftly climb the academic ranks. She received early promotion with tenure to associate professor in 2000, and early promotion again to full professor in 2005. Throughout, she continued to devote considerable time and effort to teaching and mentorship, and in recognition of these efforts, she was named to a chaired professorship in 2009 as the Arthur F. Thurnau Professor of Mechanical, Biomedical, and Materials Science and Engineering. Sastry received numerous prestigious honors as a faculty member, including the National Science Foundation's prestigious Presidential Early Career Award in Science and Engineering (1997); the American Society of Mechanical Engineers (ASME) Gustus L. Larson Award (2007) and the Frank Kreith Energy Award (2011); and the University of Michigan's Henry Russel Award (1999) and Faculty Recognition Award (2005). In 2004, she was named an ASME Fellow.

Sastry developed the first analytical solutions to the percolation of particle systems involving the triaxial ellipsoid and long-fiber geometries found in a multitude of disordered porous materials. She concurrently developed the simulation techniques to determine the percolation properties of such materials. The publications from these bodies of work have become classic references, and irrevocably altered the way that disordered particulate and fibrous materials are modeled, in applications ranging from heat transfer to electrochemistry to mechanics of materials.

Using her modeling and characterization expertise, and research support from the

National Institutes of Health and the Whitaker Foundation, Sastry partnered with colleagues in biology and medicine to solve critical problems in collagen stiffening in diabetics, evolutionary structure optimization in marine invertebrates, and intracellular transport of ions involved in cellular signaling. The latter Sastry conducted as the co-director of a $2 million Keck Foundation Center grant she secured for her innovative simulation studies of the nanoscale sensing and modeling of intracellular transport. Sastry also continued her fundamental research at the University of Michigan in materials design with sponsorship from NSF and defense agencies, determining that the connection points in fused porous networks are the most critical determinant of material response. As of 2015, Sastry's more than 100 archival journal publications and book chapters have been cited more than 3500 times by the global academic and research community.

It is in electrochemistry that Sastry made her most profound scholarly contributions. The heterogeneous multiphase modeling, optimization, characterization and control algorithms she developed span the full spectrum from the nano-scale of battery electrode structure to the macro-scale of electric drive vehicles powered by lithium battery packs. Sastry's research delivered the first comprehensive physics-based model for the thermal management of a battery cell, which forever changed the field by demonstrating that several disparate areas of physics and mathematics—kinetics, mechanics, heat transfer and optimization—could be combined into a single predictive framework for realistic materials architectures. Her teams' highly efficient algorithms thus enabled better material selection and improved control of battery cycling, degradation, and capacity utilization.

Sastry's academic work in electrochemistry and energy storage culminated in two important university-spanning initiatives at Michigan. In 2009, she founded and served as the first Director of the Energy Systems Engineering (ESE) Masters of Engineering distance-learning graduate program. The ESE program, which has graduated hundreds of students to date at the University of Michigan, facilitates the education of automotive, energy sector, and other engineering professionals with traditional academic backgrounds with the cross-cutting skills and coursework needed to solve the technological challenges associated with electric mobility, compact portable power, and energy production from renewable resources. Students from the program have gone on to become leaders in clean energy technologies across the globe.

Concurrently, Sastry founded and directed the $5 million Department of Energy–funded Automotive Battery Coalition for Drivetrains (ABCD) research center between General Motors, the University of Michigan (UM), and other partnering institutions. The ABCD center brought together industry, higher education, and government to accelerate the design and testing of advanced batteries for electric vehicles.

In 2007, Sastry's attention turned to solid state battery technology, based on the mathematical potential of these systems. Focusing not only on physics and engineering properties, but also on cost and the need to create affordable energy storage, Sastry made the decision to spin out a battery startup company from her research laboratory, the Ann Arbor–based Sakti3, to develop and scale the technology. With over $50 million in support as of 2015, from prominent investors including Khosla Ventures, Dyson, General Motors Ventures, and Itochu, Sastry and her team translated the conceptual discoveries in her university laboratory into realization, announcing in 2014 a thin-film solid-state battery, produced with a scalable patented vacuum vapor deposition technology with a record-breaking energy density of over 1100 watt-hours per liter. Under Sastry's direction as Sakti3's chief executive officer, the company is moving into pilot production of solid-state lithium cells for consumer electronics applications.

Presently Sastry resides in Ann Arbor, Michigan, with her husband and their two children. Her husband is a professor in the UM Department of Civil and Environmental Engineering and program director of Environmental and Water Resources Engineering. The family also enjoys many recreational pursuits, including downhill skiing, mountain biking, and wakeboarding at her family's lakeside home in Brighton, Michigan.

Source: Communication to the author, February 2015.

•••

Scrosati, Bruno
(1937–)
Beyond lithium-ion batteries

Bruno Scrosati was born on August 5, 1937, in Ortisei, in South Tyrol in northern Italy. His family soon moved to Rome, where he was educated first in junior school and then at the "Liceo Classico" high school. His studies included Latin and ancient Greek, two subjects which turned out to be very useful for completing his intellectual preparation.

He completed his education at the University of Rome La Sapienza. His mentor was the late Professor Filippo Accascina, at the time a well-known expert in ionic conductivity, who inspired him to become interested in electrochemistry.

In 1961, Scrosati obtained a degree in chemistry at the University of Rome, discussing a thesis on the physical chemical properties of aqueous solutions. After his graduation, he spent two years (1964–65) at the University of Trondheim, Norway, where he investigated molten salt electrochemistry and completed his knowledge of this field by serving as postdoc (1965–66) at the University of Illinois in Urbana with Professor Herbert Laitinen, who further influenced his commitment to electrochemical research.

Returning to Rome University, in 1969 Scrosati obtained his Libera Docenza (PhD) in electrochemistry. During the summers of 1970 and 1971 he was a visiting scientist at Bell Telephone Laboratories in Murray Hill, New Jersey, where he developed a solid electrolyte having a very fast silver ion transport. From 1980 until 2012 Scrosati was full professor of electrochemistry, University of Rome La Sapienza. Here he established a laboratory for advanced batteries and fuel cell technology.

In the early 1980s Scrosati and his team at La Sapienza began to work on extending the range and energy density of rechargeable lithium batteries, searching for improved nonmetal electrodes. By 1988, they had begun to develop a polymeric electrolyte on a polyepoxy basis.

By the 1990s, they had produced a composite, ternary, polymeric system formed by intimately mixing a polymeric compound, a metal salt, and a ceramic additive acting as agent promoting the transport features (conductivity and ion mobility). This culminated, by 1997, in a thin-film lithium polymer battery, patented by the United States of America as represented by the Secretary of the Air Force.

During this period, Scrosati became recognized for his achievements. From 1988, he was vice-president and president of the International Society of Solid State Ionics (1988–1991). A visiting professor at both Minnesota and Pennsylvania Universities, in 1996, he was awarded an honorary doctorate "honoris causa" by the University of St. Andrews, Scotland. From 1996 to 1998, he was president of the Italian Chemical Society (SCI). In 1997, he received the Research Award from the Battery Division of the Electrochemical Society.

Bruno Scrosati remarried in 1997 with a spectacular wedding ceremony in Yellowstone Park in the U.S.

Not content to rest on his laurels, with the new millennium, Scrosati and his team concentrated their energies on the use of pentacyclic anion salt in electrolyte compositions. This led in 2012 to a rechargeable lithium sulfide electrode for a polymer tin-sulfur lithium-ion battery, whose energy density is three times that offered by common lithium-ion batteries and plastic design. The anode and cathode of this battery are separated by an electrolyte formed by a membrane containing a solution of a lithium salt in aprotic organic solvents with the addition of lithium sulfide and/or lithium polysulfides until saturation, this solution being trapped in a polymer matrix.

In 2003–2004 Scrosati was president of the Electrochemical Society (ECS). In 2006 he was awarded the Alessandro Volta Medal of the European Section of the Electrochemical Society. In 2004 he won the XVI Edition of the Italgas Prize, Science and Environment, with the citation, "His studies provide consistent evidence that the new, morphologically optimized materials approach the performance levels requested for batteries and fuel cells designed for electric vehicle applications."

In 2007 he was a member of the Evaluating Committee of the Consolidated Research Institute for Advanced Science and Medical Care, Waseda University, Tokyo, Japan. In 2008 he was awarded an honorary doctorate in science and technology by the Chalmers University of Technology, Goteborg, Sweden. In 2009, he was a member of the evaluation panel of the Energy Frontier Research Center (EFRC) at the Department of Energy, USA.

In 2012, Scrosati, aged 75, was a member of the Advisory Committee of the TUMCreate Center in Singapore, and a member and visiting professor of the Advisory Committee of the Helmholtz-Institute Ulm Electrochemical Energy Storage (HIU) in Ulm, Germany. He also received the De Nora Award of the Electrochemical Society. He was awarded by the Sigillo d'oro medal of the Italian Chemical Society. In 2012 he received an honorary doctorate in science and technology from the University of Ulm, in Germany.

Scrosati was European Editor of the *Journal of Power Sources* and a member of the editorial boards of various international journals, as *Solid State Ionics*, the *Journal of Applied Electrochemistry*, *Progress in Solid State Chemistry*, *Ionics*, and *ChemElectroChem*. He is author of more 550 scientific publications, 30 books and chapters in books, and 22 patents.

Scrosati has been included by Reuters news agency company among the world's 3,300 most cited scientists and more recently among the "World's most influential scientific minds" in the materials science category.

Presently, Scrosati is visiting professor at the Italian Institutes of Technology, one of the most famous and established research institutions in Italy, where he continues to work in advanced lithium batteries, including graphene-based systems.

Bruno Scrosati's main hobby is model trains, N-gauge. He likes to design train landscapes and build them in the attic of his country house North of Rome.

Source: Information provided by Bruno Scrosati, February 2015.

Sinsteden, Wilhelm Josef
(1803–1891)
Working principle of the lead-acid battery

Wilhelm Sinsteden was born on May 26, 1803, as the fifth of nine children, in Kleve, a town in the Lower Rhine region of northwestern Germany. His father, Michael Fran Severin Sinsteden, was a diplomat at the Knights of the Order of Saint John of Malta and later district administrator in Kleve. In 1804 his father purchased the secularized Cistercian abbey, Graefenthal, where the family still lives today.

Sinsteden was given private lessons, then attended the Jesuit Colleges in Colonia and Kempen from 1811 to 1816. From 1817 to 1823, he attended the high school at Kleve, enrolling at the Friedrich-Wilhelm Institute in Berlin to study medicine and surgery. This institute specialized in military medicine. In 1827 he passed the midterm examination (tentamen) at Berlin University in psychology, logic, chemistry, mineralogy, zoology, botany and physics. From 1827 he was a junior surgeon at the Royal Charité Hospital (now the Campus Charité Mitte). In 1828 he qualified as doctor of *medicinae et chirurgiae* (medicine and surgery) with the dissertation *"Physico-medica sistens ationem gravitatem inter et vim vitalem"* ("The nature of the force of gravity between the physico-medical systems and vitality"). In 1828 he joined the army as a company surgeon (Compagniechirurg) with the 4th Dragoon Regiment in Potsdam.

In 1836 Sinsteden was promoted to staff surgeon and three years later he was transferred as regimental surgeon to the Queen's Cuirassiers (Pomeranian) No. 2 to Pasewalk (about 150 km north of Berlin). In 1839 Sinsteden married Cäcilie Weiß (1815–1893); they had three children. He participated in the Schleswig Wars against Denmark in 1848–49 and 1864, then against Austria in 1866.

The then-commandant of the Queen's Cuirassiers laid particular emphasis on the military-technical education of his officer corps. This included Sinsteden, who investigated optics and the theory of electricity awareness. He constructed inductors and one of the first electric motors. In order to provide the quantity of electricity during his experiments he used galvanic cells with Pt, Ag, Ni, Zn and Pb electrodes and measured the generated gas volume.

In 1854, Sinsteden published his findings on the use of flat lead plates as electrodes and of dilute sulfuric acid as an electrolyte in the German periodical *Annalen der Physik und Chemie* 92 (1854): pp. 1–21, pp. 220–37. He described that over the course of a number of

Wilhelm Josef Sisteden was a surgeon in the Germany Army (Wiki).

charge-discharge cycles, the storage capacity of his lead-acid cell (~18 cm² and 10 mAh) increased. On investigation he found that the charge cycle formed lead dioxide on one plate and pure lead on the other. By increasing the area of the lead plates, he increased the output current.

In 1870, Sinsteden served again as a surgeon to the German Army in its war against France. Ironically, by this time a Frenchman, Raymond Gaston Planté (see Planté entry), took up Sinsteden's crucial findings and developed the rechargeable lead-acid battery, although he did acknowledge Sinsteden's pioneering work.

In 1871 he retired as Prussian surgeon-general in Pasewalk, where he decided to live for the time being near one of his married daughters. In 1879 he moved to Xanten (Lower Rhine region in Germany), where he died on November 12, 1891. He was buried in Asperden-Goch.

Source: *German Annals of Physics and Chemistry* 92 (1854): pp. 1–21, pp. 220–37. With additional information researched by Dr. Jürgen Garche.

....

Skyllas-Kazacos, Maria
(1951–)
"Lady Vanadium"

Maria Skyllas was born on the Aegean island of Kalymnos, Greece, on October 26, 1951. Her father George Skyllas was a fitter and toolmaker who was born in Athens, but moved to Egypt with his parents at the age of 4. Exiled during the Suez Crisis in Egypt, and then again by the civil war in Greece, like many other Europeans at the time, the family decided migration was the only hope for a better life. Skyllas and his family emigrated to Sydney, Australia. With her father working as a fitter and turner, Maria used to watch him working with his tools and machines, but unlike her two brothers, never showed any interest in his hobbies. Instead, she developed a passion for art, poetry and drama and saw herself as having a career in arts.

Skyllas-Kazacos: "Like all Greek families, my family put a high value on education and encouraged their children to work hard at school. With my sister Tina, we were privileged to be accepted into Fort Street Girls' High School, one of Australia's top academically selective girls' high schools. In my junior years, my favourite subjects were Art, Literature and Drama. Although I was always good at Math, I always lacked confidence in my abilities, despite topping the class each year."

In those years, very few girls were finishing school and going to college, so as a teenager, Maria thought she might also leave school at 16 to become a hairdresser, or a fashion designer, or even a commercial artist. It was only after being encouraged by her parents and teachers to stay on at school that she began to enjoy the more academic subjects. In the senior years, science and math became much more rigorous than during the junior years, and this appealed to Miss Skyllas.

She found herself loving these subjects, but continued her passion for the arts and literature, so her choice of career was not clear-cut. She thought about studying art or drama, but her father convinced her that it would be very tough to have a career in these areas. Being quite a pragmatic person, Maria applied to do law, but was discouraged by a lawyer friend of the family. She finally settled on a scientific degree and initially enrolled in chemical engineering at the University of New South Wales in Sydney, where she was one of only 3 girls in a class of 100.

Despite finishing in the top 3 students of her class at high school, Maria still felt that she could not compete academically with boys, so in her first year at the university, she thought that she must work very hard just to pass. To her surprise, she topped most of her first-year subjects and received a number of awards. Of course, she thought that this was just a "fluke," so all through her university years, she continued to feel that she had to work hard so as not to disappoint her parents and professors, who had great expectations for her.

Maria Skyllas-Kazacos, inventor of the vanadium redox battery (Skyllas-Kazacos Collection).

By the end of her first year, Maria decided that a career in chemical engineering might be too difficult for a girl, so she changed to the industrial chemistry program, which turned out to be more than 80 percent chemical engineering. Although she did not really enjoy the engineering subjects that she was studying, she wanted to finish what she had already started, so she persevered and gained her enjoyment from her general studies subjects that allowed her to take drama and art history as part of her study program.

Despite her earlier insecurities, Maria graduated with a first-class honors B.S. degree and the University Medal in Industrial Chemistry in 1974. By her final year at the university, the science and engineering courses had become much more relevant to her interests, and she could now see herself pursuing a career in the chemical industry. Moving back to Greece, Maria obtained a job as a chemist almost immediately; she worked for E. R. Squibb and Sons Pharmaceuticals, in Athens, as a production manager.

But following the hostilities of Turkey's invasion of Cyprus and the threat of war with Greece, the Skyllas family decided it would be better to return to Australia. Once again, they packed up and moved back to Sydney. During a visit to her former university, one of her lecturers, Professor Barry Welch, encouraged her to do a PhD, suggesting she research the electrochemistry of molten salts. Her laboratory work exposed her to practical experiences that she had never previously encountered, including winding high-temperature furnace elements, glass-blowing, soldering electronic circuit boards to build her own instruments, and programming the new computer for data analysis.

During her studies, Maria met and married another analytical chemist, Michael Kazacos. Their first son, Nicholas, was born in October 1977, just days after she had completed her last experiment for her PhD. For several months after his birth, Maria's mother Kaliopi helped to baby-sit Nicholas so that Maria could complete the writing of her thesis. In the meantime, her supervisor and Mentor, Barry Welch, encouraged her to apply for a postdoctoral position overseas so that she could gain the relevant experience for an academic position.

Having obtained her PhD in 1978, and receiving a prestigious CSIRO Postdoctoral Fellowship, Maria Skyllas-Kazakos left Australia for New Jersey, where she was offered a position as a member of the technical staff at Bell Telephone Laboratories at Murray Hill. A short time later, Michael was offered a position in the Battery Department at Bell Labs, so Maria's mother Kaliopi joined the family in New Jersey to baby-sit Nicholas for 6 months, with Michael's mother Zambetta taking over for a further 4 months.

During her time at Bell Laboratories, Maria had the privilege of working with Adam Heller and Barry Miller in the new area of liquid junction solar cells. Maria thought that solar energy research would allow her to use her training in electrochemical engineering to solve an important social and environmental problem of energy production for the future, but realized also, through the battery research program at Bell Laboratories, that energy storage was equally important.

Working in John Broadhead's battery group, Maria gained a lot of valuable experience in lead-acid batteries and managed to identify a new ionic species that forms as an intermediate during the charge-discharge reactions at the positive electrode. This led to her first single-author paper published in the *Journal of the Electrochemical Society*, which was to later earn her the Royal Australian Chemical Institute's Bloom-Guttmann Prize for the best young author under 30. Her work with Barry Miller and Adam Heller produced 3 additional journal publications and her first joint patent on a new process for electrodepositing CdSe semiconductor thin films.

As the postdoctoral fellowship drew to an end, Maria was offered a permanent position at Bell Labs, but, once again, Australia would call her back home. In 1980, she obtained Australia's most prestigious Queen Elizabeth II Fellowship that allowed her to continue her research in liquid junction solar cells in the School of Physics and the University of New South Wales. During this period, their second son George was born, and after a 5-month maternity leave, Maria's parents took over the babysitting of both boys to allow her to return to work. In 1982 she was appointed as a lecturer in the School of Chemical Engineering and Industrial Chemistry at the University of New South Wales to replace her former PhD supervisor, who had accepted a chair in New Zealand.

As a new lecturer, Maria was given the task of establishing a new research group in electrochemical engineering while also taking over some of Barry Welch's activities in aluminum smelting, a very important industry in Australia. With the support of her mentor, Maria was able to secure her first industrial grant from the Australian aluminum smelting company, Comalco, a subsidiary of Rio Tinto. But a fellow lecturer in the school, Professor Bob Robins, was to renew her interest in batteries by inviting her to join a research project on lead-acid batteries recently funded by a grant from the National Energy Research Development and Demonstration Council of Australia.

Chlorides of vanadium were generated in 1830 by Nils Gabriel Sefström, who thereby proved that a new element was involved, which he named "vanadium" after the Germanic goddess of beauty and fertility, Vanadís.

The use of vanadium in batteries had been suggested earlier by Pissoort, by NASA researchers and by Pellegri and Spaziante in 1978, but no one had previously used vanadium redox couples in a working flow battery. A reason for this was the low solubility of pentavalent vanadium compounds in acidic solutions, which would limit the practical energy density of such a system. The fact that vanadium exists in several oxidation states, however, made it an excellent candidate for a single-element flow battery that might overcome the problem of cross-contamination observed with the Fe/Cr battery by NASA researchers in the 1970s and '80s.

Skyllas-Kazacos recalls:

> It was the early NASA work on the Fe/Cr system that drew my attention to the new flow battery concept. It all began with a Master's student, Robert Brand, who was working on the Fe/Cr flow battery with Professor Martin Green, a world leader in silicon solar cells at the University of New South Wales.
>
> Bob asked me to co-supervise him for his Master's thesis and it became quickly obvious that cross-contamination was an inherent problem for all flow batteries that use a different element in the two half-cells. This could only be overcome by using the same element in the two half-cells, so a quick examination of the periodic table and the electrochemical series produced a short list of potential candidates. My colleague, Bob Robins, had been working on the extraction of vanadium from various minerals at the time, so vanadium seemed a good starting point.

Maria decided to set this research topic as a 4th Year Honours project in 1983, but before giving it to an undergraduate student, she began some preliminary electrochemical studies on vanadium electrolytes over the summer vacation that year to confirm its viability. Her preliminary studies with VCl_3 solutions in H_2SO_4 showed good reversibility for the V(II)/V(III) and V(IV)/V(V) couples, but further research was needed to optimize the solution chemistry in order to achieve a practical system. The 4th Year Honours project student, Elaine Sum, screened a number of supporting electrolytes during 1984 and confirmed that sulfuric acid gave the best results, although the low solubility of V(V) compounds still appeared to be a limitation.

Maria explains, "In parallel with this, with my colleagues Robert Robins, Martin Green and Anthony Fane, we jointly applied for a grant under the Australian National Energy Research, Development and Demonstration Council (NERDDC) to further investigate the feasibility of an All-Vanadium Redox Flow Battery for remote area power systems."

Although the application was initially unsuccessful, it was resubmitted the following year, and with the promising results from the preliminary studies, it was granted in 1985. With the new funding, Maria set out to explore the possibility of producing concentrated V(V) solutions by oxidizing 2 M $VOSO_4$, a much more soluble form of vanadium. Together with the newly appointed research fellow, Dr. Miron Rychicik, a 2 M vanadium electrolyte was produced and tested, the results giving rise to the filing of the first All-Vanadium Redox Flow Battery patent in 1986. The key patent was taken out by M. Skyllas-Kazacos and R.G. Robins, "All Vanadium Redox Battery," U.S. Patent No. 849,094 [1986], Japan Patent Appl. [1986], Australian Patent No. 575247 [1986].

This was the start of a 25-year program at UNSW that continues today. During the early years, development efforts were hampered by the lack of suitable off-the-shelf membranes and other cell components. In particular the use of $VOSO_4$ for production of electrolyte was found to be uneconomical from the outset, so one of the first tasks was to develop a process that would allow the use of the much cheaper V_2O_5 compound for electrolyte production ($5/kg compared with more than $400/kg for $VOSO_4$). Her pioneering work thus saw her rolling up her sleeves to personally take charge of tasks such as producing electrolytes, novel plastic electrodes, and new modified membranes, as well as developing mathematical models and designs for battery technology and components, through to prototype testing and manufacturing trials in conjunction with industrial licenses.

From early on in her research career, Maria had a particular concern with the environment: "I really wanted to do something that I could see as important for the environment and for society. As a physical scientist and engineer, I suppose the most important social contribution you can make is to the environment—particularly from my own area of expertise as distinct from the medical or other social areas." Maria's battery has the lowest ecological footprint because it doesn't use heavy metals, which makes it the most eco-friendly battery in the world

She would in turn become a senior lecturer in 1986, associate professor in 1988, and professor from 1993. In 1987, a small feature article on the VRB in the university's magazine, *Uniken*, attracted the interest of the local media in Australia, and almost overnight, the VRB was featured in newspaper articles around the world.

She recalls: "I had just recently given birth to our 3rd son, Anthony, so I needed more help to continue research while maintaining a large lecture load and keeping up with all the media attention at the same time. It was at this point that my husband Michael decided to leave his job in the Analytical Laboratories of the State Department of Health to join our research team at the University and also provide more support with the family."

This partnership provided valuable continuity to the research team (that is difficult in a university environment that relies on fixed term grants and research contracts) and also led to more state and national government funding and several improvement patents on improved electrodes, electrolyte processes and sensors.

Maria continues: "By working part-time, Michael was able to look after the boys after school, allowing me to pursue my full-time research career with the security of knowing that the family was in good hands. Despite the support of husband and parents, however, juggling career and family was not always easy and many sacrifices were needed while the boys were young, For years, our social life was restricted to activities that revolved around the boys and there was limited travel to overseas conferences to disseminate the group's research results."

Although it would take almost 20 years for the vanadium battery to become known in the international scientific community, the ongoing media interest was to generate very early commercial attention. In 1987, the Australian vanadium mining company Agnew Clough Pty. Ltd. acquired an exclusive international license to the VRB technology that led to 3 years of industrial funding to further develop the VRB at UNSW. Financial problems in the company led to the return of the technology to the university in 1991. In 1993, the Thai-based construction company Thai Gypsum Products was granted a license to the technology for the Southeast Asian region. Around the same time, Kashima-Kita Electric Power Corporation, a subsidiary of Mitsubishi Chemical Corporation, Japan, was attracted to the VRB technology as a way to use vanadium waste extracted from power station soot. By using orimulsion produced from vanadium-rich Venezuelan pitch as the fuel for the power station, large quantities of vanadium waste from the soot could be recycled into an electrolyte for VRBs that could be used for load-leveling at the power station. This valuable synergy led to the granting of a license to Kashima-Kita Electric Power Corporation and Mitsubishi Chemicals in 1993 that was followed by a 5-year R&D collaboration program between the Japanese companies and the UNSW research team, leading to further advances in stack design, improved materials and control systems.

Maria continued at the University of New South Wales as professor at the School of Chemical Engineering. In 2000 she founded the Centre for Electrochemical and Minerals Processing, serving as director until 2007.

From 1993 a number of field trials of the vanadium battery were undertaken both by UNSW and the university's licensees in Thailand and Japan. As part of the R&D collaboration programs with the licensees, regular trips between Sydney, Bangkok and Japan maintained a close relationship that culminated in several field trials, the first of which was the installation of a 5 kW/15 kWh VRB in the first vanadium-powered solar demonstration house just outside of Bangkok. The battery was fabricated at UNSW by members of the VRB development group that included Michael Kazacos, Rui Hong, Chris Menictas, John Chieng, Jim Wilson and Rod McDermott. Integration into the solar house was done with the assistance of Rob Largent from the School of Electrical Engineering at UNSW, who was also responsible for the design and fabrication of the battery controller that managed the pumps and battery operation.

In order to demonstrate the vanadium battery in a mobile application, a 36-volt vanadium battery prototype was installed in a commercially available electric golf cart at UNSW in 1994, where it was subjected to over 2½ years of off-road testing by the VRB development tram. A new improved 3 M vanadium solution had been undergoing bench-testing since late 1997 and was subsequently evaluated in the golf-cart battery. Preliminary results were very promising, but further long-term testing would still be needed before a practical 3-molar vanadium electrolyte with energy density of over 35 Wh/kg would be available for commercial application. Further research into air regeneration of the positive electrolyte was also explored as a means of doubling this to over 70 kW/kg (9).

In 1998, however, the VRB patents were sold by UNSW to the Australian-listed company Pinnacle VRB, but rather than speeding up the commercial development of the VRB, a range of corporate restructures and takeovers followed that saw the patents acquired by the Canadian company VRB Power and later Prudent Energy in China, with no further involvement of the UNSW team in its commercialization.

In the meantime, Maria was keen to explore new electrolytes for a high energy density VRB, and in 2001, she filed the first patent on a new Vanadium Polyhalide Flow Battery that led to the Generation 2 vanadium bromide flow battery with almost double the energy density of the original vanadium sulfate system. The technology was licensed to the Australian company V-Fuel Pty. Ltd., but difficulties in attracting investment income in Australia saw the company folding in 2010 with the patent rights returned to the university. Further development of the G2 V/Br is continuing as part of an R&D collaboration between UNSW and Nanyang Technological University in Singapore, and significant progress has already been made with new low cost bromine complexing agents and membranes.

Maria Skyllas-Kazacos's contribution is widely recognized. She is a fellow of the Australian Academy of Technological Sciences and Engineering, a fellow of the Royal Australian Chemical Institute and of the Institution of Engineers, Australia. She is a chartered professional engineer, a member of the Electrochemical Society of the USA, and has been a member of the Australian Electric Vehicle Association.

In 1999 she was made a member of the Order of Australia. Her research has gained her many honors, including the R. K. Murphy Medal in 2000, again from the Royal Australian Chemical Institute; the Chemeca Medal of the Institution of Engineers Australia; and the Castner Medal, awarded by the UK Society for the Chemical Industry in 2011. In 2009 she was also invested as Grand Lady of the Byzantine Order of Saint Eugene of Trebizond, reconnecting her to her Greek Byzantine roots and heritage.

By 2007, more than 20 medium- to large-scale VRB systems had been installed by

Sumitomo Electric Industries in Japan, USA, Europe and Australia for the storage of wind and solar energy and for load leveling at power stations and back-up power. The largest of these was a 4 MW/6 MWh VRB integrated to a wind farm on the Japanese island of Hokkaido. Several companies are now manufacturing or are in the process of setting up production of the VRB in China and Europe, while a grant from the U.S. Department of Energy was awarded in 2010 for the installation of a 6 MWh VRB installation at the Painesville Municipal Power Plant in Ohio using the UNSW technology.

Several other companies—including Cellstrom, a subsidiary of the German company Gildemeister, Cellenium in Thailand, and Rongke Power in China—have already implemented VRB technology over the past decade. The Chinese corporation, Prudent Energy, that had purchased the UNSW patents along with the assets of the Canadian company VRB Power Systems in 2008, continues to develop and commercialize VRBs throughout China and North America, while other groups have also been developing VRB products using original UNSW patents that expired in 2006.

Since that time, Maria and her team have developed and patented some improved VRB designs that will help to achieve significant cost reduction to make the battery economically viable for a wider range of grid-connected applications. In 2013 the University of New South Wales licensed these improvements to another Chinese company, Vanadis Energy, that has set up a factory to produce VRB systems for worldwide application.

Sumitomo Electric Industries has also announced that it has now developed a fully commercial VRB system that it will market around the world from early 2015.

Maria has over 250 publications including more than 40 patents and patent applications. She is currently a professor emeritus at the University of New South Wales, where she continues to supervise up to 10 PhD and honors students in aluminum smelting and flow battery projects. She is also continuing to assist the university with new licensing enquiries for the improved VRB technology developed at UNSW over the last few years.

With several companies now commercializing the VRB technology, Maria is being sought after for technical advice and personnel training. Since 2013, she has been providing courses on the VRB technology to a number of these groups, helping them to train their engineers and scientists to develop, install, commission, operate and maintain VRB installations for a wide range of energy storage applications.

Despite the success of the VRB around the world, Maria has other preoccupations: "Michael and I started dancing classes about 5 years ago (ballroom and Latin) and this is one hobby/sport that we have been enjoying." She regards her role as mother, and more recently as grandmother, to be the greatest blessings and her life's greatest achievements. Each week she looks forward to seeing and playing with her precious granddaughters Eliana and Kristyn and hopes to be blessed with more grandchildren in the future. She is now also caring for her elderly mother Kaliopi, who has been such a strong support for her family throughout her life.

"Michael and I have also been doing a lot of travel over the last 10 years—mainly on business and to present at conferences—and this is also something we really enjoy, since it takes us to many wonderful places and allows us to make new friends from all around the world."

Sources: From an article by the author published in *Batteries International*, Winter 2013/2014, based on information supplied and updated by Maria Skyllas-Kazacos.

Smee, Alfred
(1818–1877)
Silver zinc sulfuric battery

Alfred Smee was born in Camberwell, London, on June 18, 1818, the second son of William Smee, accountant-general to the Bank of England. He attended St. Paul's School from 1829 and in October 1834 he became a medical student at King's College, London, where he carried off the silver medal and prize for chemistry in 1836, and the silver medals for anatomy and physiology in 1837. He then left King's College, and entered St. Bartholomew's Hospital. He was a dresser to the surgeon, William Lawrence, and obtained a prize in surgery. He received his diploma of member of the Royal College of Surgeons of England on April 24, 1840, and he began to practice as a consulting surgeon in Finsbury Circus suburb, devoting his attention more especially to diseases of the eye.

Smee lived the greater part of his student life in the official residence of his father within the Bank of England, and it was here that he carried out his work into chemistry and electro-metallurgy. One of his first innovations was a method of making splints out of plastic materials, known as "gum and chalk," which was only superseded by the use of plaster of Paris.

During this period, many attempts were being made to produce an electric battery that was compact, durable and safe. During the late 1830s, still in his early twenties, Smee developed what he called a "Chemico Mechanical Battery." It was composed of six cells, and its positive plates were made of amalgamated zinc and the negative plates were coated in a finely divided layer of platinized silver, thus ensuring perfect contact with the exciting liquid: dilute sulfuric acid. This liquid was found to be far more efficient than sulfate of copper or muriate of soda.

Built for the eye surgeon by Edward Palmer, normally a microscope manufacturer of Newgate Street, Smee's battery was first reported in the *London Journal of Arts and Sciences* (1840), and was awarded the gold medal of the Society for the Encouragement of Arts.

In his book, *Elements of Electro-Metallurgy: or The Art of Working in Metals by the Galvanic Fluid* (December 1, 1840), Smee wrote: "To cross the seas, to traverse the roads, and to work machinery by galvanism, or rather electro-magnetism, will certainly, if executed, be the most noble achievement ever performed by man."

As he continued his career as a surgeon, Smee's only other main invention was an improved ink for printing bank notes. In later life, he devoted himself to horticulture at his experimental garden at Wallington in Surrey, publishing his results in a magnificent work, *My Garden; Its Plan and Culture* (1872). He describes the planting of the garden at "The Grange" in Wallington on the banks of the River Wandle, as well as the natural history and archaeology of the area. Alfred Smee died on January 11, 1877.

Sudworth, James
(1939–2013)
Missionary for the sodium sulfur battery

James Lowe Sudworth was born in January 1939 in Ashton-in-Makerfield, near Wigan in the north of England. His father was a foundry worker. It was at Ashton Grammar School that the chemistry teacher inspired Jim with an enthusiasm for this subject. Leaving school at 16, Jim obtained a job as a technician at ICI Widnes, working in the analytical chemistry laboratory. Although he had left school early—or what we would call early nowadays—he had ambitions to advance himself. He studied on day release at Widnes Technical College for the Royal Institute of Chemistry (now the Royal Society for Chemistry) qualification.

At the same time, and unusually for the 1950s when most Britons rarely crossed the English Channel abroad, he traveled widely across Europe, using his passion for cycling to power his way across the continent.

After graduation, Sudworth worked on the synthesis of hydrogen cyanide, which is a key raw material in the manufacture of polymethyl methacrylate (Perspex) at the laboratory and pilot plant scale. In 1962 he had a big year. That year he married Sheila after a three-year courtship. They would have four children, two boys and two girls.

It was also the year that first brought him into professional contact with sulfur, the periodic element that was to dominate most of the rest of his life. Between 1962 and 1963, Sudworth was employed as a scientist at Schenectady Midland, a tar distillery, in Wolverhampton. "I worked on the removal of sulfur from phenols by solvent extraction of a solution of their sodium salts, taking the process to the pilot plant scale," he later recalled.

From 1965 to 1967, he worked at Chloride—one of the biggest names in batteries at that time—at its plant at Swinton. Sudworth concentrated on sealed nickel cadmium cells, and then on the stability of the platinum electrode in the hydra-zinc/air aqueous fuel cell.

Perhaps his biggest break—and certainly one that was to affect the course of his life—came in 1967, when he joined British Rail. "They were opening a new research center in Derby and advertised for electrochemists. Their plans were exciting: they were interested in developing a new battery, for powering locomotives, the sodium sulfur battery."

The next step came from the Ford Motor Company, Dearborn, Michigan. Two researchers into auto-catalysts, Neill Weber and Joseph T. Kummer, formerly investigating the Fischer-Tropsch synthesis at the Mellon Institute, had

James Sudworth (*Batteries International*).

demonstrated a major "breakthrough in developing a feasible power source for electric vehicles," according to an announcement in October 1966:

> The heart of the new system is a Ford-developed crystalline ceramic electrolyte composed largely of aluminum oxide and based on a material known as beta-alumina.
>
> Further development of the Ford battery should lead to an economical, rechargeable battery system which, when adapted to a vehicle will provide greatly improved acceleration and range capabilities than now available from existing batteries.

U.S. Patent 3413150 A (1966): "Battery having a molten alkali metal anode and a molten sulfur cathode."

British Rail, however, was more focused on locomotive applications, and Sudworth's first task in the late 1960s was to build and test a cell that would replicate the results of Weber and Kummer.

To do this he needed the ceramic electrolyte, beta alumina. "I found out that a ceramicist at English Electric, Hamish Duncan, was working on ways of eliminating this from alpha alumina ceramics used as radomes as it was an efficient absorber of radio waves. I persuaded him to join me at BR and by creating the opposite conditions to those he used to eliminate beta alumina, he was soon able to fabricate ceramic discs from the material. At this point, the acting head of the electrochemistry section was promoted and I was offered his job."

During the next 15 years, based at the British Rail Technical Centre in London Road, Derby, Sudworth was responsible for directing a team of 20 to 40 scientists and technicians in the development and production of beta alumina, cells and batteries. "When we looked at what the characteristics of a battery needed to power a locomotive would be, it was clear that it would have to store several megawatt hours of energy. It had to be recharged in a couple of hours. Even for the sodium sulfur battery, that was a huge challenge."

The BR team came up with the idea of a hybrid locomotive, with a diesel engine running at constant speed and maximum efficiency and the battery taking care of the peak power requirements. They built several batteries but never got to the point of installing them in locomotives (although over 20 years later, General Electric did build a hybrid locomotive using a different type of sodium battery, as described below). One major problem that had to be overcome was to make the sodium sulfur battery safe enough to use in mobile applications.

In 1971 Sudworth took out his first patent. Then in 1973, with John Gibson, who worked for him at BR, he wrote his first book: *Specific Energies of Galvanic Reactions and Related Thermodynamic Data*. It was published by Chapman & Hall. In the years to come, Jim Sudworth would write numerous papers and as inventor/co-inventor take out numerous patents on high-temperature batteries.

Sudworth recalls:

> The first milestone at BR Research was to reproduce the results of Kummer and Weber, which we achieved in 1969. The next milestone was to build a battery. We weren't the first to build a full-size battery capable of powering a vehicle. That was achieved by Wynne-Jones and his colleagues at the Electricity Council in the UK, who installed it in a Bedford van. Subsequently, however, we developed a high rate sulfur electrode capable of rapid charging, came up with the safety features which overcame the tendency for these batteries to catch fire, and overcame the problem of short cycle life and increases in the internal resistance of the battery.

Abruptly, in 1981, the project at BR was closed down before Sudworth and crew could test their battery on trains. BR had been in a cooperative government-supported program with Chloride Silent Power (CSPL) and AEA Harwell. CSPL decided to tie up with General Electric, which was also developing the battery. This resulted in the breakdown of the cooperative agreement and ended BR's rationale for continuing development of the battery.

Sudworth later recalled:

> I suggested to Hamish Duncan and another of my colleagues, Roger Tilley, that we should go for a management buyout and to continue developing the battery for other organizations. We went public and as a result were approached by companies interested in funding the development. We were also approached by Ron Dell who was in charge of Harwell's battery programme. He told me that they had been using beta alumina tubes we supplied them on a separate battery programme funded by DeBeers, the South African diamond mining company and Anglo American. Dell introduced us to Roger Wedlake, the DeBeers programme manager.

Sudworth led the negotiations with Anglo American, which culminated in the signing of an agreement to do contract research on a new battery and in the formation of Beta Research & Development Ltd. in January 1982.

Up to this point, Anglo American had refused to disclose what the new battery system was, but the agreement included a six-month contract to develop the battery for them. On the basis of this, Sudworth and his two colleagues persuaded the key members of the BR team to join the new company. "BR were generous enough to lease us the laboratory we had been working in and to sell us all the equipment."

On January 4 the new team assembled in their lab to meet Johan Coetzer, the inventor of the new Zebra battery, and to hear what it was they would be working on. "This turned out to be the sodium/ metal chloride battery, which then was in a very early stage of development, so much so that I couldn't imagine how it could be commercialized and was convinced that it would be abandoned by Anglo American in favour of the sodium sulfur battery. We soon realized the potential of Johan's invention and in cooperation with his group in South Africa and Harwell, we went on to commercialize it."

As chairman and managing director, Sudworth was responsible for all aspects of the development of the Zebra battery and its transfer to production. The first challenge was that the positive electrode was fabricated by passing chlorine over an iron/carbon body—not exactly a practical commercial process. Moreover, the cell could only operate in a narrow temperature range. Two key developments were to change the metal to nickel and to build the cell fully discharged, meaning that the positive electrode was a sintered body of nickel and salt and no elemental sodium was necessary. The nickel electrode had a wide operating temperature range as well as a higher voltage.

Within 18 months, Sudworth's team had built a sodium nickel chloride vehicle battery, and in 1987 Anglo American, who by that time had exercised their option to buy Beta Research & Development Ltd., started a collaboration with AEG.

The next challenge was to increase the specific power of the battery to meet Daimler's requirements for passenger car operation. This was achieved by changing the round beta alumina tube to a cloverleaf cross section tube and changing to a mixed nickel/iron positive electrode.

In 1984, Zebra Power Systems (ZPS) was formed in South Africa from the CSIR team. A multi-kWh battery was tested in a vehicle.

In 1985, with Roger Tilley, Sudworth co-wrote the seminal book *The Sodium Sulfur Battery*, published by Chapman and Hall; a Russian edition was published in 1988.

In 1986 further advances were made, in particular the development of 30kWh and

50kWh Na/FeCl batteries, and a 30kWh Na/NiCl battery was tested by Daimler-Benz engineers. Sudworth was part of the team that negotiated the joint venture agreement and was responsible for ensuring that the battery-powered Suzuki van met the performance parameters that Anglo American had given to Daimler-Benz.

In 1989 Anglo American Corporation formed a joint venture company with AEG with the aim of industrializing the Zebra battery. At that time AEG was being absorbed into Daimler-Benz, who evaluated the battery for electric vehicle applications.

There had been a long-term engagement by Ford into the use of sodium sulfur in electric vehicles such as the Ecostar, which was a small van based on the Ford Escort. The Ecostar of the early 1990s used ABB sodium sulfur battery technology pioneered by Wilfried Fischer in Heidelberg, Germany. Also approved for the Ford Ecostar was a Chloride sodium sulfur battery pioneered by Wynn Jones.

The test fleet of over 100 cars was operated on public U.S. roads by ordinary people and mostly used ABB technology. The Ford/ABB Ecostar sodium sulfur test fleet was a highly professional and successful program that focused on controlling the safety concerns of high-energy density sodium sulfur. Over 500 full-size traction batteries (approximately 40 kWh each) were built for the operational vehicles and for durability and safety testing.

The DB team led by Dieter Sahm, however, had a chemistry that was inherently safer, and they suggested a redesigned cell with a higher power-to-energy ratio than the 100Ah cell then being used. AEG Anglo Battery Holdings (AABH), a joint venture company, was formed to industrialize the battery.

Between 1990 and 1995, Daimler-Benz's fleet of Mercedes cars, using Na/NiCl2 slim-line cells, totted up some 100,000km of road testing. During this time, energy and power were improved and pilot lines went into operation in the UK and Germany. Beta R&D, under Sudworth's supervision, developed a high-power cell (monolith) which was transferred to pilot lines.

By 1997, alongside a new generation of batteries (>150W/kg) suitable for series production, the 80 Zebra-powered test vehicles had completed 1.6 million kilometers. By 1998 AEG Anglo had taken the development of the Zebra battery to the point where it was ready to be put into production.

"The pilot lines in Derby and Berlin were producing batteries at the rate of up to 20 per month, the electric vehicles were performing very well and the customers were pressing for a commitment for volume production," he recalled. At that time, however, the two parent companies of AABH were redirecting their strategies away from peripheral activities and towards their core businesses. For a time it looked as though the project would be terminated.

Then in 1999, a Swiss company called MES-DEA acquired the Zebra technology, including the production and development equipment and Beta R&D. Sudworth remained as the managing director to oversee Beta's role in support of MES-DEA's plan to relocate battery production to a new factory in Switzerland.

Beta took over the former AEG Anglo Batteries ceramic plant in Derby and recommenced beta alumina production. MES-DEA set up a factory in Stabio, southern Switzerland. By September 2002, having installed larger equipment, including moving the positive electrode plant from Derby, the Stabio factory was set up to manufacture 900 batteries per year, with an eventual target of 33,000 batteries/year depending on market demand.

Meantime, in July 2001, Jim Sudworth retired and Roger Bull took over as managing director. But retirement didn't last long—especially since there was still so much more to do: "In April 2003, I was invited by my former colleagues to lead the management buy-out of Beta R&D from MES-DEA and to take the job of research director because by then it had become clear to us that Carlo Bianco, the owner of MES-DEA, wanted to bring all the battery work together in Switzerland including the R&D and would close down the UK operation."

Putting the team back together, "Roger Bull, Roger Tilley and myself thought that we could make a business doing contract research on sodium batteries. I negotiated an agreement with Bianco for Beta Research and Development to become the UK agent for their sodium/metal chloride batteries and Beta once again became an independent company."

In January 2003, Sudworth was awarded the Earnest Yeager Memorial Award from the International Battery Association. He received this at the IBA-HBC Earnest Yeager memorial symposium in Hawaii: "For outstanding contributions to the development of sodium metal chloride (Zebra) batteries."

As an independent company, Beta R&D was then able to widen its scope to include R&D contracts with government, EU, and commercial companies.

Under the UK government contracts, with their UK partners, Beta developed a sodium metal chloride battery for down-hole operation in the oil and gas industry. This included a hybrid power source comprising a solid oxide fuel cell and a sodium metal chloride battery. Under one of their EU contracts, Beta developed a high-power version of the battery for hybrid vehicle operation. In the commercial field they worked with Rolls-Royce to provide a sodium metal chloride battery to power a NATO rescue submarine which is now in operation, and they did sub-contract research for GE's Global Research Center on their hybrid loco project.

In September 2007, Beta R&D was acquired by General Electric Transportation Division, and is assisting in the development of sodium batteries for telecom, UPS, hybrid locomotive and utility applications.

In 2010, GE Energy Storage invested over £1.7 million ($2.6 million) and created more than 50 new jobs at its Durathon battery research facility in Burton-on-Trent as it expanded its battery technology into new applications.

After over 40 checkered years, Jim Sudworth was working towards the ultimate success of Beta's sodium metal chloride battery program, when he died suddenly in November 2013. He was 74. By that time GE's $250 million factory in Schenectady, New York, was up and running. At full capacity the battery factory will employ 350 people and produce 10 million cells annually.

Sources: article published in *Batteries International*, Summer 2013, based on information supplied to the author by the late James Sudworth in the spring of that year.

••

Takeuchi, Esther Sans
(1953–)
Lithium/silver vanadium oxide (Li/SVO) battery

Esther Sans (Latvian: Laimdota Alma Estere Sāns) was born in Kansas City, Missouri, on September 8, 1953. Her parents, Rudolf Sans, an electrical engineer, and his wife Mary (who had a degree in economics) fled Soviet-occupied Latvia for Germany in 1945, living in a refugee camp for several years, ultimately immigrating to the United States. Rudolf Sans's first job was in Kansas City, Missouri, where he worked first in a coffin factory and then at TWA. Later the family moved to Akron, Ohio, where he worked at Goodyear Aerospace for many years.

As a child growing up in Akron, Esther, ever curious, once took a hammer and smashed open some polished river stones in her family's driveway, revealing the multitude of colors inside. She also rubbed off the outside of stray golf balls she collected from a practice field to find the yards and yards of rubber band at the centers. She would follow her father everywhere wanting to see everything he did as he fixed things around the house, and her father was happy to oblige; as a result, Esther felt as though she could accomplish and achieve anything she set her mind to.

After graduating from Old Trail High School in Bath, Ohio, Esther attended the University of Pennsylvania, where she earned a bachelor of arts degree in with dual majors in chemistry and history in 1975. She then worked on her PhD in organic chemistry at Ohio State University until 1981. In her dissertation research, focused on organosilicon materials, she conducted mechanistic studies on nuclephilic attack.

During this time she met Kenneth J. Takeuchi, who graduated from Ohio State University with a PhD in inorganic chemistry. They both pursued postdoctoral research at the University of North Carolina and were married on May 15, 1982.

Kenneth Takeuchi became a regional and national award-winning SUNY Distinguished Teaching Professor and a nationally recognized expert in synthesis and characterization of innovative materials.

After completing postdoctoral training in electrochemistry at the University of North Carolina at Chapel Hill and the University of Buffalo, in 1984 Esther Takeuchi found work at Greatbatch Inc. in Clarence, New York. As one of the senior chemists working at the Clarence, New York–based company, with funding from Wilson Greatbatch (see Greatbatch entry), Takeuchi was part of a team to improve the autonomy of the cardiac defibrillator battery.

Takeuchi: "They were using a battery at the time to demonstrate that the concept (the implantable cardiac defibrillator, ICD) would work. But it turned out that the battery that was initially used, only lasted maybe a year or a year and a half, while the goal was to target approximately five years. To replace the battery requiring annual surgery was never a safe idea."

By 1987, Takeuchi and the team had invented and refined the life-saving lithium/silver vanadium oxide (Li/SVO) battery technology, utilized in the majority of today's implantable cardioverter defibrillators (ICDs). In Takeuchi's innovation, the cathode material employs two metals, silver and vanadium, rather than just one, allowing for more energy. In addition, the Li/SVO chemistry lets the ICD monitor the level of discharge, allowing it to predict end of service in a reliable manner. Several key patents were issued around the technology, describing a range of topics from the battery design to the synthesis of the active material. In 2005 Greatbatch introduced its new "Q Series" battery, which moves away from using only silver vanadium oxide, combining it with another material, carbon monofluoride.

In 2007, Esther Takeuchi joined academia as the Greatbatch Professor of Advanced Power Sources in the Departments of Chemical Engineering and Electrical Engineering at the University of Buffalo in Buffalo, New York. With $1 million funding from the National Institutes of Health, she continued to develop new cathode materials for improved ICDs. This involved fine-tuning bimetallic materials at the atomic level, such as silver nanoparticles.

Takeuchi reports:

> We are actively pursuing new battery ideas. We are investigating new material concepts where the structure and molecular dimensions are carefully controlled. We are working with materials in the nano-scale to provide facile access of ions and electrons to the core of the materials. We have also incorporated silver ions in the active material. When the battery is activated, it forms silver metal within the matrix of the cathode. This enhances the conductivity by 15,000 times and allows the battery to deliver current faster. We may be heading toward a time when we can make batteries so tiny that they—and the devices they power—can simply be injected into the body.

Since then, she has received many honors. She was awarded the 2009 National Medal of Technology by U.S. President Obama for her innovations in lithium battery technology and their impact on biomedical devices. To this has been added membership in the prestigious National Academy of Engineering, fellowship of the American Institute for Medical and Biological Engineering, and in 2011 membership in the National Inventors Hall of Fame, alongside icons such as Thomas Edison and Steve Jobs. She is also a recipient of the E.V. Murphy Award in Industrial and Engineering Chemistry awarded by the American Chemical Society. Regardless of the exact number, Takeuchi currently holds the title of the American woman with the most patents (at least 150).

In 2012, Takeuchi moved to the Departments of Materials Science and Engineering and Chemistry at SUNY's Stony Brook University in Stony Brook, New York, and took on an additional post as chief scientist at Brookhaven National Laboratory's Global and Regional Solutions Directorate. Her research focus: novel power sources including development of new materials and investigation of faradaic and non-faradaic mechanisms relevant to battery systems. Her research involves continued collaboration with Kenneth Takeuchi, who designs most of the synthetic approaches to the new materials that they study. She also works closely with collaborator Dr. Amy Marschilok, research associate professor, who is involved in material characterization as well as electrochemical assessment.

Takeuchi has a particular interest in the mechanisms that affect the lifetime of batteries and in mechanistic studies. Current research includes the investigation of discharge as well as in-situ methods. Further, the group is exploring the use of low cost earth abundant materials for possible battery use.

In June 2014, Takeuchi received notification from the U.S. Department of Energy that her proposal for a multi-institutional Energy Frontier Research Center (EFRC) would be financed to the tune of $10 million. Known as the Center for Mesoscale Transport Properties (m2M), it houses labs where basic science research is being conducted to understand and provide control of transport properties in complex battery systems with respect to multiple length scales, from molecular to mesoscale (m2M), and to minimize heat and maximize work of electrical energy storage devices. This project is a multi-institutional effort that involves top scientists from around the country.

Esther has several hobbies including collecting depression glass. She and her husband make a point of walking every day to take time to discuss the events of the day while getting exercise. Takeuchi maintains boundless optimism about the future possibilities of science, and of energy storage in particular. The field is exciting as ever and the new analytical methods that are becoming available will provide new insights into the complex chemistry and physics of energy storage.

Sources: Communication with the author, December 29, 2014.

Thackeray, Michael Makepeace
(1949–)
Lithium-ion battery cathodes

Michael Makepeace Thackeray was born in Pretoria, South Africa, on January 20, 1949. He is a distant cousin of William Makepeace Thackeray, a Victorian novelist and satirical writer, particularly well known for *Vanity Fair*. His parents, David and Mary Thackeray, emigrated from England after World War II in 1947 to the outskirts of Pretoria, South Africa. David was to become director of the Radcliffe Observatory, at the time home to the largest 74-inch reflecting telescope in the Southern Hemisphere.

The 52-acre observatory plot was ideal for developing Michael's passion for the African bush and outdoor life, as were the scientific environment and the family's love of classical music for nurturing his interest in science and the arts. Michael was educated at Waterkloof House Preparatory School (WHPS) in Pretoria and at Michaelhouse in the Natal Province, where he matriculated in 1965 at the age of 16.

Given his young age, he spent a postmatric year at Michaelhouse before being conscripted into the South African Army's 6th Signal Squadron in 1967. He enrolled at the University of Cape Town (UCT) in 1968, where he graduated with a B.S. with honors (1971) and M.S. (1973), majoring in chemistry.

Uncertain of where a degree in science would lead him, Thackeray recalls a moment in his second year during a crystallography class in the geology department when he felt a strong connection to the beauty of the crystalline world, gemstones and the history of the Earth. "I was enticed to UCT's Chemistry Department, where Professor Luigi Nassimbeni, a flamboyant and outstanding lecturer, convinced me of the important role that crystallography could play in practical materials science and structure-property relationships."

Hesitant of the future importance of crystallographic organo-metallic chemistry that he used for his master's thesis, Thackeray left the academic environment and headed for South Africa's major national laboratory, the Council for Scientific and Industrial Research (CSIR), where he joined the Crystallography Division of the National Physical Research Laboratory (NPRL) in Pretoria, his home town.

Thackeray started work at the CSIR in August 1973. Fortunately, he got off to a good start, quickly unraveling two light atom structures that had eluded the efforts of others.

Realizing that he was the right age to travel before getting bogged down in a career; Thackeray gambled and asked his supervisor, Geoff Gafner, if he could take a year's unpaid leave. Gafner was generously supportive, saying, "We'll hold your job for you—see you in a year's time!" So at the end of January 1974, Michael headed for Durban, where he joined a young Swedish yachtsman and his girlfriend who were sailing around the world and hitched a ride to Cape Town—a seven-day trip with gale force winds and mountainous waves, windless moments in becalmed, mirror-like seas, and a near collision with a fishing fleet on approaching Cape Town.

In Cape Town, he collected and married longstanding girlfriend Lisa Suzanne Kreft—traveling around Europe for six months on an extended honeymoon in a makeshift van, and returning penniless to South Africa in December 1974. Over the next 10 years, they produced three daughters, Caryn, Anna and Lara.

Michael Thackeray, co-pioneer in lithium-ion battery cathodes (Argonne National Laboratory).

From an early age, Thackeray always believed that developing interests and maintaining mental activity and bodily fitness made a powerful combination to cope with the pace of modern life and its day-to-day stresses. He has been a running enthusiast his whole life, representing his university and province at track, cross country and marathon events, and completing South Africa's ultra marathons—the highly scenic Two-Oceans marathon in Cape Town (35 miles) and the hilly Comrades marathon (56 miles) run between Durban at the coast and Pietermaritzburg inland, 10 and 14 times, respectively. He is a sub–4-minute metric miler (1500m) and sub-2:30 marathoner.

Thackeray resumed his career at the CSIR in January 1975, by which time Johan Coetzer had also returned to CSIR's Crystallography Division after a short break managing his family's farm in Pongola, Natal. The time coincided with the first oil crisis in the Middle East, which spawned intense worldwide efforts to find other forms of energy storage besides fossil fuels, notably rechargeable batteries. By the time Thackeray returned, Coetzer had initiated studies of silver-ion solid electrolytes that showed anomalously high ionic conductivity at room temperature.

Thackeray used this project for a PhD thesis, gaining his degree through the University of Cape Town in 1977, while Coetzer embarked on high-temperature studies of lithium-sulfur and sodium-sulfur cells, embedding the sulfur in the pores of a zeolite matrix in attempts to reduce corrosion and enhance the safety of the cells. After completing his PhD, Thackeray assisted Coetzer and, in a parallel effort, initiated an investigation of high-temperature lithium-metal oxide cells.

Coetzer's and Thackeray's studies heralded the start of a twenty-year period when

CSIR and South Africa would make major contributions to electrical energy storage concepts and technologies. Their early studies also received the attention of South African industry, De Beers and Anglo American Corporation, the mining giants of diamonds and precious metals. Imagining the possibility of mass electrified transportation by the turn of the century, De Beers and Anglo American joined and supported CSIR's efforts to develop advanced high-energy batteries.

By 1980, significant progress had been made at CSIR. Coetzer's high-temperature sodium-zeolite sulfur concepts had been redirected to sodium-iron chloride chemistry that was compatible with a conventional sodium-sulfur cell design in which a solid sodium-ion conducting solid electrolyte, beta-alumina, was used to separate the molten sodium and sulfur electrodes. By contrast, in the sodium-iron chloride cell, later code-named the "Zebra" cell, the solid beta-alumina ceramic was used to separate the molten sodium electrode from a solid iron chloride electrode and a molten sodium ion conducting electrolyte, $NaAlCl_4$.

At the same time, Thackeray's high-temperature studies of lithium-transition metal oxide cells had revealed that iron oxide electrodes showed remarkable electrochemical stability, operating by reversible lithium insertion/iron extrusion reactions into and from a stable oxygen close-packed array to yield metallic iron and lithia (Li_2O) via intermediate spinel and rocksalt phases. Because lithium/iron oxide cells (1.1 V) provided a significantly lower voltage relative to Zebra sodium/iron chloride cells (2.35 V) and subsequently sodium/nickel chloride cells (2.6V), De Beers and Anglo American opted to focus on sodium batteries rather than lithium technology. By the early 1990s, in partnership with Daimler-Benz (Germany) and Beta R&D (UK), Zebra batteries had been demonstrated in electric vehicles. These batteries are currently being produced by FIAMM for electric transportation in Europe, and by General Electric in the United States, primarily for stationary energy storage applications under the new brand name "Durathon Batteries."

Despite the exciting progress being made by his CSIR colleagues in high-temperature sodium-metal chloride technology, Thackeray was more strongly drawn to lithium electrochemistry:

It offered greater prospects for undertaking crystallographic studies of electrode materials and for probing structural phenomena during electrochemical lithium insertion reactions. Moreover, at that time, the first generation of room temperature, primary (non-rechargeable) lithium cells was being produced by industry. Therefore, in late 1980, with the support of CSIR, the South African Inventions and Development Corporation (SAIDCOR) and Anglo American, I wrote to Professor John B. Goodenough [see Goodenough entry], who had recently pioneered the discovery of $LiCoO_2$ as a lithium insertion electrode at the Inorganic Chemistry Laboratory, Oxford University in England to ask if I could spend a post-doctoral period with him to learn the art of room temperature lithium electrochemistry. Goodenough responded warmly with an invitation for the visit.

Thackeray arrived at Oxford in October 1981, with his wife and, at that stage, two daughters Caryn (2½) and Anna (6 months); they found accommodation in Wolvercote on the outskirts of the city with a beautiful panorama of the Thames and Wolvercote Common, the spires of Oxford in the background. It was to be the start of one of the most intellectually stimulating periods of his life.

Because his earlier research at CSIR on the electrochemical behavior of iron oxide electrodes in high-temperature lithium cells had shown that, in the charged state, iron oxide spinel structures were formed, Thackeray had arrived in Oxford with several spinel samples in his possession, including magnetite, Fe_3O_4, and hausmannite, Mn_3O_4.

Thackeray: "My first meeting with Goodenough, I suggested my research plan to investigate the electrochemical behaviour of spinels at room temperature. Goodenough responded gently with the comment, 'Well, you do know that spinels are like gems, stable line-phases ... so where is the space in the structure to accommodate the inserted lithium ions during discharge? By all means try, but I suggest that you look around the laboratory to see what other projects are going on.'

The mineral "spinel" ($MgAl_2O_4$) is a semiprecious gem, one of the most famous being the misnamed Black Prince's Ruby, dating back to the 14th century, which is positioned above South Africa's Cullinan II Diamond on the Imperial State Crown, one of the British Crown Jewels. Goodenough then left for a visit to India, returning some two weeks later.

Thackeray immediately set to work, first conducting a chemical reaction of lithium with Fe_3O_4 at room temperature to mimic the electrochemical reaction. To his delight, Thackeray observed that the magnetic Fe_3O_4 particles, which clung to the magnetic stirrer in the reaction vessel, gradually fell away from the stirrer on the addition of the lithium reagent, n-butyl-lithium—evidence of iron reduction and reaction between lithium and the spinel structure. On obtaining the powder X-ray diffraction pattern and a compositional analysis of the lithiated product, Thackeray determined that, on lithiation, the cubic unit cell of the Fe_3O_4 host structure had expanded by approximately 3 percent and that there were changes in the relative intensities of the diffraction peaks, confirming the lithium insertion process.

On John Goodenough's return from India, Thackeray bumped into him close to the laboratory where the experiment had been conducted. Thackeray recalls: "I told him that lithium was indeed going into the spinel, Fe_3O_4. Goodenough immediately laid his hand on my shoulder and led me into his office, saying, 'Sit down, tell me all.'"

A few days later, Bill David, a highly talented physicist and crystallographer from the nearby Clarendon Laboratory, who had also recently joined John Goodenough's research team, introduced himself to Thackeray—he had heard of the Fe_3O_4 results from Goodenough. David had access to the "Wiseman" computer program—software written by Phil Wiseman, who had worked on Goodenough's earlier $LiCoO_2$ project, to undertake structural refinements of powdered materials with X-ray diffraction data. Refinement of the $Li_xFe_3O_4$ data showed that during the lithiation of magnetite, $Fe_{tet}[Fe_2]_{oct}O_4$, the $[Fe_2]_{oct}O_4$ spinel framework (with iron in octahedral sites) had remained intact, whereas the iron that resided in tetrahedral sites outside the framework were displaced into neighboring empty octahedral sites to make place for the uptake of one lithium ion to generate a rock salt structure $(LiFe)_{oct}[Fe_2]_{oct}O_4$; i.e., without iron extrusion as in high-temperature cells. Thackeray and David reported the results of the refinement to Goodenough with similar findings for hausmannite (Mn_3O_4) that, on lithiation, formed the corresponding ordered rocksalt structure $(LiMn)_{oct}[Mn_2]_{oct}O_4$.

The results had immediate scientific and technological implications. Goodenough, familiar with the spinel structure from his earlier research on their magnetic properties, suggested an investigation of the lithium spinel $Li_{tet}[Mn_2]_{oct}O_4$, which accommodated lithium by the same principle as Fe_3O_4 and Mn_3O_4 to form the ordered rocksalt configuration $(Li_2)_{oct}[Mn_2]_{oct}O_4$; in this case, the interstitial space of the $[Mn_2]_{oct}O_4$ spinel framework contained only lithium ions that could migrate, unimpeded, through a three-dimensional network of face-sharing tetrahedra and octahedra, providing fast kinetics and a high-power electrode. This reaction occurred electrochemically at 3 V in a lithium cell. Because the concept of spinel electrodes had originated at CSIR, Goodenough graciously agreed to cede title of the spinel patent that was filed to SAIDCOR, one of the South African sponsors of Thackeray's visit to Oxford, later to be licensed to industry. Over recent years, $Li[Mn_2]O_4$ has been widely exploited. It is often used as a blend in the cathodes of lithium-ion batteries, notably for portable electronics and electric vehicles, such as the all-electric Nissan Leaf and the hybrid-electric Chevy Volt.

Shortly after the discovery that spinel structures could act as insertion compounds for lithium at room temperature, Peter Bruce, an electrochemist from the University of Aberdeen, Scotland, joined the Oxford team, contributing to the evaluation of the electrochemical properties of the electrodes. It was a golden twelve months, a happy band of four—each contributing to a shared and impactful outcome of spinel research in different ways. Thirty years on, the four scientists are still in close communication with one another.

Thackeray returned to South Africa at the end of 1982. The Zebra team was on the verge of leaving the CSIR site to become an Anglo American–owned company, Zebra Power Systems, outside Pretoria. Thackeray remained at CSIR, where he established a new battery team to build on the lithium battery materials research he had initiated, while providing R&D support to the South African battery industry, including, amongst others, Zebra Power Systems; Willard Batteries, a producer of lead-acid batteries; and Delta EMD, a manufacturer of electrolytic manganese dioxide (EMD) for the alkaline (Zn/MnO_2) battery market.

Over the next 10 years, Thackeray and his CSIR team continued to innovate the design of new lithium battery electrode materials, structures and compositions, first focusing, on his return from Oxford, on the family of lithium spinels containing manganese, vanadium or iron. He demonstrated, in particular, that lithium could be extracted electrochemically from $LiMn_2O_4$ at an attractive 4 V. In 1987, there were indications that Sanyo and Sony Corporation were starting to pay particular attention to the manganese spinel, $LiMn_2O_4$. By then, it had been established that stoichiometric $LiMn_2O_4$ had significant problems, notably manganese dissolution that resulted from the dissociation of trivalent manganese ions into soluble divalent ions and insoluble tetravalent ions. Furthermore, lithium insertion into $LiMn_2O_4$ induced a severe crystallographic (Jahn-Teller) distortion that compromised the stability of the electrode particle surface and the reversibility of the reaction at 3 V.

Thackeray addressed these problems with Rosalind Gummow and Annemarie de Kock—they made significant improvements to the operational stability of $LiMn_2O_4$ by adding excess lithium (and other multivalent cations) to increase the average oxidation state of manganese in the starting spinel electrode above 3.5+. In 1994, Ernst Ferg, Gummow, de Kock and Thackeray demonstrated that safe 2.5 V lithium-ion cells could be fabricated by coupling a lithium titanate spinel anode ($Li_4Ti_5O_{12}$), which operates 1.5 V above the potential of metallic lithium, with high-voltage cathodes, notably a stabilized $Li_{1+x}Mn_{2-x}O_4$ spinel—a system that is currently being exploited for devices requiring high-power batteries, such as hybrid electric vehicles.

Recognizing the cost and stability advantages of manganese over cobalt and nickel oxide electrodes, the CSIR team adopted strategies to engineer and patent new lithium insertion materials, which included manganese oxide electrodes with one-dimensional, two-dimensional and three-dimensional pathways for lithium-ion transport. They were successful on all three counts, designing and evaluating lithia-stabilized alpha-MnO_2, lithia-stabilized layered-MnO_2 and lithia-stabilized spinel-MnO_2 electrode materials, respectively. Anhydrous layered MnO_2 structures were unknown at the time. Of particular significance was that Thackeray's approach to use the layered rocksalt structure of Li_2MnO_3 ($Li_2O \bullet MnO_2$) as a precursor to fabricate a Li_2MnO_3-stabilized layered MnO_2 electrode was the forerunner to further materials advances made by him and his team at Argonne National Laboratory a few years later.

While in South Africa, Thackeray was presented with several awards for his research contributions. In 1983, he was awarded a Silver Medal from the South African Institute of Physics for significant achievements for a scientist under the age of 35 for his seminal work on spinel electrodes. In 1990, he received the CSIR Outstanding Achiever Award and three years later the International Battery Association Research Award for significant contributions to the development and understanding of manganese oxides and vanadium oxides. Other awards followed. In 2005, Coetzer and Thackeray appeared as two of 11 notable South African scientists and innovators for contributions to world science and technology on the commemorative wall at Africa's first internationally accredited science park: the Innovation Hub. Indeed, visitors to the new Innovation Hub in Pretoria, South Africa, can drive down streets named after Michael Thackeray and Johan Coetzer.

In 1992, Thackeray was informed by senior management that despite the success of the lithium battery research being conducted at CSIR, a decision had been made to terminate further funding, ostensibly because there was no industry in South Africa to capitalize on the technology. It appeared that CSIR management was oblivious to Sony's introduction of the first lithium-ion battery products into the market in 1991 (see Hatazawa entry), and the need for high-energy batteries to power the impending boom of portable consumer electronics devices. It was therefore fortuitous that, at an Electrochemical Society Meeting in Toronto in October 1992, Thackeray met Don Vissers, head of the Battery Department at Argonne National Laboratory. Unaware of Thackeray's dilemma at CSIR, Vissers invited Thackeray to lead a materials R&D effort at Argonne for a new lithium-polymer battery project to be sponsored by the U.S. Department of Energy and the United States Advanced Battery Consortium (USABC). Thackeray, sensing a bright future for lithium battery technology and recognizing an excellent opportunity, accepted the invitation.

He and his family packed their bags and left South Africa for Chicago in January 1994. The decision was not easy—it meant leaving close-knit family and friends in midlife at a time when South Africa was undergoing daunting but exciting changes under Nelson Mandela's leadership. It also meant leaving a country with its diverse, colorful and vibrant population, beauty and splendor—and, particularly, a shared beachside cottage at Pringle Bay with its spectacular view over the Cape Peninsula, and access to the African bush and game parks, such as Pilanesberg outside Pretoria, where the nighttime silence of the bush and brilliant Milky Way overhead would be broken by the sounds of the wild—an aspect of life that had become, and are still, part of Michael's inner being.

Michael, Lisa, Caryn (15), Anna (12) and Lara (9) arrived at Chicago's O'Hare airport in February 1994. By this time reality had set in—they were on their own, not knowing a soul and far from family and friends. As the American Airlines aircraft approached the landing strip with the wheels a few feet from touchdown, the pilot opened the throttle and took the plane back into the air. There was a stunned silence in the aircraft—but Lisa, looking at Michael at her side, said quietly—"Thank God, we're going home!" (There was another aircraft on the runway.)

Thackeray settled quickly at Argonne—the cultures and scientific intellect of the

South African and American national laboratories were similar. Lisa, despite the heartache of leaving her homeland and family, acclimatized over time. She had become deeply involved in adult education in South Africa, helping those who had suffered a lack of education during the apartheid years. On her way to Johannesburg International Airport, a friend had mentioned that she knew the director of an adult literacy agency, Literacy Volunteers of America–Du Page, "somewhere near Chicago." Remarkably, it transpired that the literacy agency was in Naperville, just a stone's throw from the Thackerays' lodgings. It was meant to be—Lisa volunteered, later becoming program director of the organization until her retirement in 2012.

Like at CSIR and Oxford, Thackeray got off to a quick start—within two months of his arrival, while working on a high-energy, all solid-state, lithium-polymer battery project for electric vehicles supported by the U.S. Department of Energy, 3M Corporation, and Hydro-Quebec (HQ), he had identified a lithia-stabilized vanadium oxide cathode material (based on his earlier research at CSIR) that provided the 3M/HQ cells with 30 percent more energy and superior power relative to the original material being used. This materials technology was subsequently transferred to, and scaled up by, 3M and implemented by Hydro-Quebec/Avestor in commercial battery products for stationary energy storage. However, subsequent problems related to lithium dendrite formation and short-circuiting on long-term cycling ultimately led to the withdrawal of the batteries from the market.

During his early years at Argonne, Thackeray also received support from the Office of Basic Energy Sciences of the U.S. Department of Energy. With Christopher Johnson and others, he used the funding to continue his unfinished research of lithia-stabilized alpha-MnO_2, spinel-MnO_2, and layered-MnO_2 electrode structures. Towards the end of the 1990s, noticing that other research groups were initiating studies on Li_2MnO_3, Thackeray, Johnson, Khalil Amine, Jaekook Kim and an expanding Argonne team intensified their efforts to exploit composite "layered-layered" $xLi_2MnO_3 \bullet (1-x)LiMO_2$ (M=Mn, Ni, Co) and "layered-spinel" $xLi_2MnO_3 \bullet (1-x)LiM_2O_4$ (M=Mn, Li, Ni, Co) electrode structures, which formed the basis of a broad patent portfolio. Argonne's intellectual property was subsequently licensed worldwide to major lithium battery materials and cell manufacturers. The first generation Chevy Volt, in particular, uses a lithium-ion battery with a blend of the Argonne composite materials and stabilized $LiMn_2O_4$ spinel in the cathode.

In March 2007, Thackeray received an invitation to meet President George W. Bush at the White House for round-table discussions with eight others on his energy policy relating to lithium-ion batteries and bio-fuels. Also in attendance were Samuel Bodman, the Secretary of Energy; Karl Rove, the president's former senior advisor and deputy chief of staff; and Steven Chu, the future Secretary of Energy in the Obama administration. Thackeray stressed to the president that the U.S. had fallen way behind Japan, Korea and China in lithium-ion battery technology, despite the ability of the U.S. to continually innovate in the field; that lithium-ion batteries were becoming a strategic commodity; and that it was necessary for U.S. national laboratories, industry and academia to come together to address the issue, to play "catch up" and narrow the technological gap. Bush looked at Thackeray and said, "You are asking me for greater financial support?" to which Thackeray responded in the affirmative. A short conversation with Sam Bodman followed. Thackeray was subsequently asked to write a white paper for the White House outlining a strategy to address the needs for lithium-ion battery technology in the United States. President Bush was exceptionally hospitable, taking the nine invitees to the Oval Office, where he spoke candidly of the challenges and responsibilities of being president, particularly in defending the liberty of the United States and the free world.

A month later, the U.S. Department of Energy's Office of Basic Energy Sciences held a workshop on electrical energy storage to identify the basic research needs and opportunities underlying batteries, capacitors, and related energy storage technologies, with a focus on new or emerging science challenges with potential for significant long-term impact on the efficient storage and release of electrical energy. These events in 2007 heralded the start of a significantly increased investment and commitment by the United States government to support energy storage research and development. The workshop resulted in the instigation of five DOE Energy Frontier Research Centers (EFRCs) on Energy Storage in 2009, of which one was awarded, under a five-year contract, to Argonne National Laboratory with Northwestern University and the University of Illinois at Urbana-Champaign as institutional partners. Thackeray was appointed Director of the EFRC, the Center for Electrical Energy Storage—Tailored Interfaces. The prime mission of the Center was to acquire a fundamental understanding of electrode/electrolyte phenomena that control electrochemical processes to enable dramatic improvements in the design of new electrode/electrolyte materials and architectures, and in lithium battery performance. Among the Center's achievements was the design and characterization of several new silicon and silicon-carbon architectures for lithium-ion battery anodes, one of which led to the formation of a start-up company, SiNode, in Illinois.

Since arriving at Argonne, Thackeray has been honored with several additional awards: the University of Chicago Distinguished Performance Medal for contributions to lithium battery technology (2003); the Electrochemical Society Battery Division Research Award (2005); an R&D 100 Award: "Composite Electrode Materials for Plug-in Hybrid- and All-Electric Vehicle Batteries" (2009); the U.S. Department of Energy R&D Award—Office of Vehicle Technologies (2010); and the International Battery Association's Yeager Award for lifelong achievements in lithium battery electrode materials research and development (2011).

Thackeray is currently a distinguished fellow, senior scientist and group leader at Argonne. To date, he has published more than 200 scientific papers and is an inventor on 48 patents, several of which have been licensed on an international scale or sold to industry.

Regarding the future, Thackeray, now 64, believes that there is still much more to be done by the next generation of chemists, physicists, materials scientists, theoreticians and engineers to push the envelope of battery science and technology in an interdisciplinary manner even further: "I've spent thirty-five years in the battery game and I have been extremely fortunate to have worked with, and learned from, some of the best and brightest minds, both young and old. My experiences with lithium-ion technology can be likened to surfing a wave—a wave that is still building and has not yet broken. The challenges to increase the energy capacity of batteries further and to store the energy in smaller and smaller containers—safely—will be difficult, but not insurmountable. The 21st century will be about harnessing clean energy, a matter that is of growing environmental, economical and strategic importance for the future of the planet and humankind."

Sources: From an article by the author published in *Batteries International*, Spring 2014, based on information provided by Michael Thackeray.

Tobias, Charles W.
(1920–1996)
Nonaqueous solvents

Charles W. Tobias was born in Budapest, Hungary, on November 2, 1920. He received his diploma in 1942 and his doctorate in 1946 from the University of Technical Sciences in Budapest. He escaped to the U.S. in 1947 just as the communists were taking over Hungary, following his brother Cornelius, who was a faculty member in medical physics at UC Berkeley, California. Pursuing postdoctoral studies, Tobias was hired by Dean Wendell Latimer of the College of Chemistry to join the faculty of the nascent Chemical Engineering Group.

Tobias met his first wife, the former Marcia Rous, while living in Berkeley's International House after his arrival. They had three children, Carla, Eric, and Anthony.

In 1954, Tobias founded an electrochemical research program at the Lawrence Berkeley National Laboratory, which soon included collaborations with Charles Wilke and Donald Hanson, fellow chemical engineering faculty members. Tobias sought to replace these empirical, almost mystical approaches, introducing the methods of exact science. He studied fluid flow, electric potential fields, thermodynamic and materials properties, and mass transfer, linking his findings into a new discipline. Computers came into use during those years. Tobias and his colleagues pioneered in the use of computers to design and model electrochemical systems.

Tobias and his co-workers also did pioneering research with solvents. Up to that time, solvents had been water-based, but they had disadvantages. They ruled out the use of a number of promising electrode materials, which could react with the water to create hydrogen gas and an explosion. But Tobias discovered lithium, sodium, and potassium cannot be combined with an aqueous solvent but can safely react with the nonaqueous solvents. Decades later, this opened the way for the lithium battery.

As chair of the Berkeley Chemical Engineering Department from 1967 to 1972, Tobias placed strong emphasis on broadening the department to cover the newer subfields of chemical engineering, in particular the processing steps involved in semiconductor manufacture. This interest meshed well with the development of Silicon Valley and led to close ties between Berkeley chemical engineering and that growing industry. He also was acting dean of the College of Chemistry in 1978.

Tobias's graduate students produced 32 master's theses and 34 doctoral dissertations. His PhD graduates have literally populated the academic electrochemical engineering faculty of the succeeding generation. Thus in many ways he was a father of his field. He had more than 150 publications and patents.

Charles Tobias was elected to the National Academy of Engineering in 1983 and served shortly thereafter on NAE's Committee on Electrochemical Aspects of Energy Conservation and Production. He was president of the Electrochemical Society (1970–1971); a fellow, honorary member, and recipient of the society's Acheson Award (1972); the first Henry B. Linford Award for Distinguished Teaching (1982); and the Vittorio de Nora Diamond Shamrock Award for Electrochemical Engineering and Technology. He was president of the International Society for Electrochemistry (1977–1978). From the American Institute of Chemical Engineers he received both the Alpha Chi Sigma Award for distinguished research and the Founders Award.

After his wife Marcia's untimely death in 1981, Charles Tobias married Katalin Voros. He died on March 6, 1996, at his home in Orinda, California, after a long struggle with emphysema. He was 75.

Trouvé, Gustave Pierre
(1939–1902)
Sealed reversible battery

Gustave Pierre Trouvé was born on January 2, 1839, at La Haye-Descartes (the central French Department of the Indre et Loire). He was the son of Marisse and Jacques Trouvé, a wealthy cattle dealer. From his childhood, Trouvé held a fascination for making anything mechanical. With only needles, hairs and bits of lead, he produced a miniature steam engine of which an old tinder box made up the generator and which, despite the size of its elements, worked very well. Two self-taught skills would prove to his advantage—an ability to draw and an intricate skill with his fingers.

Trouvé studied at the Collège de Chinon before joining the Ecole des Arts et Métiers in Angers. In 1859, aged 21, he arrived in Paris and was apprenticed to a clockmaker.

On 8 May 1865, Trouvé took out his first patent:

Monsieur Trouvé (Gustave), watchmaker, living in Paris, rue and hotel Montesquieu, 5, has conceived of animating jewelry, clockwork and other objects d'art by the application of electricity and he has invented a wearable Lilliputian battery especially for this application. Here is the specification for his industrial application.

This electric battery is cylindrical. It is made up of a tube whose length is double that of the piece of zinc and carbon used inside the upper part. This device enables that in the vertical position, the liquid placed in the lower part has no contact with the carbon and zinc, while in the horizontal position, on the contrary, with the immersion taking place, the battery immediately starts to work. With this device, the battery does not wear out and lasts as long as it is not working, while in general, other systems of battery wear out without even being used.

Another advantage of this battery is that Mr. Trouvé reduces it as required infinitely small, and so easily transportable. In addition, it can be placed in a hardened rubber pouch, which completely encloses the cylindrical tube, in such a way that if it has just broken, the liquid in the battery cannot escape.

… As each object carries an engine in itself in an annex, it is easy to understand how the inventor succeeds in animating, by this process, birds, flowers and general objets d'art, from the moment they are in contact with his battery. These objets d'art being either for hanging, office ornaments, etc.

Patent Granted July 1st 1865 N° 67294 Duration: fifteen years.

Ministry of Agriculture, Commerce and Public Works. For the Minister. The Associate Director.

Trouvé did not know that over in Brussels, a Belgian inventor called Georges Leclanché (see Leclanché entry), exactly the same age as the Parisian, was working in a shed on a battery based on zinc and carbon activated by a solution of ammonium chloride. It was extremely similar to that of Trouvé. Leclanché patented his battery just six months after Trouvé. The Belgian telegraph service and the Netherlands Railways soon made use of it and Leclanché opened a factory for its production—unlike Trouvé, who was not interested in business potential. Leclanché's battery became known as the forerunner of today's dry cell battery and his name entered into history. Until recently Trouvé was not acknowledged for having invented the ubiquitous AA-sized battery in use throughout the world today.

Before long, Gustave and his elder brother Jules were able to set up their own precision-engineering business, making scientific observation instruments, with the particular innovation of powering them by electricity. Their first main product was an ingenious instrument for swiftly locating and extracting bullets or other projectiles from servicemen. Commissioned by the respected 60-year-old Professor Jules Gavarret, it took Trouvé only three weeks to assemble. It was in fact the prototype metal detector.

Soon after, in 1867, working with Gaston Planté (see Planté entry), Trouvé came up with the *electric* polyscope, ensuring the diagnosis of illnesses of the mouth, the throat, the ear, the eye, the nasal cavities and other lower organs. Several years before Edison, Trouvé succeeded in keeping the light of his battery-powered polyscope cool and longlasting. Today this is variously known as the otoscope, auriscope, opthalmoscope, etc.

Gustave Trouvé, French electrical genius (Musée EDF Electropolis, Mulhouse).

At the same time, the Trouvé brothers felt they should also make an appeal to the popular market, with some form of electrical trinket. Using their little sealed carbon-zinc battery the size or a cigar, they began to produce electro-mobile jewels, capable of making more or less complex movements with miniature electromagnets. Mounted on tiepins, these could be activated at will by the wearer; the mini-battery was hidden in the waistcoat pocket and linked to the jewel by an invisible wire. The owner could light up a butterfly, make a little grenadier beat a drum, or a monkey play a violin. Trouvé's *bijoux électriques* soon became the rage of Paris and London! (Their lithium-powered lead-based descendants, known as wearable technology, are now made in Asia).

Trouvé's sense of humor is exemplified the word he chose for his brand name. The initial of his first name added to his family name, G. Trouvé, translated as j'ai trouvé ("I have found [it]"), Archimedes's famous exclamation in Greek, εὕρηκα (heúrēka), would from now on be engraved on almost all the instruments he would conceive and make. It was easy to recognize a Trouvé instrument because it displayed the words "Trouvé—Paris" and then the Greek word for "I've found it!" *Eureka*, with its packing case in purple velveteen.

But perhaps Trouvé's key invention was a compact electric motor and its applications (Patent, 8 May 1880–Numéro 136,560). Its innovative feature was the electromagnets

Trouvé's electric tricycle on trial in downtown Paris in April 1881 (Musée EDF Electropolis, Mulhouse).

made of soft iron and tempered steel. With his larger batteries, Trouvé made some tests in boat trials up and down the River Seine. At first he used two motors to turn paddles. Then he used a propeller and placed it in a false mobile rudder placed sometimes in front, sometimes behind the rudder. "It's the rudder including the propelling unit and its engine, forming a movable whole, easily removable from the boat," he explained. This "gouvernail moteur propulseur" was the first outboard engine in the world.

And as if this was not challenging enough, in the spring of 1881 Trouvé electrified an English Coventry-Rotary tricycle. The two smaller wheels were each driven by a little 5kg motor: a Faure battery (see Faure entry) of six accumulators gave the current; the apparatus increased the weight of the vehicle to 160kg (350 lb.) and gave a speed of 12 km/h (7 mph).

A journalist called Henry de Parville wrote in *The Officiel* newspaper on April 20, 1881: "One of Trouvé's friends tried the new velocipede on the tarmac of the rue de Valois. He ran up and down the road several times at the speed of a good carriage." And this has since come to be regarded as the first lightweight electric vehicle in the world.

That a Trouvé-engined boat could make an extended voyage, was demonstrated when the yawl of Monsieur Schlesinger made an upstream voyage between Chatou and Besons. Trouvé also equipped Schlesinger's Paris house with battery-powered electric lighting.

For the International Exhibition of Electricity later that year, Trouvé devised a featherweight 220 gm electric motor constructed entirely of aluminum, except for the parts like the electromagnetic pole in iron which enabled the aeronaut Gaston Tissandier to make his first model balloon-airship demonstrations in one of the exhibition halls. Two years later, Tissandier and his brother would make three pioneer flights in their full-scale airship-balloon.

One journalist wrote: "*Mon sorcier s'appelle M Trouvé; il y a trois siècles, on l'eut brulé, aujourd'hui on l'apprecie comme l'inventeur le plus savant, l'electricien le plus ingénieux que nous possedons.*" ("My sorcerer is called M Trouvé; three centuries ago, one would have burned him, today one appreciates him as the most knowledgeable inventor, the most ingenious electrician that we possess.")

While visiting the Exhibition, the legendary American telephone inventor, Alexander Graham Bell, met Trouvé in Paris. Bell told Trouvé: "I wanted to surprise you amongst your works that I so much admire. In addition, I want to take away to America, a complete collection of all your inventions, because for me they make up the highest expression of the perfection and the ingenuity of the electric science in France."

Indeed, Trouvé was once hailed as "the Gallic Edison." But unlike Edison, this son of a cattle merchant was not interested in accruing wealth, merely in electrifying anything which had previously worked by human, clockwork or steam power.

To crown his successes, at the end of 1881, Trouvé was made a Chevalier of the Légion d'Honneur, one of many awards he received.

In the years which followed, people visited Trouvé at his workshop in central Paris, to commission a variety of objects: a photophore or frontal head-torch developed with Dr. Paul Hélot of Rouen, pioneer of ENT (ear-nose-throat medicine). There were improvements to the telephone; his auxanoscope for projecting drawings or photographs up onto a screen (macography); an electrically-lit front gunsight and projector for nocturnal hunting; an electric gyroscope for correcting the marine compass (1886); a light switch; an electric safety torch for miners; an orygmatoscope for the inspection of subterranean geological strata, initially used for exploration in Mozambique; and an underwater lamp, used during the building of the Suez Canal.

Alongside Alexander Graham Bell, among those who must have inspected Trouvé's inventions at the Paris Universal Exhibition and read up about them was a French science-fiction novelist called Jules Verne, who includes a variety of electric vehicles, submarines and airships (*The Clipper of the Clouds*) in his novels. Indeed, when Verne's comic novel *Kéraban-le-Têtu* was turned into a ballet and the dancers "illuminated" à la Trouvé, audiences spoke more about the special effects than about Verne. The latter therefore forbade electrics for subsequent performances!

Throughout the 1890s, his diverse brilliance continued: an electric piano, a battery-powered lifejacket, a domestic acetylene lighting system; ultimately a total of 75 innovations.

With Dr. François Victor Foveau de Courmelles, Trouvé helped create what is today known as "puvatherapy." This involved the concentration and filtering, with colored glass and quartz, of certain rays of electric light for therapeutical purposes. Working at the St. Louis Hospital in Paris, de Courmelles reported this electrotherapy had healing effects on patients suffering from tuberculosis and lung-infected diseases.

Then there was chronophotography or time-lapse, initially used for medical and scientific purposes, soon developed into cinematography. Trouvé took out a patent for its electrification and this was used at the Salpêtrière Hospital in Paris by Professor Charcot.

Perhaps his last innovation was his most beautiful: "*les fontaines lumineuses*," a choreography of colored lights playing like ever-changing fountains but *without water* and electrically automated! Although such a special effect was initially created in battery-powered miniatures for dining-room tables, in 1892 Trouvé was commissioned to provide a monumental unit for a stately home in south Wales. Its owner was Adelina Patti-Nicolini, then the most famous and influential opera singer in the world. Her Welsh château, Craig-Y-Nos Castle, was bristling with modernity, and in her giant winter pavilion glasshouse rose up the luminous fountains of Monsieur Trouvé—weighing in at 10,000 kg with the bottom basin some 20 feet (6 meters wide)!

Eight years later, Trouvé's *fontaines lumineuses* had been taken to their most unforgettable level of development. To herald in the new century, the Paris Exposition Universelle of 1900 required something very special indeed. Situated at the Champs de Mars, beside the Palais de l'Electricité and in the shadow of the Eiffel Tower, Trouvé's "fontaines lumineuses" were his way of saying goodbye to a world he had ingeniously helped to make electric.

In the summer of 1902, this modest inventor cut his thumb and index finger while working on a chemical radiator to cure lupus. It appears his hand became gangrenous. Doctors wanted to amputate, but he refused, saying that without his hand, he could no longer draw and create his inventions. On July 14, he went out to celebrate Bastille Day with some friends. Apparently he drank some ice-cold drinks. Result: that night he woke up with a cerebral and pulmonary congestion. He died on July 27, almost two weeks later, in the Hospital de Saint Louis, where, only months before, Dr. Henri Danlos had carried out the very first radium treatment on dermatological cases, thanks to Marie Curie. He was only 63. His body was taken back to his native town of La Haye-Descartes for a funeral several days later.

Many battery-powered items in our world of the 21st century can trace their ascendancy back to one or several of Monsieur Trouvé's instruments.

Source: Kevin Desmond, *Gustave Trouvé: French Electrical Genius* (Jefferson, NC: McFarland, 2015).

··

Urry, Lewis F.
(1927–2004)
Long-lasting alkaline battery

Lewis Frederick Urry was born on January 29, 1927, in Pontypool, north of Oshawa, Ontario, Canada. His ancestors originally hailed from the Isle of Wight. "He developed his interest in things mechanical while helping his father tinker with cars in his local garage. His dad (Oman Urry) sold the first Ford Model T in the area when he operated a garage in Beaverton," his sister Ada later recalled.

Between 1946 and 1949, Lew served in the Royal Canadian Army, later achieving the rank of captain in the Army Reserve. He then read for and obtained a B.S. in chemical engineering at the University of Toronto in 1950. A few months later, in July, he went to work in an office at the Union Carbide Corporation (later Eveready), on Davenport Road in Toronto.

In 1955 Urry was dispatched across the border to the company's battery research laboratory in Parma, southwest of Cleveland, Ohio. His mission: to discover a way of extending the life span of the zinc-carbon battery. Toys ran on them in those days, but their short life span had been seriously damaging sales. Urry realized that developing a new battery would be more cost-effective than developing the old ones further.

Throughout the 1950s many engineers had experimented with alkaline batteries, but nobody had been able to develop a longer-running battery that was worth the higher cost of production. Urry began by making a mock-up alkaline battery from an empty flashlight shaft. After testing a number of materials, he discovered that manganese dioxide and solid zinc worked well coupled with an alkaline substance as an electrolyte. His main problem was that the battery could not provide enough power.

Lewis Urry (Eveready, *Batteries International*).

"My eureka moment came when I realized that using powdered zinc would give more surface area," he later recalled in an interview with the *Washington Times*.

In order to sell the idea to his managers, to demonstrate his battery to his boss, Urry went to a local toy store and bought two battery-operated model cars. He put a conventional D-cell battery in one car and his mock-up alkaline battery in the other. Then, with R.L. Glover, the Eveready vice president of technology, watching, Urry set the cars loose on the floor of the factory cafeteria.

"Our car went several lengths of this long cafeteria," he said, "but the other car barely moved. Everybody was coming out of their labs to watch. They were all oohing and aahing and cheering," Urry recalled in an interview with the Associated Press in 1999. Eventually spectators became so bored with the successful car going and going that they returned to work.

Glover later provided his own demonstration of Urry's alkaline battery to an executive in the products division in New York City. He loaded one flashlight with a standard battery and one with an alkaline battery, then he left the flashlights on overnight. The next morning, only the alkaline-powered flashlight was still glimmering.

Eveready now began production of Urry's design at their Asheboro factory in North Carolina. The first Eveready alkaline batteries went on sale in 1959. They were labeled "Eveready Alkaline Energizer—the Long Life Power Cell."

The following year, with Energizer batteries started to be used in transistor radios,

Eveready batteries over the years (Eveready, *Batteries International*).

watches and hearing aids. Lew Urry married Beverly Ann Carlock and so became a U.S. citizen. They were to have three sons and eighteen grandchildren.

But the test of time can be a source for further improvement. The mass production of alkaline batteries was facing problems with cell-venting and leakage. As they rolled off the assembly line, some began to smoke and others to explode with a popcorn pop. For six months, a team of scientists were stationed at Asheboro sorting out the manufacturing problems. Their names should be included in this story–Hal Hirt, Walt Rauske, Jerry Winger and Bob Scarr. For example, one of Jerry Winger's most significant contributions was a sealant to eliminate leakage of the alkaline element.

In 1962 Lew was transferred to the Edgeware Development Laboratory.

Several years later, P.R. Mallory and Sam Ruben (see Ruben entry) switched their battery from the more troublesome mercury-alkaline system to the alkaline version devised by Urry.

In 1980 the brand was renamed Energizer. Since then, chemical improvements have made them 40 times longer-lasting than the ones that went on sale in back 1959. Urry held 51 patents, including several in the 1980s related to the development of rechargeable lithium batteries.

Eventually Lew Urry was transferred to the Westlake Technology Lab near Cleveland, where he continued to innovate with carbon/zinc and magnesium cells, but also with thionyl chloride/lithium cells contributing key ideas to cell designs as well as in other areas of nonaqueous batteries. In December 1998 he was name senior technology fellow.

Following his wife Beverly's death in 1993, Lew lived in Eaton Township, a rural community in Lorain County, Ohio. In addition to being a proud grandfather of an ever-increasing number, he had ample room to pursue his hobbies of gardening and auto repair.

In 1999, forty years on, Urry donated his first prototype battery, along with the first commercially produced cylindrical battery, to the Smithsonian Institution. Both cells are now displayed in the same room as Thomas Alva Edison's light bulb.

By the time he retired, Urry had been named as inventor and co-inventor in 51 patents. He died on Tuesday, October 19, 2004, after a short illness. He was 77 years old. He is buried in Butternut Ridge Cemetery, in North Olmsted.

Not long before, Lew Urry had told a friend, "I still have some breakthroughs on the horizon!" Indeed, his last patent was issued to him posthumously in 2006. In short, he was rather like the unstoppable toy car which had made him world famous!

Source: From an article by the author published in *Batteries International*, Winter 2010, from information and pictures supplied by the Eveready Co.

•••

Volta, Alessandro Giuseppe Antonio Anastasio
(1745–1827)
Inventor of the battery

Alessandro Volta of Como, Italy (Musée EDF Electropolis, Mulhouse).

Alessandro Volta was born in Como, Italy, on February 18, 1745, to Count Filippo and Countess Maddalena Inzaghi. He was baptized in the San Donnino Church, a few hundred meters away from the family mansion.

Volta's childhood was spent in the house of barometer manufacturer Ludovico Monte. The boy had severe speech problems and it was only by the age of seven that Alessandro had learned how to speak fluently. At 13, following the death of his father, Volta's uncle, also Alessandro, took over the education of his nephew at home, while he also attended the Jesuit School at Como. Both his uncle's efforts to persuade him to take up legal studies, and those of Father Gerolamo Bonesi to enter the priesthood, soon proved useless. Already his main interest was in physics.

In 1761 Volta joined the Royal

Benzi Seminary, Como, where he was encouraged by family friend Canon Giulio Cesare Gattoni. From 1765, Gattoni, whose residence was an old stone tower, allowed Volta to use his scientific instruments and books for the purpose of research, particularly into electricity. On April 18, 1769, aged 24, he wrote a treatise, "On the forces of attraction of electric fire" (*De vi attractiva ignis electrici ac phænomenis inde pendentibus*), in which he put forward a theory of electric phenomena.

In 1774 Volta accepted a post as professor of physics at the Royal School in Como, where he continued his experiments on electricity. In 1775 he devised a "perpetual electrophorus" that could transfer a static charge to other objects. His promotion of it was so extensive that he is often credited with its invention, even though a machine operating on the same principle was described in 1762 by the Swedish experimenter Johan Wilcke.

In the years between 1776 and 1778, Volta studied the chemistry of gases. He discovered methane after reading a paper by Benjamin Franklin of America on "flammable air," and Volta searched for it carefully in Italy.

In November 1776, he found methane at Lake Maggiore and by 1778 he managed to isolate the gas. He devised experiments such as the ignition of methane by an electric spark in a closed vessel. Volta also studied what is now called electrical capacitance, developing separate means to study both electrical potential (V) and charge (Q), and discovering that for a given object, they are proportional. This may be called Volta's Law of Capacitance, and it was for this work the unit of electrical potential has been named the volt.

In 1779 he became a professor of experimental physics at the University of Pavia, a chair that he occupied for almost 40 years.

Volta's early work had already made him a well-known scientist, but his greatest contribution to science was the voltaic pile, which he invented as part of a scientific dispute with Luigi Galvani.

In January 1781, Luigi Aloisio Galvani, a physician and anatomist based at the Bologna Academy of Sciences, was experimenting with dissected frogs' legs and their attached spinal cords, mounted on iron or brass hooks. In most of his experiments, the frog legs could be made to twitch when touched with a probe made of another metal. The frog legs would also jump when hanging on a metal fence in a lightning storm. These observations convinced Galvani that he had found a new form of electricity, which was being *generated by the frogs' muscles.* He called the phenomenon "animal electricity."

Initially galvanized by this work, Volta replaced the frog's leg with brine-soaked paper, and detected the flow of electricity by other means familiar to him from his previous studies. In this way he discovered the electrochemical series, and the law that the electromotive force (emf) of a galvanic cell, consisting of a pair of metal electrodes separated by electrolyte, is the difference between their two electrode potentials (thus, two identical electrodes and a common electrolyte give zero net emf). This is now known as Volta's Law.

Volta thus argued that the frogs' muscles were simply reacting to the electricity, not producing it. He set out to prove Galvani wrong, and sparked a controversy that divided the fledgling Italian scientific community. In doing so, he invented the voltaic pile, an early electric battery which produced a steady current.

Volta had determined that the most effective pair of dissimilar metals to produce electricity was zinc and silver. Initially he experimented with individual cells in series, each cell being a wine goblet filled with brine into which the two dissimilar electrodes were dipped. The voltaic pile replaced the goblets with cardboard soaked in brine.

In announcing the discovery of his voltaic pile, Volta paid tribute to the influences of William Nicholson, Tiberius Cavallo, and Abraham Bennet.

In 1781–1782 Volta traveled to Switzerland, Alsace, Germany, the Netherlands, Belgium, Paris and London. In Paris, he demonstrated what he called his "artificial electric organ," emphasizing that animal tissue was not needed to produce the current. He was welcome by the great naturalist Georges-Louis Leclerc de Buffon and scientists Pierre Simon Laplace and Antoine-Laurent de Lavoisier. At the Royal Society of London, he lectured on his "capacitor," a talk subsequently printed in English in the journal,

Luigi Aloisio Galvani of Bologna, Italy (Musée EDF Electropolis, Mulhouse).

Philosophical Transactions. In 1784, he crossed the Alps with his colleague Antonio Scarpa, professor of anatomy at the University of Pavia, and they were received in Vienna by Emperor Joseph II. The following year he was elected rector of the University of Pavia by the students for the academic year 1785–1786.

As for Galvani, following the death of his wife Lucia in 1790, he withdrew from public research, wounded by Volta's criticism of his efforts. He entrusted his nephew, Giovanni Aldini, to act as the main defender of the theory of animal electricity. His star was to fall even further in 1797 when, as a university professor, he refused to swear loyalty to the French Cisalpine Republic and found himself plunged into obscurity, removed from the academic offices he had held, which took every financial support away. Galvani died in Bologna, in his brother's house, formerly his childhood home, depressed and in poverty, on December 4, 1798. He was buried alongside his wife at the Corpus Domini Church in Bologna.

By this time, in 1794, Volta, 49 years old, had married an aristocratic lady also from his native Como, Maria Teresa Peregrini, with whom he raised three sons: Zanino, Flaminio and Giovanni.

The Voltaic pile was a huge success. Not only did it swing the scientific community to his side in the debate with Galvani, it was immediately recognized as a useful device. In 1800 William Nicholson and Anthony Carlisle used the current generated by a battery to decompose water into hydrogen and oxygen. Sir Humphry Davy also studied the same chemical effect. In the 1830s Michael Faraday would use a battery in his groundbreaking studies of electromagnetism. Other inventors made improvements on Volta's original design, and soon it was powering telegraphs and doorbells.

However, this cell also has some disadvantages. It is unsafe to handle, since sulfuric acid, even if diluted, can be hazardous. Also, the power of the cell diminishes over time

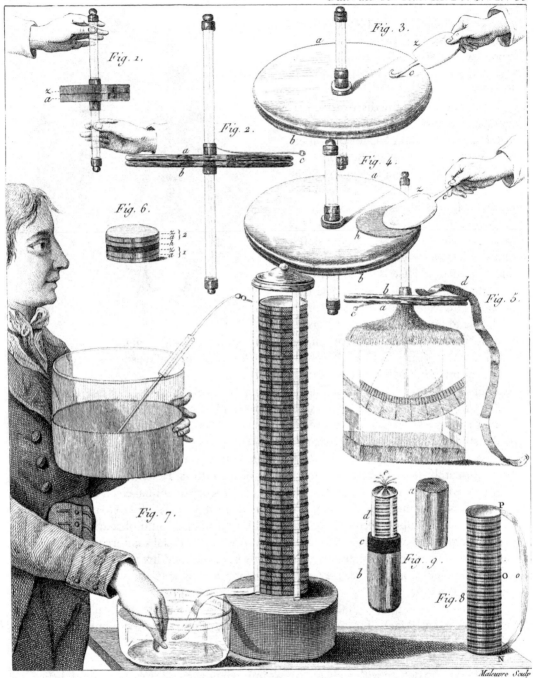

Volta's pile (Musée EDF Electropolis, Mulhouse).

because the hydrogen gas is not released. Instead, it accumulates on the surface of the silver electrode and forms a barrier between the metal and the electrolyte solution.

Napoleon Bonaparte was so impressed by Volta's experiments that he persuaded the professor to visit Paris and demonstrate his invention to the members of the Institute of France. The Emperor himself helped with the experiments—he drew sparks from the pile, melted a steel wire, discharged an electric pistol and decomposed water into its elements. An overly enthusiastic Napoleon made Volta a member of the Institute, and a member of the Legion d'Honneur. In 1809 he was appointed a senator of the Kingdom of Italy, and the following year he was made a Count of the Kingdom of Italy, with the title transmitted to his offspring by direct order. In 1815 the Emperor of Austria named him a professor of philosophy at Padua. In 1816 Volta's works were published in five volumes by Vincenzo Antinori in Florence.

The invention of the battery brought him great renown, but Count Volta seems to have preferred a quiet life. In 1819, he gave up most of his research and teaching, retiring to his estate in Camnago, a frazione (subdivision) of Como, Italy, now named "Camnago Volta" in his honor. He died there on March 5, 1827, aged 82. Volta's remains were also buried in Camnago Volta.

Since his death, Volta's portrait has appeared on the Italian 10,000 lira note (no longer in circulation, since the lira has been replaced by the Euro) and stamps. In 1881, the International Electrical Congress, now the International Electrotechnical Commission (IEC), approved the volt as the unit for electromotive force.

Volta's legacy is celebrated by the Tempio Voltiano memorial located in the public gardens by the lake. There is also a museum which has been built in his honor, and it exhibits some of the original equipment that Volta used to conduct experiments. Not far away stands the Villa Olmo, which houses the Voltian Foundation, an organization promoting scientific activities.

Nor has Galvani been forgotten, despite the misfortunes of his later years. Since 1879, a statue of Galvani, studying books and frog's legs, can be found in the Piazza named after him in Bologna. His name lives on: "Galvanization" was once used to describe the administration of electric shocks, but in the present day is used when somebody is galvanized into sudden, abrupt action.

Although this book places Volta almost last, he was among the first!

• •

Voss, Ernst Christian Hinrich
(1923–2004)
The discovery of α-PbO$_2$

Ernst Voss was born on August 29, 1923, in Nortorf (Holstein, Germany). His father was a merchant. He attended the primary and secondary school in Nortorf from 1930–1937. He finished the grammar school in Rendsburg with the school-leaving examination in 1942. Drafted into the German Armed Forces in 1942, he was taken prisoner in 1944, and detained at Camp Carson, Colorado, until the Armistice.

Voss's interest in chemistry was born already during his grammar school time and so he wanted to study chemistry after the Second World War. Unfortunately all university places for chemistry at Hamburg University were already occupied in 1946. So for the next two years, he obtained a free chemistry university place with studies in classical philology at Hamburg University. He was the first university student in his family.

Finally he could start his chemistry study at Hamburg University in 1948; he finished in 1953 with the degree of Diplom-Chemiker. In 1955 he was awarded a doctorate from the same university. His doctoral thesis, devoted to structures of hexafluorometallates, was inspired by the lectures of Professor Hans Heinrich Bode (see Bode entry). It was Bode who supported Voss in his electrochemical ambitions by finding him a post as co-researcher in the central research laboratory of Accumulatorenfabrik AG Kelkheim near Frankfurt am Main, Germany. That same year Ernst Voss married Ruth Steiner, their daughter Erdmuthe born in 1958 and their son Wolfgang in 1963.

For the next nine years, Ernst Voss was engaged in all aspects of research into lead-acid batteries. In 1964, he became manager of the department for product research and development and widened his activities to include studies on nickel/cadmium cells.

In 1973, he was appointed manager of the technology department for primary and new systems. This position allowed him to become acquainted with many different types of primary systems including zinc/carbon, alkaline manganese, zinc/silver oxide, and lithium/organic cells. Despite this added responsibility, Ernst Voss still pursued his research and developmental studies on both lead-acid and nickel/cadmium cells.

In 1978, Ernst Voss was given the position of department director. Simultaneously, he received the authorization to represent VARTA Batterie AG in legal matters. During 1976–77, he participated in a research program on the lithium/iron sulfide molten salt battery at the Argonne National Laboratory, Illinois. After this visit, he established and inaugurated a similar program at VARTA's R&D lab. This work was continued for many years under his supervision.

Ernst Voss was appointed a director of the research and development center of VARTA Batterie AG in Kelkheim in 1981. Information, planning, patents, government contracts and contacts with universities came within the orbit of his responsibilities.

Mainly Voss was working in the field of understanding the behavior of lead-acid batteries. He was the inventor, or a co-inventor, of 47 patents. These included: Brightening and stabilizing the color of metal salts of naphthene and ethylhexanic acids and their solutions (1957–1960); lead storage battery with solidified electrolyte and process of making same (1963–64); galvanic cell with solid fluoride ion-conductive electrolyte (1975–1976); polyacetylene cell with ceramic solid electrolyte (1983–1985).

His work was reported in 54 papers that have been published in various prestigious scientific journals. In one of his early papers he reported together with H. Bode about his discovery of α-

Ernst Voss (courtesy Wolfgang Voss).

PbO_2 in *Zeitschrift für Elektrochemie, Berichte der Bunsengesellschaft für physikalische Chemie* 60 (1956): 1053. α-PbO_2 is distinguished from the α-PbO_2 modification by its capacity and lifetime. Practically he dealt permanently during his work life with phosphoric acid additives to sulfuric acid of lead-acid batteries (see his review in *J. Power Sources* 24 (1988): 171). Together with August Winsel he developed the "Kugelhaufen Modell" (aggregate-of-spheres model) of the PbO_2-$PbSO_4$ electrode (*J. Power Sources* 30 (1990): 209), explaining the capacity dependence on currents and additives on a theoretical basic.

In 1985 he was elected to work as an expert on batteries and fuel cells for the Commission of the European Communities, Directorate XII, in Brussels. In 1987 Voss collaborated with Hiroshi Shimotake as general editor of *Progress in Batteries and Solar Cells*. He also served on the Editorial Board of the *Journal of Power Sources*.

Erenst Voss retired from VARTA Batterie AG on September 30, 1988, after 33 years of employment with that company. He continued to work for VARTA as consultant till 1993 and was among others responsible for scientific grants of the Herbert-Quandt-Stiftung der VARTA AG. During this time he was still active in attending international battery conferences. During the LABAT meeting in 1989, Voss was selected to become the first recipient of the prestigious Gaston Planté Medal, awarded by the Bulgarian Academy of Sciences.

After his retirement, Ernst Voss finally found more time for topics apart from chemistry, such as philosophy and history, which interested him practically his whole life, starting with his study of classical philology in Hamburg in 1946. He continued these studies, "interrupted" by his almost 40 years of successful chemistry life. He attended various lectures at Frankfurt University, mainly in literary history, and took a course in Chinese. In 1999, the death of his daughter Erdmuthe from cancer deeply affected Voss, and the following year he started to show the first signs of dementia, which worsened until his death on April 8, 2004, in Liederbach (Germany), his residence for 40 years.

Source: document sent to the author in January 2015 by Juergen Garche and Wolfgang Voss.

•••

Whittingham, M. Stanley
(1941–)
Lithium rechargeable batteries

Michael Stanley Whittingham was born near Nottingham in the UK in 1941. He got his interests in science from his father, who was a civil engineer, and from Major Lamb, who was his chemistry teacher in school. During the 1950s he was educated at Stamford School in Lincolnshire before going to New College, Oxford University, to read inorganic chemistry. He obtained his B.A. in 1964, his M.A. in 1967 and his DPhil. in 1968.

Whittingham recalls his days in Oxford:

Initially we were studying catalytic activity, and how all that changed with the changes in the electronic properties of the material. There was a great deal of interest in the crystal structure, or rather the band structure, that controls the catalytic activity. We chose a very, very simple reactant: mainly oxygen atoms, and we just looked at how they recombine at the surface of tungsten bronzes, NaxWO3, because it was very easy to change their catalytic behaviour by changing the amount of sodium. And this was at the time of Sputnik and the U.S. Air Force paid for the research through their London office. They were interested in how various gaseous species reacted on the surface of their space ships. That was for my Master's degree.

Oxford always had a very active program in solid-state. There were three or four faculty there interested in solid-state. His DPhil continued on tungsten oxides and tungsten bronzes and looked at the same materials as catalysts potentially for gas production. And the Gas Council paid for that research. But within a few months of his starting the research, they struck natural gas in the North Sea and the emphasis changed: "I studied the mechanism of reduction of the tungsten oxide bronzes, to form tungsten metal."

Whittingham realized that to obtain an academic or an industrial job, he must go to the USA, and what better place than the warmth of California! In February 1968 he became a postdoctoral fellow, investigating solid-state electrochemistry under Professor Robert A. Huggins at Stanford University. He recalls, "That was quite a switch. In England, France, and Germany, solid-state chemistry was a respectable subject. Chemistry departments did solid-state chemistry. In the U.S. you could count the number of solid-state chemists on the fingers of one hand. So I went to a materials science department, not to a chemistry department."

For relaxation Whittingham traveled almost every weekend to the national parks in California and Oregon. He met his wife, Georgina, in San Francisco after he went to Stanford. She came to Stanford to get her PhD in Latin-American literature. Their two children were born in California, and they moved back west after finishing high school. They now have four grandchildren, also all Californians.

In 1971, Whittingham's published findings on fast-ion transport, particularly in the conductivity of the solid electrolyte beta-alumina, won Whittingham the Young Author Award of the Electrochemical Society.

Whittingham: "Soon after this, I was approached by Ted Geballe, Professor of Applied Physics and associated with our Materials Department. He had been asked to find people to go to Exxon who were starting up a new corporate research lab in Linden, New Jersey. They wanted to be prepared since oil was soon going to run out. Exxon really had very few chemists and physicists at the time. So I did an interview at Exxon and one at Cornell, and I was offered a job in the Materials Science Department at Cornell, not the Chemistry Department."

But Exxon made Whittingham an offer he could not refuse. They included him in a six-strong interdisciplinary group, led by physical chemist Fred Gamble, who had also been at Stanford, alongside an organic chemist and several physicists. Whittingham: "If you needed something for your research you asked for it, and it would be there in a week. Money was no issue. They invested in a research laboratory like they invested in drilling oil. You expect one out of five wells/ideas to pay off."

The Exxon research team began to look at tantalum disulfides. They found that by intercalating different atoms or molecules between the sheets of tantalum disulphide, they could change the superconductivity transition temperature. The potassium compound showed the highest superconductivity. He realized that this compound was very stable, unlike potassium metal, so the reaction must involve a lot of energy. This suggested the possible use for this intercalation reaction for electrical energy storage.

Whittingham: "We looked at lithium and sodium, not potassium, because it turns out that potassium is very dangerous. We also looked at the titanium disulfides, because

M. Stanley Whittingham, a father of the lithium ion battery (Whittingham Collection).

they are lighter in weight than tantalum, and moreover were good electronic conductors. During this time, a Japanese company had come out with a carbon fluoride battery, which they used for fish floats. They fish at night and they need to see where their floats are. And that was a primary battery. This was the beginning of interest in lithium batteries."

In the fall of 1972 Whittingham and his colleagues informed their Exxon bosses that they had a new battery, and patents were filed within a year. Within a couple of years the parent company, Exxon Enterprises, wheeled out a prototype 3W 45Ah lithium cells and started work on hybrid diesel vehicles.

The Exxon battery promised to make a huge impact. At the time, Bell Labs had built up a similar researching group, again made up of chemists and physicists from Stanford. Exxon and Bell were competing head-on for a while, also in publications. Examination of their publications on the battery reveals a lot of basic science with no mention of batteries at all. Exxon came up with the key patents early on. These early batteries were quite remarkable, and some of the smaller ones, used for marketing, are still operating today, more than 35 years later.

Whittingham: "We had an incredibly good patent attorney. They would write up your invention and then ask you: why can't you do it this or that way? And they provoked us into building a battery fully charged or fully discharged." The latter is the way almost all of today's batteries are constructed.

In 1977, Whittingham teamed up with John B. Goodenough (see Goodenough entry) to publish a book *Solid State Chemistry of Energy Conversion and Storage*. To better disseminate information about the field, in 1981, Whittingham launched a new journal, *Solid State Ionics*, which he would edit for the next twenty years.

Whittingham:

> Exxon had one good thing about them. It was run by scientists and engineers, not by lawyers or MBAs. Their philosophy was that if you were a good scientist then you might also be a good director. So within a few years I became director of their chemical engineering division. I was responsible for technology, for synthetic fuels in those days, chemical plants, and refineries. It sounded challenging at the time and I stayed there four years. At that time there began to be much interest began in the shale oil and coal gasification. It was a booming period. My job was to employ as many chemical engineers as I could lay my hands on. But soon the writing was on the wall and the slump was coming. We started laying off people.

By this time Whittingham was missing doing any pure scientific research himself. In 1984, he went to work at the Schlumberger-Doll Research Center in Ridgefield, Connecticut. Schlumberger was the Rolls-Royce of the oil field. They built very expensive analytical "logging" equipment which they put down oil wells to determine whether there was in fact any oil down there, and what the rock foundations were like. They would put these probes worth millions of dollars down the well, pull them up very slowly, and take readings that could help determine whether a particular well was feasible to develop. It was a very low-key company. In those days they probably made more money than all but two or three of the biggest oil companies.

Whittingham: "What they did not have were chemists, those who tried to understand what these measurements actually meant. They did have a large number of physicists and electrical engineers building the instruments. Then they decided to build up a basic rock science group, the job of which was to try to understand what was measured."

For the next four years, Whittingham headed this analytical group, bringing together instrument builders and chemical engineers, which he found more satisfying than his managerial post at Exxon. Whittingham: "But as my wife said, I was doing far too much travel. Schlumberger had labs in Texas, Connecticut, Tokyo, Paris, and Cambridge, England. During my first year I was in the U.S. maybe half of the time."

Four years later, with U.S. industrial research activities going downhill, Whittingham realized that the writing was on the industrial wall. After 16 years in industry, in 1988, he joined the Binghamton campus of the State University of New York as a professor of chemistry to initiate an academic program in materials chemistry. By this time Japanese companies, in particular SONY, had made great strides in the commercialization of lithium rechargeable batteries (see Hatazawa entry). When Whittingham returned to battery research, the Japanese lead was becoming dominant, embodied in a raft of patents.

For five years, he served as the university's vice-provost for research and outreach. He also served as vice-chair of the Research Foundation of the State University of New York for six years.

Whittingham's group developed a strong effort in the hydrothermal synthesis of new materials, initially of vanadium compounds, then used this technique for making cathode materials, which is now being used commercially for the manufacture of lithium iron phosphate by Phostech/Sud-Chimie in Montreal, Canada. The group also developed a fundamental understanding of the olivine cathode and of a new tin-based anode.

He co-chaired DOE's study of Chemical Energy Storage in 2007, and is now director of the Northeastern Center for Chemical Energy Storage, a DOE Energy Frontier

Research Center at Stony Brook University. This center has as its goal a fundamental understanding of the electrode reactions in lithium batteries. Without such an understanding the ultimate limits of energy storage will never be met. The center comprises top scientists from around the country, including MIT, Cambridge, Berkeley and Michigan. This center has now moved to Binghamton with renewed funding through 2018.

Regarded as a father of the lithium-ion battery, Whittingham received from the Electrochemical Society the Battery Research Award in 2004, and was elected a fellow in 2006 for his contributions to lithium battery science and technology. In 2010, he was awarded the American Chemical Society-NERM Award for Achievements in the Chemical Sciences, and the GreentechMedia top 40 innovators for contributions to advancing green technology. In 2012 he received the Yeager Award from the International Battery Association for his lifetime contributions to lithium batteries. In 2015 he received the NAAbatt Award for lifetime contributions to batteries.

Still at Binghamton, 73 years old, M. Stanley Whittingham has been focusing recently on the synthesis and characterization of novel microporous and nano-oxides and phosphates for possible electrochemical and sensor applications. He still travels a lot, visiting around the world, as well as his relatives in England and his children and grandchildren in the west of the U.S.

In 2012 he co-authored *History, Evolution, and Future Status of Energy Storage*, which describes the evolution of lithium batteries and probes into the future (IEEE Proceedings, 100, 1518).

In his own website, Whittingham explains:

The research interests of the materials chemistry group are in the preparation and chemical and physical properties of novel inorganic oxide materials, using in particular soft chemistry (chimie douce) approaches. Much of our effort is targeted at finding new materials for advancing energy storage and production. Recently we have reported the first layered vanadium and molybdenum oxides containing organic cations, simple layered alkali manganese dioxides formed from the hydrothermal decomposition of permanganates, and hydrothermal synthesis methods for the formation of a group of iron phosphates that are being used as the cathodes in a range of commercial applications.

The chemistry of materials is one of the two areas of chemistry experiencing the greatest growth at the present time both in academic institutions and industry. This popularity can be associated with the pervasiveness of solids throughout our lives, from semiconductors through energy storage to geological/biological systems, and to a number of recent breakthroughs, including high-temperature inorganics superconductors.

One of our goals is to find new synthetic routes to prepare metastable compounds that cannot be prepared by traditional techniques. Primary emphasis is on reacting ions in solution with solids, so that the ions diffuse into the solids giving, for example, enhanced superconductivity. In many cases it is possible to form previously unknown open structures, such as layered VO_2, by diffusing ions out of existing structures creating vacant tunnels or layers in which chemistry may be performed or separations/catalysis carried out.

Another goal is the understanding and exploitation of ionic motion in solids and its use in electrochromic devices and batteries. Here much emphasis is on intercalation compounds of the transition metal oxides, Alk_xMO_y, where M includes V, Mn, Fe, Mo etc. Closely related is an investigation of aluminosilicates which can swell in the presence of water and other solvents and have been implicated as playing a critical role in diagenetic processes. These compounds are excellent systems for performing chemistry on the molecular level, and have the potential for revolutionizing the area of nanocomposites.

Source: From an article by the author published in *Batteries International*, Spring 2013, based on information supplied by M. Stanley Whittingham, updated in 2015.

Wollaston, William Hyde
(1766–1828)
The reserve battery

William Hyde Wollaston was born on August 6, 1766, in East Dereham, Norfolk, England, the son of the priest-astronomer Francis Wollaston and his wife Althea Hyde. He was the 7th child of 17 children. Theirs was a financially comfortable family, which was well positioned in British scientific and religious circles. His great-grandfather William Wollaston was a well-known theological author; his uncle Charlton Wollaston had been physician to the queen's household; and his father was a vicar of the Church of England, a competent astronomer, and a fellow of the Royal Society of London.

William was raised in an intellectually vibrant household, educated at Charterhouse School in London, and studied medicine at Gonville and Caius College, Cambridge. Here he did some work himself in his own rooms and in the laboratory of his brother, Francis, also studying at Cambridge. In this way, he began to accumulate his scientific knowledge, opening the way to his own genius in experiment.

He obtained a doctorate in medicine from Cambridge in 1793, working as a physician, first in Huntington, then in Bury in rural Sussex. Unhappy as a physician, because of both the constant demands on his time and the physician's inability to do much to alleviate pain, in 1797 Wollaston moved to London.

During his studies, Wollaston had become interested in chemistry, crystallography, metallurgy and physics. In 1800, after he had received a large sum of money from one of his older brothers, he dropped medicine. He concentrated on pursuing his interests in chemistry and other subjects outside his trained vocation.

He discovered palladium in 1804, rhodium in 1805, and ductile platinum. In spectroscopy he worked on the Fraunhofer lines in the solar spectrum. But he also investigated electricity. In 1801, for example, he performed an experiment showing that the electricity from friction was identical to that produced by voltaic piles.

From 1813, Wollaston redesigned and improved Volta's pile (see Volta entry). By joining cells of his battery in series, he was able to construct very large batteries. To do this, he doubled the copper plates by bending them into a U-shape with a single plate of zinc placed in the center of the bent copper.

William Wollaston, a former physician (Musée EDF Electropolis, Mulhouse).

The zinc plate was prevented from making contact with the copper by pieces or dowels of cork or wood. In his single cell design, the copper U-shaped plate was welded to a single overhead bar, replacing the single handle arrangement that was then mounted to two adjustable ring stand type uprights. This unit formed a trough, and was considered an elementary galvanic cell. Wollaston experimented with element sizes until he found that one inch square was sufficient to ignite a wire of platinum one three thousandths of an inch in diameter. The solution used in the cell by Wollaston was sulfate of copper ($Zn + CuSO4 = ZnSO4 + Cu$). This chemical reaction left a deposit of copper as a black powder (oxide of copper) on the zinc plate, which then had to be constantly scraped off in order to maintain an acceptable current amplitude. Wollaston's design was considered the best battery at the time.

Wollaston never married. Beyond appearing at the meetings of learned societies he took little part in public affairs; he lived alone, conducting his investigations in a deliberate and exhaustive manner, but in the most rigid seclusion, no person being admitted to his laboratory on any pretext. Towards the close of 1828 he felt the approach of a fatal malady—a tumor in the brain—and devoted his last days to a careful revisal of his unpublished researches and industrial processes, dictating several papers on these subjects, which were afterwards published in the *Philosophical Transactions*. Before his death he presented the Royal Society with £1,000 funded stock, the interest of which was to be used to fund scientific experiments. He died in London on December 22, 1828. and was buried in St. Nicholas Churchyard Chislehurst, England.

Source: William Wollaston, "Description of an Elementary Galvanic Battery," *Thomson's Annals of Philosophy*, 1815.

• •

Yai, Sakizou
(1863–1927)
The dry cell battery (Japanese)

Sakizou Yai was born in Nagaoka, Niigata Prefecture, in 1863. In 1875, at the age of 13, he became an apprentice at a watch shop in Tokyo. In 1885, at the age of 23, he invented a battery-powered clock that kept accurate time, which was called the "continuous electric clock" and was patented (Japanese patent No. 1205) in 1891. This was Japan's first patent related to electricity. The battery used in this clock was a liquid one, like the Daniell cell (see Daniell entry), with the disadvantage of being unusable when it froze in the winter. Hence Yai began his quest to manufacture a dry battery.

During the day, Yai worked for the company, and at night, he worked on developing a battery, and for three years he got an average of three hours' sleep a night. He became an assistant at a science university laboratory, where he worked diligently. In this Sakizou Yai was able to consult at length with professors, and he was probably the first pioneer of cooperation between industry and academia. There were difficult problems to overcome—chemicals were leaking out of the positive terminal, the metal became corroded and unusable. Yai tried desperately to impregnate paraffin in a carbon rod, until in 1887 he succeeded in the impregnation, resulting in the first dry battery invention in Japan. He would not patent it until 1892 (Japanese patent No. 2,086). Therefore, the first patent holders for a dry battery were Carl Gassner (Germany) and Frederik Hellesen (Denmark) (see Gassner and Hellesen entries).

In 1893, Yai's dry battery was installed in the seismograph (assembled by Imperial University of Science, presently University of Tokyo). When this was exhibited at the World's Columbian Exposition, it attracted considerable international attention. The Imperial Japanese Commission to the Exposition gave it to the Smithsonian the following year.

The Sino-Japanese War broke out in 1894, and an extra edition of the newspaper one day reported the great success of the military version of the Yai battery used in Manchuria. The newspaper reported that "our victory in Manchuria relies in no small measure upon the dry-battery." Reporters of the newspaper learned that this dry battery was the very one invented by Sakizou Yai, and the next day they ran a story about him.

In 1910, Sakizou Yai established the sales division of his Yai Dry Battery Limited Partnership Company in Nishiki-cho 1-chome, Kanda-ku, Tokyo, and at the same time he built a factory in Kamiyoshi-cho, Asakusa-ku, Tokyo, which grew to the largest in Japan with the annual production volume of more than 200,000 units as of 1921. This was the birth of the Japanese battery industry. Yai's company dominated the domestic market in Japan and he soon became known as the "king of the dry battery."

Unfortunately, however, in September 1923 the Great Kanto Earthquake of magnitude 7.9 struck the Kanto Plane, as a result of which all facilities of his company were burnt to ashes. Nevertheless, Yai soon managed to rebuild a new factory in Kawasaki near Tokyo, where numbers of commercially successful batteries were produced.

In 1927, possibly as a result of his arduous efforts since he was young, Sakizou Yai developed stomach cancer complicated by acute pneumonia, and he passed away at the age of 66. The Yai Dry Battery company was not inherited by his successors, and the name of Yai Dry Battery disappeared from the registry of the Dry Battery Industries Association in 1950.

Information kindly supplied by the Battery Association of Japan.

Yeager, Ernest B.
(1924–2002)
Sodium amalgam–oxygen fuel cell

Ernest B. Yeager was born in Orange, New Jersey, on September 24, 1924. He considered a career in music and was a talented pianist, winning a statewide piano competition. He even helped finance his college education by leading a small band. He also played timpani in his college marching band and concert bands as well as their symphony orchestra. But in the end Yeager decided to pursue mathematics, physics and chemistry. Graduating summa cum laude, with a double major B.A. degree from New Jersey State Teachers College at Montclair in 1945, Yeager enrolled as a graduate student in chemistry at Western Reserve University in Cleveland, with the express purpose of studying with Professor Frank Hovorka. His PhD, obtained in 1948, concerned modifying an ionic vibration effect observed when ultrasonic sound waves are applied to electrolyte solutions. Yeager then joined the faculty of the department of chemistry, becoming a full professor ten years later. He would remain there for the next forty-two years.

From 1947, he wrote a succession of papers about the application of ultrasonic waves or colloidal vibration to the study of electrolytic solutions, mostly for the Office of Naval Research, among whose key workers was Jeanne Burbank (see Burbank entry). This work often involved massive machinery in a stone building; one of the rigs for measuring ionic potentials was the size of a small swimming pool. Yeager became a fellow of the American Association for the Advancement of Science and the Acoustical Society. He also received the Biennial Award of the Acoustical Society of America (1956) and a Navy Certificate of Commendation, for work as a member of the committee on undersea warfare. He was a NATO senior fellow and a visiting professor at the University of Southampton in England. The last of his 50 ultrasound papers was published in 1978.

He also served as chairman of the Physical Electrochemistry Division (formerly the Theoretical Division) of the ECS from 1955 to 1957, and he was chairman of the Cleveland Section from 1954 to 1955.

Yeager soon became known for his contributions to understanding the electrochemical oxygen reduction reaction mechanisms which directly related to fuel cells, metal air batteries, and energy storage systems. He served as a consultant to numerous organizations, including Union Carbide, the Institute of Defense Analysis, NASA, Argonne National Laboratory, General Motors Corp., and Eveready Battery Co.

In the late 1950s, working at WRU's Morley Chemical Laboratories, Yeager and WRU graduate students Dietrick and Witherspoon developed the sodium amalgam–oxygen fuel cell. Although a top-secret Naval project, their U.S. Patent 3,161,546 A, obtained in 1964, refers to a "continuous feed primary battery."

In 1965 Yeager was elected president of the ECS, four years later also becoming president of the International Society of Electrochemistry. From 1969 through 1972, he served as chair of the chemistry department and chair of the CWRU Faculty Senate in 1972 and 1973.

In 1976, Yeager founded the Case Center of Electrochemical Sciences at his university.

That year in the magazine *Plain Dealer*, Yeager commented that electrochemistry would play a major role in meeting the nation's energy problems and in helping to conserve natural resources. He believed that electric cars would become more common in years to come and that high-performance fuel cells and storage batteries would be needed to power these cars. Much of his research focused on developing these advanced power systems.

Ernest B. Yeager (Case Western Reserve University Archives).

He was awarded the Edward Goodrich Acheson Medal and Prize in 1980 and the Vittorio de Nora (see di Nora entry) Award in 1992. In 1994, Case Center of Electrochemical Sciences was rededicated in his honor as the Ernest B. Yeager Center for Electrochemical Sciences.

During nearly 50 years on the Case Western Reserve faculty, Yeager mentored 80 doctorate students and 45 postdoctoral fellows. He was considered by students, staff, and faculty to be a generous person, whose life revolved around his campus activities. He was a dedicated teacher and a stickler for detail, known for his uncompromising demand for excellence in research and scholarly writing.

He would stay on campus later than 11 p.m., holding office hours to meet with students who needed help. He would entertain his holiday party guests with his piano skills. Following an appendix operation, his students lined up outside his hospital room taking turns visiting him. He often joked that he only needed four hours of sleep.

Yeager authored 270 scientific papers and edited or co-edited 20 books. Dr. Yeager was editor of the Electrochemical Society monograph on electrode processes. Ernest Yeager died on March 8, 2002, in Cleveland, Ohio, after a long struggle with Parkinson's disease. He was 77.

Source: Thomas Gilligan and Joe H. Payer, *The Life and Legacy of Professor Ernest B Yeager* (Yeager Center for Electrochemical Sciences, Case Western Reserve University).

....

Zamboni, Giuseppe
(1776–1846)
Battery-powered clocks

Giuseppe Zamboni was born on June 1, 1776, in Arbizzano, a small village at the foothills of Verona. He was sent to study philosophy and theology, as often happened in those days, since the seminar also provided a good cultural preparation. This was the first occasion that he demonstrated his precocious personality, completing his studies for the consecration of a priest a year earlier than canon law.

After completing his studies in the seminary at Verona, in 1800, at the age of 23, Padre Zamboni was appointed abbot and called to teach philosophy in the municipal school of St. Sebastiano, equivalent to the local university. (Today the ancient façade fronts a more recent building which houses the headquarters of the public library where Zamboni's manuscripts, books and articles are archived.)

Becoming interested in physics, and in particular electrology, before long Zamboni had obtained the post of teaching experimental physics and applied mathematics at the Imperial Royal Boarding School established by the conquering Emperor Napoleon I.

He carefully studied the Volta battery. Noting its unpredictable unreliability from the corroding effect of sulfuric acid on the zinc, he began to look into a way of improving the supply.

Of course the idea of eliminating chemicals that corrode the metal cup was not new. It had been tested by Johann Wilhelm Ritter (see Ritter entry), Jean-Baptiste Biot (who used potassium nitrate as a conductor), by G.B. Behrens (with copper, zinc and gold paper) in 1803, by Jean Nicolas Pierre Hachette, by Charles-Bernard Desormes (with single pairs of zinc and copper separated by starch glue), and in 1809 by Jean André De Luc (with wet paper silver and zinc).

Eventually Zamboni came up with his version. Each was composed of 2,000 or more disks made with sheets of commercial paper called "silver paper" (on which was spread a thin layer of tin or an alloy of copper and zinc called "tombac") on the surface of which was spread a paste made of soft wood charcoal powder, mixed with water or worked with nitric acid. The moisture of the paper served as a conductor.

By pressing a large number of such discs together in a glass

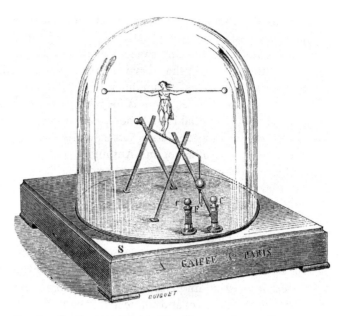

Zamboni's pile, 1812 (Musée EDF Electropolis, Mulhouse).

tube, Zamboni was able to obtain an electromotive force sufficient to deflect the leaves of an ordinary electroscope. By bringing the terminal knobs of the pile near each other and suspending a light brass ball between them, he devised what he called an electrostatic clock. The device was so named because the ball oscillating between the knobs looked like a pendulum.

In 1812 Zamboni delivered to a trustworthy Veronese printer the first version of his "Dissertation on the dry electric battery."

Following a correspondence with Volta, Zamboni experimented with zinc sulfate powder dissolved in water, then tested out brittle and black oxide of manganese dissolved in water with a little glue starch. The main problem was the fact that manganese dioxide fixation was made to adhere to disks with different substances, or mixtures associated with rapeseed oil or milk or honey. The mixtures were then eventually suspended in a highly concentrated solution of zinc sulfate. The discs were inserted in a glass tube. The overlapping discs were painted internally and externally with insulating putty.

After many trials Zamboni found that the common paper worked very well as a separator material between the metal pairs. The wetness it contained was sufficient to permit the passage of electricity. The small amount of humidity and the adhesion of the particles to the soaked paper only has an effect on the metals after an extended period; also the thin layer of oxide that was produced to serve as protection against further oxidation increased. The pile was then covered with melted resin (or colophony, a resin which takes its name from the pine trees of Colophon, an ancient Ionic city), then plastered with beeswax, which does not absorb moisture over time, and then covered with two or three coats of insulating varnish.

Two years later Zamboni had his second paper about the pile printed, titled "Description and Use of the Perpetual Motor." It was not in fact a hypothetical perpetual motion device, as all action would eventually cease when the zinc was completely oxidized or the manganese exhausted.

By this time, there was no doubt about the long-lasting efficiency of the Zamboni pile. But what about its applications? Zamboni and his staff came up with one idea. Why not use the almost maintenance-free battery to power clocks. Indeed, in his "dry cell" paper, he had written that "beyond the perpetual oscillations in the mechanical engine, there may be some useful application."

In this new project he was helped by a watchmaker called Carlo Streizig, physics teacher at the Imperial High School. The prototype they built in 1814 seemed to have the potential of running endlessly. Subsequently, encouraged by Zamboni, both the Veronese clockmaker John Bianchi and Antonio Camerlengo, Director of the Academy of Agriculture and Commercial Arts in Verona, built several copies. A full-battery pendulum original dated 1830, still functioning in 1930, is preserved at the Museum of the History of Physics of the University of Padova.

For the next thirty years, Zamboni meticulously attempted to perfect these electric devices. He stated that some of his clocks were powered by batteries in operation for years without stopping. One was put into action May 18, 1839, at the Institute of Physics of Modena and worked for almost 100 years. This electromotive perpetual device consisted of a pendulum pivoted on an axis moving between two platinum electrodes at a distance of some 3 cm and connected to batteries. The pendulum consisted of a platinum wire about 10 inches long and two concentric metal rings rigidly interconnected with a central axis light lying on two horizontal supports of quartz.

The small size of his battery enabled cramming thousands of couples to increase the voltage. For this Zamboni developed the tools to build and shape them, and boxed them with the most suitable sealants. In fact, he managed to sell his batteries to several colleagues for their physics cabinets, as well as to schools, and even individuals who put them in their home as a mere object of curiosity with pendulums and gears that moved the batteries.

Zamboni's batteries became known not merely in Naples, but in Russia, France, Austria, and England, which countries we find mentioned in his private correspondence. In one of his trips to Vienna, he demonstrated his electric motor to the Emperor Francis I and Metternich. In 1822 he traveled to Paris, where he lectured to the Academie des Sciences.

Giuseppe Zamboni died in Venice on July 25, 1846. In Verona he is remembered by a plaque on the house he lived in until his death. There is also a marble bust in the hall of the Academy of Agricultural Sciences and Letters.

In the Oxford Electric Bell experiment at the Clarendon Laboratory at Oxford University, the terminals of what is believed to be such a pile are fitted with bells that have been continuously ringing since the device was set up in 1840. It has been chiming throughout the development of the electrical battery narrated in this book.

Appendix: Timeline

Although single names have been given to the innovators below, it goes without saying that with the passage of time, the majority of them led an increasingly large team of assistants.

AD 800: Jabir ibn Hayyan (Geber): sulfuric acid
1745: Ewald von Kleist: Leyden jar
1746: Van Musschenbroek: Leyden jar
1746: Andreas Marggraf: zinc
1751: Benjamin Franklin: the words: battery, charge, conductor, positive, negative and condenser (capacitor).
1751: Baron Axel Frederik Cronstedt: niccolite
1780: Luigi Galvani: animal electricity
1800: Alessandro Volta: the voltaic pile
1802: Johann Ritter: electrochemical dry cell
1807: Humphry Davy: aluminum (later aluminum); the word electrochemistry
1812: Giuseppe Zamboni: battery-powered clocks
1813: Humphry Davy: The Great Battery
1814: William Wollaston: reserve battery
1817: Johan August Arfwedson: lithium
1817: Friedrich Stromeyer: cadmium
1820: Robert Hare: "galvanic deflagrator"
1831: Nils Gabriel Sefström: vanadium
1834: Michael Faraday, adopting terms created by the Reverend William Whelwell, such as ion, anode and cathode; adds the words electrode and electrolysis
1836: John Daniell: an improved battery
1838: William Grove: "gas voltaic battery" or fuel cell
1840: Alfred Smee: platinum silver zinc sulphuric battery
1840: Anyos Jedlik: switch-over battery
1842: Robert Bunsen: carbon pole battery
1843: Alexander Bain: earth battery
1848: Nicolas Callan: Maynooth battery
1854: Wilhelm Sinsteden: working principle of lead-acid battery
1859: Gaston Planté: regular storage lead-acid battery
1861: Charles F. Kirchhof: earliest patent for storage battery
1865: Gustave Trouvé: wearable miniature battery
1866: Georges Leclanché: carbon-zinc wet cell battery
1869: Dmitri Ivanovich Mendeleev: periodic table of elements
1873: Joseph Clark: standard mercury cell
1881: Camille Faure: rechargeable secondary battery

Batteries through the years (Musée EDF Electropolis, Mulhouse).

1881: Carl Gassner: dry cell battery (zinc-carbon cell) (Austrian)
1883: Jules Thiébaut: battery with both the negative electrode and porous pot placed in a zinc
   cup
1883: Charles Renard: the flow battery
1887: Frederik Hellesen: dry cell battery (Danish)
1887: Sakizou Yai: dry cell battery (Japanese)
1889: Ludwig Mond and assistant Carl Langer: fuel cell using coal-derived "Mond-gas"
1895: W.M. Jewett: paper-lined commercial dry cell
1897: William Jacques: coal battery
1899: Waldmar Jungner: nickel-cadmium rechargeable battery
1900: Karl Liebenow: experiment on forced flow of electrolyte
1901: Thomas Alva Edison: nickel-iron battery
1907: Charles Burgess: improving the dry cell (U.S.)
1919: Gilbert Lewis and Frederick Keyes: discovery of the nonchargeable lithium isotope
1931: James Drumm: traction battery
1932: Henri André: rechargeable silver-zinc battery
1935: Horace Haring: lead-calcium alloys for battery construction
1941: Sam Ruben: mercury button cell battery (later Duracell)
1944: Dr. Georg Otto Erb: the molten-salt battery
1947: Georg Neumann: sealing the NiCd cell
1949: Lew Urry: longer-lasting alkaline-manganese battery
1954: Gerald Pearson, Calvin Fuller and Daryl Chapin: first solar battery
1954: Tom Bacon: practical hydrogen-oxygen fuel cell
1955: Charles Tobias: nonaqueous solvents

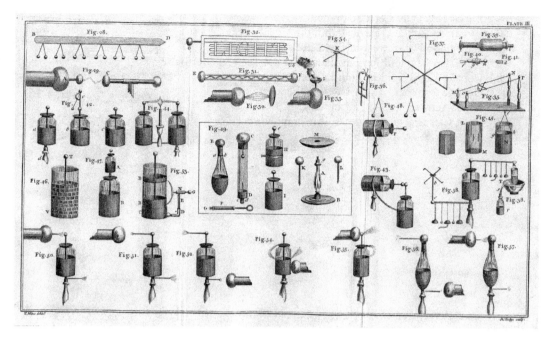

Batteries, 19th century lithograph (Musée EDF Electropolis, Mulhouse).

1957: Karl Kordesh: alkaline primary battery cell
1958: Otto Jache: the gel-filled battery
1958: Hans Bode: longer-lasting lead-acid battery
1960: Wilson Greatbatch: implantable pacemaker
1960: Jeanne Burbank: X-ray diffraction studies of electrodes
1962: Vittorio de Nora: dimensionally stabilized anode
1964: Ernest B. Yeager et al.: sodium amalgam–oxygen fuel cell
1965: John Devitt: sealed lead-acid battery
1968: Elton Cairns: lithium sulfur cell
1969: David Feder: cylindrical lead-acid cell
1969: Jim Sudworth: beta alumina, cells and batteries
1971: Henry Sampson: gamma electric cell, nuclear battery
1973: M. Stanley Whittingham: commercial lithium rechargeable batteries, electrode intercalation
1975: R. David Prengaman et al.: low antimony maintenance-free battery grid alloy
1982: Stanford Ovshinsky: "Ovonic" nickel metal-hydride battery
1983: John F. Cooper: zinc air refuelable battery
1984: Andrew Green and Stuart Wenham: buried contact solar cell
1985: John B. Goodenough et al.: the lithium ion battery
1985: Johan Coetzer et al.: sodium–iron chloride cell, later code-named the "Zebra" cell
1986: Maria Skyllas-Kazacos: all-vanadium redox flow battery
1987: Esther Takeuchi: lithium/silver vanadium oxide battery
1991: Brian Conway: "the Supercapacitor"
1991: Randell Mills: hydrino hydride battery
1991: Tsuyonobu Hatazawa: lithium ion polymer battery
1991: Michael Grätzel and Brian O'Regan: dye-sensitized solar cell
1996: Theodore O. Poehler and Peter C. Searson: all-plastic battery
1999: Michael Thackerary et al.: lithium ion "layered-spinel" battery
2002: Andre Geim and Koystya Novoselov: graphene

2004: Kurtis Kelley: lead acid foam battery
2005: Lan Trieu Lam and David Rand: the UltraBattery
2009: Tsuyonobu Hatazawa: bio-fuel cell
2009: Lan Trieu Lam and Jun Furukawa: the commercial UltraBattery
2009: Donald Sadoway et al.: liquid metal battery
2012: Hongjie Dai et al.: nickel-iron/graphene battery
2012: Bruno Scrosati: lithium air battery
2013: Elton Cairns et al.: lithium-sulfur/graphene cell

Bibliography

Bagshaw, Norman. *Batteries on Ships*. New York: John Wiley & Sons, 1982.

Bain, Alexander. *A Short History of the Electric Clocks*. London: Chapman & Hall, 1852.

Barak, Montefiore. *Electrochemical Power Sources, Primary and Secondary Batteries* (IEE Energy Series). The Institution of Engineering and Technology, 1980.

Barbier, Jean Paul. *"Bonaparte et les savants. De la pile de Volta a la grande pile de l'Ecole Polytechnique (1800–1812)"* Bulletin d'Histoire de l'Electricité, no. 34, 1999.

Berndt, Dietrich. *Maintenance-Free Batteries, Aqueous Electrolyte Lead-Acid, Nickel/Cadmium, Nickel/Metal Hydride, Lead-acid, Nickel/Cadmium, Nickel/Metal Hydride*. Norman E. Bagshaw, ed. Taunton, UK: Research Studies Press, 2003.

Bode, Hans Heinrich. *Lead-Acid Batteries* (Electrochemical Society Series). New York: John Wiley & Sons, 1977.

Böhnstedt, Werner. *Handbook of Battery Materials: Separators*. Wiley-VCH Verlag GmbH, 1999.

Bunsen, Robert. *Gasometry, Comprising the Leading Physical and Chemical Properties of Gases*. London: Walton & Maberly, 1857.

Davy, Humphry. *Consolations in Travel or The Last Days of a Philosopher*. London: John Murray (1830).

_____. A late fragment, probably written when he knew he was dying, in *Fragmentary Remains* (1858).

_____. *Researches, Chemical and Philosophical, Chiefly Concerning Nitrous Oxide, or Dephlogisticated Nitrous Air, and Its Respiration*. London: Bristol, Biggs & Cottle, 1800.

Davy, John. *The Collected Works of Sir Humphry Davy*. London: Smith, Elder, 1839.

Dell, Ron, and David Rand. *Clean Energy*. Cambridge: Royal Society of Chemistry, 2004.

_____ and _____. *Hydrogen Energy: Challenges and Prospects*, Cambridge, UK: Royal Society of Chemistry, 2008.

_____ and _____. *Understanding Batteries*. Cambridge, UK: Royal Society of Chemistry, 001.

Dell, Ron, Pat Moseley, and David Rand. *Towards Sustainable Road Transport*. Amsterdam: Elsevier, 2014.

Desmond, Kevin. *Gustave Trouvé: French Electrical Genius*. Jefferson, NC: McFarland, 2015.

Dicks, Andrew, and James Larminie. *Fuel Cell Systems Explained*. New York: John Wiley & Sons, 2000.

Dolezalek, Friedrich. *The Theory of the Lead Accumulator*. New York: John Wiley & Sons, 1900.

Franklin, Benjamin. *Experiments and Observations on Electricity Made at Philadelphia in America*. London: R. Cave, 1751.

Garche, J., C.K. Dyer, P.T. Moseley, Z. Ogumi, D.A.J. Rand, and B. Scrosati, eds. *Encyclopedia of Electrochemical Power Sources*. 5 vols. Amsterdam: Elsevier, 2009.

Garche, J., K. Wiesener, and W. Schneide. *Elektrochemische Stromquellen*. Berlin: Akademie-Verlag, 1981.

Glasstone, Samuel. *An Introduction to Electrochemistry*. New York: D. Van Nostrand, 1947.

Goodenough, John B. *Witness to Grace*. Publish America, 2008.

_____ and K. Huang. *Solid Oxide Fuel Cell Technology, Principles, Performance, and Operations*. Cambridge, UK: Woodhead Publishing, Ltd., 2009.

Greatbatch, Wilson. *The Making of the Pacemaker: Celebrating a Lifesaving Invention*. Amherst, NY: Prometheus Books, 2000.

Green, Martin. *"Solar Cells Operating Principles, Technology and System Applications."* Prentice-Hall, 1982.

_____. *Third Generation Photovoltaics Advanced Solar Energy Conversion*. Berlin, New York: Springer, 2003.

Kabanov, Boris Nikolaevich. *Elektrokhimiya metallov i adsorbtsiya* (The Electrochemistry of Metals and the Adsorption). Moscow, 1966.

König, Wilhelm. *Im verlorenen Paradies: Neun Jahre Irak.* Rudolf M. Rohrer, Baden bei Wien, 1940.

Kordesch, Karl, ed. *Batteries—Vol. 1: Manganese Dioxide.* New York: Marcel Dekker, 1974.

_____, ed. *Batteries—Vol. 2: Lead-Acid Batteries, Electric Vehicles,* New York: Marcel Dekker, 1977.

Kordesch, Karl, and Günter R. Simader. *Fuel Cells and Their Applications.* Weinheim: Wiley, 1996.

Liebhafsky, H.A., and E.J. Cairns. *Fuel Cells and Fuel Batteries. A Guide to Their Research and Development.* John Wiley & Sons, New York, 1968.

Moseley, P.T., and David Rand. *Encyclopaedia of Electrochemical Power Sources,* 5 vols. Amsterdam: Elsevier, 2009.

Moseley, P.T., and J. Garche. *Electrochemical Energy Storage for Renewable Sources and Grid Balancing.* Amsterdam: Elsevier, 2014.

Park, Benjamin. *The Voltaic Cell.* New York: John Wiley & Sons, 1893.

Pavlov, Detchko. *Lead-Acid Batteries—Science and Technology.* Amsterdam: Elsevier, 2011.

Rand, D.A.J., P.T. Moseley, J. Garche, and C.D. Parker. *Valve-Regulated Lead-Acid Batteries.* Amsterdam: Elsevier, 2004.

Rand, D.R., R. Woods, and R. Dell. *Batteries for Electric Vehicles.* Taunton, UK: Research Studies Press, 1997.

Reddy, Thomas B., ed. *Linden's Handbook of Batteries,* 4th ed. New York: McGraw-Hill Professional, 2011.

Reynier, Emile. *The Voltaic Accumulator.* New York: E & F.N. Spon, 1888.

Schallenberg, Richard H. *Bottled Energy Electrical Engineering and the Evolution of Chemical Energy Storage.* Philadelphia: American Philosophical Society, 1982.

Schlesinger, Henry. *The Battery: How Portable Power Sparked a Technological Revolution.* New York: Harper Perennial, 2011.

Skundin, Alexander M., and Galina A. Tsirlina. *V. S. Bagotsky's Contribution to Modern Electrochemistry.* Journal of Solid State Electrochemistry, 2014.

Sudworth, James, and Gibson, John. *Specific Energies of Galvanic Reactions and Related Thermodynamic Data.* Chapman & Hall, 1973.

Sudworth, James, and Tilley, Roger. *The Sodium Sulfur Battery.* London: Chapman & Hall, 1985.

Tobias, Charles W., and Gerischer Heinz. *Advances in Electrochemistry and Electrochemical Engineering.* New York: John Wiley & Sons, 1984.

Treadwell, Augustus, Jr. *The Storage Battery.* New York: Macmillan, 1898.

Wade, E. J. *Secondary Batteries, Their Theory, Construction and Use.* London: "The Electrician" Printing and Publishing Company Ltd., 1902.

Whittingham, M. Stanley, and John B. Goodenough. *Solid State Chemistry of Energy Conversion and Storage.* Washington, D.C.: American Chemical Society, 1977.

Williams, K. R. *Francis Thomas Bacon, 21 December 1904–24 May 1992,* Biographical Memoirs of Fellows of the Royal Society, 1994.

Wisconsin Historical Society, *Charles Frederick Burgess 1873–1945.*

Index

255

CPSIA information can be obtained
at www.ICGtesting.com
Printed in the USA
LVHW081507290423
745601LV00006B/633